In seventeenth-century France, land took on new importance for the practice of politics and rituals of court life. As a sequestered aristocracy promenaded in great formal gardens, the French military moved across the landscape, marked the boundaries of the state with fortresses, and refigured the topography of the interior with canals and forests. In her major new book, Chandra Mukerji highlights the connection between the two seemingly disparate activities of engineering and garden design. She shows how, at Versailles in particular, the royal park showcased French skills in using nature and art to design a distinctively French landscape and create a naturalized political territoriality. She challenges the association of state power with social and legal structures alone, and demonstrates the importance for Louis XIV and his state of a controlled physical site and a demarcated French territory within the wider European geopolitical continent.

Territorial ambitions and the gardens of Versailles

Cambridge Cultural Social Studies

Territorial ambitions
and the gardens of Versailles

Chandra Mukerji

University of California, San Diego

CAMBRIDGE
UNIVERSITY PRESS

PUBLISHED BY THE PRESS SYNDICATE OF THE UNIVERSITY OF CAMBRIDGE
The Pitt Building, Trumpington Street, Cambridge CB2 1RP, United Kingdom

CAMBRIDGE UNIVERSITY PRESS
The Edinburgh Building, Cambridge, CB2 2RU, United Kingdom
40 West 20th Street, New York, NY 10011-4211, USA
10 Stamford Road, Oakleigh, Melbourne 3166, Australia

First published 1997

Printed in the United Kingdom at the University Press, Cambridge

Typeset in 10/12½ Monotype Times

A catalogue record for this book is available from the British Library

Library of Congress Cataloguing in Publication data
Mukerji, Chandra.
    Territorial ambitions and the gardens of Versailles / Chandra
Mukerji.
        p.   cm. – (Cambridge cultural social studies)
    Includes bibliographical references.
    ISBN 0 521 49675 6 (hardback)
        1. France – Politics and government – 17th century.   2. Parc de
Versailles (Versailles, France) – Pictorial works.   3. France – Court
and courtiers – History – 17th century.   4. Gardens – Symbolic aspects –
France – History – 17th century.   5. Military engineering – France –
History – 17th century.   6. France – Boundaries.   I. Title.
II. Series.
DC126.M85   1997
944'.033–dc21   96–37156   CIP

ISBN 0 521 49675 6 hardback
ISBN 0 521 59959 8 paperback

To all those who have died because of territorial politics

Contents

Illustrations

Acknowledgments

This work is the result of a long research process, filled with many twists and turns, so I naturally owe debts to many people who have helped me in different ways. There were those who nudged me into the gardens, those who thought it interesting for me to stay there, those who recognized when I needed a hand getting out, and those who helped me refine the argument so I could finish the book. None of them is responsible for the flights of theoretical fancy or the excessive empirical details of this book. None can help excuse my odd approach to French gardens.

I began this work with the encouragement of Charles Saumarez-Smith and Mary Walshok. Mary, as the Dean of Summer Session, wanted Charles and me to teach a joint summer course at the Victoria and Albert Museum, and thought it exciting to focus on gardens. Charles' casual optimism about the intellectual value of the project and Mary's institutional support for designing the course stimulated my earliest efforts to formulate a sociological approach to gardens. Soon after, I received more encouragement from Pierre Bourdieu and Raymond Moulin, both of whom saw possibilities in gardens as a topic in the sociology of art. Still, I was surprisingly settled into this project by a research assistant, Silvio Waisbord, who was interested in politics and culture, and who knew enough French to help me explore this topic. I became so immersed in the volumes of material he carted from the library that I could only get out by writing a book.

Once set in the project, I received the most help from Bruno Latour. To my delight, he thought studying French gardens was a beautiful project. He saw immediately that the sociology of art could meet the history of science and technology in the gardens, where land was made plastic and political through localized human effort. His generosity in making our stays in Paris easier and more pleasurable was impressive and essential to the project. His intellectual seriousness combined with his deep commitment to studies of technology and material culture made my work all the more interesting and important to me. Bruno's colleague at the Centre de Sociologie de l'Innovation, Antoine Hennion, in his turn, pushed me to think about why French music was so ubiquitous to noble gardens during the seventeenth century. I became convinced somehow that when I could explain the significance of Lully's music wafting through the trees and over parterres at Versailles, I would better understand the political life of that particular time and place. This exercise forced me to keep re-examining relations between two extra-linguistic forms of culture (music and gardens) to think about how humans impress their will and social ambitions onto the world through transforming nature. This was a crucial turn in the work.

I was socialized into doing work in France with the help of a research assistant from the Ecole de Paysage in Versailles, Isabelle Mourré. Isabelle worked on me like a patch of bad soil, trying to rid me of unhealthy attributes of an awkward American as I followed her to French archives and libraries. She took me to Versailles' public library, the Bibliothèque Nationale, the Bibliothèque Mazarine, the regional archive in Versailles, the small libraries in the Paysage and Horticulture schools in Versailles and the great science library at the Natural History Museum by the Jardin des Plantes. Best of all, she took me to the National Archives in Paris and shared my delight in finding the immense plumbing plans for the gardens at Versailles. These documents made it clear that there was enough evidence of French formal gardening technique there to warrant my continued attention. This introduction to French sources and sites for research proved invaluable in the coming years as I returned to France and worked on my own.

I was sustained as I first tried to write on these materials by the support of a few scholars, particularly, Paul DiMaggio, Tom Gieryn, Elizabeth Long, Vera Zolberg, Sharon Zukin, and Roy Ritchie. I am also grateful to John Brewer, Roy Porter, Thomas Haskell, and Richard Teichgraeber III, who asked me to speak on the culture of consumption at their conferences. They gave me opportunities to refine my arguments in the company of some extraordinarily gifted scholars, including (notably) Jean-Christophe Agnew and Joyce Appleby. I owe all of them a debt.

Michael Schudson has once again been an inspiration and help with this project. He has managed to steer me away from some of my analytic excesses while conveying such an optimistic view of my work that I have been able to recognize and correct deep failings in the project. I have also received valuable feedback and help from other colleagues in the Communication Department, namely, Dan Hallin, Helene Keyssar, Vince Rafael, and Dan Schiller.

I have learned more than I can specify here from members of the long-standing sociology of culture reading group, including Bennett Berger, the late Fred Davis, Murray Davis, Ana Devic, Harvey Goldman, Joe Gusfield, Doug Hartman, Bennetta Jules-Rosette, Dick Madsen, Laura Miller, Anna Szemere, Christina Turner, and Silvio Waisbord. They have slowly made me a more rigorous and broad student of culture. I am also indebted to members of the current culture study group: Marnie Dillon, Jerry Doppelt, Dan Hallin, Rebecca Klatch, George Lipsitz, Dick Madsen, Bud Mehan, Jann Pasler, and Michael Schudson. I must single out Jann Pasler and Joe Gusfield for special thanks. Jann Pasler has taught me enormous amounts about French music and culture, and shares with me the pleasures and pains of French archives and libraries. Joe Gusfield has transformed my work in the sociology of culture over the years because he embodies such a taste and capacity for fine sociological theorizing with such a deep knowledge of art history that he makes clear how good the sociology of art/culture can be. I have benefited as well from the rough and tumble feedback on this work from colleagues in the Science Studies Program, UCSD, including Adrian Cussins, Jerry Doppelt, Martin Rudwick, Steve Shapin, Bob Westman, and many visitors.

There are many others elsewhere who have helped or encouraged me with this project, too. They include in Paris Luc Boltanski, Mary Noelle Bourguet, Denis Duclos, Bernard Lepetit, Ilana Löwy, Antoine Picon, and Claude Rosenthal. I also owe thanks to David Antin, David Bakhurst, David Brain, Howie Becker, Steve Epstein, Bruce Hackett, Sharon Hays, Kathryn Henderson, Karin Knorr-Cetina, Kristin Luker, Michael Lynch, Marianne MacDonald, Naomi Oreskes, Gianfranco Poggi, Leigh Star, Sharon Traweek, Cynthia Truant, Loïc Wacquant, Peter Whalley, and Doug and Lillyann White – all of whom have helped me think through parts of this project. Howie, in particularly, needs thanking for turning me toward the sociology of art at the beginning. He probably was successful in large part because he did not make clear to me how difficult this work would be. Maybe for him it was easy; maybe he was just a good teacher.

I also owe much to my graduate students who, over the years, have shaped my thoughts on culture. They include Tedi Bish, Patrick Carroll, Ana Devic, Alex Halkias, Douglas Hartman, Chris Henke, Rick Jonasse, Moses Kaern, Jill MacDowell, Laura Miller, Nic Sammond, Joey Scures, Rachel Shaw, Bart Simon, Susan Sterne, Anna Szemere, and Suzanne Thomas. I am particularly indebted to Patrick Carroll, Suzanne Thomas, Rick Jonasse, Rachel Shaw, and Tedi Bish whose interests have been so close to my own that their education has also been mine. They have brought as many books to my attention as I have ever assigned to them for a class. All these students are too smart for their own good. I hope they can endure it.

I want also to recognize the indispensable help of Jill MacDowell after I broke my back. Her cheerful demeanor made it easier to go on; her trips to the library made it possible for me to do research; and her intellectual engagement made writing seem worthwhile. I also want to express my appreciation to Patrick Carroll, Bart Simon, and Charis Cussins for their kindness and lively conversations during that awful summer. I also owe much to the long soul- and back-strengthening walks I have taken with Becky Cohen, the photographer for the project. She taught me new ways to see the gardens at Versailles, and gave me study photographs to examine later that were as lovely to view as they were informative. Even when we had no vistas or sculptures to discuss and no food or wine for punctuating our talks, the promenades were still lovely. Becky's wise eyes continue to be an inspiration and an indispensable part of this project. I am deeply grateful.

I could not finish these acknowledgments without also mentioning the helpfulness of Catherine Max at Cambridge University Press. Her kindness and guidance in this project has made publication a pleasure for me. She sustained me while I was hurt, has endured the delays in finishing the project, and always – to my surprise and delight – taken the illustrations as a serious part of the work. I am also grateful to the editors of the series, and to the editors at Cambridge for accepting the costs and size changes in the book to make the visual parts of the argument as accessible to readers as the verbal ones.

In the end, of course, I owe the most to my family. I must thank my children, Kenneth and Stephanie Berger, for letting me work when I needed to, and learning to pull me away from the computer when I was getting too brittle from obsessive thought. I am also grateful to them for enduring more time in Paris than they wanted just so I could indulge my need for old books and archives. They learned valuable lessons from attending French schools, but it was not easy for them to be there. So, I thank them both. Kenneth and Stephanie also made garden research more of a delight by accompanying me on garden walks, wearing their rollerblades – entertaining the fashion-loving Parisians with their high-tech grace and disturbing the keepers of order in the gardens. Research is not all serious. I am indebted to my nephew, Jadu Jagel, and his girlfriend, Paula Pralinsky, too, who came to Paris to take care of Stephanie and Kenny while I was working long hours in the archives and library. Most of all, I am indebted to my husband, Bennett Berger. It is not just that I owe most of my thoughts about the gardens to conversations both actual and imagined with him – although that is not to be discounted. More centrally, this was a project born during a period of deep family crisis. More suffering and illness dogged our small inner circle than I can bear to remember. Only my husband knows how much he and this research project sustained me through the most difficult times. Once recently, Bennett said that I argued with him about culture and gardens as though my life depended on it. In some mysterious way, he is right. So, I owe him the greatest debt of all.

Glossary of French terms

allée: a garden walkway or alley

appartements, appartemens: evenings of informal entertainment in the king's chambers at Versailles

ballet de cour: dance performed by members of the court

bosquet: forest room, walled with trees and bushes and filled with statuary and waterworks

cabinet de curiosité: a room housing a collection of artworks, papers, and/or specimens from nature.

carrousel: a ritual event in which feudal military contests take place

cloche: a glass bell used in gardens to protect and provide heat for tender plants like melons and cucumbers

collation: a display of foods and the opportunity to consume them

colonnade: an array of columns, used both in the Louvre design by Perrault and in Mansart's bosquet at Versailles

coquillage: displays of shells in gardens

courses de bague, courses de tête: the feudal contests most often used at French carrousels

demi-lune: a small outlying piece of a battlement wall system

divertissements: parties for the nobility performed frequently in the garden

étoile: a star shape, used frequently in military architecture

éstang: a holding pond or reservoir

faïence: hand-painted and glazed pottery or tableware

faïenceries: manufacturing centers for faïence

fête: a party, usually organized around a narrative theme

fossé: a ditch used in battlement wall systems

fusil: a kind of gun used by infantry soldiers

grand couvert: the most formal of the king's meals

grand habit: fine dress for noble ladies at court with tight lacing and low-cut necklines

honnête homme: the ideal for a French courtier, desiring to please and having the grace to do it well

intendants: the king's representatives in the provinces, placed there permanently under Louis XIV

jardin potager: the kitchen garden, providing fruits and vegetables for the court

justacorps, justaucorps, justaucorps à brevet: a costume for men with special embroidery on the sleeves to denote high social standing

lac, pièce d'eau: a large reflecting pond in the garden

levée: the rituals surrounding the king's rising in the morning

manufacture royale, manufacture du roi: companies given special authority to manufacture goods for the court

mascarade: a court dance, at first denoting a dance in which narratives or symbols were enacted, but later referring only to a costume ball

mousquet: a gun for the infantry, a precursor to the fusil

opiat: soothing medicines given the king in the morning, presumably with opium in it, but mixed with a variety of herbs. Used after the king began to suffer from both pain and emotional strain.

orangerie: an indoor space, usually but not always with glass doors, used to house delicate palms, citruses, and other bushes or trees during the winter

parterre: low garden bed with complex designs made from cut bushes, flowers, colored gravel, water, or grass

petit académie: the group of secret advisors to Colbert on intellectual and cultural matters

petit couvert: the less formal ritual meal of the king and/or royal family

petit parc: the older and more highly decorated area of the garden of Versailles between the château and the canal

plans-relief: clay models of fortresses or towns used for military planning with highly accurate renderings of the plants and building materials as well as spatial relations of the site

points de France, poincts de France: French lace

politesse: good manners, refined style

pompe: a pumping system, often using river current to power the pump to raise water from the river for human use

potager: another name for the *jardin potager* or kitchen garden

pré carré: Vauban's term for the France he wanted to engineer with fortresses to make it a great nearly-square feature of the European continent

précieuses: salon women of Paris

Roi Soleil: the Sun King

sape: a raised area of dirt along a trench to protect soldiers moving through the trench

serres: the glass covering garden areas, particularly hotbeds, for starting seedlings and protecting tender plants

tapis vert: a large area of plain green grass in the middle of the Allée Royale, running between the Latona fountain and the Apollo fountain

1

The culture of land and the territorial state

According to Saint-Simon, Louis XIV on his deathbed expressed regret about the pain caused others by his overwhelming passion for building and war. For Saint-Simon, this was only a passingly sympathetic moment. He was more concerned about the suspect moral character of a king who would inflict so much suffering on his people to follow his own passion, and who would wait until death to renounce his weakness. The deathbed confession was followed soon in Saint-Simon's diary by the descriptions of the general glee in France and throughout Europe that followed the announcement of the king's death – a mirror, we suspect, of the author's own elation.[1]

Saint-Simon's contempt aside, Louis XIV's confession was more than an act of moral purging by a king distressingly prone to set out monuments to himself and seek military reasons to erect them. It pointed to a shift of attention to the built environment as a site for political action. Building and war were particularly potent tools for constructing a territorial state over which Louis XIV could be absolute monarch. In seventeenth-century France, government transformation of the French landscape – with the construction of fortresses, factories, garrisons, canals, roads, and port cities – imprinted the political order onto the earth, making it seem almost an extension of the natural order. Political power in this moment was not just invested in the bureaucracy and Colbert's supposed rationalization of taxes, laws, and the military, but was also embedded in reconstituted social relations to "nature" that we in the West work from (and against) today.

Part of what Louis XIV so passionately wanted to build and what he wanted to fight for in war was an uncontested and identifiable political *location* for accumulating and exercising power: a territorial state. His passion for building and war was part of a desire for domination, a lust for power, that he shared with many political leaders before and since, but his ambitions took on a shape, a trajectory, that was not so historically constant. In the emerging system of European geo-politics, building and war were particularly material means for mobilizing landmasses and artifacts as political resources. Appropriately, the French military engineer, Sébastien Le Prestre de Vauban, was a major architect of this new, territorial France. He constructed a great string of fortress cities around the perimeter of the country, holding the state's land within a ring of artificial barriers located primarily where natural features did not already neatly mark or protect state boundaries.[2] Great earthworks and diversions of rivers were part of his schemes; the conquests of the French army were not just marked on maps, but dug into hillsides and dredged along waterways, transforming French borders into physical features of the landscape. The French countryside was made into a recognizable political space to help define France as a singular power.[3]

The techniques used to transform French land into a site for politics were perhaps surprisingly showcased in the formal gardens around the royal residences, particularly Versailles. In these parks, aesthetic displays of control over natural forces yielded stunning visual effects that dazzled foreign visitors from throughout the world.[4] But the gardens were not just marvels to transfix the viewer; they were laboratories for and demonstrations of French capacities to use the countryside as a political resource for power. In grading the earth to make terraces, they showcased military engineering techniques for which France was becoming renowned. At Versailles, the gardens acquired a water system even more elaborate than – but still based on the same principles as – the one joining the hillsides around Paris to serve that city's growing needs. The statues in the royal gardens were commissioned and designed by Le Brun to be exquisite exemplars of French taste and fashion that could mark what was French with a distinctive style. Even the flower-beds with their complex patterns inscribed models of French design onto the land itself, significantly using imported exotic plants that testified to the reach of French trading networks. No wonder the gardens became sites of diplomatic rituals and celebrations of war victories, where territorial engineering and design could be made manifest to foreigners and locals alike as a basis for determining what was France. In the microcosm of the garden, the tools of French land-based politics were revealed in all their glory.

Versailles was a model of material domination of nature that fairly shouted its excessive claims about the strength of France. The great château and gardens were crafted and then represented in printed propaganda and pictures as marvels, wonders of the world, that were testimony to the greatness of the monarch who built them. The gardens housed collections of rare shells, plants, rocks and statues that made manifest the geographical and cultural reach of the French state. They served as stages for elaborate fêtes and rituals that, while celebrating the monarch, flaunted the political discipline of the aristocracy under this regime. Wonders and riches of nature were packed into this miniature realm to suggest all that would lie in the French countryside beyond. Versailles was an elaborate earthwork, import depot, and architectural feat, a dramatic piece of material culture that was born of a passion for building and war placed in the service of the accumulation of power within the territorial state.

The material culture of the territorial state

To create the modern state, a centralized bureaucracy to claim and manage a vast and complex territory, place and power had to be allied in a new way. In the old system, leaders dominated land by linking a radiating network of power centers – fortresses, towns or cities. These centers regulated trade, maintained military routes, standardized political relations, and afforded protection from invaders. It had worked well for empires that stretched over vast distances; the newly captured margins of such territories could be reached, if not fully managed, through the network of centres. State territory was different; it was more clearly bounded and closed, and it could be more immediately controlled. If the land of empires was known by its power centers and expansiveness, the land of the state was known by its boundaries; it was the product of a kind of political "enclosure" movement that identified a particular, marked part of the European continent with the state.[5] Any ambiguity about the placement of its boundaries was welcomed as an opportunity to go to war. France, as a political *location*, needed a standing army to guard its borders; it had to be measured precisely in latitude and longitude by the scientists of the observatory; it required surveying and recording on maps by military engineers and cartographers; it had to be integrated by canals, roads, and bridges and had to have its land drained and improved to give it wealth; it required managed forests, harbors, arsenals, and shipyards to support a navy; and, for all this, it needed to be shaped and reshaped on the battlefield so its boundaries would be grand and clear to everyone. Like the Roman Empire, France was as much an engineering feat as a political one. Unlike the Roman Empire, the territorial state mobilized a more contained and controllable parcel of land, whose resources could be explored and displayed in new ways. Controlling land through war and engineering was a strategy for gaining power that was not without precedent, but was resuscitated to new ends in the political culture of early modern France. It led to a rash of experiments in building and war that transformed a landmass into a new kind of political resource.[6]

The existence of a political culture of territoriality in early modern Europe would be easy to overlook as ahistorical or unremarkable (and hence easy to erase from French history), if one assumed that humans were by nature territorial creatures or that they always held feelings of political ownership about places.[7] But neither of these static views of power and place would explain the shifts in cartography that appeared in Europe during the sixteenth and seventeenth centuries. Surveyors began to be commissioned in growing numbers to make ever more detailed images of states and estates, using new measurement techniques and modes of cartographic rendering. The results were often treated as much more than repositories of facts. Some were used to plan wars, build canals, or organize forests. Others simply pointed to the importance of their contents with elaborate decorations, including signs of the powers inherent in nature and pictorial inventories of the social and natural resources of the mapped regions.

The desire for careful measurement of topography was itself a tribute to the growing importance of land and its systematic use in the period. It was not that people had not surveyed before or cared about their domains and fields. Certainly the Doomsday Book in late medieval England was a dramatically complete land inventory. But something changed during the sixteenth and seventeenth centuries. Lines of demarcation across the earth took on new significance. Before that time domains were certainly politically significant landholdings, but they were identified by their centers more than their peripheries. Old maps were marked with castles and towns, centers of commerce and social action, and with the rivers, roads and seas along which one could pass from center to center. The newer maps of the sixteenth and seventeenth centuries were

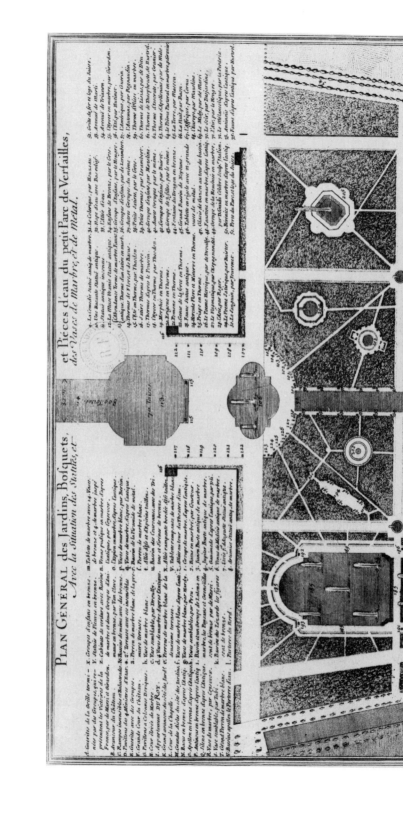

PLAN GÉNÉRAL des Jardins, Bosquets, et Pièces d'eau du petit Parc de Versailles, des Vases de Marbre, et de Métal, Avec la Situation des Statües, etc.

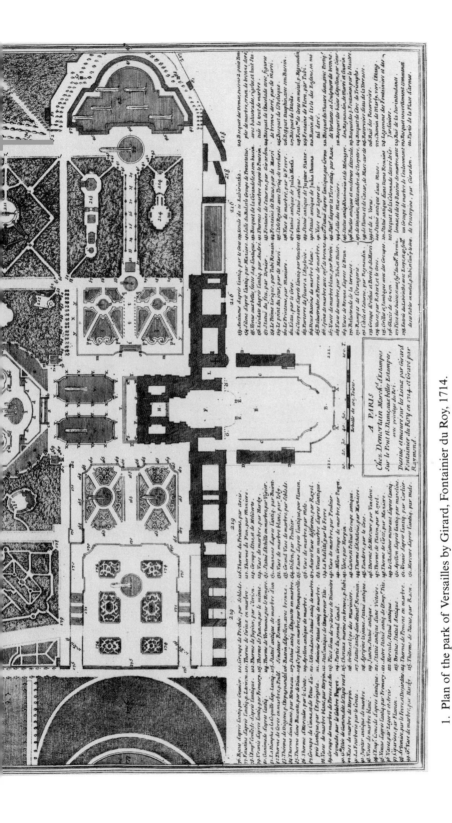

1. Plan of the park of Versailles by Girard, Fontainier du Roy, 1714.

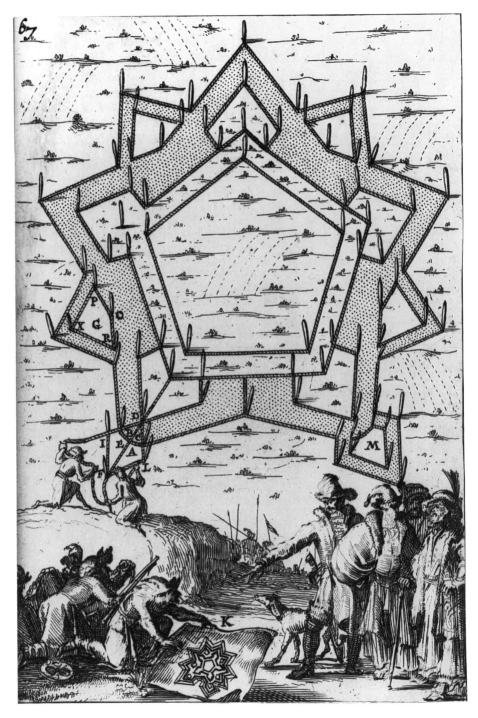

2. Laying out the design for a new fortress (Mallet, *Les Travaux de Mars ou l'Art de la Guerre*, 1684, p. 167).

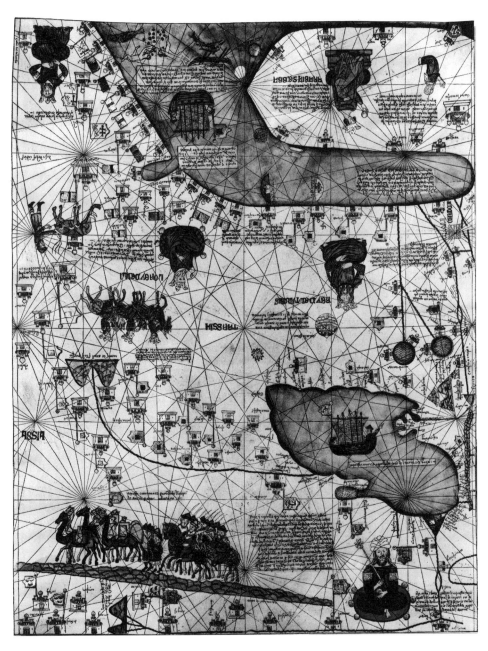

3. Catalan Atlas, 1376.

different. They started to mark boundaries with clear lines (and to use color changes to emphasize them). Grid structures on maps were revived from Ptolemaic sources and were used not only to measure the earth in scientific terms but to locate borders more precisely.[8]

While in England surveyors most often made maps of estates for economic purposes, in France the vast majority of them did map-making for military or other institutions of the state. Louis XIV shared with other French military leaders an obsession with political maps and models; they filled their châteaux with maps and globes that described, not so much their own private land holdings, but either political territories of foreigners (friends or enemies) or land that they had annexed in war. In addition, they had constructed the most terrifyingly elaborate models of their own and others' towns and fortresses that could be used for strategic planning; techniques for making these clay constructions were illustrated in books on fortress-centered warfare.[9] Military books were joined on French shelves by primers written by surveyors on how to use triangulation techniques for warfare, linking the measurement of territory to the techniques for capturing more of it. At the end of the century, the government even contracted for a great national survey to be made to lay claim to and embody the territorial reach of the French state. The techniques of military control of land obsessed the entire nobility and pervaded the cartography of France during Louis XIV's reign.[10] These political maps developed with and helped to constitute the territorial state.

French formal gardens as laboratories of power

In an odd way, one of the clearest (albeit not immediately obvious) expressions of the new political interest in land in the period lay with the massive gardens that began to be constructed around the great royal châteaux of France. The gardens in seventeenth-century France grew dramatically in size and cultural importance. They became highly articulated and deeply structured forms, emerging from châteaux as quasi-architectural features and continuing along pathways and beyond sculpted masses of trees toward the horizon. They delineated living spaces and ceremonial stages beyond the walls of buildings; they constituted a site for an aristocratic way of life that linked social standing to territorial control and the accumulation of property. It seemed that buildings in this historical moment were no longer large enough nor complex enough for the new cultural possibilities of the age. Something more was needed to contain the sculpture, fountains, and plants; a bigger stage was required for the elaborate fêtes (or even frequent but modest promenades or hunting parties) that were part of court ceremonial life. Not just buildings but land itself needed attention and celebration, requiring ingenious decorative strategies and engineering feats, and embodying new visions of natural order. Enormous energy and passion were harnessed to bring together garden designers, gardeners, trees, shrubs, sculptures, and water systems to facilitate a massive restructuring of hills and valleys. This kind of activity seemed so important that Louis XIV began building the great gardens at Versailles before he began expanding the château there.[11] The political territoriality that developed in France in the period was simultaneously a form of material practice and of political representation.

We tend to think of territoriality as a state of mind, a way of feeling about a portion of land, but the territoriality that developed in seventeenth-century France was, first of all, a form of material practice, a way of acting on the land that helped to make it seem like France. Land was politically mobilized as territory in the period, using engineering skills to reshape it and in the process alter its meaning. Land was measured and fitted within the languages of maps so it could be carried on pieces of paper and made a public image; it was marked and bounded with military fortresses so its breadth would be visible and its relation to state power tangible; and it was suffused with humanly engineered waterways and roadways that gave it internal orderliness and tied it to an economic rationality that was also associated with the state. In all these ways and more, defining state territory for France and making it useful for the state was an activity, not the consequence of a propaganda campaign but the result of a new way of life in which the state intervened in the landscape and gave it new form. Land was not just *seen* in a new way in the seventeenth century; it was handled differently, and this made it represent simultaneously a new materialism and new political trajectory.

The territoriality of these gardens was visible enough. Seventeenth-century French formal gardens were much like the new maps of the period. They consisted of measured areas, organized internally, carefully bounded, marked by waterways and walkways, and filled with lines that simultaneously marked divisions and defined meeting points.[12] Visual rhythms in the gardens were created by the relations of *parterres* (garden beds that looked like carpets), and the *bosquets* (or forest rooms filled with statues and waterworks) that lay beyond. Their geometries were used to integrate diverse elements into a common whole, a corporate or communal unity that transcended all the separate components that went into it.[13] They were built from reappropriated land – farms, cemeteries, and even whole towns – that stood in the way of their formal designs. The finance minister from the early part of Louis XIV's reign, Fouquet, commissioned at Vaux-le-Vicomte what was to become the prototype for all the French formal gardens. To fashion a grand enough tribute to himself and his power, he bought and tore down three villages, and employed 18,000 laborers to make his garden. Nothing short of major military campaigns were equal in their ambitions and consequences for the land. For his hubris and the corruption it represented to the king and Colbert, he was jailed, and his designers taken over by the young king who employed them to articulate at Versailles and other royal residences the new political power of France and its king.[14]

The importance of the gardens to Louis XIV's reign was underscored by the itineraries written to direct visits to the gardens at Versailles. Some of the few pieces written in Louis XIV's own hand were itineraries for promenades that he penned for use on diplomatic occasions; the king wrote these guides himself apparently because he placed great weight on the ritual tours of the park. The promenades were formal affairs, at which distinguished visitors were fed and entertained as they followed the prescribed paths through the gardens. What they did and saw in these circuits was somehow meant to inform their assessments of the king and his court. The promenades constituted an important, if obscure, means of doing politics in and for the new state.

In spite of their tantalizing importance to the king, the itineraries have been

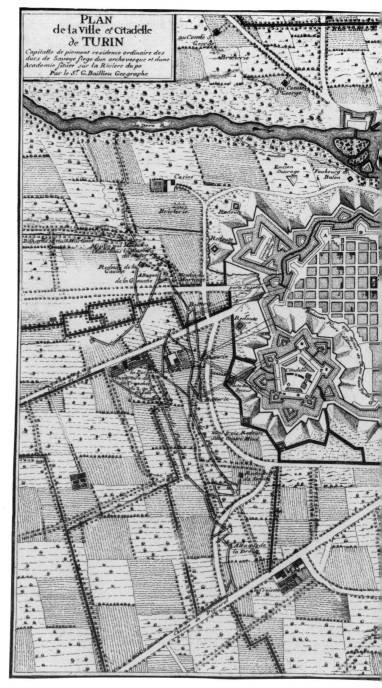

4. Plan of Turin, seventeenth century (Sr. G. Baillieu).

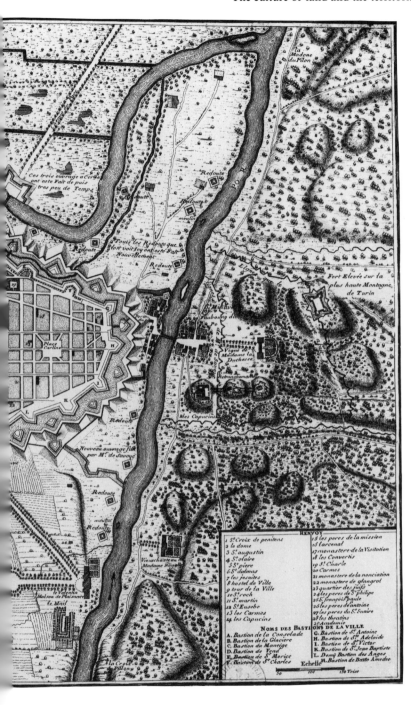

Ces trois ouvrage ou Corset ont este fait de puis tres peu de Temp

Redoute

Redoute moulin

Touts les Redoute que l'on voit Icy ont este fait Nouvellement

Redoute

Redoute

la Madone du Pilon

Redoute

Fort Eleveé sur la plus haute Montagne de Turin

Place Carline

Milieu faubourg du Po

Vigne Madame la Duchesse

Retranchment

les Capucins

Redoute

Nouveau ouvrage fait par M.r de Savoye

Redoute

moulin Redoute

Vieuxchasteau de Madame Royale

Valanne Maison de Plaisance

le Mail

la Croi Pillons

RENVOY

1 S.te Croix de penitens
2 le dome
3 S.t augustin
4 S.t olaire
5 S.t piere
6 S.t dalmas
7 les jesuites
8 hostel de Ville
9 tour de la Ville
10 S.t roch
11 S.t martin
12 S.t Eusebe
13 les Carmes
14 les Capucins

15 les peres de la mission
16 l'arcenal
17 monastere de la Visitation
18 les Convertis
19 S.t Charle
20 Carmes
21 monastere de la nonciation
22 monastere de gfangrot
23 quartier des juifs
24 les peres de S.t philipe
25 S.t françois paule
26 les peres de antoine
27 les peres du S.t Suaire
28 les theatins
30 Academie

NOMS DES BASTIONS DE LA VILLE

A. Bastion de la Consolade
B. Bastion de la Glaciere
C. Bastion du Maneige
D. Bastion de Yend
E. Bastion de S.t Morice
F. Bastion de S.t Charles

G. Bastion de S.t Antoine
H. Bastion de S.te Adelaide
I. Bastion de S.t Victor
K. Bastion de S.t Jean Baptiste
L. Demij Bastion des Anges
M. Bastion de Beate Amedee

Echelle

50   100   150 Toise

5. Plan-relief under construction (Mallet, *Les Travaux de Mars*, 1684, p. 175).

6. Aerial view of Vaux-le-Vicomte (Amis de Vaux).

appropriately described by Thacker (1972) as problematic to use in understanding gardens, since they were developed as systems for showing the park, not explaining it; they provided no guide for analyzing the meaning of the garden, its statues, or its layout. Instead they told visitors how to walk in a semi-circular pattern through the parterres and bosquets of the *petit parc*, and where to look as they moved. When they approached intersections of walkways they were told how to turn to appreciate a view or to see the artwork or château from a different angle; they had their attention focused on the garden's spatial design and the objects punctuating it. Thus they were taught to inventory the lands and wealth of the French king.

How did the visitors respond to their tours? Madeleine de Scudéry, in her fictional account of a garden walk, suggested how surprised and delighted foreigners could be with the gilded fountains, intricate plantings, complicated water system, and classical statues brought from Italy (not to mention the collection of rare trees, the elaborate topiary, and other planted marvels to be found there). Presumably, this salon writer was currying favor with the king by her praise. Nonetheless, she was also conveying impressions of Versailles that were actually experienced and noted by journal-writing tourists from England and Italy. Martin Lister came away from the gardens gushing about the natural and aesthetic wealth at Versailles, which he claimed now surpassed anything found in Italy. Most others spoke more about the sheer monumentality of the gardens, and the overpowering combination of beauty and scale found there. The vast

array of fountains, the elaborate garden architecture, the huge canals, and impressive collections of rare trees and animals were the impressive features to visitors such as John Locke, Ellis Veryard, and Richard Ferrier. John Locke was most taken, in his tour, with the water works – the fountains, aqueducts and pumps that ran them; he was overwhelmed by their technical daring and success. Nature was *made* miraculous through French ingenuity apparent in the glittering fountains, marble furniture dripping with cool rivulets of water, the enormous Orangerie, and the stately grotto at Versailles.[15] These sites encompassed everything one could expect of the land of a Sun King, and suggested what wonders could lie in the countryside beyond. As a representation for propaganda purposes of French cultural and technical achievement, the gardens were clearly effective.

Some scholars have downplayed the significance of the promenades as forms of symbolic education, arguing instead that the itineraries were only practical necessities required because of the technical limits of the water system. Fountains had to be turned on and off as the visitors progressed through the garden "rooms" and *allées* to keep the water pressure high enough to make the jets work to full effect. But why was the full effect of the fountains so important if the garden walks were just for fun? And why were the grounds at Versailles made so grand that it strained the water supply? Why were distinguished visitors taken to the gardens in the first place? Why was Versailles made more and more elaborate during the period of the king's reign? Certainly, the itineraries had practical advantages; they helped to coordinate the movements of water valves, cooks, servants, sedan chairs, and food required to make these rituals as lavish and well run as possible. They also insured that politically important guests would not overlook any part of the gardens, and not miss even one of these triumphs over nature. But these practical considerations were meaningful not in themselves but in light of the social purposes of the promenades.

Garden historians have searched the itineraries in vain to see if they could find an overall narrative structure in the gardens at Versailles to explain their sociocultural significance. They have met with little success. There was apparently no hidden history of the reign or morality tale about the power of the king that an itinerary was meant to reveal. The routes Louis XIV chose for different occasions were not exactly the same, making it hard to argue that the garden had any essential narrative order that he wanted guests to see. Even the descriptions of the gardens written by Félibien (official publicist for the building projects of the king), which explained in some detail individual statues and decorative artworks, did not ascribe any narrative form to a prescribed walk in the gardens. He only pointed to the Sun God/Apollo-theme that was elaborated in a range of statues and fountains.[16] The king's military prowess was certainly celebrated in the garden. New bosquets or fountains were often erected to hail the king's return from a military campaign. But many elements of the garden from the new kitchen garden (the potager) to the new Orangerie (a proto-greenhouse) had no direct relationship to the military fate of France. Over time, the gardens simply realized ever more breathtaking technical feats. New water pumps wrested new heights from fountains; espalier techniques in the potager forced earlier fruits from trees; retaining walls set vast terraces into the hillsides (as in the new Orangerie); and great ponds and

8. L'Isle Royale during a promenade (F. Delamonce).

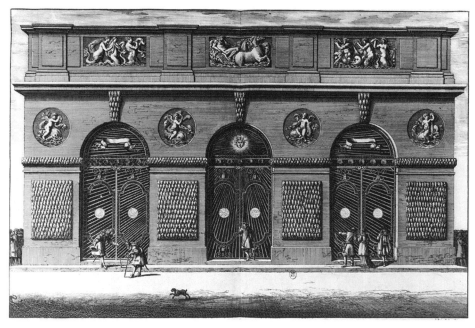

9. Front of the Grotto with the Sun King emblem (Le Pautre 1672).

reservoirs (like the Pièce d'Eau des Suisses) kept swampy regions drained so they could be used productively. With the notable exception of the *Colonnade*, which the great garden designer Le Nôtre ridiculed as simply architectural, newer garden features tended to express an increasing capacity of French artisans, laborers, soldiers, and gardeners to control and manipulate the *land*. That is why, when the king was on a military campaign and wrote back to Colbert to learn how the gardens were coming along, he was not just inquiring about forthcoming efforts to celebrate his military prowess or (on the other hand) turning away from the hardships of war to dreams of an idyllic landscape, but rather engaging in a search for territorial control that was continuous from the garden to the battlefield.

The social significance of land and territorial control

To say that the gardens were expressions of a new French political territoriality is only to beg an important question. What made land so vital to the politics of the period that territoriality became central to both political culture and gardening? One clear source of its importance was the centrality of landholding to the definition of nobility. As new social mobility was making definitions of rank vexed and complicated, markers of high standing gained social salience. Land was clearly implicated in this change.

A striking amount of social mobility, created by the expansion of trade, was throwing members of the bourgeoisie into the world of the aristocracy, creating political and cultural instability.[17] Early in the century, the state tapped the new wealth of the bourgeoisie by selling estates and titled offices in order to raise money, particularly for war;

Perry Anderson estimates that in 1620, 38 per cent of the state income came from the sale of offices.[18] This practice provided a means of bourgeois social mobility while serving the military ambitions of the nobility. The extent of these sales and the scale of the resulting social mobility were greater in France than elsewhere in Europe. This made the mix of class cultures in the French court particularly rich and problematic, and called into question traditional ideas of political legitimacy and aristocratic privilege.[19]

The feudal hierarchy on which noble status depended might have relegated finance and trade to the lowly Third Estate, but this stratification system could not be sustained with the political rise of so many merchants and financiers; neither could the feudal hierarchy be ignored since political legitimacy still rested, albeit less and less comfortably, on the theological presuppositions of the divine right of kings. Business activities were needed to augment the general wealth and power of France, but high standing could not be derived simply from wealth. Instead, the French began to associate high rank with "natural virtue" that conveniently but not exclusively flowed through noble blood.

Justifying the growing power of non-noble elites could have been a severe political problem. In the town of Romans during the late sixteenth century, peasants had railed against the spread of aristocratic privileges to upwardly mobile bourgeois families.[20] Comparable distrust of social mobility also fueled the passionate opposition by nobles to the power of Mazarin during Louis XIV's minority. A notion of "natural virtue" was cultivated inside this new social order, and provided a means of stabilizing it. Natural virtue described a personal nobility of character that could leak beyond bloodlines. Some people were thought to be part of a "true" aristocracy, even though they had not been born to that station. The *"honnête homme,"* whose good character was deemed inherent but not predetermined by blood, had such a natural superiority of character that it defied simple social location. The cult of *honnêteté* in France allowed nobility of character to parallel the social mobility of individuals, while maintaining allegiance to a conception of social ranks as based on natural differences.[21]

In this slippery field of mutually adjusting social values and roles, the bourgeoisie gained some necessary but not decisive political power in France. Simultaneously, aristocrats began to find ways to nibble at the edges of finance and trade. Those of high standing who claimed aristocratic privileges were still restricted from engaging directly in either manufacture or trade, leaving the bourgeoisie in essential control of the economy. Financiers could and did buy aristocratic titles and state or military offices, but then they, like the nobles, had to give up some economic freedom. They were only permitted to trade in products from their estates if they wanted to remain free from taxes and other responsibilities. Even given these incentives, many wealthy Parisians did not choose nobility because they preferred trade to titles, and some impoverished nobles gave up their hereditary rights in order to enter trade. The rights, obligations, and social functions defining social ranks remained intact, while families moved across them.

Colbert's response to the potential political instability arising from this mobility (following Mazarin's earlier moves) was to concentrate power and legitimacy within the

10. Louis Le Grand celebrated for military victories.

state: a political institution outside the hands of both the traditional nobles and new merchant/financier elite; it was an overarching structure that kept both groups from developing an alternative political base.[22] This system of state power could promote capitalist development and yet contain the political disruptions resulting from it by solidifying noble rights while simultaneously undermining the exclusiveness of aristocracy.[23] The problem with this strategy was that it undermined the feudal bases for political legitimacy. If the king transferred his power to a state administrative structure, then what happened to the divine rights of kings? His personal will was supposed to be authoritative because it was meant to be a direct extension of God's Will, but that legitimation did not extend to ministers like Colbert or Louvois. Building a state bureaucracy created fundamental problems of legitimacy that all his fuming and fussing to express his will could not erase. Louis XIV's government commissioned much flagrant propaganda to make the regime seem necessary.[24] But what gave the state more legitimacy was the transfer of authority from the heavens to the earth. The state was made to seem natural. The systematic management and military articulation of French territory not only helped to mark French land, but also began to locate France as a chosen part of the earth whose existence was an expression of God's Will. If divine right was no longer so clearly authorizing the power of the king, the earth could at least be used to legitimate state-based territoriality as a political extension of Creation. The legitimacy of state authority lay in its claim to custodianship of the earth. Louis XIV still acted as though his authority were feudal. He saw and projected himself as express-ing *personal* will through the state, embodying God's Will on earth. But the Sun King, Apollo, was no servant of the Christian God; he was a force of nature that could move the heavens and affect the earth. No wonder the king and Colbert associated the authority of the absolutist state with the land and its improvement: canal building, fortress construction, factory sponsorship, warfare, and colonial land management. All of these gave new material form to the state, and set it on the earth, where the lines between the natural order and the social order could be blurred.

The material culture of state control was particularly effective in linking feudal and commercial cultures around a celebration of land.[25] It linked capitalist conceptions of property to feudal ideas of the relationship of power to the king's domain; managing state territory worked to embellish and improve the king's landholdings, while enhanc-ing the economic value of the domain. There were seeds of this new relation to land in the reign of Henri IV, the Protestant king whose legitimacy was made so rocky because of his faith. His early commitment to Protestant values and simultaneous investment in noble authority perhaps made him and his ministers particularly interested in land-improvement policies imposed by the state. His ministers explicitly began to explore the potential of treating the state as a grand estate, whose properties could be put to better use. This turn to the land, using the tools of a property manager but tied to dreams of state power, may have set France uniquely on the path toward intervention-ist, land-based politics. In any case, by the reign of Louis XIV, territorial politics entered the French court, not as a threat to the king, but as a way to associate his legit-imacy with the management of the state.[26]

Engineering of land for the pursuit of ever more power was the impulse behind the elaboration and extensive use of both French royal gardens and the territorial state. Just as the state was restructuring the political map of France, Le Nôtre was designing a new spatial and technical orderliness for French formal gardens. And just as old polit-ical regions were tied more firmly to a system of *intendants* that were the representa-tives of the central state in the provinces, old garden spaces were being integrated into and superseded by new and larger systems of spatial relations. Similarly, while wars were used to expand and re-articulate the boundaries of France, towns and hamlets were being destroyed around châteaux to produce the new great gardens. The royal gardens could be a diplomatic vehicle for the French court because they eloquently equated land with the state.[27] They testified to a French capacity to control both natural and social forces within a single political culture of territoriality and a cen-tralized political bureaucracy to administer that domain.

Gardens and changing definitions of the natural

So far, the discussion of territoriality and state power has focused on the social strains and cultural responses to them that led the seventeenth-century French to experiment so enthusiastically with technologies of land control both inside and outside the garden. No account of legitimacy, order, power, and French gardens would be com-

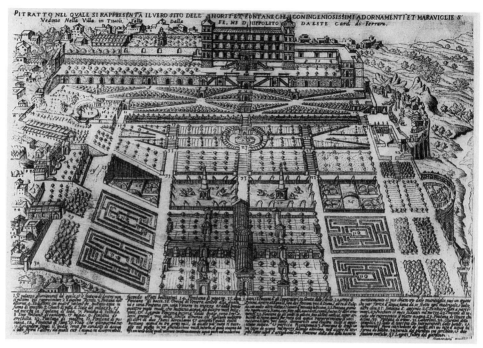

11. Tivoli Gardens, Italian garden design.

plete without reference to the natural world on which this experimentation took place – for the power of the state was rooted in the natural resources of the territory. It took harnessing the powers of nature for political ends and the equation of political order with nature's lawfulness to make the state seem an inherent part of the landscape. To articulate the natural bases of political power, French gardeners, designers, propagandists, and artists called upon conceptions of nature being expounded within the "new science."

Keith Thomas describes a fundamental transformation in the meaning of nature that occurred during the early modern period (sixteenth to the eighteenth century) that might seem at first blush able to explain what the new science meant to French gardeners. At the beginning of the period, Thomas argues, most Europeans saw nature as a dominion set up by God for Man (Adam and his male descendants); increasingly they learned to see nature as a system of forces and relations distinct from the human world, set up by God but available to humans through sense perception combined with reason. In the first view of nature, land was God's Creation given to man to manage in His name. In the latter, land became property with impersonal qualities that could be learned through study and employed for human improvement. Neither view treated nature or land as a political resource.[28] The first view of nature described by Thomas mapped well onto traditional descriptions of the early Edenic Italian garden. The second fits the later property-oriented English gardens, but neither accounted for the seventeenth-century French garden. We will see why in a minute.

The Renaissance pleasure garden followed very closely the Christian view of nature

12. Villa Borghesia, Italian garden design.

described by Thomas. They used circles and squares as geometries of perfection to express the spiritual qualities of these sites. Many of the gardens were actually built for clerics and played on Edenic visions of the garden as the locale for idealized human pleasures, a site for innocent and not so innocent delight. They were also a naturally masculine domain, a gift from God to men, constructed as a playful space, which worked out themes of hierarchy and domination. These Italian gardens were full of jokes; they made funny noises, created illusions, sprayed visitors with water, and tricked them with mazes. They exercised God-like control over those who visited them. Their tricks, which disarmed the unwary, demonstrated that a larger power was at work in the garden. Only the designer of the garden (to continue the image of Eden) or his agents were able to anticipate what the automata would do, where the mazes would lead, and where the unsuspecting visitor would get wet. The garden, like Eden, was both perfect and treacherous because it was controlled by a non-human power.[29]

At the same time, Renaissance gardens were spiritual and mysterious. The presence of Greek and Roman gods in the statuary might make one think that Christian spirituality had no role here, but the Renaissance pleasure garden was clearly an embodiment of a Christian ideal. It was not just that the gardens were idyllic (although they were certainly that). They were vertically open: situated on hillsides that allowed visitors to see the connection of the sky above to the earth below. (The garden plans from the period depict them as nearly flat, but they were on quite steep hillsides.) They were also protected by enclosing walls, trellised walkways and recessed grottoes that sheltered guests from the outside world and contained the Edenic beauty of the flora and

13. Stowe, English garden.

fauna. They were intimate spaces with small garden beds set out in geometries of perfection, expressing a formality of idealism rather than power.

The Mannerist garden in Italy picked up most of these Renaissance qualities but began to break beyond the walls of the earlier pleasure garden, making the claims to land in these gardens greater. Mannerist, and then later, Baroque garden designers wanted something grander and more integrated than small walled gardens would allow, so they built larger walled gardens with sweeping vistas and long walkways. Baroque gardens resited the house within the garden, locating it as a center for viewing this domain. The garden still celebrated Creation, even if it also testified to the power of the family that could set out such a fantastic tribute to God. [30]

In contrast, the English landscape garden was based on what Thomas sees as a rational/scientific conception of nature, a nature that had its own ways, shape, and truth that could be learned through individual contemplation and study. The landscape garden was less personal and less controlled than its Italian counterparts. Nature, in the English garden, was available through the senses as a knowable world, but it was not a representation of nature revealing hidden scientific truths. Drawing on ideas from Chinese gardens, English landscape garden designers emphasized the autonomous, surface qualities of nature. They felt beauty was located in the curve of the hill, the shape of a tree, the sudden vista that opened up when rounding a corner of a path. This garden was a site for contemplation and appreciation through thoughtful admiration of nature's integrity. Land was no longer Adam's responsibility, but an autonomous

14. Stourhead, English garden.

place in the order of things. It was also land for the apprehending individual, the lone thinker or viewer who could know and own it.

This English garden was at the same time property that people could measure, own, and improve using rational skills. It had a value apart from the individual viewing it, but its value could be enhanced by improvements, particularly the addition of small Greek or Roman temples and other icons of the classical tradition that celebrated European rationality and moderation. When themes from antiquity were used for garden architecture, the Renaissance tradition of reclaiming the classical past for humanist reasons was both evoked and ruptured for the pursuit of property relations.

To be "natural," these gardens had, ironically, to be honed carefully from the landscape and designed to control the movements of guests with precision. Paths drew visitors past a series of views that approximated paintings. Strolling along them, guests would pass by a clump of carefully planted trees and suddenly encounter a view or scene that looked like a tranquil landscape. In these vistas, the objects had to look natural; water had to fall and flow, not spray into the air; animals had to roam loose, not be displayed in unnatural menageries or aviaries; and lawns had to be trimmed and trodden by cows and deer. The English landscape garden ran toward the horizon, like the French garden, suggesting it was continuous with nature itself, but there was no boundary marked with a statue or gate at the end of the owner's domain. Instead, a ha-ha (a deep ditch surrounding the property) was used to keep the cattle and sheep in place without showing the property line. The English garden provided an image of

15. Ha-ha at Versailles used to replace a wall, presumably in the eighteenth century.

property-holdings so vast that some of it could be left unproductive. There was no walled Eden here, just an ideal vision of the country that was simultaneously a representation of nature itself and the fecund property of its owner.

In this garden, the line between wildness and cultivation became increasingly difficult to draw. It was not just that the boundaries of the garden were made obscure; it was that the line between cultivated areas and the wilds was made problematic. With the decline of stag-hunting and the growth of fox-hunting, great forested areas were no longer a necessary part of the land around great houses (and not a likely sight in England's deforested countryside). So trees in the English garden started to be planted in small groves which dotted the rolling hills. Wildness was encouraged in these groves, and put alongside great green lawns and the house itself. Nature had many faces, just as the garden had many views, and this new image of natural diversity gave the landscape garden a rhythm, in spite of the lack of garden beds or walls to mark bounded garden spaces.[31]

What was the role of the French formal garden in relation to the gardens of the Italian Renaissance and eighteenth-century England? In terms of Keith Thomas' models of nature, it had no distinctive position; rather, it seemed to embody elements of both systems of culture and cultivation. They imposed even greater order on the land than Renaissance gardens, and they were clearly pleasure gardens, full of surprises and delights. They made water do tricks; they fashioned garden beds to look like rugs rather than patches of wild flowers. At the same time, they were vast and open, moving toward the horizon. They were meant to represent nature as an autonomous system, full of its own order and diversity. They were designed with long walks, providing lovely views, which alternately opened and closed. They created quiet places to sit and think.[32] But unlike both Renaissance Italian and eighteenth-century English gardens, they were not private property; they were open to the public (including peasants) during much of Louis XIV's reign.[33]

One could think of the French formal garden as a hybrid, holding Thomas' contradictory cultural tendencies together, but that would not do justice to the innovative character of the style and its uses. The garden at Vaux-le-Vicomte was no muddle, forming a bridge between Italy and Britain (see plate 6); the French formal garden presented a distinct vision of nature. It was certainly related to Italian gardens of the sixteenth and early seventeenth centuries, being rooted in the symmetries and complex formal structures from the Italian Baroque. But French gardens had a more restrained geometry. Long walkways cut across the countryside, making the overall scale and spatial relations of the gardens visible. The walls that had been prevalent in late medieval and early Renaissance gardens were revived and divided the interiors of the gardens, but now they were made with natural materials: hedges, trees, and trellises filled with vines. The complex space was finally organized around a now-expanded central *allée* and was finally bounded with statues and gates at the extremes of many walkways, helping to hold the huge site together.[34] The result was the territorial garden – a dramatic display of spatial order.

What conceptions of nature were active, then, in French formal gardens? While the great garden architect under Louis XIV, André Le Nôtre, did not write about nature and garden design, one of his immediate predecessors did: Jacques Boyceau. The latter prescribed a system of training for young gardeners that Le Nôtre followed, and was the senior royal gardener when André began his career. There is every reason to believe that he established many principles guiding French formal gardening throughout the seventeenth century.

Boyceau argued that designs for pleasure gardens should realize a scientific vision of nature by containing a diversity of plants and presenting them within a lawlike geometry of space. The inherent rationality of the natural world was to be depicted through the garden's geometry, and nature's abundance was to be expressed through the diversity of plant materials and forms.[35] The parterres, or figured garden beds, provided the richest site for depicting abundance because they were set out in elaborate patterns and were made with a variety of shrubs, flowers, and colored sand. Nonetheless, they had

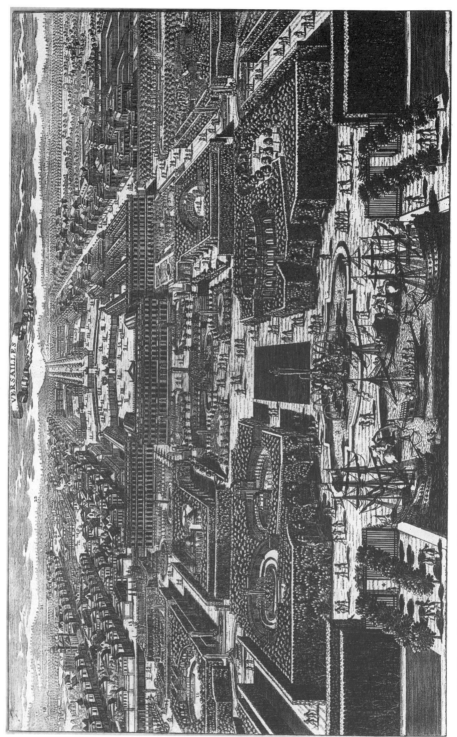

16. View of the petit parc at Versailles from the canal with details of the bosquets (Aveline n.d.).

17. Medieval-style garden.

symmetrical structures that gave them an underlying order – just like that which Boyceau assumed to exist in nature. On the other hand, the bosquets or forest "rooms" – open spaces circumscribed with trees, hedges, and trellises – were carefully laid out in apparent, if not always real, bilateral symmetry with the "rooms" getting larger as they were set farther from the house. These garden features emphasized the geometrical form of the gardens[36] (see plate 1). Still, they were filled with sumptuous statuary and elaborate waterworks that were ample exemplars of superfluity. The resulting parks were not explicitly tied by the garden literature to the political organization of France, but they had a combination of wealth and orderliness that was strikingly comparable to Colbert's goals for the French state. No wonder these vast and sumptuous landscapes were constructed by Le Nôtre under Colbert's supervision. And no wonder they proliferated just as the new system of state-based political order was being developed. They enrolled bits of forest and lawns, canals and walkways into new and ambitious patterns of territorial management.[37]

The land in the French formal garden was measured but not in ways that would become typical for English gardens in the next century. English gardens were carefully delineated areas on privately owned estates. They were pieces of property freed from the burden of productivity – places set aside for learning, not scrubbed and ordered up for political duty. The French formal garden, in contrast, contained land that was very much in use: surveyed and measured, and stamped as something under human control. The French garden was neither an Eden evoking the sacred nor a fertile field left to

Jacques Mollet Inuentor   1 2 3 4 5   10 .toises

18. Parterre pattern by Jacques Mollet.

19. Théâtre d'Eau, a bosquet at Versailles.

reveal nature's inner truths; this land was dominated in order to glorify its ruler and to mark itself as French. It was a politically imbued, closed space designed for power, not wealth or spiritual health. In this, it was a bit like the land annexed in war or the estates acquired by Parisian financiers in the seventeenth century. Both these spaces were acquired to secure political status. The noble seigneuries bought by Parisians were a means for translating economic power into *political* power; they were not estate lands in the English sense designed to secure agricultural wealth or stable incomes from rent. They embodied a more deeply political and corporate view of land, and projected a more spatialized view of political relations.[38]

There was a wild, corporate nature in French gardens, too, but one different from the untamed woods of English gardens. According to Carolyn Merchant, nature (particularly in popular culture) was seen prior to this period by most Europeans as a woman or female: a wild, spiritual, inviolate, holistic, productive, responsive, and integrated being. With the scientific revolution, this popular female presence was supposedly displaced; nature was tamed, secularized, dissected, exploited, made orderly, harnessed for pragmatic ends, while also being made part of a culture of gentlemen.[39] In seventeenth-century French gardens, however, *both* the female/corporatist and male/mathematical conceptions of the natural world were mobilized. While nature's orderliness and pragmatic value (for politics) were self-consciously evoked in the formality of the gardens, the female, organistic, wild conceptions of nature were realized in garden statuary. France was frequently depicted – always as a female figure and often with bounties of nature or fruits of war placed around her. She embodied a France that was corporate, inviolate, whole, productive, responsive, wild, but integrated – just like nature. She was met in the garden by other female figures, many of whom represented elements of the natural world. The Marsy brothers' statues of the times of day, the four elements, and the four seasons were all women. These figures, presented as physically comparable to France, helped to naturalize the state, using a female principle of power.[40]

Together, the statuary and garden structure conveyed a richly layered view of the landscape as a site of power that was part natural, part social. French formal gardens may have looked on the surface a bit like their Italian predecessors because of their formality, and they may have shared some of the expansive and intellectual qualities of later English landscape gardens, but they embraced the forces of nature in a unique fashion and placed them in a distinctively French way on the human plane of power.

Gardens and the study of material power

What good does it do to turn to gardens and ask these kinds of questions about material relations in European political life? Clearly, one purpose is to illuminate aspects of the growth of the seventeenth-century French state that have not been given adequate attention. But how can gardens help with this? Gardens are sites where people reflect upon and experiment with relations between the built and unbuilt environment. They are places where managing the natural world is a matter of everyday concern, and where social relations to nature can be both forged and contemplated. Gardens use engineering and cultivation practices to make "nature" unnatural; and then they recon-

20. *France's Victory over Spain* by Girardon.

21. Le Gros, *L'Eau* (1681). One of the four elements.

stitute a "second nature"[41] honed to human purposes through their artifice. Gardens are complex laboratories, where new cultivation techniques are explored, new approaches to engineering entertained, new aesthetics mobilized, and new demonstrations/representations of power tendered; they are places where human will and the natural order are co-constructed. Gardens address, in other words, some fundamental ties between human action and the material, "natural" world, so they have surprisingly important tales to tell about human societies.

French formal gardens are (or ought to be) particularly salient to social theorists for the way they can illuminate state territoriality: that aspect of seventeenthth-century French state formation which has been surprisingly resistant to conceptual development. While the material relations of the sort made visible in French formal gardens may seem just ephemera, the restructuring of the landscape to give it a political identity was itself an experiment in territoriality that had much more consequence. The gardens demonstrated ways in which land could be made a more vital force in politics; they also helped to naturalize the imposition of political order on the countryside by making it seem continuous with nature's own forms and forces. Territoriality in the seventeenth century was, as Finer (1975) notes, related to military power, but it was cultivated where military ambitions, the natural world, and engineering skills met – not so much in battle but in the preparations for it – in fortress engineering, bridge-building, and other earthworks that preceded and followed moments of armed conflict. Importantly, it was this territoriality, the material politics of land-based power, that was explored in French formal gardens where claims to French greatness were made using a combination of military engineering, land cultivation, and French aesthetic ambition. So, while it might seem at first blush more precious than important to study gardens, essential social processes are illuminated in them that are just not easy to study elsewhere.

Understanding territoriality as a form of politics is difficult without attention to its material dimensions, and gaining a fuller sense of the workings of territoriality in modern politics is hardly a frivolous project, given the numbers of people who have died to secure lands in which to invest their political hopes and identities. We need vocabularies for explaining these struggles that will make sense of both the social development of political passion and the uses of land to legitimate and instantiate political relations. And French formal gardens, where the French countryside and political will were merged through art and engineering, provide some clues for addressing these issues.

Studying European gardens also provides an opportunity to think more generally about material relations and political culture. Historians and social scientists, who are loath to admit that culture can be a significant force in history, may not find this issue compelling, but scholars, who take culture seriously but assume that it works through discourse or thought, should find value in considering it. This book is dedicated to unearthing fundamental cultural dimensions of material relations whose consequences are not so much mediated through thought or language as located in an ordering of the material world itself. If the first modern state was indeed a territorial as well as an administrative entity, then physical transformations of material environment helped to produce it. The cultural engineering of a material world designed to serve new forms of political relations was, in this time and place, consequential for history.

Social scientists and historians of many stripes already take it for granted that social relations must always include (if not always be based upon) economic uses of the natural world. We know that human beings must eat, consume water, and find shelter to survive. We know that we take these things from nature. Most social theory recognizes this fact by saying that large-scale social systems must have economies. Through patterns of extraction, human communities get adequate resources to survive. This means intervening (either on a small or grand scale) in the natural world. Too often, terms like "economy" and "field systems" provide analytic means for describing these processes while allowing the natural world to drop out of sight. Economies become equated with money and power, and through conjuring tricks of language, the natural world recedes in importance. Plant cultivation becomes associated with different types of agriculture. The growing things themselves drop from view. Similarly, cutting through the landscape to build roads and canals becomes infrastructural work. After we make these reductions, we can then speak fluently about agriculture, manufacture, and infrastructure as though we can now ignore topsoil, cold winters, gravel roads, and people working in fields. We construct analytic languages to reinforce and purify the assumed split between nature and culture. The elements of nature we care about (plants, minerals, and waterways, for example) get new names so they can be brought inside social life (agriculture, raw materials, and transportation systems). Plants, minerals, and water can be forgotten. We can talk about growing foodstuffs without worrying about nature – at least until there is bad weather or terrible diseases that wipe out what is growing in the fields. Then, viewing the social chaos, we remember that people depended on the crops, not the language of economic analysis.

We also need, as cultural analysts, to include material practices as part of the world of meaning-making.[42] We should try to approach material culture without reducing objects to instantiations of discourses or realizations of cognitive representations. Where culture is treated as ideas and beliefs or discourses of power, the end result is the disappearance of the material world behind language. That is comparable to the loss of things in economic analysis. Meanwhile, we live in built environments, and we make sense of ourselves and others not just by what we say and write but also by our actions in the material world. Building a fence can say volumes. So can shooting weapons at someone. We often figure out whether or not we are privileged or oppressed members of our social worlds by assessing the material resources at our disposal. We are not, however, just vain and greedy creatures who live in a frenzy of material desire. Certainly, we can buy too many worthless consumables, and we can thoughtlessly litter the countryside with old wrappings and cigarette butts (or at worst, toxic chemicals), but we also build schools, hospitals, homes, parks, and we even sometimes for good reasons leave the environment alone. Self-consciously or not, we and our predecessors have made the very landscape that we now live on, value, curse, and worry about. We live in an artificial world, even in most areas of the countryside. The many forests in depopulated areas filled with young trees, all more-or-less the same age, did not just grow that way by magic. Most sprang up where earlier farming communities died out.

22. Girardon's *Apollon et les nymphes*, designed for the Grotto.

The woods once were fields, and the young trees emerged together as seedlings in abandoned meadows, reclaiming those spaces. Rolling hills that remain open and seemingly endless are often the remnants of a devastating deforestation that has not been rectified over time. History is visible in the material environment, whether we recognize it or not, because human life has a material dimension that is not usually taken seriously.

It is easy to see why great pleasure gardens built by princes – of all the material environments to consider – would be ignored by history. Princes are rare, and pleasure is not usually thought by intellectuals to be serious enough to contemplate at length. But French formal gardens in the seventeenth century were both impressive sites of power, and gained much of their effectiveness from their sensuality and delights. The gardens could instruct foreigners in the power of France because they could lure them into this pedagogical space with seductive visual effects; they could attract nobles to the center of Louis XIV's court by making it glitter with parties, costumes, and entertainments. Hazlehurst contends that the gardens of Le Nôtre were gardens of illusion, which played on visual surprises to capture the visitor's interest. Their orderly severity and their political import were both tempered and furthered by an intentional and very serious playfulness.

The social mobilization of nature in the gardens of Versailles may have been in part a seduction, but it was in the end important because of its social use for politics: *geo*politics. Of course, land had been central to power before and used to manage the relations between states. People had developed new weapons of war before, and the results were important to the outcomes of wars and the fates of princes. It was not that infra-structural improvements had not been used in the past to improve the land. But in seventeenth-century France, these things were organized into *a single system of material culture dedicated to the accumulation of power*. The measure of power in this regime came to be a material one; the search for power centered on technological innovations; and the realization of power came through successful intervention into the realm of nature, making it the object of territorial ambition. Geopolitics brought the earth to the center of the struggle for power, where techniques of intervention, destruction, and control over nature were no longer in the range of local action but became the business of states and important sources of state power.

2

Military ambitions and territorial gardens

The formality of seventeenth-century French gardens has generally been attributed to Cartesian rationality: a geometrical order imposed on the land. Yet while the gardens may have flourished in post-Cartesian France and created measured landscapes, their order was derived less from an abstract pursuit of scientific truth than from the design and construction of military fortresses. French gardens, depicted from a bird's-eye view or on two-dimensional plans, did indeed have geometrical forms that could easily be equated with a mathematically structured natural world. But the parks' three-dimensional shapes had military sources. French formal gardens were constructed with complex grading like fortresses to embed their surface geometries into the earth. Their elaborate terracing gave the gardens an important and imposing hierarchical structure that was in spirit much more feudal than Cartesian. The designs were dug into hillsides and put up with retaining walls, creating complex contours even where the natural landscape was quite flat. Gardens had high points that commanded clear views over the surrounding countryside, and also depressed areas with canals, fountains, and statues that were masked from view until the visitor came near. This kind of systematic structuring of visibility and invisibility through grading was derived from the design of battlements. In fortresses, staying out of sight of the enemy while being able to see them clearly provided strategic advantage. The transfer to formal gardens of military techniques for strategically manipulating vision helped to give purpose and meaning to the vertical relations among spaces there. French garden topography was less the realization of some Cartesian impulse than an expression of military engineering in garden architecture that spoke obliquely but effectively to French prowess in war.

Gardeners writing in the seventeenth century were quite clear that building a great garden had to begin with the land. The first chores of gardeners were earthworks to make the landscape tractable. Those setting out new gardens had to level the planting areas, remove excess stones and water from the soil, cut down trees in some places and plant them in others, erect retaining walls to hold back hillsides and raise terraces, divert whole rivers and streams to connect or contain planting areas, and cut canals or ditches into low-lying regions to sculpt the landscape and drain potentially arable land. At the same time, plumbers had to lay pipes for waterworks, and engineers had to

23. Grading used to articulate the garden geometries near the Latona fountain.

design a system of reservoirs and channels to create an adequate water supply. With these elements in place, planting could begin in earnest.[1]

But how were these elements to be put in place? What techniques could be called upon to make the earth more amenable to the plans of gardeners and the will of their patrons? Many approaches were derived from the Ancients. Much of the hydraulic engineering, for example, had roots in Roman practices. Reservoirs, pumps, aqueducts, and canals were all known features of Roman culture. Nor were retaining walls particularly new. Classical designs for fortified cities provided models of grading and earth-moving that were easily used to construct gardens. These traditions had been elaborated upon in Renaissance Italy, and were self-consciously transferred to France.[2]

In the early seventeenth century, the garden theorist, Jacques Boyceau, solidified this transfer by making it fashionable in France to discuss garden design in terms of classical culture. He was a highly educated man whose position as a royal gardener perhaps was too modest for a person of his recognized abilities. He articulated a theory of garden design that equated landscape design with architecture. Architects were already considered artists and were clearly distinguished in this period from builders, but gardeners were still deemed to be part agricultural workers. To make his occupation more lofty, Boyceau pointed to classical interest in gardening, and argued that designers of aristocratic parks should be trained in classical thought and art to refine their tastes and techniques. He elaborated a program of education for young gardeners with considerable emphasis on the Great Tradition, drawing upon Renaissance interest in using education to distinguish arts from trades, artists from ordinary people. If gardeners were schooled to be artists, reflective theorists of their own practices, they could do better work, gain greater respect, and receive better positions at court. For this, they needed training in both mathematics and architecture – not just for the practical value of these subjects but for the connections of these disciplines to the Great Tradition.[3] As we will see, his educational program, whatever its intended purposes, necessarily turned young gardeners like André Le Nôtre toward classical engineering, including the military sources and ramifications of design.

His pivotal position in bringing military architecture to formal gardening may seem ironic, since Boyceau was more interested in connecting gardens to modern science than feudal models of military power. He forcefully argued that gardens should reflect the order of nature known to the new science – whatever that meant to him. But Boyceau's classicism had a more powerful effect on his work and the future of gardening in France. Once young designers turned for inspiration to the Ancients, particularly the Romans, they were confronted with classical military engineering and architecture. If the same students also sought to familiarize themselves with contemporary French architecture, they would have found themselves faced with other military influences, too. There was still only a blurred distinction in France between the architecture for houses and that for fortresses. Châteaux contained many elements of both. The French Renaissance residences of the Loire Valley, such as Azay-le-Rideau, Serrant, Villandry, Chambord, and Le Plessis-Bourré, still retained some of the references to castle architecture already disappearing in Italy.[4] Seventeenth-century houses built in the Ile de France by financiers and merchants were often designed on similar

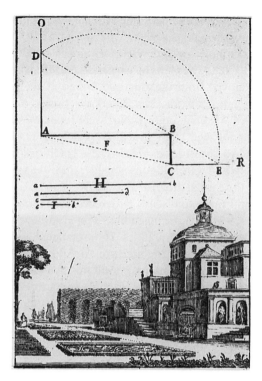

24. Geometry and garden
design from Le Clerc's book
on mathematics (Le Clerc
Practique de la geometrie,
1669, p. 177).

principles. For young men faced with the job of laying out gardens for this kind of property-owner, there was every reason to use and no motivation to eschew elements of military architecture or fortress engineering in reshaping the landscape.

Young landscape architects urged to train themselves in mathematics would have learned many of the same lessons. To study the combination of pure mathematics and survey geometry needed for designing formal gardens, they would have had to use geometry books written primarily for teaching military strategy and fortress design to young aristocrats anticipating a life-time in the army.[5] Mathematics books commonly contained lessons for measuring the trajectories of cannon or for setting out battlements along a fortress wall. No young gardener getting properly schooled in mathematics could miss the illustrations of battlements and discussions of siege warfare. No wonder the young André Le Nôtre, future designer of the gardens at Versailles, after being educated according to Boyceau's principles, used military land-management techniques in his gardens.[6]

Military engineering was probably also attractive to those dreaming of massive garden projects in the seventeenth century because the essential skills needed to make earthworks for military purposes were beginning to be publicized in the period. As army engineers gained experience in grading – setting up new wall systems around old citadels or erecting wholly new fortresses – numerous books on military architecture

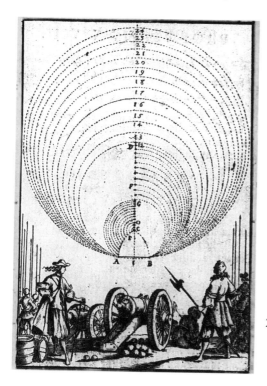

25. The use of geometry for
setting cannon (Le Clerc
Practique de la geometrie,
1669, p. 91).

and strategies of siege warfare were being printed in the vernacular. These texts made widely available both classical ideas on the subject and the results of more recent experience.[7]

What possibilities for garden design could fortress builders provide? The fortifications generally consisted of a complex set of raised flat terraces, interspersed with deep ditches or canals. The walls systems were constructed – like a garden – with back-filled stone or brick. The fortresses themselves had a distinctive star shape comprised of bastions (protruding wall segments), demi-lunes (outlying, often triangular sections of fortress wall), dry *fossés* (ditches), water channels (moats around the walls and demi-lunes), and reservoirs to capture water for the channel systems.[8] These forms were not a fundamental part of the garden's surface geometry, although they sometimes appeared there. The grading, however, was strikingly comparable in form and purpose in gardens and fortresses in the seventeenth century. Land was engineered to manage vision as well as physical access in both sites. Terraces, ditches, and canals became central features of Le Nôtre's gardening idiom.

The growth of military engineering and fortress design during the seventeenth century in France was dictated in large part by the increasing use of cannon to break down the tall, thin stone walls of old cities and citadels. Traditionally designed, unreinforced stone walls simply crumbled under this fire, but sloping walls back-filled with

26. Grading in fortress construction (Mallet, *Les Travaux de Mars*, 1684, p. 49).

soil could withstand the attacks. Fortress design was influenced, too, by the ideal city tradition, which was revived from the Ancients by Renaissance scholars and put to work in Italy. Ideal cities were known for their star-shaped patterns of defenses, which made direct assaults by enemies more difficult (see plates 4 and 5). Although geometrical ideals remained at stake in this tradition, the ramparts for seventeenth-century French fortresses took increasing advantage of local physical conditions, integrating local natural features with constructed ones. Under Vauban's tutelage, French military edifices came to embody what garden commentators in the period would have called a marriage of art and nature. Using land and building techniques, they mobilized the countryside for France.[9]

The military wall systems erected in France during the seventeenth century generally increased the scale of the fortifications, recruiting more land into the system of control.[10] Stones and brick, water and soil, trees and weapons, animals and soldiers were all spread over the landscape, making the structures ever more visible parts of France. Perhaps the technical finesse and grandeur of these projects stirred Le Nôtre to build his ambitiously grand gardens. The French formal parks under his command certainly grew in scale, too, using the same kinds of stone and soil, water and brick, trees and laborers as any fortress. Both citadels and gardens claimed the land, using retaining walls, canals, plantings, and a complex system of grades. Both kinds of edifices were first drawn onto and then carved into the landscape. And both gave French noblemen terraces for surveying the countryside and simultaneously enhancing and signifying the power of the French state.

While Le Nôtre was clearly instrumental in bringing military engineering and military allusions into the French formal garden, it is not obvious why he was the one to make this shift. There are some clues. He was, as mentioned earlier, trained according to the program championed by Boyceau, exposing him to military architecture, mathematics, and engineering at least in their classical forms. Some text books, such as R. P. Bourdin's *Cours de Mathématiques dédié à la noblesse* (1661) could have taught him explicitly how to grade terraces like military architects. The techniques illustrated in that text mirrored exactly the ones used later by Le Nôtre and his followers in French gardens.[11]

Other points of exposure to land-control techniques came elsewhere in Le Nôtre's education. Thierry Mariage suggests that when André went to the Louvre for his training in painting, he probably encountered the instrument-builders, land surveyors, and mathematicians who were located there, helping to measure and render France cartographically for military use. He would have seen in their shops or studios both new survey instruments and techniques of survey geometry being developed for measuring and managing territories.[12] Le Nôtre may also have learned some engineering directly from the aging Boyceau. The charismatic senior gardener could well have supervised Le Nôtre in his early days as a royal gardener. But Boyceau himself was not a great sculptor of the landscape like his younger colleague. André Le Nôtre most likely cultivated an independent fascination with the material techniques of war, which made him think about their aesthetic possibilities for gardening.

In the late seventeenth century, when cultivated gentlemen were *supposed* to think about war and French nobles still considered themselves part of a warrior caste, Le Nôtre was probably only following the norms of the day in taking an active interest in war and military engineering. In any case, he became connoisseur enough of sieges to accompany his father-in-law, a *Conseiller ordinaire de l'artillerie de France,* to watch the siege of Valenciennes. There he certainly could see earthworks and firepower placed in contest. He also collected medals, many of which commemorated battles.[13] And Le Nôtre was sanguine enough about using soldiers for his projects at Versailles to dig and carry trees, stones, and soil. He clearly took advantage of soldiers' experience in building defensive military structures. It is important to realize, however, that none of these activities could have initiated his turn to fortress engineering. He had already begun to use military techniques long before he came to Versailles.

Le Nôtre's tendency to employ military engineering was already a hallmark of his first great garden: Vaux-le-Vicomte. There was no apparent pressure to use military themes in that park. His patron for the project, the finance minister Fouquet, was a Parisian gentleman whose military experience was limited and whose strategic power lay in the navy, not the army. Moreover, Fouquet never identified himself as a warrior; he was a Parisian sophisticate, who cultivated cosmopolitan tastes and wanted to bring them into the countryside. Le Nôtre, a royal gardener trained to serve nobles, probably knew and cared more about the military than Fouquet. On the other hand, Fouquet had no reason to shrink from military allusions in his gardens if they elevated the stature of his estate. As a well-known patron of the arts, he was predisposed to encourage Le Nôtre's aesthetic experimentation at Vaux. In this surprisingly open context, Le Nôtre seems to have established a signatory gardening style. He made a landscape that was distinctively French, startlingly beautiful, and ambitiously territorial in large part by exploring the design possibilities of military engineering.

What made Vaux so military was its pattern of terracing, which paralleled grading systems used in battlement walls. In fact, it reproduced in form, if not scale, a complex of walls illustrated in Allain Manesson Mallet's seventeenth-century book, *The Art of War* (1684). The shape of Mallet's fortress and the layout of the gardens were, of course, entirely different when viewed from above. The fortress in Mallet's book was star-shaped, while the garden at Vaux was more rectangular. Still, the cross-section (or terracing) of the battlements followed the grading of the garden in an uncanny fashion. The high point at Vaux beyond the canal, farthest from the house, was similar to the exterior bulge of the bastion wall in Mallet's design. The low *fossé* or ditch next to this bulge in the defense system was comparable to the canal at Vaux. The main garden area rising behind the canal did not begin with a uniform raised *sape* like the fortress, although there was a small terrace to one side of the garden at just this point. Still, the low-point behind the *sape,* if elongated, paralleled the main body of the garden. This garden plane ended just before the house with a small elevation, a drop into the moat, and a rapid return to an even higher terrace for the house. A comparable set of grades characterized the last set of terraces in the battlement plan, although this final plane had a *sape* sticking up approximately where Vaux had a moat dug into the ground. The details in the heights of the walls and scale of the garden or fortress might have differed, but the general pattern of grading, the sequence of elevations and ditches, clearly

27. Profile of a grading system for fortress walls (Mallet, *Les Travaux de Mars*, 1684, p. 63).

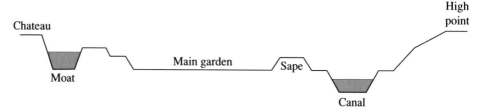

28. The basic grading system used at Vaux-le-Vicomte.

showed Le Nôtre's gardens playing on the wall systems designed for siege warfare.

If we cannot be sure why Le Nôtre used these design elements to make his gardens veer away from Italian precedents, we certainly can see why Louis XIV would have been attracted to them. He was, as Saint-Simon suggested, obsessed with the arts of building and war. We can understand more clearly as well why the young king, visiting Vaux-le-Vicomte for the first time, would have seen Fouquet as a dangerous man, and would have wanted Le Nôtre to design the great parks for his own royal residences. Henceforth, Versailles would become the showpiece for Le Nôtre's talents, and formal gardens would enter into the king's program of building and war.

Military power and the French state

France has often been considered the first modern state because of its efforts to centralize and professionalize both the army and its finances. It helped to articulate a relationship between the two for what has been inelegantly but usefully called the fiscal-military state.[14] This state has been characterized as little more than a means for financing and organizing military conflict, not (as one might expect looking at Versailles) an administrative mechanism with a tax system designed to feed the king's penchant for luxury. More than half of the budget of the new European states of the early modern period was devoted to paying the bills for the military. Colbert commented on these expenses in the early part of the reign, but learned to accept them. Saint-Simon bemoaned the willingness of the king in his later life to sanction whatever military moves were counseled by Louvois, the minister of war.[15] The problem, of course, was as much structural as personal. Integrating principalities into larger state units was a militarily costly enterprise; the claiming of land near unclarified boundaries of states often required military action (and expenses); and setting up colonies or trading stations beyond the European continent required fighting forces to guard them. These actions might eventually bring in revenues, but they would start by requiring expenditures. Acquiring and managing land to exert political authority was an expensive and difficult business.[16]

The displacement of organized violence from the feudal nobility into a professional army was crucial to this new system of power. In traditional feudal life, the military was the center of the reciprocal relationship between nobles and the king; fighting forces were made up of or supplied by members of the nobility doing their duty to the crown. The new French army consisted of paid fighting men, working for the state; it

29. View of Vaux from the side, showing grades near the château (Israel Silvestre, *Veue de Château de Vaux par le Coste*).

30. View of Vaux, showing grades near the canal.

gave the state the legitimate might to exert its will both in France and beyond, but it could only be trained and used with steady revenues, and this meant, of course, that tax funds were needed.[17]

Nobles could and did fight in the new military, but they had to pay heavily for military posts, and they had to be willing to undergo intensive training. In both ways, they put themselves in service to the state. The monarchy was less dependent on them than they were dependent on the king for their military posts. With this system, noble autonomy was diminished, the state's power was enhanced, and yet the noble culture celebrating military virtues was not only sustained but elaborated. A standing army that was continually available for strategic planning, physical training, military contests, or public parading could easily develop new military rituals and rethink battle planning in ways that would not have been possible before, just because there was time and

31. Different ranks of soldiers under the regime of Louis XIV.

money devoted to the purpose. Nobles could glory in the pageantry and in the military victories; they could raise their own infantry, if they were appointed as colonels in the army; but in the end, this fighting force fought to claim land for a French territory that was a resource and responsibility of the state.[18]

With this war machine, the state no longer had to depend for its territorial power on the traditional loose set of alliances among nobles who sustained quasi-independent political centers. These alliances were too fragile for a strong state. If there was a fragmentation of power groups, dissident nobles could set up separate centers of power, as they had done in the past. Soldiers were more reliable within a professional army as well; both regular pay and new garrisons to live in produced a loyalty among the soldiers that was generally stronger than before. It had not been uncommon in this century for groups of soldiers, let loose after military engagements and already poorly paid, to become renegades and take over small citadels. This kind of small-scale guerrilla warfare made the political allegiances of many areas difficult to define. A professional soldier who was continually employed was less likely to become a renegade. With a state-funded army, control over both legitimate violence and the countryside was enhanced.[19]

The standing army also trained soldiers more effectively. Soldiers were not only drilled in formation marching and battlefield formations, but were also taught techniques for attacking fortresses. They dug, dragged, and exploded enemies out of their strongholds, and built new structures to protect their newly won territory.[20]

The state military put particular emphasis on the use of natural resources and local natural features for land engineering: stones and soil for fortresses, waterways and crags for natural protection, forests to hide in and to provide wood for building more fortresses, ores for forging weapons, chemicals for making gunpowder and animals for carrying the weapons, soldiers and supplies for battle. Part of accumulating a great fighting force and making it effective depended on the cultivation of the engineering, forestry and artisanal skills to supply materials for the army and transform them into the resources for war. Fighting and winning wars no longer depended so much on the ability to recruit and organize human brute strength, but more on a capacity to put revenues to work in engineering victories, wresting power from nature to make weapons and wage war. These forces were then used to impose military orderliness back onto nature, to claim the French countryside.[21]

Engineering and military power

During the reign of Louis XIV, the famous architect of so many of France's fortresses, Sébastien le Prestre de Vauban, became the first titled military engineer in France. His appointment to this post and his argument for the permanent cultivation of engineers in the army were responses to the palpable importance of engineering skills for warfare in the period of Louis XIV. Vauban began his career, ironically in retrospect, as a soldier for the Grand Condé during the uprising against the monarchy known as the Fronde. Because of his skills in building and undermining battlements he was forgiven, after his capture, for his treasonous activity and accepted into the royal army. He gained an appointment as a military engineer, and after 1659, began developing fortifications for the army.[22] From that time through the 1690s, he built defenses along the northern and eastern frontiers of France, and improved and fortified major port cities both in the north and south of France. Throughout this period, he followed a dual policy of destroying citadels in the interior of France and constructing or reconstructing fortresses along its boundary, which helped to define the whole territory as part of the state.[23]

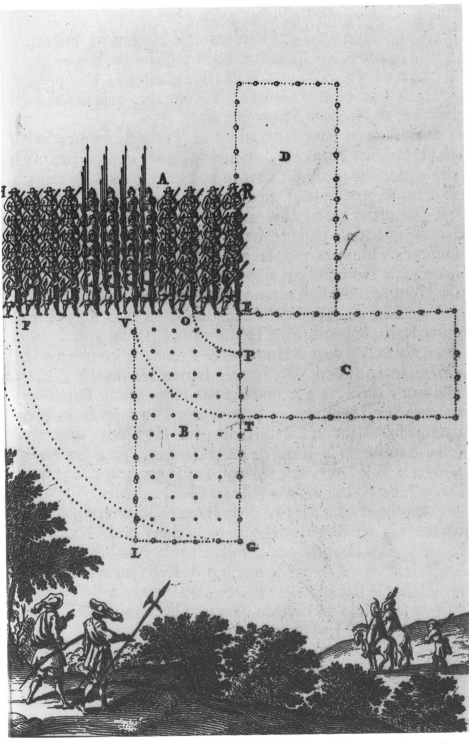

32. Formation marching and geometries of land control (Mallet, *Les Travaux de Mars*, 1684, p. 97).

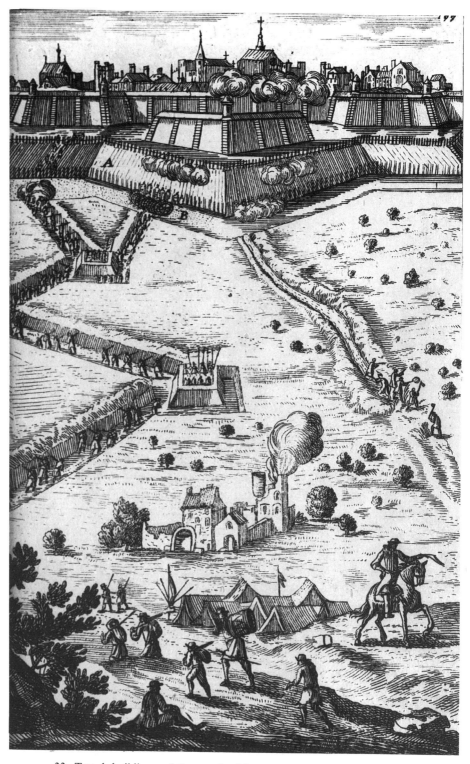

33. Trench-building and the attack of fortresses (Mallet, *Les Travaux de Mars*, 1684, p. 107).

The development of these defenses was in some ways a response to earlier changes in the technology of warfare. The growth of firepower, the development of both cannon and hand-held firearms, had not just affected wall systems around cities, but also the strategies of war. Open-field conflict between opposing cavalry forces could no longer be the mainstay of war. Infantry equipped with guns could easily level even armored men on horseback, creating an unthinkable egalitarianism in warfare that had to be stopped. No longer were aristocrats on horseback better protected than their foot soldiers by their mounts and armor, so they had to be used more sparingly in the field. That way ordinary soldiers would continue to bear the major brunt of injuries and deaths. Soldiers with pikes and with *fusils* or *mousquets* made up the new infantry. Meanwhile, aristocrats turned toward sieges as the primary sites for pursuing glory, and Vauban engineered their victories.[24]

At first, Vauban built fortified cities where they were strategically needed to defend newly won land and to keep outside enemies at bay. Soon, he constructed them where regional populations were only reluctantly under the control of France. He also built garrisons for soldiers in or near fortresses so that these men, if paid well and well armed, could keep both potential invaders and local discontents from filling up any power vacuums that developed along the borders of France.[25] Then, during the 1660s, Vauban began to imagine building not just single citadels for strategic purposes, but a system of defenses. He proposed to construct two fortified lines along the vulnerable northern and eastern borders of France, setting up artificial barriers where there was a deficit of natural ones. The Pyrenees, the Alps, the Atlantic, and the Mediterranean already marked the other sides of the territory. With this project, Vauban hoped to engineer a French territory that was simultaneously defensible and natural. This France Vauban called the *pré carré*. The term *pré* meant a meadow, particularly a dueling meadow; it described a landscape imbued with warrior values. The term *carré* meant square, orderly, self-evident; it was used to refer to plots in a garden, ranks of soldiers, and geometrical orderliness. The square was the perfect form for a natural-ized, measured, and militarily defined territorial state. The systematic building and destruction of fortresses by Vauban and his cohort in pursuit of this ideal of a seam-less French territory began to make the French state not just a political regime but a material entity built into the landscape.[26]

Although it might seem counter-intuitive, Vauban's reputation as an engineer was just as much a product of his offensive strategies as these building projects. Attacking fortresses that had newly elaborated systems of ramparts required digging under walls rather than going over them. It was a job for a mining engineer. Vauban had a flair for that too. Elaborate systems of ditches were used to approach fortified cities or citadels. Behind the attacking army, protective walls or ditches were constructed to prevent local sympathizers from attacking from the rear. For the sieges themselves, the trick was to use earthworks and constructions to control vision and access – in a way comparable to the control used in fortress design. Soldiers had to dig long trenches to approach their target, building walls in front of them with the excavated soil (*sapes*) to keep the defenders from seeing their troop movements. These trenches with *sapes* created a series of blinds that not only kept attacking soldiers from being easily seen but also helped them get near their target without being hit by gunfire. Where ditches could not be dug or they were not large enough for the attacking army, soldiers also used movable blinds on wheels for protection. They also employed portable bridges as well to get closer to their targets, where they were faced with deep ditches, small rivers, or channels. Finally, when the offense was well planned and executed, some soldiers could get close enough to dig under the barricade walls and the attacking troops could enter the town.[27] This was the art of war in which Vauban excelled. For him, war was a matter of engineering a physical environment favorable to French interests – whether offensive or defensive.

Vauban started his career in the military as a regular soldier. He gained the attention of his superiors by showing exceptional bravery and daring. He was assigned to work on fortifications, and only then seems to have learned to see war through the eyes of an engineer. He started to recognize strategic advantage in physical manipulation of the environment. He found that, if the steps to victory were carefully engineered, sieges could be won with less blood shed by his own troops. Because he began his military career as a foot soldier, he identified with these men more than the aristocrats he served. He sought for new technical solutions to strategic problems in part to reduce the loss of life and injury for soldiers. He was particularly concerned with engineering temporary defenses behind attacking troops because counter-attacks from behind were particularly dangerous for the men. His practical humanitarianism led to such successes in war that he seems to have cultivated it too well. He ended his life in disgrace, shunned by the king, for speaking on behalf of ordinary people. He tried to promote a more equitable tax system for the common Frenchman – with disastrous results. He wrote to the king that, while traveling through most parts of France for his various projects, he had noticed that the people were suffering from poverty. This was because the part of the population that could least afford it paid the most taxes. He suggested that the king should and would want to remedy the situation. Of course, he was wrong. At court, where the king lived among the aristocrats who benefited from the tax system, this proposal was an outrage. For his offense, Vauban lost his standing with the king, and apparently died a very unhappy man.[28]

It was not his humanitarian streak, then, that made Vauban a powerful figure in the late seventeenth century even though it shaped his work and perhaps should have influenced the king. Rather, it was his ability to use material means to exercise power and delineate political spaces. His military thinking and engineering projects were central to the growth of territoriality in France under Louis XIV. Vauban did not just treat France as a place to be won by wars, but as a physical reality to be studied and constructed from soil, stone, trees, water, and people. He worked to make France into a great square shape (the *pré carré*) because he felt that the simple geometrical form would give the physical state a kind of abstract legitimacy.[29] The boundaries once set, France could be improved through "works." The country could be engineered to make it better. He worked for Louis XIV on a number of engineering projects from canals to forest management systems, from his strings of border fortresses to the physically improved and protected ports of the Atlantic and Mediterranean.[30] What made Vauban so consequential to the future of France was not so much his siege victories as

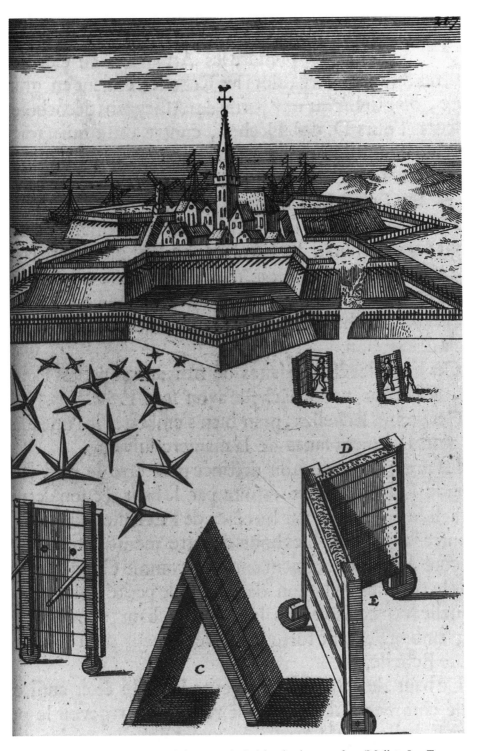

34. Movable blinds and the control of vision in siege warfare (Mallet, *Les Travaux de Mars*, 1684, p. 217).

35. Portable bridges (Mallet, *Les Travaux de Mars*, 1684, p. 223).

his demonstrated conviction that power could be *more easily* derived from manipulating land than sacrificing people. Vauban's tactics yielded a form of warfare where military might was not just measured by the strength of the soldiers or even by their weapons, but by a new factor: engineering skills.[31] This was a lesson about French power that would be generalized not just to gardens but (as we shall see later) to many areas of French state politics.

In terms of fortress engineering itself, Vauban's contribution was surprisingly small. Admittedly, he added small v-shaped forms called *tenailles* to the extant system of *demi-lunes* extending in front of the central battlements, but this was a minor flourish. What he did that made him seem such a great engineer was to take military engineering seriously as a way of "doing politics."[32] His military constructions were a way of embedding politics in the landscape, not unlike what Le Nôtre was doing in the garden. Both were means for transforming land into territory under the control of and testifying to the glory of the king and the French state.[33] No wonder fortress grading systems were such an appealing addition to garden architecture, and that military themes would become important to royal parks.

Military engineering and the gardens at Versailles

The militarism at Versailles in the late seventeenth century is easy to overlook because the château built there by Louis XIV was much less fortified than its predecessor. The early château had a moat, high walls and turret-shaped corners, all suggesting it could be used as a military stronghold. The grand residence built by Louis XIV, in contrast, was broad and open with large windows looking directly out onto an unprotected terrace. The moat that had surrounded the early château was filled in and replaced with terraces and fountains. The interior was made surprisingly visible and accessible to the garden, and the nearby parterres themselves were made enough like carpets or floral fabrics to blur the distinction between interior and exterior. Even the land of the estate was made more open to please the young king. Stone walls that had enclosed the park during the period of Louis XIII were partially razed as the estate expanded, sometimes being replaced by or transformed into decorative fences. Medieval forms gave way to baroque and classical ones. All this seemed to signal that the medieval period of fortress-houses for the nobility was over. And it was. Nonetheless, the military references were still there – not in the residence but in the garden, and not in the commonly recognizable feudal forms.

The military heritage of Ancient Rome was the new source of inspiration for seventeenth-century French architecture. The ideal city tradition not only provided models of fortress design and urban battlement systems that influenced French military architecture and gardening, but also established a basis for redesigning residential architecture. Where cities had exterior battlements, individual houses could be more open because they did not need their own protective walls.[34] With the land around the château at Versailles now filled with military references and elements of military engineering, the château could be pierced with great glass doors, exuding a kind of smug optimism about the safety of the inhabitants. The military engineering of the gardens

36. View of the château at Versailles from the Orangerie, showing its accessibility.

at Versailles significantly predated the remodeling of the château, enveloping this favorite royal residence safely in reminders of French power.

It is important to note that, while the Italians were familiar with much the same military engineering that the French used for their garden architecture, they did not use it so explicitly for making political claims with their pleasure gardens. Italians seeking Edenic perfection did not waste time highlighting their skills in military engineering. Classical engineering did help them build their gardens, but whether or not it was *military* engineering was apparently not an issue to them.[35]

In contrast, at Versailles, the traditional military culture of the aristocracy was celebrated, and any classical reference to the military glory of Rome or any use of classical forms of military engineering were welcomed and often highlighted.[36] The star-shapes common to fortress architecture may not have been the organizing principles for the whole *petit parc* at Versailles, but a pentagon, one of the most commonly used geometrical forms for battlement wall systems, provided the fundamental structure for the *Etoile*.[37] Fragments of bastions were also ubiquitous to French formal gardens. Protruding points of masonry, hedge, and water intruded into terraces, garden beds, ditches, and waterworks. These decorative flourishes may have seemed just pieces of baroque fancy, but combined with changes in the gardens' grades, they helped to give French gardens their military character. At Versailles, these geometrical shapes sometimes imparted a surprisingly somber quality to otherwise very bright parts of the garden.

37. The *Etoile* with its pentagon shape.

The topography of the *petit parc* provided another subtle link to French military culture. Many changes in elevation in these gardens were only a few feet in height, apparently just reinforcing the surface geometry of the garden. But they also provided some miniaturized ramparts for appreciating the details of parterres. In these sites, there was no grand expression of French military power. In fact, many of the walls

38. Miniaturized bastion shapes, grades, and cascades at Vaux-le-Vicomte near the canal.

were sheathed in hedges that had been trimmed to the same height as the wall, so they seemed to merge into the landscape. But these features also encouraged people on a promenade to step periodically onto high points in the garden to survey the land around them – just like a soldier would do from the ramparts of the fortress. They supported moments of military practice through very muted forms of military architecture.

In other parts of Le Nôtre's gardens, the uses of military engineering were dramatically forefronted. Great terraces were erected at many of his royal gardens to allow

39. Bastion-type wall behind the Latona fountain with topiary "guards" along the
top.

people to see spectacular views of the countryside – just as they would from a fortress.
The Orangerie at Versailles, for example, held up the great terrace to the south of the
château. It was unusual to dig orangeries into hillsides this way, so the structure could
not have been just an outgrowth of gardening practices. At the same time, this design
clearly helped to enlarge the terrace, and provide a dramatic viewpoint from the top.
The Orangerie was obviously no battlement wall, but the huge arches around the doors,
which actually held up the structure, were in fact quite military in style. They were
staple forms of support used by military architects since the Romans to build bridges
or aqueducts.[38] The result was a great retaining wall structure with clearly martial roots
that could also house tender plants in winter.

Simple battlement-type walls with their grand and slightly sloping surfaces of stone
made their most obvious appearance at Versailles in the great wall (with double
inclined carriageways) behind the fountain of Latona. This wall retained the main
terrace directly behind the château. It set out the central vista which ran from the residence down the Allée Royale, past the *petit parc*, over the canal, and to the hunting
forests. The top of this wall might have appeared to be merely a convenient spot for
viewing the expanse of the garden below, but the construction itself was identical to
that used in the back-filled barricade walls built for military purposes elsewhere in
France. This wall was a more powerful architectural feature than any of the retaining
walls used in Italian gardens like Villa d'Este in Tivoli, Villa Lante in Bagnaia, Villa
Farnese in Caprarola and the Boboli gardens in Florence. These Italian gardens were

built on inclines, and had to have walls to hold them up. They unfolded in layers down the hill, like a cascade made with greenery, sculptures, water, and flowers. Each terrace provided a momentary stop on the hill and a new garden environment. The retaining walls were technically necessary, but they provided aesthetic problems to the gardeners, who tried to decorate or hide them. The terrace walls were generally broken up with criss-crossing staircases, niches full of statuary, fountains shooting water into the sky, or rivulets of water running along walkways. The decorative elements pointed not toward something as practical as the retaining wall itself, but toward the sky. For an Edenic garden, the relations between heaven and earth were at stake more than the different uses of the earth.

In contrast, the wall behind the Latona fountain at Versailles was made a massive presence (see plate 39). The stairs and carriageways coming down from the terrace curved respectfully away from the center of the wall. The structure was unmarked by statues, and the center was unadorned with niches. It was partially sheathed only in simple hedges. It might have seemed only a quiet backdrop to the Latona fountain, if the wall did not threaten to overpower even that massive multi-level fountain. Rhythmically spaced rows of topiary bushes were planted along the top of the battlement and followed its contours. They drew attention to its massive presence. Statues set along the carriageways were dwarfed by the walls. The château slowly disappeared from view behind this barrier when people descended the ranks. The wall's solidity stood in contrast to the openness of the remodeled château, protecting the seat of the court with the might of the military.

The battlement form had another and even more unusual site at Versailles: the *jardin potager*, or the kitchen garden. This garden has not usually been discussed in art histories of the gardens at Versailles, in spite of the fact that the king was extremely proud of the garden and took distinguished visitors there. The *jardin potager* was a site in which intensive gardening techniques were furthered, particularly espalier techniques for encouraging fruit trees to grow along walls to create earlier and sweeter fruit. Walls were central to the design of this garden. Espalier trees needed walls, not just to support them but to absorb and retain heat.[39] There was no reason why these walls should be thick enough to walk along, but the king insisted that the garden be built with battlement-type walls all around and through it. Visitors to the garden could promenade along them and look down at the plants below. The result was that the kitchen garden was made more like a fortification than any other part of the garden.[40] Its walls surrounded and crossed it in a way that clearly resembled the walls at the fortified Château Trompette after it was rebuilt by Louis XIV in 1680.[41]

The wall systems at Versailles both in the *petit parc* and the potager mobilized French military culture. France was already known for its experiments with military technique and for the professional training it provided the army. So, when soldiers marched across the terrace above Latona, as they did for fêtes and promenades, viewers were primed to see military strength on parade. They were ready to see the wall as a small-scale barricade and the soldiers as guards, marching along the top of a fortification. But the garden walls had no real defensive purpose; their massively visible staircases and roadways made their heights readily accessible. There was no barrier between

40. The potager wall-system with espalier fruit trees. The walls were thick enough
for the king and his visitors to walk along the top.

the king and the countryside typical of medieval castles (suggesting that the king
needed military defenses from the people). The Sun King was supposed to draw people
to him, not send them away. Still, like Vauban's fortified towns, the gardens at Versailles
presented to the world marvels of French engineering that spoke directly to the might
of France and its ability to control its territory.[42]

Military themes in garden features

The reasons why the king and his courtiers would have found militarily inspired
gardens like those at Versailles interesting are quite obvious. The nobility of France
still imagined itself to be primarily a warrior class, and saw surprisingly little distance
between the lives of courtiers and military duties. The passion for war that Saint-Simon

identified in Louis XIV was not so much a taste for violence as a thirst for personal glory that was part of his noble heritage. Noblemen took to the battlefield to confirm their greatness. In fact, Louis XIII had been much more of a military man than his son; he had reveled in military engagements and the strategies for winning them. He was personally involved both during the Thirty Years War and in the campaigns against the Huguenots. His wife felt he had no interest in coming home.[43] In his campaigns, much blood was shed, much new thinking about warfare was pursued, and many of Louis XIII's goals were achieved. But all this was accomplished at a high price. France in the end, like much of the rest of Europe, had been exhausted.[44] The result was political unrest that plagued Louis XIV's late childhood, the period when his memories were shaped and his political education began in earnest.

Noble military virtues were all the more important during the reign of Louis XIV because of earlier political threats to both the crown and nobles of the sword. Political instability had periodically threatened the power of the French crown even before Louis XIII's time. Henri IV's Protestant faith was a political irritant, and added to the religious strife in France. His death, leaving a regency under the ambitious Cardinal Richelieu during Louis XIII's childhood, did nothing to add to the power of the crown. Louis XIII's politics, when he gained the throne, temporarily seemed to stabilize the monarchy, but, as we have seen, the economic costs of his military adventures had the opposite effects. Moreover, his early death left another regency. While Mazarin was running the government during this second regency, some nobles and Parisian businessmen rebelled against the Cardinal, expelling him from the country and threatening to reduce monarchical authority. This was the substance of the revolt called the Fronde. The rebellion was quashed but the turn toward political stability only began after Mazarin's death, when Louis XIV took over the military governance of France.

The young Louis XIV was no great young general, like Alexander, come to restore France and build a French empire (although he dreamed of the latter and Le Brun depicted him that way). But he nonetheless built a powerful army that underscored the military character of French elite culture and could address French geopolitical interests.[45] Louis XIV's memoirs are filled with discussions of political intrigue, warfare, and the aggrandizement of French power and territory.[46] He did indeed want to make France the seat of the next Holy Roman Empire, inheritor of the Habsburg Empire. So having a taste, if not a flair, for war was both important to the king's schemes and the effectiveness of this regime.

Versailles, when it became the seat of the French court, also became the center for French military life. The Place d'Armée in front of the château contained barracks for the king's guards on one side and the Swiss guards on the other.[47] The guards formed the backbone of the army. They did not just protect the king and perform rituals at court, but they also fought in his battles. They were always with him when he was leading the army, and they often represented him when he was not in the field as well.[48] While many French soldiers were garrisoned at fortified border and port towns, defending strategic locations along the boundaries of French territory,[49] the king's soldiers were housed and trained at Versailles. These men carried the weapons of war

41. Van Clève et Raon, *Combats d'animaux*, 1687, Fountain of the Animals.

when they drilled or marched by the château, and they wore uniforms that made their political loyalties physically visible. They also displayed in their actions the training that was becoming increasingly necessary in the complicated new world of warfare.[50] As they paraded in the courtyards and gardens, they helped to claim the landscape for the king and state.[51]

As if to draw more attention to the military power of France, the surface of the gardens at Versailles was littered with artworks and plantings with military allusions. Many of the waterworks, topiary bushes, bosquets, and the statuary in the gardens symbolized warriors, land, or achievements in war.[52] Le Nôtre's park had topiary bushes and statuary set out like guards along the perimeters of garden areas. Parterres and bosquets themselves were visibly bounded landmasses, like state territories – marked and surrounded by bushes, trees, and walls. The topiary bushes were often clipped to stand in formation, and statues were frequently set out in ranks like infantry. Some sculptures showed wild animals engaged in life or death struggles like soldiers. Others depicted Achilles, Apollo, Hercules, Diana, and other gods and heroes whose

42. Allée Royale: the Latona and Apollo fountains, linked by the *tapis vert*.

physical strength was important to their fame. All these images spoke in allegorical fashion to the value placed on military power in this regime.

The most important set of figures addressing military themes in the *petit parc* were the Latona and Apollo fountains, set along the Allée Royale running from the château down the hill to the canal. In their final setting, these two great works faced each other across the long expanse of the *tapis vert*. This ensemble spoke eloquently to the military might and ambitions of the king and state. The central statue of the Latona fountain showed a delicate and beautiful young mother with her children (one of which was Apollo as a baby) surrounded and attacked by quite horrifying figures of angry peasants, frogs, and lizards. This daunting construction was one of the earliest garden features, and in spite of the many reworkings of the park, it was never toppled. It was an image of vulnerability that was balanced in the Apollo fountain by an image of complete and utter adequacy. Apollo, in his fountain, was already a young man, thoroughly competent not only to take care of himself but to carry responsibility. He was set in his chariot, drawing the sun from the underworld into the sky. The counterpoint of the two fountains, contrasting youthful vulnerability and adult potency, provided an interesting comment on the Sun King's coming of age.

The classical myth alluded to in the Latona fountain helps explain its enduring importance to the gardens at Versailles. The story goes that young Latona and her chil-

43. The Latona fountain, showing peasants attacking the young family and being turned into frogs (Balthazar and Gaspard Marsy, *Latona with Diana and Apollo*, 1668–70, pedestal setting by Hardouin-Mansart, 1686).

44. The Apollo fountain depicting Apollo as a young man and powerful god (Jean-Baptiste Tubi, *Apollo*, 1668–70).

dren, Apollo and Diana, were trying one day to use a pond, when they were suddenly attacked by peasants. Before this confrontation, Latona had already been expelled unjustly from the garden in which she had been placed by Jupiter. (His jealous wife had resented the favors the god had given to this attractive family and had driven them from their rightful home.) Now, peasants pummeled the family with dirt, while the young Apollo (the symbol of the Sun King, here just a baby) recoiled in horror from the assault on himself, his mother, and his sister. Latona implored Jupiter for help, the attackers were turned into frogs and lizards, and the embattled family was saved from death (but remained expelled from their garden).[53]

Some art historians claim that the fountain symbolized the Fronde, that moment of instability that rocked Louis XIV's childhood. Certainly, this event was traumatic, and caused the royal family to flee unceremoniously from Paris. The monarchy was saved, but not without a severe break between the crown and some of France's most esteemed families. Some say that this uprising was so horrifying that it soured Louis' trust in Paris and drove him to establish his court at Versailles.[54] The Latona fountain could mark this move, but then it would stand for a moment of retreat and fear, hardly the kind of thing to be given such a central spot in the garden. The fountain could alternatively be read as a kind of negative political lesson, showing the vulnerability of a weak monarchy and indirectly legitimating the accumulation of new power inside the French state. Read this way, the fountain could sanction the development of the polit-

45. The Latona fountain with the water turned on.

ical and military strength of France and its monarchy. That was a lesson that the king would surely want to convey to the world.

In the fountain's original setting, Latona and her children stood at ground level on a reflecting pond, looking up toward the château that rose dauntingly and unresponsively before them. Perhaps the fountain, placed this way, was indeed meant to be a reminder of the Fronde. It could, after all, encourage the young king to become ever more powerful for the sake of his family. But the statuary did not remain in that configuration. The fountain was rebuilt, and the young family was both raised on a pedestal and turned away from the château to face the Apollo fountain. The two fountains were set in a kind of distant conversation with each other across the long and open *tapis vert*. Apollo on his chariot, representing the adult Sun King, was poised to charge up the hill toward Latona, seemingly ready to bring relief to this young family. He was not so much an emissary from the heavens as a warrior from the earth. This grown Apollo was made a powerful figure, a beautiful and muscular hero with the will and ability to come to the aid of his family. The weakness of Latona and her children was still evident enough to beckon to Apollo, but with the fountain's new setting, the sense of threat to the family was visually reduced. This trio was placed on a pedestal closer to the gods than their attackers. Moreover, when the water was turned on, it covered the young family with a protective cover of water jets. The principle of their vulnerability was sustained, but the sense of imminent danger was diminished. Now, with the fountain of Apollo just on the other side of the *tapis vert*, they seemed almost safe, but not yet aware of it. The allegorical assault from the peasants was only a passing threat that functioned as a reminder of how necessary it was for the royal family to exercise its rightful use of power.[55]

If the king's direct kin (depicted symbolically in the Latona fountain) could not depend without peril on the goodwill of those around them, they needed independent means of defending themselves and of regaining control over the land given to them by the gods. Just as Apollo could use his horse and chariot to save Latona, the king could use the state and its military to restore the land of France to its proper monarch.

The role of the *tapis vert* (the "green carpet" of grass stretching from the Latona to the Apollo fountain), has not usually been assessed in relation to the two fountains, but it perhaps should be. Given the intricacy of the parterres on either side of the château, it seems a bit odd that Le Nôtre chose to make the central Allée Royale, dominating the vista from the château to the horizon, so simple. Why was it not made the most intricate and extended parterre in the *petit parc* instead of an area resembling an over-grown road with a grassy center-strip and two side ruts of gravel? Mariage suggests that this design was actually based on the roads that began linking châteaux and gardens in early seventeenth-century France.[56] Certainly, in her description of Versailles, Mlle de Scudéry commented that broad avenues were one element that could make gardens more beautiful, but she was much more ecstatic in describing the parter-res full of flowers, the gilded balustrades of terraces, the elegant fountain statuary, the baroque grotto, and the bosquets filled with treasures in the gardens at Versailles.[57] A simple grass-filled road (even carefully manicured and exploded to supernatural scale) would hardly have seemed elegant enough for the main axis of this garden at the seat of the French court. Le Nôtre was even praised widely for this design. Would enlarg-ing a traditional roadway and filling it with grass invite such comment and delight?

The simplicity of this area makes sense if the *tapis vert* somehow brought a repre-sentation of the French countryside itself to the royal garden. That gesture would have filled the simple space with vast political meaning. The *tapis vert* was after all a kind of meadow like the one evoked by Vauban's *pré carré*; it even looked square from the ter-races behind the château. Smaller grassy meads had in the past carried large meanings in European gardens. Medieval cloisters had frequently used knolls of grasses and wildflowers to represent Creation.[58] It was not such a leap to use this kind of grassy area to represent the French countryside and to celebrate both its natural fecundity and political import. The *tapis vert* viewed this way would have added to the impact of the Latona–Apollo grouping. As Apollo charged in his water-splashed chariot up the hill to save Latona, he would have been crossing and claiming the French landscape, holding it under his power as the rightful domain of the royal family.

Other clearer allusions to military life in the gardens added to the political flavor of the *petit parc*. Along the walkways of Versailles, statues of classical figures were set out like guards in the landscape. These marble hunters and warriors were prepared for battle, armed with swords and shields. They functioned in part as ties to the "classical tradition," adding to the claims that France was the new Rome. They were heroes, men and women of valor, showing what kinds of glory were meant to usher in the new age of French greatness. As guards in the landscape, interspersed with the trees, these

46. Statues guarding a bosquet. One side of the *tapis vert* at the canal end of the
Allée Royale.

figures resembled soldiers on duty as well. They made French military power seem
somehow both blessed by and connected to the gods and heroes of the past.

   Some military references in the garden were less allusion than straightforward. The
Arc de Triomphe drew on Roman design precedents for commemorating successful
battles, and was erected to celebrate the king's achievements in war. It embodied a traditional vision of success that could be used to cover up a less glorious reality. The
bosquet des dômes with its classical architectural forms was decorated along its central
balustrade with images of shields and helmets. These were common decorative elements in triumphal arches. It is telling that they managed to find form in this rather
tranquil bosquet. The point of these decorations was to signal the continuities of the
garden with the Great Tradition *and* to fill the landscape with appropriate signs of military prowess.

Tree planting and military culture

Tree planting in French gardens was also part of a complicated story of tree use,
forestry management, garden design, and military aspiration in France. The massive
wooded hunting grounds at the back of the park at Versailles, the intensive plantings
of single species of trees both in the potager and other areas of the gardens, and the
organization of bosquets into wooded rectangular forms all had connections to a new
forest management system being developed under the watchful eye of Colbert.

47. Apollo and his chariot in the bosquet of the Arc de Triomphe (Cotelle, *Bosquet de l'arc de triomphe*).

France put great store in its forests during this period, particularly because rivals such as the English and Dutch were suffering from deforestation. It was not just that woods represented a kind of wealth. Trees were the source of the lumber necessary for shipbuilding and fortress construction. These were essential to state power. Even world trade depended on lumber – masses of it – to provide the navies to protect merchant vessels and to build those commercial ships as well. Navies in particular had voracious appetites for trees because naval vessels needed very specialized kinds of timber, and fighting ships were so often sunk. Now that the European states which gained their livelihood from sea trade were beginning to feel the pinch of their deforestation, Colbert thought France could become more competitive in world trade and colonial settlement, using its forests and building its navy. Needless to say, France needed *more* than just a forestry policy to begin creating a vital navy. It had to create safe and deep harbors for building and launching large fighting vessels. The forests were nonetheless a large part of the program, and one that Colbert personally supervised.[59]

Before Colbert's intervention, French forests had already been regulated to control their growth and lumbering, but the rules had not been enforced and the policies were short-sighted and often ill-conceived. According to the ordinances, forest lots of equal sizes were supposed to be marked out and harvested in turn without regard to the differences in the species growing there. This system had encouraged clear cutting and a low level of concern about re-seeding the scarred forests. Most frustratingly to Colbert, these regulations had not protected the slow-growing pole pines and oaks that were particularly useful in shipbuilding. In fact, most timber had been felled without any method at all, and in quantities well beyond what was permitted, leaving some areas functionally deforested. What trees had not been damaged or used in war were destroyed by private individuals seeking profits from timber sales. Even poor people, living along the boundaries of the royal holdings, sometimes claimed traditional rights of usage and felled the trees with no thought to replanting. But the worst offenses were by the forest masters who had been formally responsible for the trees but who had used the woods as their own economic resources, cutting what and when they wanted. The end result was that the forests were in disarray when Colbert began to survey them.[60]

Colbert hired new forest masters and surveyors to go first to the thick woods of Normandy and the north of France, and later to the more devastated south to document the state of the forests. Louis de Froidour, the most frequently employed and best known of these environmental inquisitors, tried to account for the trees. While he checked old records to see what the forests had once contained, his surveyors walked through the woods, checking the dimensions of the forests, the trees they contained, and their general health. On the basis of this information (which was not always accurate or reliable), the foresters assessed the level of fines to be imposed on those who had illegitimately profited from timber sales and usage. In some ways, this exercise was a fund-raising measure. Colbert saw the forests as a hidden economic resource that was being lost by graft. Best of all, assessing fines for past offenses usually extracted money from aristocrats who were not subject to taxes.[61]

While this reform of the forests was a revenue-raising activity for the state, the purpose of the regulations was primarily to serve military interests. No longer could forests located near the oceans or major rivers be cut without first getting state sanction. The navy had first rights to those trees that were near enough to the water to float to shipbuilding ports and that were appropriate species for this kind of construction. When a forest in protected regions was cut, a representative of the navy could mark some trees to keep standing for future naval use. Colbert not only now enforced policies to this effect that had already been on the books, but expanded the areas placed under these regulations. The rest of the forests were characterized by the types of trees growing in them, and once again divided into square parcels. But now the trees were to be harvested at different periods, depending on the growth characteristics of the trees and uses to which the timber was to be put.[62]

Importantly, these regulations drew together all of French forests into a common system of control. Forests might not have been treated differently because of their growth characteristics, but they were all subject to the same system of regulation. The royal forests were expanded as the state reclaimed much land that had been illegally sold in earlier periods, bringing these properties under direct control of the crown. But more importantly, the policies regulating private felling stood as a reminder to local elites of their regulation by and subservience to the central government, and the state's claims to all of France's territory.[63]

Once the studies were finished and fines assessed, Colbert had the old roads that had separated forest plots restored, and built new ones where none had existed. Undesirable trees were felled to increase the health of the desired species, creating something closer to monocultural forests in France than naturally grew there. New roads were cut to facilitate harvesting the trees, particularly where engineers could link forests containing mature trees to rivers that could carry large timbers to the sea. The result was that French forests took on a new look. They were more uniform spaces, containing similar trees, cut into squares, triangles, or rectangles with roads that both marked the different planting areas and facilitated movement through them.[64]

French forestry and garden design

There were provocative parallels between the shapes and uses of French forests and patterns of garden design in the sixteenth and seventeenth centuries. Throughout the sixteenth century and into the early seventeenth, French garden designers laid out pleasure gardens with square garden beds that had undifferentiated sizes and design functions. Each knot or parterre in the garden had its own design, but the different beds were used as interchangeable design elements. Space in these gardens seemed to be organized in much the same way that French forests had been under the old regulations. In both cases, an underlying repetitive geometry held the spaces together, and gave them equal weight and uses.

The newer theories of garden design that came into force during the seventeenth century paralleled the new forestry system. Gardeners began dividing spaces up in new ways. Parterres were set closest to the house and large bosquets or hunting forests were placed at a distance. The parterres were meant to be smaller, contained short flowering plants, trimmed hedges and topiary trees, and had square to rectangular forms. These spaces were in a fascinating way almost completely "deforested." They often had boxed trees from the Mediterranean region rolled into them in the summer (and kept in an orangerie in winter), but they were primarily open areas filled with flowers and low hedges. The bosquets beyond were forest "rooms" with large architectural sculptures and fountains surrounded by taller and permanent trees. Each bosquet had a different

48. View from the top of the Orangerie at Versailles, showing the sequence of different tree species and their uses, from the château to the distant countryside (Martin, *La Pièce d'Eau des Suisses et l'Orangerie*).

The general Disposition of a Magnificent Garden all upon a level

49. Dezallier d'Argenville's plan of a formal garden, showing an ideal progression from parterres to bosquets to forests (*La Théorie et la practique du jardinage*).

function or use, although they shared common exterior shapes. Inside, the kinds of fountains, sculptures, seating, and open areas made their social uses distinct. Beyond the bosquets lay the hunting grounds with their thick forests and larger plots of local trees, reaching in extended rectangles (sometimes cross-cut by radiating roads) to the bounds of the estate. These areas had roads both for marking the boundaries of the bosquets and for providing transportation through the woods.[65]

The parallels between gardening patterns and forestry systems existed probably because they were both derived from common French ideas about estate management of the sixteenth and early seventeenth centuries. (These ideas are discussed in chapter 4.) Following these strictures, both French forests and royal parks in the late seventeenth century participated (albeit differently) in restructuring the French landscape. They equally made trees and their cultivation more valuable to the state, particularly to the military.

Colbert used forestry management techniques as well as plans to develop the woods at Versailles. Sustaining the forests in this difficult valley constituted an ongoing problem for the minister. The land there was muddy in the winter, rotting the roots of trees, and dried to hardpan in the summer. It did not happily sustain lush forest growth. The terrible, prolonged cold periods at the beginning and end of the reign of Louis XIV also killed off even larger numbers of trees and bushes than normal. Even hedges for the parterres had to be replaced along with trees for the bosquets and hunting forests to make "nature" fit the proper image for the king's estate. So, Colbert was regularly faced with the problem of finding new trees and keeping old ones alive.[66]

Large numbers of trees and bushes were transferred on a regular basis to the gardens, many of them full grown rather than saplings. The roads leading to the front of the château were lined with young trees, but many garden walkways were bounded by newly planted full-grown trees. Bringing such huge plants to the garden would have been a technologically demanding process in any period. It was made even more difficult in that the roads were not good and applicable technologies limited. Moving large trees from even nearby forests was a task requiring a huge labor force. This problem once again brought the military to the garden. The army was recruited to move the thousands of trees required for the replanting, ostensibly so that Colbert could reduce some of the costs of maintaining the grounds for the king. In truth, only the military was capable of realizing the scale of land manipulation needed for the gardens.

Military imagery also pervaded the uses of trees in the garden. *Allées* and bosquets often had double rows of trees along their boundaries, reproducing the style of planting used on the barricades of French fortified towns. These long lines of trees constituted a kind of symbolic standing army, guarding garden features, just like trees that stood sentry along barricades, guarding and standing in for French soldiers along the walls of French fortresses.

Old prints showed topiary bushes also set out in rows this way around parterres or fountains. These plants were cut, not in the familiar cone shape used today, but with three tiers of spheres, the middle sphere having two arm-like branches on the side. The resulting constructs looked like fanciful sentries, standing guard along the edges of

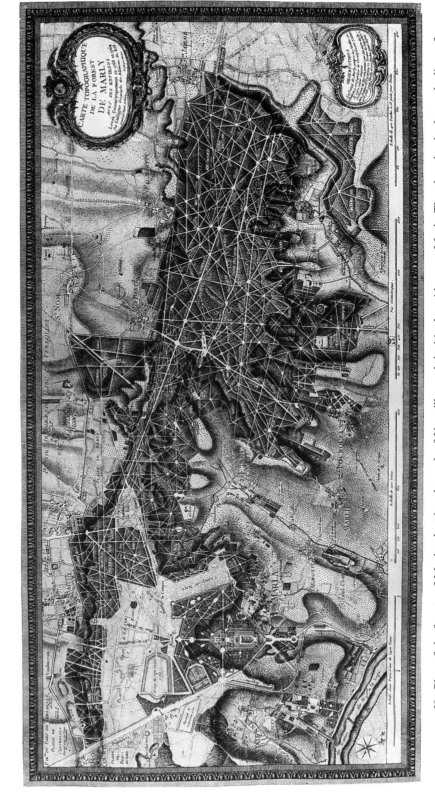

50. Plan of the forests of Marly, abutting the park of Versailles and the king's residence at Marly. The plan clearly shows the lines of sight through the forest (*Lассinто, Geographe des batimens du Roi*, 1768–69).

51. Topiary guards set along a path on the north parterre at Versailles.

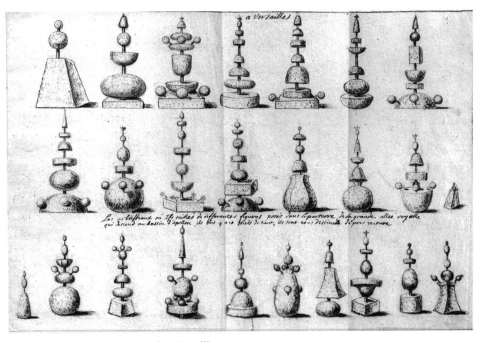

52. Topiary designs for Versailles.

garden features. They provided an interesting contrast to the kinds of trees used around parterres from earlier in the century. The latter were most often placed around or among the flowers or herbs of parterres, and were depicted in prints as delicate and spindly specimens – often fruit trees. Not so the topiary of the French formal garden. Even when they were made quite playfully eccentric, these bushes were distinctively more hardy-looking and clearly embedded in the earth. They provided a permeable but still daunting barrier that marked the boundaries of garden beds and visually underscored the park's lines.

Colbert's job as minister gave him the responsibility for both the royal forests and the king's buildings. No wonder he took such an interest in the lushness of the king's hunting grounds and the thickness and health of the trees in the bosquets at Versailles. These sites were important for showing visitors the health of French forests.[67] Since this was strategically important information to convey in a period when trees were a vital resource for military power, healthy forests at Versailles were a necessary goal for Colbert. Trees had become a strategically significant element of French political life, so they emerged as an essential part of French gardens.

The pleasures of military culture

French gardens may have had serious political uses and been built with military engineering, but they were nonetheless pleasure gardens that carried their messages in seductive forms. This is not to say that the military aspects of the garden were masked or made oblique to emphasize the sheer beauty of the place. On the contrary, military culture was central to *enjoying* the gardens, and seeing them as beautiful and wondrous. A visitor trained in military techniques for assessing the contours of a landscape and possibilities for moving through them was exactly the kind of guest most prepared to be dazzled by the complexly ordered landscape of the formal garden. This was the kind of person who would notice the nuanced grading of the parterre areas, and take pleasure in the visual surprises set into the woods beyond.

As French gardens moved away from the strict geometries of Italian and early seventeenth-century French gardens, they abandoned the use of walkways laid out in squares, rectangles, and circles. The new *allées* nearer the canal were laid out in lines of sight (see plate 1). Diagonal walkways cut across wooded areas and intersected with shorter walks that marked the depths of the forests. The *allées* were carefully measured and related to others, but they did not form simple geometries. There were few walkways to l'Encelade, the Salle de Conseil, the Galerie, and the Colonnade (this in a garden not known for its economy and simplicity). Where the walkways crossed, viewers could quickly gauge the size of the garden simply by looking at the vistas opening and closing around them, and following the punctuation of sculptures and gates. This was part of the pleasure embedded in the visual structure of the gardens. Seeing and surveying, looking and measuring by eye, finding visual surprises and making sense of them, were all part of what guests could discover in the gardens to make them both enticing and delightful.

The existence of a visual culture to support this kind of playful surveying by eye

Jardin de la Maison de Mr de St Poange rüe des petits Champs,
De l'invention de Monsr le Nautre

53. Topiary "guards" set out along a parterre designed by Le Nôtre.

54. Double lines of trees along the Pièce d'Eau des Suisses.

makes some sense for this period. Michael Baxandall has already argued that a kind of visual culture of measurement developed in Renaissance Italy when merchants needed to estimate the bulk of trade goods by eye. Artists paid increased attention in the period to the scale and size of figures as part of this new relation to the material environment. Similarly, Svetlana Alpers (1983) has claimed that the Dutch in the seventeenth century cultivated a particularly cartographic visual culture. They sought to make careful description of perceived objects and developed techniques to render them systematically in two dimensions. In France, perhaps a comparable culture of visual estimation developed in the seventeenth century around siege warfare, focusing on the spatial relations of objects in the landscape.[68]

Sébastien Le Clerc wrote a seventeenth-century book on survey technique which indicates how informal surveying could have produced a complex visual culture in the period.[69] The author was a famous mathematician of the day who conducted surveys both for state military projects and for the water system at Versailles. He seemed to try in his book to teach paper and pencil mathematical techniques to replace and improve upon familiar sorts of estimation mathematics. At one point in the text, the illustrations abandon their initial uses of geometrical figures drawn on drapes held up by putti. These images were replaced with pictures showing geometrical figures floating in the sky above towns, landscapes, and formal gardens. With these illustrations, the author drew a connection in principle, if not in practice, between the desire to see measured relations among objects in the world and knowing the mathematical operations with which to measure them. The illustrations changed again farther in the book, now

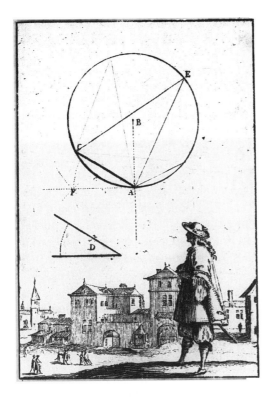

55. Gentleman appearing to survey a town (Le Clerc, *Practique de la geometrie*, 1669).

showing gentlemen in the foreground of pictures who seem to be surveying spaces by eye. The combined set of images suggests that noblemen of the period indeed wanted to estimate the contours of the landscape by sight, but could not always do it accurately, using mental calculations. With survey mathematics, they could become more precise in judging spatial relations. Le Clerc's book, in this light, was not meant to teach gentlemen to *begin* thinking in terms of surveys, but to learn how to use calculations to do it well.

The inclusion of garden views in Le Clerc's illustrations is extremely provocative (see plate 24). Seeing the landscape with a surveyor's eye seems to have been central not just to the design but also to the delight of the gardens. Visual surprises met garden visitors as they strolled through Le Nôtre's parks because the subtle grading and complex plantings kept shifting visual relations among garden features and making design elements appear and disappear in a matter of a few paces. The topography of the garden could seem absolutely simple and clear in one moment – and then the promenader would come upon a huge drop, where a canal cut across the landscape. The whole structure of the park would suddenly be revealed to be vastly different from the one the visitor presupposed. Le Nôtre's complex garden spaces, filled alternately with illusions and revelations, seemed always to be toying with the efforts of visitors to produce a stable vision of the land. A seemingly closed walkway would suddenly open up in a new direction or an apparently empty piece of forest would be filled with spray from a fountain. These garden details would be most surprising and delightful to a viewer already prone to assess land in terms of measured spaces and visibility, particularly one who was trained to engage in mental mapping of spaces. The gentleman-surveyor was the perfect type to revel in Le Nôtre's formal gardens.

There was plentiful evidence that such a social type existed. "Views and Perspective" prints of the period, for example, which were commonly used to depict estates or gardens, often showed aristocratic hunters in the foreground, resting on a hill, looking into the picture, studying the domain before them, and apparently engaging in a kind of surveying for pleasure.[70] The prints seemed designed to be sold to members of a military visual culture that located pleasure in surveying and taking the measure of lands.

Even the inaccuracies in garden prints point interestingly toward the cultural salience of surveying to garden appreciation. These prints not only show details of the gardens' contents, but also significant distortions of the space. It is not at all surprising that many illustrations of formal gardens made them seem more grand and imposing by dwarfing the people in relation to the garden features. Royal parks meant to display the king's power could do it better through exaggeration. But why was the grandeur routinely expressed through a change of scale rather than, for example, a manipulation of content? Why were there the correct numbers of statues or stairways? The objects in the parterres and bosquets at Versailles remained surprisingly stable across prints, even though the apparent scale of the gardens varied widely. This pattern would make sense if scale was a particularly *salient* part of the local culture of perception. Determining scale, of course, was the essence of surveying.

Perhaps the most direct evidence of how the gardens were perceived in the period came from Mlle de Scudéry's *Promenade à Versailles* (reprinted 1979). Since the author was explicitly determined in the essay to monumentalize the king's achievements, aligning his military successes with the gloriousness of the gardens, the text reeked of feigned adoration and delight. Nonetheless, the elements of the park she chose to highlight, and the kinds of praise she felt appropriate to her task provide some hints about how visitors might actually have responded to Versailles' gardens in her period. At one point, the beautiful fictional stranger, who is being taken on the promenade, comments on the visual surprises in the garden and the ways they contribute to the pleasures there. Her male companion replies that variety is what makes the place so pleasant, apparently missing her delight in the element of surprise. "Mais comment est-il possible, dit la belle Etrangére, qu'un si grand & si beau jardin se soit dérobé à mes yeux pendant que j'estois sur le corridor du palais, d'où j'en ai découvert tant d'autres. C'est assurément, dit Telamon, une des grandes beautez de Versailles, que la variété des jardins & des bosquets; car il y a de tout ce qui peut rendre un lieu agréable" (p. 89).While the woman seems to revel in the illusory quality of the garden, the man does not. The passage is suggestive, but hard to read as a definitive statement on surveying and promenades. At another point in the text, the visitors show interest in the structure of the walkways. They note that, at the borders of the park, the walks stopped at lovely grillwork gates, beyond which one can see the countryside. They also say that they had encountered on their stroll a hundred intersections of radiating walkways, large and small, with fountains in them. They were apparently looking down *allées* and making informal inventories of the length of the walks, where they ended, how they were laid

56. The taking of Mons by the king, showing the aristocrats surveying the
battleground (*La Prise de Mons, Capitale de Hainaut par le Roy en Personne, Le
VIIe Avril, 1671*).

in relation to each other, and what lay beyond them. They even seemed predisposed to
estimate the quantities of *allées* and intersections – even if only to exaggerate the
number. "Elles prirent-garde qu'au bout de toutes les allées on a mis des grilles, au delà
desquelles on découvre des païsages agréables, qui font paroître les jardins plus beaux,
& aprés avoir trouvé cent étoiles d'allées grandes ou petites avec des fontaines, nous
retournâmes au canal des cygnes, dont on ne peut trop admirer la beauté" (p. 90).

It may well be, then, that informal surveying helped organize aristocratic relations
to land in seventeenth-century France (just as informal measurement of the volume of

goods affected merchant life in Renaissance Italy). Certainly, visual skills in estimating distances and heights of objects would have facilitated the planning of sieges. The same capabilities would also have been useful in designing and enjoying gardens – particularly ones built with a surface geometry following survey lines and terraces arranged in grades that made their topography intriguing. No wonder Abraham Bosse's book on the "applied" uses of perspective found a market in France (through the efforts of Desargues, 1648). It illustrated how gentlemen could see spaces in measured terms, using the author's ideas about geometrical forms, point of view, and perspective.

The itineraries devised and used by Louis XIV certainly would make more sense in this visual context. When visitors went on promenades in the royal gardens, using one of the king's itineraries, they moved from one site to the next, studying views, appreciating statues, and looking at the château from different positions. They followed a set of scripted movements that told them where to turn, how far to walk, where to stop, and what views to admire. It is not surprising that the script told them what statues and fountains to study, making sure they would see all the wonders of the gardens, but the itinerary frequently told them to turn to look down *allées* toward a distant fountain or at an intersection in the walkways. There is no indication of why this would be an interesting thing to do.[71] The itineraries read more like choreographies for a dance than directions for a tour. They said nothing about what fountain statuary was supposed to mean or what visitors should appreciate in the views.[72] Given all the propaganda for the regime that played on classical mythology to celebrate the king and his reign, it was a mystery why the itineraries were so unconcerned with these issues. Perhaps the answer lay in the taken-for-granted habit of informal surveying within the aristocracy. Perhaps these scripts assumed that visitors of the period would know to *survey* the gardens in the promenade. They would not need to be told to make an inventory of the wonders of the bosquets, to assess the massiveness of the plantings, and to peer through passages in the landscape to measure the gardens' immensity, comparing the distance along one *allée* to the distance of another. They would take pleasure in the way the grading system would make vistas appear and disappear.[73] Changing relationships of space and land would provide cognitive pleasures in estimation measurement skills for those steeped in military life. Certainly, the gardens' apparent openness made surveying seem simple; their complex control of vision made resurveying interesting; and perhaps (with the itineraries) the organization of promenades also made this kind of surveying socially necessary as well.

Some different connections between the delights of the garden and military culture were brought out in Mallet's military strategy book, *Les Travaux de Mars ou l'art de la guerre* (1684). The title page showed a garden terrace in the middle of which was a statue with the title of the book etched on its base. Scattered around this statue were nobles talking, pointing, looking, walking, standing and taking their leisure, while in the background a battle is in progress. This image drew an interesting equation not just between war and gardens but between both these sites and aristocratic pleasures. Mallet treated these two social spaces as part of a single world set out for the diversion of gentlemen.[74]

Mallet's illustrations depicted, among other things, the construction of *plans-relief*:

57. Gentlemen exercising techniques of perspective viewing (Bosse in Desargues 1648).

Les
TRAVAUX
de
MARS
ou
L'ART de la GUERRE
Tome Premier.

A Amsterdam 1685

58. Title page of Mallet's *Les Travaux de Mars ou l'art de la guerre.*

clay models that the nobility built as strategic planning devices. These models copied in detail the appearance of every house, wall, and alleyway in the cities they represented. They showed topography and plantings, battlements, churches, rivers, roads, hillsides, and even details of the texture and color of individual building exteriors, so providing an inventory of the material contents of the land. Such models were serious tools of war. Mallet's treatise being about the art of war, it was entirely appropriate to find directions there for making these models. What was arresting was that the first illustration, showing a gentleman starting his model, depicted him at a small table in his formal garden. This picture suggested that making models was a *leisure* pursuit of gentlemen, linking their peacetime pleasures with the arts of war.[75] At the same time, the illustration showed that both the garden and model had visible grading systems that provided visual pleasures for aristocrats.[76]

Model fortresses in their own right were noble playthings that also entered French formal gardens in the late seventeenth century. As moats disappeared from the architecture of châteaux (but remained a standard feature of fortress cities), miniaturized moat-like features migrated into the gardens. These were not exact reproductions of feudal citadels or their moats, but rather spaces that alluded to both. At Versailles, for example, the early Salle des Festins had at its center a delicate stone esplanade shaped like the "footprint" of an older castle (a rectangle with rounded turret-like shapes in the corners). This was set in a pool of water (the moat?). From a bird's-eye view, the parterre looked like a plan for one of the châteaux found in Du Cerceau's book on sixteenth-century French houses. It was flat like a plan, but materialized on a small scale. Nobles could walk out onto this island and look across the mock moat to the rest of the garden, playfully surveying the king's lands. In the Salle des Festins, where aristocrats attended parties, they danced and amused themselves on a similar castle-shaped island. When the French arrived in costumes that allowed them to take on the character of ancient warriors or early medieval heroes, the fantasy element was complete. Make-believe linked the military past to the meant-to-be glorious present. Even in the Galerie d'eau and the Obélisque, where water features themselves were given the shape of a fortress, both the power associated with the shape and its playfulness coexisted. These areas were leisure spaces, sites for living out dreams, and not real defense systems. They carried the pleasures of France's military heritage, but they also signified French success in seeking power through warfare.

The exquisite metal fountain statuary at Versailles which might have seemed only sensual outgrowths of Italian fountain sculpture were nonetheless products of the arsenal. Italian fountains usually had marble statues, but the fountains at Versailles were made in gilded lead or cast bronze. Stylistically, the difference was not wrenching. The classical deities of the Fountains of the Seasons and the Apollo fountain were entirely continuous in both content and style with Italian precedents. But the change in medium was significant because many of the statues at Versailles showed off the technical finesse of the metalwork from the arsenal. Some of the famous sculptors of the period, Coysevox and Girardon, were paid specifically for work done at the arsenal to supply art for the king and court. Each new effort to make statues for the garden was an opportunity to develop skills in working with media used for making cannons

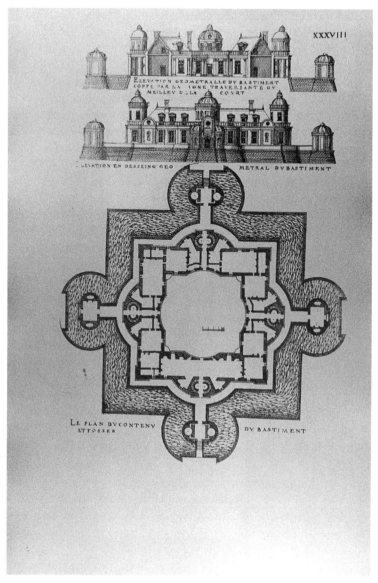

59. Fortress design from Du Cerceau.

and cannonballs. And each new sculpture completed with finesse and beauty provided visitors with new sources of delight derived from military culture.[77]

The Parterre d'Eau ended up in its last configuration as an elegant tribute to French metal-casting. Surrounding a giant reflecting pool were great statues in bronze, representing the major rivers of France, water nymphs, and children. The pieces carried the names of the Kellers, the men who cast them, as a tribute from the artists who designed them. Set on the terrace directly behind the château of Versailles, these fountains were

60. Salle des Festins at Versailles with its fortress footprint (Cotelle, *Salle des Festins*).

always visible from and around the house. No cannons needed to be set out around this royal residence to announce the power wielded by the state; the statues there told much the same story. The smooth and elegant bodies of the river gods were sublime embodiments of French taste and talent, but they were also flawless examples of what French forges could do. Aesthetic pleasure and the art of war met beneath the windows of the château of Versailles.[78]

The allusions to war during the fêtes in the garden also provided many satisfactions for the guests who came. These great parties included military games played by nobles to display their prowess. The contestants wore costumes to mark their allegiance to their team, which represented a great fighting unit of the past such as the Romans or Turks. This bit of theater symbolically evoked a whole history of military life and placed it in their contests. In 1674, when the king and court celebrated the victories in the Franche-Comté, cannons were shot over the canal while miniature military vessels floated late at night to the strains of music. And when these fêtes were over, there were extensive firework displays. Explosions filled the air with the sounds and sights that now typified armed conflict.[79] All the joys of war and few of its dangers could be found in the gardens of Versailles.

61. The *Obélisque* bosquet, containing stairs shaped like a fortress around the central fountain.

Military might and formal gardens

The military presence in the gardens at Versailles thus had many levels, from the most symbolic to the most concrete, from the most grand and dramatic to the most playful. The reason was that the military had such deep political meanings in seventeenth-century France that military culture pervaded this social world. The military had helped to solidify the power of Louis XIV and the absolutist French state by distancing the nobility from the military sources of state power, expanding the territory of France, engineering fortress cities and ports around the state's boundaries, and providing a model of discipline over people and nature that testified to the power of the state. The military elements in the gardens gave this space an ordered solidity and authority, a power that was comforting to those with hopes for the French state. The formal garden was not a place for expressing the love of God or private property, but a site for claiming authority for a political system and showing a French love for glory. It was a tribute to the military heritage of the nobility and a vehicle for state politics.

That is why the garden was used to entertain Queen Marie d'Este of England (wife of the deposed Catholic king of England, James II), when she was waiting anxiously for her husband to return from his French-sponsored expedition to regain his crown. She was taken on a promenade, using a route apparently written out by Louis XIV himself for the unhappy queen. She had been to Saint-Germain and was reported to be depressed. Now she was taken to Versailles to get some more immediate distraction.

62. Regnaudin's *Fountain of Summer* or *Ceres*. One of the Fountains of the Seasons in gilded lead.

What better way to cheer her up than take her out into this elegant, ordered, and powerful garden, and to have Louis XIV at her side.[80]

The promenade was set to begin, as was conventional, on the back terrace. While the king was waiting for the queen to appear, he was entertained by a display of military marching. Since the French soldiers parading there so elegantly were the kinds of military men placed by Louis XIV in the service of her husband, James II, their skilled and disciplined marching could have been quite an inviting lure to the garden for the worried queen. When she arrived, the party began by touring the Parterre d'Eau. The stunning perfection of the bronze statues projected both military might and an easy assurance. The technical skill in casting spoke to the quality of French cannons, and the relaxed demeanor of the river gods suggested a self-assurance that could also engender faith in the powers of France.

63. Tubi's *Rhône river* in the Parterre d'Eau, cast bronze.

The company then made a tour of the terraces, studying the views, particularly the central axis of the *petit parc*. They stopped explicitly to look across the Latona fountain, down the *tapis vert*.[81] The queen must have been met with a smashing view of the young Apollo charging up the hill to defend his château and the center of the French court. Waiting for her husband, Marie d'Este may have felt a bit like Latona cowering before her enemies, not knowing if her husband was dead or alive, and whether they had forever lost their throne. But if she looked beyond Latona, she would have seen Apollo, that symbol of Louis XIV, coming to the aid of Latona and looking terribly impressive. Perhaps this gave her reason for reassurance. Help from the Sun King himself seemed in sight. The rest of the promenade took her to the nearby bosquets and parterres of the *petit parc*. The effects of the gardens must have been all the more attractive to the nervous queen where they exuded markers of order and power. Her afternoon in the garden was not a mindless confection for a spoiled princess, as some might suggest, but a way to help her regain her composure under great stress. This walk in the garden was expected, of course, to be entertaining, but it was neither casual nor apolitical. It was an element of the geopolitics of the period. The queen needed distraction because Louis XIV wanted a Catholic king to the north of France, and her husband was available for the position. A walk in the garden was appropriate for her entertainment because the *petit parc* embodied the territorial optimism and technical expertise on which French military geopolitical action was based.

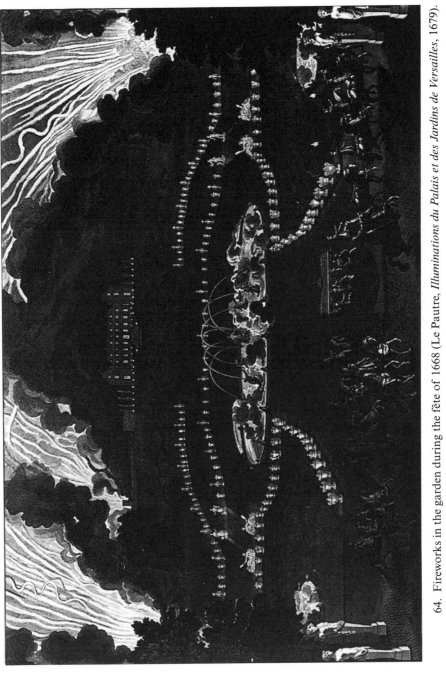

64. Fireworks in the garden during the fête of 1668 (Le Pautre, *Illuminations du Palais et des Jardins de Versailles*, 1679).

3

Material innovation and cultural identity

The fat cherubs, excessive gilding, cavorting figures, and massive piles of grapes, shells, gems, and flowers in the statuary in the gardens of Versailles, overlaying the strict geometries of Le Nôtre's designs, partially disguised the military elements in the park, and made the space seem playfully exorbitant. This was a pleasure garden so filled with delights that even the most indulged nobles were unlikely to have seen anything like it before. Great gilded fountains spewed quantities of water above the young trees of newer bosquets. Seemingly endless walkways were lined with classical sculptures, either imported from Italy or copied from originals there. Whole amphitheaters and grottoes were decorated with rare shells and minerals that glistened in the open air or reflected candlelight off giant enclosed chamber walls. The effects would have been astonishing, even if they had been only signs of a Dionysian abandon or unbridled greed inside the French aristocracy. In fact, they represented much more. They embodied a pressure toward sumptuousness and public display that fed the growing system of state-based power. As Norbert Elias has suggested, regulated patterns of consumption contributed to a disciplining and impoverishment of the aristocracy in seventeenth-century France that reduced its independent powers. Even the new manufactures built by Colbert to satisfy noble demand for luxury goods and to decorate Louis XIV's properties helped to empower the state by giving France a new, unified cultural identity. The decorative elements in the gardens at Versailles associated this culture of things with French territory by inserting exemplars of French taste and style into the French landscape.[1]

At first, some of the sculptural excesses of the garden at Versailles were aesthetic gifts of the Italian Baroque. Many of the early fountain statues, particularly on the north side of the château, dotted the French earth with the writhing limbs and sumptuous decoration typical of that style.[2] But the decoration of the garden began to change from the 1660s to the 1680s, making it a showplace for French design. The material superfluity and aesthetic ambition of the Baroque at first had a propaganda value that made it seem appropriate to celebrate the glory of Louis XIV's reign. Bernini's Rome was built, after all, as a massive architectural tribute to the power of the Church. But Louis XIV was determined to make French culture surpass anything Italian, and specifically demanded that the painting, sculpture, music, dance, architec-

65. Rockwork cascade in the Salle de Bal.

ture, fashion, design, and gardening for his court all become distinctively French. By the end of the regime, much of the wealth of France lay in an array of politically coded material things. These included, of course, Vauban's stone fortresses, garrisons, canals, and military hospitals, but also Colbert's manufactures and the artworks produced by the newly organized *Académies*. The first marked the land of France; the second gave it a cultural form. This location of French political identity in the world of goods, of course, seemed a disastrous policy for the French peasants at the end of the regime who were starving from crop failures and dying in the brutal winters. But state power – at least at that moment in history – was cultivated not through investing in the needs of citizens but from the political crafting of a geographical territory and a world of goods which defined the state as a unified actor in European geopolitics. The price for this choice would be paid later.[3]

The sumptuous park at Versailles was the perfect setting for displaying a seventeenth-century material identity for France. Collections of artworks were set into the landscape to claim power, glory, and cultural coherence through the aesthetic mobilization of a country valley. The formal garden gave the land a form and filled its geometrical matrixes with statuary and decorative touches that marked it as distinctively French. French territory in this site was not only measured, graded, and put into order, but also made more appealing and somehow more substantial through the stunning display of arts and manufactures.

In what way could this turn toward the world of goods serve political unification in

France? Although we now equate political territoriality with a culture of nationalism, France in the seventeenth century was not yet a nation. What kind of political identity could Europeans associate with the increasingly well-articulated and aggrandized French state? The population saw itself as belonging to diverse local communities. France was made up of regions with profoundly (and fiercely defended) independent traditions of law, agriculture, social relations among the ranks, manufacture, and trade. How could the state make these regions not only function in some coherent way politically, but also feel unified to the population or to outsiders who visited there? At the same time, how could France, claiming to be the rightful heir to the classical tradition, to the glory of Rome, distinguish itself from the other European countries around it, particularly from Italy? How could one think of the Midi as more like Normandy than Turin without thinking of them all as part of a greater Western civilization or a common Christian culture?[4]

The gardens at Versailles provided some surprising and illuminating clues about how these difficulties were negotiated and how place was imbued with meaning in this regime. At Versailles, as in the countryside, massive manufacturing, planting, and building projects were covering the land with objects that were expressions of a new and decidedly French taste. *Académies* were defining new French art, music, and dance forms, while *faïenceries* and lace factories were inventing distinctive French pottery and lacework. Just as land was being coaxed into new forms to formulate a space of power, its surface was being littered or decorated with a new material culture that was claiming a cultural style as well as superiority for France.[5]

The Italian Renaissance tradition of collecting artwork in the garden was transformed at Versailles into a political process and burdened with new significance and importance; the royal gardens boasted statues, architectural forms, decorative façades, urns, and *coquillage* in forms that aesthetically codified commonalities for France. The gardens laid out for view evidence of French taste that culturally modified the meaning of the term " French." This manifestly exuberant, materially defined culture was less wildly Dionysian and excessively narcissistic than ambitiously, monumentally, and artfully political. The France it represented, as artificial and artifactual as it was, had the political robustness to endure even through the brutal winters toward the end of Louis XIV's reign. It projected a false vision of French unity and well-being that turned out to be all too effective. The exorbitance of the French court ironically helped frighten French enemies into joining military forces to forestall the formation of a new empire. Exquisite goods and their ostentatious display were clearly taken seriously as an expression of geopolitical power.[6]

How could goods gain this political standing in the period? The rediscovery or invention (depending on how you look at it) of the classical heritage put enormous emphasis on the world of goods; *things* had carried this revered past into the present. The *objects* from Ancient Greece and Rome made this inheritance manifest; the artworks, writings, aqueducts, and road systems – all things you could touch and point to – were the measures of the greatness of the Ancients against which contemporary life was compared.[7] These enduring markers of earlier civilization were recognized as privileged conduits through history. No wonder early modern Europeans cultivated them, dreaming that their work might last for centuries (and developing aesthetics that held such monumental endurance as the highest goal).[8]

The reverence for the classical tradition gave Italians a disproportionate role in defining seventeenth-century European cosmopolitan tastes. Artists and gentlemen made pilgrimages to Italy to expose themselves to Ancient works and writings, and discovered on the peninsula not only Ancient artworks, but also Renaissance and baroque pieces derived from this tradition. This cultural tourism, while directed toward the Great Tradition, also helped to make even common Italian artifacts more central to European fashion and design. For Louis XIV and his ministers, who took French claims to greatness more than seriously, having both the Great Tradition and trends in fashion located so firmly in Italy was unacceptable. If the French state was to become a center of European civilization, not just power, it had to take on cultural leadership. So, Louis XIV followed classical precedent and had his achievements monumentalized through artworks, while Colbert manipulated fashion to make French goods desirable to elite consumers throughout Europe. Material beauty was more a matter of power and glory than an aesthetic issue to these men. It was as important to their cultural politics as being praised or feared was to the delicate balances of power among European states. French works had to surpass anything made in Italy to make this reign an aesthetic as well as military success.[9]

Of course, getting the eyes of Europe away from Italy and toward achievements in France was a difficult goal to realize. It was attempted with a mixture of military aggressiveness, extensive building projects, more than a little manufacturing, and a powerful system of patronage. Still, there was reason to do it. There seemed to be an opportunity for France to assume broad leadership in Europe. The Italians might have had the Great Tradition in their backyards, but they were also terribly divided politically, and had lost much of their political and economic standing because European trade had turned away from the Mediterranean and toward the Atlantic. England was benefiting from this economic shift, but was behind in letters and some techniques of manufacture. Dutch trade was thriving and Dutch power was great in spite of the small size of the country – but its culture could not take over the world of fashion. Protestant countries were pleased to use Dutch manufactures and to follow their styles, but Catholic courts were reluctant to imitate Dutch dress even when they used Dutch goods. They preferred to be more visibly influenced by Italian styles. The Habsburg Empire was supposed to be the great Catholic force in Europe, but it was losing its cultural and political hegemony (although it remained a substantial rival to France). Rome was the center of Catholic cultural influence, but it was a limited political force. There was an opportunity, then, for France to integrate itself politically and culturally, and provide leadership for the rest of Europe. It was part Catholic, part Protestant, part Mediterranean, part Atlantic, and it had been part of the Roman Empire. France could perhaps forge a new empire and build a great civilization in Europe, a new Rome. Success depended first on the establishment of its territory, but it also rested crucially on the development of its cultural resources.[10]

Cultural objects were important to the politics of the period in another way because of their increased diffusion through capitalist trading networks. Consumer

66. Horses by Marsy from the Grotto, with shell work in the background (print by
Stephanus Baudet 1676).

goods in the marketplace told stories about the quality of life in far-away places. A small shop-owner in Italy might not ever see France, but could probably see French goods. The power of France might not be locally manifested, but it could be estimated first by stories about successes on the battlefield (sometimes carried by consumer goods like almanacs and coins) and then by the elegance and desirability of French goods.

The availability of more objects in the marketplace, then, was providing new bases for geographical identification, aligning places and things in new ways. Trading was making visible a diversity in local cultures that many consumers had been unaware of. They could not only begin to see what other people had, but to conceive of their own material world as something other than the natural way of things. Fashionable aristocrats, who had already been cosmopolitan for generations, were certainly aware of the diversity of cultural traditions in Europe. But their tastes were becoming economically and culturally more influential. Fashions for goods were beginning to be recognized as forces affecting international trade. Governments were trying to use legislation to regulate dress as well as imports. Sumptuary laws were enacted to limit clothing choices, and trade sanctions and duties were imposed to restrict access to foreign goods. Colbert was quick to point out that elites, importing clothing and other consumer items to stay in fashion, could easily do damage to local manufacturing. States whose goods were not in fashion had their economies undermined by the tastes of their own well-dressed elites. But local artisans who crafted goods that pleased aristocratic tastes throughout Europe could benefit from the international market for their products. The state manufactures set up by Colbert were designed precisely to meet and profit from the demands of fashion; they also were set up through a state system regulating production. The new arrangement helped to transfer both cultural and economic power from independent artisans and city guilds to the state, making fashion a political tool for empowering the central government.[11]

The new manufactures (royal or state-sanctioned) being developed under Colbert produced consumer goods that were both designed for the marketplace and distinctively French. They were neither traditional wares derived from regional cultures nor slavish copies of fashionable objects found elsewhere, but rather ones made according to directives from the state. This made them an invention and reflection of France that helped to give the country both a common economic base and a rudimentary cultural unity. Colbert wanted to make mostly fine goods for aristocrats and financiers, who were the ones who had the money to spend on fashion. While Colbert was severe at first in demanding that the artisans he brought from Italy or the Netherlands should train French workers to manufacture objects that exactly imitated fine foreign goods, the successful enterprises did more than that: they married the newly learned techniques with local tastes, materials and craft traditions. They applied a cosmopolitan view of design and manufacture to this mixture of manufacturing skills and demands for quality to make innovative and highly refined pieces.[12] Colbert claimed he just wanted to get French consumers to buy French goods. To do this, he had to make the results fashionable. But with a little pressure from the king on his court to wear what Colbert's enterprises produced, and with some refinement in the manufactures

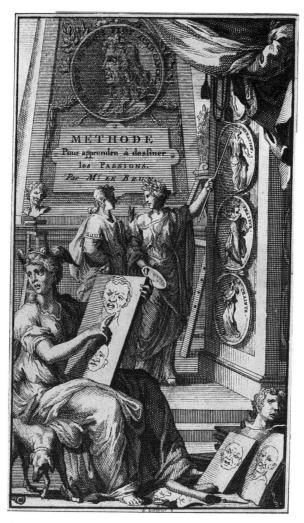

67. Frontispiece for Le Brun's text on drawing emotions (Le Brun 1727).

produced in the French countryside, the state actually brought to life a French style that was imitated throughout Europe.

Another kind of state-sponsored cultural regulation was also helping to define a French aesthetic during the reign of Louis XIV and under the eye of Colbert. Academies for art, music, ballet, and science were all founded or augmented in power during the reign, each in its own way helping to define a distinctively French style of thought, movement or manufacture. Charles Le Brun, who headed the Académie de Peinture and Sculpture, was unrelenting in his efforts to shape a common aesthetic for this reign. The highly codified education he developed for French art students was matched by his careful regulation of the artworks supplied to the king and court. Le Brun gained the reputation as a tyrannical leader, but his domineering supervision of the arts may have been what made him succeed in this very political period of French cultural life, when the cultivation of individual genius was less important to art than its political effects. Le Brun helped articulate a style of art in France that was less individual than collective, less personal than strategic. The artists in this period of French history used their work to make a reputation for their king and country more than for themselves.[13]

Finally, the growth of trade itself – the import of goods into France and the movement of goods among regions of France, both of which were increasingly regulated by the state – had consequences for the evolution of an identifiable French material culture. Restrictions placed on imports helped to stimulate more local production and consumption, while internal trade of commodities among the various regions of France helped to distribute the new items more effectively across the country. Even the imports of goods, restricted as they were, helped the French develop a distinctive culture. Elite contact with the cosmopolitan fashion system helped local producers to see what tastes were in vogue around Europe so they could follow fashion using their own products.[14]

The political apparatus of late seventeenth-century France may have been primarily organized for warfare, but it was also well positioned to regulate the production and flow of goods, from artworks to tableware. Privileges from the state were a means for intervening in the economy and developing goods to be traded there. Monopoly trading companies were formed to control trade to distant areas of the world and to keep it under the watchful eye of Colbert. Imports from other European countries were drastically curtailed or actively discouraged. Economic life was (formally and at the top) grounded on rights allocated by royal authority. What could be simpler than to make this regulation a political means for generating a distinctive culture for France?[15]

A culture of manufacture and collection in France, then, combined to produce a French style, a particular material culture and a centrally modulated system of manufacture, fashion, art education, and trade. French style not only marked French elites, but became a means for exporting French goods. Elites from throughout Europe by the 1660s were already beginning to imitate French fashions, and they continued to do so through the first half of the eighteenth century.[16]

It seems ironic that tapestries, furniture, laces, rare shells, jewels, sought-after bulbs, silk clothing, porcelain plates, citrus trees and all the other evidences of the excesses in consumption typifying this reign would have been politically significant. We know that gluttonous consumption was a guiding theme and *modus operandi* of court life, both inside the château and in the gardens, but the willingness of king and court to live a spendthrift existence at the expense of the people seemed the opposite of any effort to create a sense of commonality among the French. Nonetheless, however repugnant the idea, greed helped to produce a material culture for France that associated place with a set of tastes and objects conveying them.[17] The creation of the territorial state was a material project that began with the marking of place with fortresses and canals, but continued with the articulation of a locating culture of collection, consumption, and display.

That is why a riot of decorative objects was loaded on top of the austere and simple geometrical lines of French royal gardens.[18] The ambitious drive for cultural as well as political leadership of Europe was made manifest where visitors could see and be seduced by French style. The excesses of the Italian Baroque were eventually rejected as a matter of taste by the French court, but not because of any abhorrence of the ornamentation in the style. French claims to greatness could only be made through a cultural style that could be seen as authentically French and yet cosmopolitan enough to suit fashionable consumers in distant parts of Europe. The resulting French classicism had a restraint and solemnity that matched the strict geometrical leanings of this still quite military culture, but it was both balanced and undermined by the passionate and gluttonous consumption in France being mobilized there for political ends – notably at Versailles.

Fouquet and the politics of gardens

A great scandal at the beginning of Louis XIV's reign brought the importance of gardens, consumption, style, and social identity into the forefront of French political life. The finance minister, Nicolas Fouquet, built a lovely house and garden at Vaux-le-Vicomte, using Le Nôtre to engineer the great formal gardens, La Quintinie to set up a kitchen garden, Le Vau to design the house, and Le Brun to coordinate the project as a whole (see plate 6). The house was modest in size, if not taste, but the gardens were enormous, and contained Le Nôtre's most perfect design. When the work was complete, Fouquet brought the king to a party to see his new estate. When the visit was over, Louis had Fouquet imprisoned on charges of graft, and then took Le Brun, Le Vau, Le Nôtre, La Quintinie, and a number of less well-known artisans to build Versailles.[19]

The familiar story of Fouquet's downfall – the history of his arrest for graft and fall from political favor – can tell us about the political nature of consumption and gardening in France during the reign of Louis XIV. Ranum argues that Fouquet, the Treasurer when the young king came to power, was only following the lead of previous powerful ministers, namely Richelieu and Mazarin, in building a lovely château and beautiful gardens on his estate. They had both used graft to amass fortunes and then built great homes. They had carried the Renaissance culture of collection into France where it took root as elsewhere in Europe among those of high rank. Accumulation of beautiful things was associated with personal quality; fine taste in consumer goods was thought to be a mark of personal superiority. Fouquet was certainly ambitious in buying an estate like Vaux and decorating it so lavishly, particularly when he was so young, but his graft and self-aggrandizement had some precedent, and his concern about taste even had some positive cultural value.[20]

Nonetheless, Fouquet created a scandal at Vaux, and paid a high price for it. In a terrible breech of decorum, he brought to French noble life a sensibility from Parisian worlds of art and finance that did not comfortably sit there. Worst of all, he displayed an enormous vanity about his cultural learning that made him less than appropriately deferent toward those of higher rank. He was a bright and witty man who apparently learned quickly from those around him, but he also seemed to be quite self-indulgent and did not know when to modulate either his ambitions or his desires. He immersed himself in a world of French writers, artists and intellectuals to whom, as Treasurer, he supplied royal patronage. They fed his narcissism and passions, while also shaping his tastes. Fouquet's aesthetic inclinations were apparently not so original in the Parisian context; he seemed no genius impresario around whom artists were capable of surpassing themselves. But the Parisian cultural penchants that he applied to seigniorial life created a breathtaking estate at Vaux that was aesthetically engaging, but socially scandalous.[21]

Ranum argues that Fouquet was among a number of new financiers of France who tried to find cultural expression for their new elevated social standing through acquisition of property and its lavish development, using new aesthetics. Fouquet in fact acquired *two* large estates and accumulated an impressive array of tapestries, statues, and paintings for them. He also amassed a fabulous collection of books and a garden of plants so rare that Colbert had to hire two German gardeners to examine them after Fouquet's imprisonment. No one in France could assess their worth.[22] The ascendancy of Fouquet and his cohort supported a shift in taste and thirst for new goods because they had little inherited property to defend, no traditional culture to associate with their high status, and only personal tastes to indicate their intellectual and social superiority. Fouquet was astoundingly successful, according to Ranum, in finding the best in French culture, but Fouquet's claims to power using displays of taste were too great for his social standing. Although graft was an unspoken tradition in the office of Treasurer, the elegance of Vaux made the graft impossible to ignore. As a result of a lack of discretion in the realm of cultural politics, Ranum argues, Fouquet lost his office, his property, and his role in the development of culture in France.[23]

Fouquet's story is interesting not because the scandal was so great or Fouquet himself was personally fascinating, or even that he was a world-scale swindler, which he probably was, but because his fate can tell us a great deal about French politics, the political uses of taste, and the importance of gardens as vehicles for taste and state politics in the period. Fouquet embodied cultural currents of his day that were politically too potent to be left in his hands, and therefore contributed to his downfall.

Fouquet was part creature and part creator of the Parisian art world of the mid-seventeenth century. He was a man who mixed with the *précieuses* like Mlle de Scudéry in the salon world of Paris. He wrote poetry (albeit not good poetry), and seemed to value quite seriously the gifts of artists. Although those who were patronized by him clearly identified him as a man who had chosen administration over the pursuit of letters, they accepted his largesse on their behalf and took advantage of his political placement. They cultivated him just as long as he was in power, and some even after that.[24]

The system of patronage he administered was developed during the reign of Henri IV. This Protestant monarch had a love for learning that was put in the service of political need. Because of his shaky legitimacy as a Protestant king in a mainly Catholic country, Henri was in need of voices to praise him. Writers patronized by the king made themselves tributes to the monarch, not as propagandists per se, but as celebrants and exemplars of greatness in the Renaissance tradition.[25]

After the reign of Henri IV, this system of patronage decayed. Individuals of high social standing without much genuine interest in scholarship or language – but with the ambition to *appear* cultivated – became patrons to many less-than-distinguished literary figures. State patronage was continued, but lost its early political significance and aesthetic legitimacy. Mazarin tried to revive the system by sponsoring artists and thinkers from outside France. Ironically, this effort to demonstrate a kind of cosmopolitanism further diluted the political potency of French pensions to artists and made local recipients seem second class compared to the lofty foreigners. Nonetheless, the policy did still continue the patronage system itself.[26]

Fouquet, when he became Treasurer, entered this world of art pensions as an ardent connoisseur steeped in the Parisian milieu. He was not just appreciative of letters, but a bibliophile, plant collector, art collector, and particularly a student of history and cartography. He was heir to the cultural predilections of Richelieu and Mazarin that had made both of them impressive collectors and cultural leaders in France. He shared their vanity and thirst for refined intellect and taste. Like his predecessors, he sponsored artists, writers, and scientists because his position as Treasurer demanded it. Unlike them, he also immersed himself in French art worlds and scholarly circles, and supported French cultural achievement without reservation. He embodied the odd combination of chauvinism and cosmopolitanism that characterized Parisian culture.[27]

Fouquet's ambitious approach to connoisseurship made him an impressive collector. He built a massive library that was particularly rich in the works of political history, which he felt important for understanding and participating in politics. Fouquet's collection of books, maps, and documents in this area contained works of such serious historical value that scholars came to his estate, Saint-Mandé, to consult his bookshelves. Fouquet recognized the political need for these kinds of pieces, and proposed that his library and similar collections be identified and placed in a state depository. (Somehow he understood the political significance of his library while he did not develop a similar understanding about his gardens and house.) Although Colbert distrusted Fouquet's project at first, he eventually endorsed it and the collection became the basis for the French *Archives Nationales*.[28]

Early in his career, Fouquet also turned to gardening, not as a connoisseur of garden design, but as a collector. He assembled an enormous display of citrus trees at Saint-Mandé. It was probably the best collection of its sort in France. He brought a German gardener to help him locate and collect new specimens (which is why Germans were later brought in to assess the results). He also cultivated a botanical garden that brought unusual medicinal herbs into France; the collection was thought to be more extensive than that found in the Parisian Jardin Royal. Fouquet's estate lands at Saint-Mandé were said generally to be marvelous, being filled with artworks as well as plants, but they had no formal gardens of the sort that soon would be planted at Vaux.[29]

Although the minister was a public figure, Fouquet's world at Saint-Mandé was cultivated and private. Except for the library, Fouquet kept his collections away from general public view. He lived a mostly shadowy, if sophisticated and somewhat decadent, life at his country home. Luminaries of Parisian salon life would come there, but their exclusive world depended on private parties where literary or artistic greatness could be displayed in glittering but intimate conversation. Although an ambitious man who was not afraid of the spotlight, Fouquet at first kept his connoisseurship and ambition somewhat masked by moving in this very enclosed social world of fashion and taste.[30]

The Parisian salon life that Fouquet frequented was in many ways diametrically opposed to the life of the nobility. For one thing, salons were directed primarily by women. Aristocratic life, on the other hand, revolved nostalgically around a memory of nobles as occupying a manly, warrior rank. The former was a world of words more than action; the latter depended more on public performance than private intimacies. Salon life was an urban, educated culture, while noble life was located in land owner- ship and military duties that required little book knowledge. Both flourished from the wealth that was being brought to France through trade, and both participated equally in the fashion system, but still at the beginning of Louis XIV's reign, they held their differences dear. (This is why Molière's criticism of salon life was so pleasing to the court.)

Women were not yet leading the great salons of the eighteenth and nineteenth cen- turies, but they presided over a world of gossip, wit, and love of entertainment that brought fine taste, intimacy, superficiality, and a constrained eroticism together. Although they were called the *précieuses*, this was not because their conversation was always as precious as Molière suggested. Serious issues of cultural controversy were engaged by them both in their private social discourse and in the press; the conflict between the Ancients and the Moderns (those who believed that the Ancients had achieved all that was humanly possible and those that believed that the modern world could surpass theirs), which was at the center of intellectual life in seventeenth-century France, was a staple of discussion in salons. The *précieuses* may not have been riding horseback regularly to develop military skills like Louis XIV and his entourage, but they sharpened their wits and pens to create a refined, if sometimes trivial, social world.[31]

Elements of Jansenism also ran through salon life, challenging the traditional reli- gious foundations of French society. Mlle de Scudéry, the most famous of the *pré- cieuses* and a great supporter of Fouquet, seemed to have harbored a Jansenist belief in divine grace, a position that Catholic traditionalists saw as making Jansenism little different than Protestantism. Louis XIV turned out to be just as distrustful of Jansenists as Protestants and made efforts in his regime to suppress this lively and eco- nomically vibrant group. But for the cultural and economic elites of Parisian literary circles, Jansenism was an appealing philosophy, although not a cause for which the *pré- cieuses* fought.[32] Fouquet brought his immersion in salon life with him when he bought and developed the estate at Vaux-le-Vicomte; the *précieuses* transported their conver- sations to Vaux, where Fouquet's mistress presided over their parties. But the forms and consequences of Fouquet's new life at Vaux were not to be continuous with his previ- ous one at Saint-Mandé. For one thing, the land at Vaux conferred nobility on this young and ambitious Parisian minister; for another, Fouquet began to act more like a noble, experimenting all-too-successfully with the kinds of public events (fêtes, ballets, carrousels) that traditionally helped mark the social superiority of the nobility. Here, a man with constrained but arty tastes, daring friends, and a penchant for scandalous love affairs was trying to use his Parisian roots to speak to the nobility. His tastes and ambitions that had been cultivated in private in salon circles were now, thanks to Le Nôtre's gardens and Le Brun's designing of fêtes, strewn visibly across the French landscape. Unfortunately for Fouquet, he did his work all too well. He should have failed, building a grotesque domain where his gross ambition could have become a source of laughter; but, instead, he used the enormous cultural resources at his fingertips for his personal aggrandizement, and shaped a public profile that was too glittering for his own good (see plates 29 and 30).[33]

Fouquet's importation of Parisian salon taste into the world of the aristocracy yielded a beautiful but threatening vision. A brilliant and novel French style was fashioned in the space between the two social worlds (noble and commercial) in which Fouquet lived and worked. Le Brun was able to use his training in Italian baroque culture to begin to knit together these worlds of consumerism, learning, and power. The great city-states of Italy had already made themselves into cultural amalgams of a similar sort. Merchant wealth and a respect for aristocratic virtues had been joined there with classical ideas of nobility and valor. Le Brun went to Italy and exposed himself not only to the artworks of the Ancients but the ideas and creations of Italian artists. The young artist brought this experience to the problem of building a showplace for Fouquet, and used it to help integrate Parisian sophistication with the French noble love for staged ritual and public performance. The resulting French style was magnificent – grand, gestural, symbolically complex, and grounded in a military system of land control. Fouquet's new estate, however, had a fatal social flaw. It was intended to celebrate personal power. This might have worked well enough in his private world at Saint-Mandé, but it was a scandal for the very public and collective life at Vaux.

Fouquet's downfall may have been primarily a political tale about greed, graft, and political disgrace, but the story of Vaux's development and importance to France was different. This grand estate did more than just reveal Fouquet's character; it brought to light the possibility of a French culture that Louis XIV quickly and enthusiastically embraced. The king immediately adopted the artists and artisans from Vaux for use at Versailles. Perhaps Vaux was so extravagantly expensive that it made Fouquet's graft undeniably visible. Maybe the king did realize at the fête held in his honor that Fouquet was dangerous and disloyal, and had him imprisoned. All may have been the case, but the obviously public value of Vaux's cultural brilliance may have had different and more profound political significance. In the seventeenth-century French noble world, where politics was more a matter of performance than words, the glittering qualities of this physical space as a stage for political performance should not be underestimated. Saint-Mandé absorbed just as much graft money as Vaux, but because of its inwardness, it was no offense to the king. Fouquet's great library and collection of citrus trees were terribly desirable, expensive, and famous at Saint-Mandé, but did not lead to charges of corruption. Fouquet was already personally shaping French culture through patronage and drawing artists around him before he even purchased Vaux. What changed at Vaux was that he built a political stage of staggering proportions and very French novelty.

None of his cultural tastes and ambitions seemed to matter as long as Fouquet lived quietly. Bourgeois culture was centered on private tastes and private life. Powerful financiers and merchants who did not try to share the stage of power (even when they shared its exercise) were quite acceptable to the French nobility. As long as Saint-Mandé was private, it could be as magnificent as any estate. Fouquet could promote there any aesthetic vision he pleased. But Vaux was different. It was a seigniorial estate, and hence was meant to be a stage for French noble life. What Fouquet did there mattered, and he did a great deal. There seemed to be nothing that Fouquet would or could not get for himself. He set up a factory near his estates just to supply tapestries for his two homes, placing Le Brun in charge of the designs. If businessmen could set up factories, so could he. Molière brought comedies to Vaux at virtually the same time as he did to the royal family's nearby residence at Fontainebleau. Fouquet also hired La Quintinie, the best gardener in Paris, to set up his potager and supply him with the earliest, best, and most exotic fruits and vegetables. Both nature and commerce were mobilized to make Vaux exquisite, using tastes and techniques from French commercial life to enter noble culture. The results were stunning.[34]

The trouble with Vaux was that what Fouquet built there combined bourgeois and noble culture in ways that seemed alluringly *French*. The feminized tastes of the salon embodied in the house at Vaux, and the scholarliness of the artworks both in the residence and the gardens might have been at odds with the military masculinity of noblemen, but the battlement features of the garden, and the severity of Le Nôtre's garden design made the whole approach to land there hard to resist for noble visitors. The artful and ambitious estate at Vaux, then, was not just a sign of Fouquet's graft, but the sign of a scandalous and seductive social daring. On this estate, being educated and rich looked more grand and French than being noble.[35]

It is possible that Louis XIV and Colbert turned against Fouquet before the fête at Vaux. Colbert had already been horrified and amazed to find nothing in the treasury when the king took the reins of power. He intimated to Louis XIV that Fouquet must have been to blame, but they both should have known from Mazarin's estate where most of the money had gone. After all, Mazarin was the richest man in France when he died, even wealthier than the monarch himself. He was so embarrassed by the scale of his fortune that he offered unsuccessfully to bequeath much of his estate to the young king. Of course, it is safe to assume that Fouquet was grooming himself to follow Mazarin's lead, and would have matched the level of graft set by his predecessor, if he had been given the chance. But Colbert assured him that this would never happen and lobbied the king quite vociferously to get rid of Fouquet.[36]

Colbert specifically mentioned graft to Louis XIV, and did raise questions about the emptiness of the treasury, but he was just as personally concerned about Fouquet's ambition as he was about the money. Colbert was, after all, extremely loyal to the young king, and realized that Fouquet was a vain and calculating character, who could well put his own interests before those of the young king. Both Fouquet and Colbert were of bourgeois origins, but they clearly did not share the same values. Colbert was a provincial man from a family in the textile business. He believed in hard work, loyalty, and honesty as the guiding values in his life. Fouquet's Parisian origins made him a very

68. Stairway and statue near the canal at Vaux.

cosmopolitan man who was not terribly disciplined, but loved money and consumption. Both men shared a love of collecting and connoisseurship (a passion for things that commercial life can indeed help to instill), but they brought different resources and values to the world of material culture. Colbert disapproved of the spendthrift and immoral Fouquet, and Fouquet probably found Colbert provincial. It should be no surprise, then, that they would have been enemies at court and that Colbert would have worked to alienate the king from this charming young minister.[37]

Even before the fête at Vaux, then, there were many reasons for Colbert to feel antipathy toward Fouquet and to try to cultivate similar feelings in the king. There are fewer indications as to why these men nonetheless embraced Fouquet's tastes. Le Vau, Le Brun, Le Nôtre, La Quintinie, and many artisans from Vaux, were brought immediately to Versailles after Fouquet was imprisoned. They were joined there by

Fouquet's impressive set of artworks and extensive citrus collection. Ranum explains nicely why financiers from Paris would have liked Fouquet's Vaux;[38] but why did this style appeal to a king who was in many ways so conventional and conservative? It cannot be that the king and Colbert simply had good taste and liked what they saw at Vaux. Their subsequent rejection of Bernini's plan for the Louvre and his glorious equestrian statue for Versailles suggested quite the opposite. They could easily be contemptuous of wonderful artworks, if the political message of the work was wrong. For some reason, the political message of the style at Vaux, while wrong for Vaux, must have been right for Versailles. How could that have been the case?

Perhaps the style was simply so French and so seductive that it pointed to the political possibilities of an exquisitely French material culture competing with Italian forms. Such a culture was too valuable a resource to be left in the hands of an unpredictable minister, but it was certainly a potential asset for the king, court, and state. Vaux clearly took the best from Parisian consumer culture and married it through classical forms with the military and performative tendencies in the French aristocracy. The garden, for example, maintained the materialism of the Renaissance collector's garden, added land management systems that broke with the more spiritually inclined traditions of Italy, and became a setting for breathtakingly ambitious parties and performances in the noble tradition that made consumption an artwork in itself. It was a grand and ambitious place that spread as far as the eye could see, and then merged seamlessly into the distant countryside. It claimed both nature and art with equal vigor.[39] The grandness of Vaux may have made the graft of Fouquet more visible, but it also made the cultural resources of France more palpable (see plates 6 and 30).

The style of art used at Vaux, so French, original, grand, classical, and territorial, was a perfect tool for the state. At Versailles, Louis XIV, Colbert, Le Brun and Le Nôtre could make political use of this very seductive and distinctive culture, adjusting it to fit the realities of state politics. Although they were staunch defenders of the monarchy and traditional forms of authority, Louis XIV and Colbert were still self-consciously set to *change* politics in France. They wanted a powerful monarchy where only a weak one had existed before. They thus had reason to promote a new French political culture to support state-based absolutism. They claimed to be "restoring the monarchy" by empowering the state, but they were actually working to found a French state with unprecedented power that they hoped could be fashioned into the center of a European empire. What better way to serve these political ambitions than by taking over and dangling in front of aristocrats elsewhere in Europe the flamboyant, materialistic, territorial, and ever-so-French style of Vaux-le-Vicomte!

By Ranum's account, Fouquet's arrest was a step in the disciplining of the aristocracy that was necessary for establishing an absolutist state. It was a prelude to the enforced system of consumption in the French court that Elias says reduced French nobles to dressed-up actors in the king's political performances.[40] It made it clear that consumption was a politically powerful weapon that aristocrats and financiers ignored at their peril. The Fouquet affair politicized material identity and made it a matter of state power. With the king's control of court consumption and taste and with Colbert's control of design and manufacture in France, it was possible to create a corporate identity based on common consumption of French goods and the articulation of French tastes. Fouquet found artists and aesthetics with which to make a French material culture; he also pointed to the garden as a site for aesthetic innovation where experimentation with territorial control could be harnessed for power. In a dangerously ambitious or innocent way, he set French design into the landscape where it could help give form to the territorial state.

Consumption and identity in early modern Europe

The importance of goods – whether collector's items or vast gardens – to the processes of political unification and differentiation in this period makes more sense in the historical context of the seventeenth century. Place was already marked by goods, since so much production had been local for centuries; guild protectionism had helped to keep techniques of manufacturing located in particular places, tying regions to material cultures. The rise of capitalist trading and new opportunities for buying imported goods did not immediately undermine this regionalism because most people sought and could only afford the goods that fitted their traditional lifestyles. Still, many of them could fathom the influences of the trade around them and savor the newly visible differences in material culture. For those with little money, the marketplace may have been more a source of new sights than new goods, but even these voyeurs of commercial life could recognize elements of political geography through design and consumption.[41]

In theoretical terms, one could argue that Bourdieu's system of stratified tastes, which is used today to reproduce and make sense of social stratification, was both elaborated in this period and connected to political geography in ways that Bourdieu has not really discussed (Bourdieu 1984). Fashion in the seventeenth century was still primarily driven by the problems in stratification caused by disjunctions between traditional sources of social rank and new sources of economic and political power. Social mobility made rank more problematic and encouraged people to use elegant objects to lay claims to higher social positions. But state-formation in the period was also helping to redraw the political map of Europe, making identity problematic in new ways. Nobles who had been leaders of principalities that became part of a state or empire often kept their traditional rank but not necessarily their political identity. In this fluid situation, consumption provided a means of claiming political feelings as well as social aspirations. The choice of clothes became a means of either expressing regional loyalty or submitting to the political authority of the state.[42]

The association of geographical areas with styles of consumption became more codified in late seventeenth-century France, when both a standardized French code of dress was set at court and regional styles of clothing started to become stabilized for the first time. Aristocrats and townspeople alike were faced with the choice of abandoning or condoning tradition in their uses of goods. Some displayed regional dress to defend, codify, and employ their heritage to claim regional identity; others followed fashion to curry favor with the king. Ironically, both choices gave clothing more political significance in France. Both made material culture a means for communicating political identities along with social individual rank. In this system, taste became a more important marker of both social and political place, opening up avenues for changing group identities.[43]

Making the state of France into a territorial whole had obvious quantitative dimensions to it: measuring the landmass, counting the people and places in it, fixing its position in terms of latitude and longitude, and locating its rivers, mountains and other natural features in relation to human settlements.[44] But location had to mean something beyond mere physical siting if it was to be politically potent. France (as opposed to merely a collection of regions with pieces of common history) needed some unifying cultural base to make sense of the common institutions of government. Regionally localized material culture might have seemed an unlikely candidate for this job, given the low levels of production and trade in the pre-industrial world. But the significance of goods made even small-scale consumption visible and politically significant.

Patterns of manufacture and taste in Europe had already been instrumental in forging and projecting political identities in some Italian city-states during the Renaissance. Great cultural centers like Florence were adorned with elegant artworks as a way of making vivid the wealth and power of their bourgeoisie and the refined tastes and patronage of the local nobility. French territory, won by the state's army and defended by its fortresses, could hardly be comparably adorned with arts and manufactures. It was far too large for that. But the *petit parc* at Versailles could function as a kind of central square for all of France, and set out in public view the qualities that made France uniquely great. French artworks could be flaunted there and testify to French power and taste. Statues set out by the garden's battlement walls could connect French military power to its cultural strength. The flora and fauna collected in the park could even testify to the scale of French trading systems and the richness of French natural resources. The bosquets and parterres combined all these elements to give French territory a distinctive identity inside the larger European continent.

New manufactures and French design

While Colbert's manufacturing policies have tended to be read flatly as economic moves designed to insert some rationality into French industry, they were actually important for both empowering and glorifying the French state. The tapestries and furniture from Gobelins certainly dramatically trumpeted French taste, giving the French a reputation for elegance and luxuriousness that became well known. It is true that Colbert claimed that he was not a cultured man, and his letters show him to be a harried worrier, always obsessed with problems of economy and efficiency. Still, the same Colbert set up a *petite académie* of advisors to develop his cultural program for the regime. He realized that his work required the articulation of cultural goals, and he was determined to make French culture as vibrant as the French economy. The minister even tried to cultivate himself during his period in power, following the precedent set by Mazarin. He became such a connoisseur, mostly of rare books, that his private collections became known throughout Europe. Visitors also found more than a little of interest in his *Cabinet de curiosité*. Since he was celebrated mostly for his intellectual rather than aesthetic interests, he may have remained uneasy about the arts even after his rise to power. Still, Colbert was clearly no accountant trained to make inventories and draw up ledgers without considering the objects being counted. He knew better than that. Colbert certainly set out economic policies to make money, but he pursued this goal by improving the quality and variety of French consumer goods, tailoring French commodities to suit cosmopolitan tastes. For profit, Colbert demanded luxury goods fit for the king. He wanted nobles at court to envelop themselves in confections from French industry, but he also wanted to be sure that their dress would be a tribute to the regime.[45]

The fashion system itself was already in full swing well before Colbert began these efforts to shape the French economy and culture. Clothes, interior design, furniture, gardening, and the like were all joined in a common system of elite style and change. From the late fourteenth century, fashions had migrated across a variety of trend-setting centers, following patterns of trade and power across the European continent. At the beginning of Louis XIV's reign, fashion favored Italian and Dutch consumer goods. Catholic courts like the French one tended to be drawn to Italian styles, but French nobles were also enamored of some of the fine manufactured goods (and gardening styles) that the Dutch were making available. Unhappily for Colbert, the result was that French bullion was leaving the country in pursuit of fashion. Colbert's response was to manufacture in France the kinds of consumer goods that French elites were importing.[46]

Mercantilist theory equated a healthy economy with accumulating bullion, and fashions for imports let gold and silver leave the country.[47] In 1662, Colbert estimated that 12 million *livres* were spent on Flemish or Dutch goods, and almost an equal amount on Italian ones. An additional 1 million *livres* were spent on English imports and a comparable amount on German and Scandinavian goods. Some 26 or 27 million livres left the country that year, while only 12–18 million livres came into France from exports. Obviously, the balance of trade was frighteningly negative.[48] If the French economy was to thrive, Colbert believed, bullion had to stay in France, and wealth had to be spent on French consumer goods.

Colbert used this kind of purely economic analysis to define the problems facing the treasury, but he employed a cultural calculus to shape his industrial response. He encouraged French artisans and entrepreneurs to study and tap the desires of fashion-conscious denizens of European courts. He pointed to the economic importance of *cultural* innovation in the design and manufacture of goods, throwing tradition aside and experimenting with imported techniques. If he wanted to halt the movement of bullion out of France, he just as clearly wanted to lure new designs and techniques of production into France to fabricate a new state-based culture of consumption.[49]

To start new manufacturing ventures, Colbert began by tempting Dutch and Italian entrepreneurs and artisans to bring their skills and fashionable tastes to his country, and encouraging French elites to invest in their businesses. Colbert authorized tax reductions, tariff protection, bounties, refunds, subsidies, privileges, payment of rent, loans, gifts, wages, importation of workers, protection of noble prerogatives of investors, and the allocation of the title of *manufacture royale* or *manufacture du roi* to realize this goal.[50] He used treasury money to start these enterprises and keep them going during the early years of their growth. In return, he imposed strict rules on them to try to assure the quality of what was produced.[51] In the end, France became less an industrial giant from these policies than a center for European fashion during most of Louis XIV's reign. Colbert subsidized industries producing fine woolens, figured silks, lace, carpets, tapestries, mirrors, porcelain, and furniture, associating France with the manufacture of luxury goods. Although many of the individual projects failed, Colbert's policies and the new manufacturing centers they supported helped to give birth to a vibrant French elite culture, which had a powerful impact on European life.

The cultural impetus behind Colbert's economic policies may help to explain why Colbert's administration turned out, under close inspection, to be less than wholly rational and much more politically shaped than previously assumed.[52] Perhaps Colbert was just not a good administrator, but it is also possible that the end-product of his ministerial policies was not *supposed* to be rational bureaucracy, economic expansion, or efficient tax accumulation, but the glorification of king and state. We know that the king was traditional and vain enough to prefer glory to a full treasury. We also know Colbert strained to serve the monarch loyally, even when he found his decisions fiscally unsound. He rarely acted unswayed by the king's ambitions and desires. He obediently financed expensive military ventures that the king felt would bring him great renown – but not necessarily any riches. To the extent that Colbert's administration was devoted to constructing a legacy of greatness for France under Louis XIV, it *had* to be less directed toward the rationalization of French political life than toward the articulation of a ravishing French material culture to support claims for the ascendancy of France.

Textiles were central to this system of culture in spite of the fact that their fragility militated against their usefulness as monuments to the king and court. They were important because they were easily circulated, and could quickly contribute both to the cultural reputation of France and to the economic health of the treasury. Colbert was well prepared to use fabrics for his new industrial policy. His family came from the textile business. He already knew that cloth constituted a major item of international trade and cosmopolitan fashion. It made sense for him to manufacture woolens, silks, and laces to create a more healthy French economy and a more dominant French culture.[53]

Because woolens were the staple goods of the European textile trade, they received the greatest attention in Colbert's manufacturing schemes. Ample amounts of Dutch and English fabric had been imported annually by the French when Colbert started trying to strengthen the French economy. These materials were better quality than French wools and were extremely attractive to French elites who could afford imported goods. There was nonetheless a tradition of woolen manufacture and finishing in France that provided a skill base and proclivity for the textile trade that Colbert wanted to build upon. In Abbeville in 1665 a Protestant cloth manufacturer from Zeeland, van Robais, was allowed to import fifty Dutch workmen to start manufacturing woolens similar to those made in Spain and Holland. This entrepreneur was tempted with promises of tax relief, the right to build breweries, windmills, and watermills to serve his manufacture, 12,000 livres to start the project, and 2,000 livres for every new loom put into operation. Another project for making Dutch-style fabrics was located in Louviers, where an existing cloth town was given new work.[54] Comparable projects were spread to sites around different parts of France. Colbert contended that the natural and social resources of individual regions favored different kinds of production, so he placed his projects around France as carefully as he supervised their activities. He also calculated that the dispersing of manufacturers across many regions of the country would stimulate economic activity and increase tax revenues most efficiently. Whether he intended it or not, he also enforced a common industrial policy on diverse localities this way, and helped simultaneously to stabilize the political regime and regulate the material culture of France.[55] In Languedoc, for example, where political instability was a problem for the monarchy, Colbert set up manufacturing concerns that specialized in goods for export, mainly to the Levant. There was little local support for the venture and not such great results for the industry, but the attempt to fashion a political culture through economic policy was made particularly evident in this region.[56]

Soon the French were able to serve most of their own needs for woolens. French fabric finishing actually became so refined that English manufacturers sometimes even sent their best fabrics to France for finishing – at least until the expulsion of the Huguenots sent many textile workers from France to England. The economic effects of Colbert's efforts were not always to increase the productivity of a region or industry; some towns claimed that state intervention had stifled their local traditions of production. But state regulation of industry began to standardize and codify French products, and French textiles started to appear on the backs of aristocrats at Versailles. These manufactures became not only adequate substitutes for imports but desirable in their own right. Finally export goods sent French commodities further afield. Even if these goods did not always live up to the standards set for internally marketed luxury goods, French manufactures became a more visible part of international trade.[57]

French figured textiles may not have been the type of fabric manufactured in the largest quantities in this period, but they were associated with French style because they had such an important place in French fashion. These decorated cloths were surprisingly well suited to the political culture of seventeenth-century France; florals in particular had many of the same associations as French gardens. They mixed nature and culture, the interior and exterior, growing things and artifacts. They provided courtiers and courtesans with a way to carry nature and land – the stuff of estate gardens and territorial states – on their backs. This passion for florals was not new to European fashion, although it had disappeared for quite a while before the French revived it. During the height of the Italian Renaissance, both floral fabrics and formal gardens had come into style. In this period, when Humanist thinking was drawing cultural attention away from the heavens and toward the earth, and when Mediterranean trade was making consumption a more viable and culturally significant activity, wearing floral fabric gained importance.

Florals were not always considered so beautiful. When Burgundy was the center of fashion in the early fifteenth century, Italian florals were a cause for laughter at this haughty court. The joke was on them when the fashion center moved to Italy, and well-dressed Burgundians had to wear styles their elders had ridiculed. But Italian tastes

69. Parterre-like embroidery on clothes and the stratification of clothing styles by rank (Le Pautre).

also waned in importance when the fashion center for Europe moved from Italy to the Habsburg Empire at the end of the sixteenth century. Tastes for floral figured silks again declined and were replaced by a love of leather, dark colors, severe tailoring, and huge starched (often lace) collars. Dutch fashion, when following on the heels of Spanish tastes, translated Counter-Reformation severity into Protestant piety. The black fabrics so well loved by the Spanish were simply adapted to looser, simpler cuts of clothing. When Spanish and Dutch tastes dominated fashion, colorful patterned clothing was not completely submerged but became associated with people with less refined tastes. Even in France, where aristocrats remained more tolerant of Italian florals and figured laces, stylish elites rigorously adhered to the fashion for simpler fabrics. Yet in the period of Louis XIV, both the garden and floral prints once again drew attention to a link between the world of Creation and human decorative arts. Figured silks were the major site and source of floral designs.

French silk manufacture was at the heart of seventeenth-century French fashion, and contributed even more dramatically than other areas of fabric production to the reputation of France as a producer of refined luxury items. Increasingly, cosmopolitan connoisseurs, wanting to adopt the styles of French courtiers, chose to wear the kinds of figured silks that were in vogue at the court in Versailles. The fabrics were often light-weight, and yet had very elegant and refined designs. The French color palate tended to be more subtle than the one used earlier in Italian brocades and embroideries. So even though both the French and Italians frequently used floral imagery in structured, repeating patterns, the French goods were made clearly distinguishable. The French also often used striped silks. Drawing on the fashion for ribbons from earlier in the century, these silks were frequently striped not so much with solid lines of color, but with bands filled with repeating small floral figures. They looked just like the patterns found in the finest ribbons. While most frequently these figured bands appeared as vertical stripes, they were also woven loosely across the fabric, and interspersed with flowers and greenery. French dresses sometimes were quite tailored, and looked almost severe with their striped fabrics and clean lines. But during much of the period of Louis XIV, women wore silks in draped, almost floating layers. Heavier fabrics could be substituted for men's coats or waistcoats, but not for such dresses. With these fashions, French fabrics and styles were linked in a profitable way. Even where the silk cloth had to be heavier, as in men's waistcoats, it was frequently decorated with borders of vine-like embroideries. This gave the clothing a delicate character that was becoming associated with French design.

Not surprisingly, silks were a vital part of Colbert's manufacturing system. Silk milling had been pursued in France since the reign of François I, but this industry had languished before Colbert revived it. Various centers were established for manufacture, particularly around Lyons where crêpes, damasks, velvets, and satins started to abound. Silk ribbons were also mass produced using a recent invention that could weave up to ten ribbons simultaneously. French imitations of foreign cloth were often a great success. Even the famous Milan gold thread (not really gold but fashionable) was imitated to great effect in France, and replaced imports. In 1674, Cole claims that silks worth £300,000 were exported to England.[58] The embroidered silks made in France became quite beautiful with their organic imagery and growing diversity of colors. In the era of cold weather toward the end of the regime (a period known as the Little Ice Age), silks were used extensively because they could keep aristocrats warm and elegant at the same time, particularly when they were draped in multiple layers. The wealthiest and most fashionable consumers, then, were not just discreet users of the fabric, but massive consumers of silk, and helped establish the French silk industry before the end of Colbert's life.[59]

Lacemaking was another industry restructured in this period to very good effect. The taste for Dutch and Venetian laces among fashionable elites in Europe was very powerful throughout the first three-quarters of the seventeenth century. Great lace collars and cuffs, even lace ruffles along the bottoms of men's pants, were fashionable items that created enormous demand in France for imported goods. These laces were very expensive, draining French bullion, and they drove well-dressed French away from patronizing local manufacturers. Fashion was clearly undermining traditional lacemaking in France, and local artisans did not know how to produce patterns to satisfy the tastes of the times. So Colbert allowed three entrepreneurs, Jean Pluimer, Paul de Macq, and Catherine de Macq, to bring thirty skilled lacemaking mistresses from Venice and 200 lacemakers from Flanders to train 1,600 girls in eight cities to make lace in styles from Venice, Genoa, and Holland. What they produced was called *poincts de France*. Although there was violence against the lace bureau in Alençon and complaints that the girls at Auxerre were not disciplined enough, the French artisans generally took the training well, incorporated new techniques into their work, and began producing something that was part Italian, part Dutch in style but used techniques that remained part regional to France. The end result was something French that was a fine replacement for imported lace. It entered French fashion, where lace became an even more ubiquitous part of good dress, and the *poincts de France* became luxury goods desired in other parts of Europe.[60]

The best known, if not the most economically consequential, of the factories set up under Colbert were the Gobelins and Savonnerie. These became the celebrated centers of French luxury goods whose influence continued through the centuries. The former specialized in the finest-quality tapestries, but also yielded other decorative items like furniture, fireplaces, doors, silverware, and garden decorations. The latter made primarily fine carpets. Importantly for this analysis, both were centers of French consumer goods in the seventeenth and early eighteenth centuries influenced by and influencing garden design. We will return to that part of the story shortly.

Le Brun was placed in charge of the Gobelins shortly after Fouquet was imprisoned. He had previously managed the tapestry factory for Fouquet, and was well qualified to do the same for the king. At the Gobelins, his charge became even larger as numerous artisans were brought to the *Manufacture* to work alongside the weavers. As director of this institution, Le Brun monitored the political and aesthetic qualities of works commissioned for the state, and impressed his stamp on the style of French consumer goods. The endless sketches that he made for artists working under him testified to this hard-headed artist-administrator's creative energy and exact supervision.

Le Brun may have been the leading figure in the French decorative arts but he was not the only man to influence French design. On the contrary, Berain was the one who helped to give French style much of the delicacy, oriental flavor, and playfulness that would characterize French taste during the following century.[61] The heaviness of the Baroque and soberness of French classicism remained the most powerful currents in seventeenth-century French taste, but they already depended on the charm of work by Berain and others to give French design some of its nuance and exquisiteness.

70. Lace shop in the Louvre (print by Le Blond).

The Gobelins became famous for the large numbers of the high-warp tapestries they produced. These were the most demanding kinds of textiles to make, but they yielded gloriously refined results that filled the royal residences. The Gobelins helped to revive this art in France, and supported a community of highly skilled tapestry-makers and designers who made this medium an emblem of French luxury manufacture. Master artists of other backgrounds and skills also made their services available at the Gobelins, and would design almost any kind of decorative art object required by the king.[62] The massive consumption at Versailles was in large part a product of these *ateliers* (see plate 74).

The commissions from the state to the Gobelins provided the French artisans there with the money and incentives to hone their skills and refine their sensibilities, and to make French textiles outstandingly beautiful. The artists and artisans working at the Savonnerie and the Gobelins received annual stipends from the treasury, but they were also commissioned and paid to undertake particular projects. While the Gobelins in theory manufactured tapestries for whoever wanted them, in fact, this center did almost all its work for the king and court. An important series of Gobelins tapestries, for example, was designed to document important events in the reign, such as military victories, the birth of the dauphin, or the king's visit to the Gobelins. The resulting pieces glorified the monarchy as much as any triumphal arch or victory statue in a formal garden or provincial town square. The size and aesthetic beauty of the tapestries gave them and the histories they contained a timeless, monumental quality. They might have been fragile textiles, but they still entered into the program of civilization-building authorized by Colbert and supervised by Le Brun.[63]

The Savonnerie was another royal manufacture that provided the king with textiles, but rugs rather than tapestries. The most famous work produced by the Savonnerie was a series of carpets for the Long Gallery of the Louvre and the adjoining Apollo Gallery. It required ninety-three carpets to cover the floor of the Long Gallery. It took thirteen to fill the Apollo Gallery alone. New looms had to be brought into the Savonnerie to weave pieces of this size. Even then, it took about twenty years to deliver all ninety-three of the commissioned pieces. Between 1664 and 1684, when the great carpets for the Louvre were being woven, an average of 21,060 livres per year went from the treasury to the Savonnerie.[64]

This large-scale, in-house manufacturing may not have influenced the balance of payments in France, but it did help to draw European attention to the French court and its material splendor. This, in turn, contributed to the fashion for French goods. These centers changed the look of French elite culture, and helped to establish the French reputation for luxury manufacture. No wonder aristocrats from far and near flocked to Versailles to study French styles. No wonder they acquired or imitated the consumer goods desired by French courtiers. Once Versailles was made the permanent seat of the French court (because of the king's advancing age and problems in moving such an overstaffed bureaucracy from one royal residence to the next), French fashion gained a permanent center. Travelers wanting to learn the essence of French style could go to Versailles, just as they went to Rome to study classical style and Bernini's Baroque.[65] At Versailles, they could see the highly ritualized life at the French court, and could learn how taste, manners, and massive consumption were used in France to create both political stability and aesthetic refinement.

The victory of French fashion in the late seventeenth century was a strategic success in the struggle to control European political culture. It may not have brought France all the affluence that Colbert would have liked. Nonetheless, it elevated French taste, and made French fabric, which was at the heart of French fashion, desirable to elites throughout Europe. The result was a cultural coup with important, if intangible, politico-economic benefits.

French design innovations and the gardens

The shifts in manufacture of textiles, which led to the creation of distinctive styles of fabrics in France and the growth in the fashion for French goods, were surprisingly connected to garden design. *Parterres de broderie*, the great figured garden beds set out with low hedges, colored sand, and/or flowering plants, became identifying character- istics of French formal gardens. Parterres looked much like borders on Gobelins tapes- tries, figures on Savonnerie carpets, fine laces, the designs in brocades, and, of course, the sewn figures on the best embroidered silks. Even though they were made from natural materials, parterres constituted artificial and artful representations of nature that were in many ways comparable to the plant forms used in the other decorative arts, particularly but not exclusively textiles. According to the early eighteenth-century garden writer d'Argenville, parterres could be made with water, with hedges and colored sand or even with areas of grass. But the glory of French gardening, and the kind of parterre necessary to decorate a great residence, was the *parterre de broderie*.[66]

As the name suggests, these parterres resembled figured textiles (*broderie* means embroidery). In fact, d'Argenville claimed (and created the lasting and inaccurate impression) that these garden beds were given this name because their designs were directly derived from textile patterns. But Mariage has found that young women at court who embroidered seem to have modeled *their* designs on parterres. They appar- ently sketched garden patterns they saw from their windows or copied the parterre pat- terns from printed garden books, and used them for sewing. The direction of influence, of course, is less important than the continuity between garden designs and fabric dec- orations. Both were examples of French taste, and both helped connect nature to French style.[67]

It is hard to assess the relations between parterre designs and French fabrics of the period in part because of the arguments about the origins of parterres themselves. Thacker contends that so-called French parterres were actually elaborations of an Italian form. The ubiquitous knot patterns of Italian gardens began to take on vine- like structures in some baroque gardens. They became early parterres. But the Italians could have originally taken these figured garden beds from the French, since Italian gardeners began these experiments after working in France for François I.[68] It is most likely, however, that both French and Italian gardeners derived these forms from the Oriental carpets, textiles, or other design patterns that were being brought through trade and print from Asia to Europe by the sixteenth century. That would make the

Parterre du Chasteau de verssaille

71. Parterre design by Boyceau.

whole argument over the European origins of parterres moot. What matters is that by the late sixteenth century, parterres in Europe had *both* French and Italian traditions, and by the seventeenth century, French parterres were a distinctive genre. By the time that Le Nôtre began designing his great parks in France, figured garden beds had become so central to French formal gardening that they could inscribe on the local countryside a look that was decidedly and fetchingly French.[69]

In spite of their name, *parterres de broderie* were more often described by contemporaries as carpets, not stitched fabrics, probably because of the way they were used. They were laid out in the garden beds nearest the house, and set on terraces where the line between interior and exterior spaces was blurred. The two-dimensionality of the

72. French lace design resembling a parterre.

73. Princesse de Savoie, 1701, shown in a dress with a pronounced leaf scroll design
and set before a garden (H. Bonnart).

patterns added to the illusion that these forms were floral carpets spread outside the house. Anyone looking down on the beds from the second storey of the château of Versailles, for example, could imagine them to be giant oriental rugs or Savonnerie confections set to the north and south of the château. The *trompe d'oeil* was accentuated by the way the terraces were used. They were treated as extensions of the interior, as places where the ritual and social life of the court could transpire.

The image of parterres as carpets was enhanced under Louis XIV by the fact that Savonnerie carpets looked so much like Le Nôtre's parterres. The gardener's designs have often been described as simpler than the patterns developed by earlier Frenchmen. They were actually made less complex in their ornamentation than both Boyceau's parterre designs and oriental rugs. Le Nôtre's parterres had thicker and more scroll-like leaf figures, and used more open spaces to emphasize the organic shapes of the designs. These parterre patterns were more effective in integrating larger spaces because they were not so full of details that they needed to be studied at close range. They also had a sober and less fanciful quality that fit Le Nôtre's more majestic and militarized gardens. All these characteristics helped to give the resulting garden beds more features in common with the French carpet patterns being developed to cover the huge halls at the Louvre.

Parterre designs also started to be mirrored in the decorations for furniture, silverware, ceramics, and laces from the royal manufactures. French style seemed to emerge from the intersection of Le Nôtre's designs, Le Brun's decorative propensities and Colbert's ambitions for French manufactures. Inlaid table tops, curtain fabrics, lace collars, ceiling decorations, details of fireplace mantels, ceramic plates and serving dishes, and silverware – as each became more "French," it was covered with more lace-like figures and floral decorations. Some of the greatest designers of consumer goods in the period were also interested in garden design. Jean Berain, who was so influential in the decorative arts in France, also published a book of his parterre designs, and sold copies of it in his galleries at the Louvre. The interior of royal residences, the gardens of Le Nôtre, the espalier trees of the fruit garden, and the clothing worn by the aristocracy at the French court, then, came to share common idealized imagery of plant life, and made this look fashionable throughout Europe.[70]

Floral patterns were so popular for the decorative arts in France in part because of their centrality to Italian style. But floral patterns gained specific local significance in late seventeenth-century France. At Versailles florals were used extensively to glorify military power. In the classical tradition, garlands were frequently decked upon heroes. Victors in contests would often wear laurels on their head and garlands around their necks. No wonder the French decorative arts crafted for Versailles used so many floral or vine patterns. Louis XIV was often depicted in paintings and bas-relief portraits with a circle of flowers or laurels around him to represent the king as a great warrior.[71]

The tapestries from the Gobelins, celebrating great achievements during the reign of Louis XIV, had floral decorative borders made with entwined strings of flowers. Le Brun's famous paintings of Louis XIV's victories on the ceiling of the Hall of Mirrors at Versailles were enclosed in golden frames made of laurels or garlands. Even Mignard's destroyed ceiling for the Petite Galerie had putti carrying garlands up

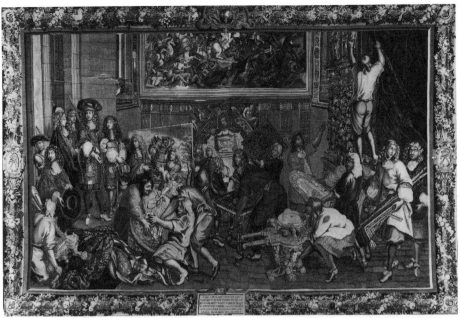

74. The king's visit to the Gobelins. This segment shows not only the kinds of manufactures made at the Gobelins but also the garland border to the tapestry.

towards a figure of the king in classical military dress. This was certainly an image of power and celebration.[72]

It is possible that part of the attraction of floral patterns in French fabrics was derived from this tradition. Men's coats and waistcoats in particular had embroidered borders that often ran around the necks and down the torso, as though constituting a golden or flowered garland, hanging about the bodies of aristocrats. In contrast, the floral patterns on women's clothing were more randomly arranged, as though women were themselves set among the flowers. As the ubiquitous large lace collar of early seventeenth-century fashion died, there developed a comparable difference by gender in French neckwear. Women often carried plain, sheer fabrics around their shoulders and neck, only perhaps delicately trimmed with lace or embroidery, while men almost always had floral-patterned laces draping about their necks. It is intriguing to think that well-dressed noblemen in their court finery were not only elegantly dressed but symbolically wreathed in garlands. For a nobility that still identified itelf strongly with the military, this would have been quite appropriate and desirable.

The densely flowered parterres in French gardens may have similarly gained significance from the association of military bravery with cascades of flowers. The militarism of the gardens and their sensuality could have met in the floral decorations that permeated the bosquets as well as parterres of formal gardens. The parterres in particular covered the landscape with sweet-scented blossoms alternating with green-leafed hedges, not just randomly thrown about, but set out in long vine-like figures that looked surprisingly like strings of flowers or greenery. The parterres made by Le Nôtre

75. Espalier branches of pear trees in the potager, showing their similarity to the garlands in decorative arts of the period.

at Versailles, with their long strands of plants, resembled garlands or laurels draped along the ground, glorifying the seat of the French court.

Parterres de broderie, as their name suggested, also looked much like the embroideries of the period, and sometimes functioned that way, too. Embroideries in the fashions for men under Louis XIV took on unusual significance. The king decided to appoint fifty men from his inner circle to an honorary rank. These men wore a particular pattern of golden embroidery over the sleeves of uniformly colored coats, identifying them as elevated members of this extremely hierarchical social world. As we will see later in chapter 5, the dress for these gentlemen was not just stylishly floral and militarily uniform, but depended for its social significance on golden garlands.

This use of codified costume might seem to have very little connection with gardens,

76. Lace and embroideries in a portrait of Colbert, illustrating the similarity with parterre patterns (C. Le Brun in print by P. Simon, 1682).

but in fact the parterres of Le Nôtre were similarly used to embroider the properties of the king's favorites. Le Nôtre only designed gardens for families selected by the king, so his parterres only marked the estates of families holding the king's highest esteem: the most valuable social resource available in the court of Louis XIV. Just as a plain coat could be made socially more potent through the application of specific kinds of embroidery, so the grounds of a château could be given new authority with the addition

77. *Faïence porrager* decorated with a parterre designs, Lille.

of Le Nôtre's patterned garden beds. Both were decked with foliage to show their rank. Thus, when gardeners dug flowering plants and box hedges carefully into the earth to make a parterre, the land was given new social value along with new beauty. French gardening in these moments dressed the earth in French style, making the land as much a carrier and captive of French fashion and social hierarchy as any courtier.

Even in winter, the parterres could sustain their connection with textiles and taste. As the gardens lost their color and the winter cold bleached the remaining plants, the parterres looked more and more like the laces that were ubiquitous to fashion in the period. The parterres printed in garden books and the patterns for laces from France were almost interchangeable at the end of the seventeenth century. Particularly after an early snowfall, when the tops of the hedges would still have been white with flakes but the warmer ground would have turned dark again, the parterres must have closely resembled these delicate bits of cloth.[73] To those looking out from the château, already predisposed to compare *parterres de broderie* with textiles, the parterres at Versailles in winter must have seemed much like the laces used by fashionable men around their necks. The hedges daintily dressed this monumental château.

Together the great swaths of flowers in the parterres of summer and the delicate lacework of hedges accented in winter would have dressed the king's lands year-round in the gardening equivalent of French textiles. The land in these garden beds was not simply made French by state power, but was attired to look French as well. In gardens at least, the earth was given a fashionable and distinctive French style.

The links between the garden and commodity design in France during the seventeenth century may have been centered on textiles, but it did not end here. The *faïence* makers in Lille also started using parterre designs in their pottery. The great gardening books of the period were facilitating this transfer of designs by including so many

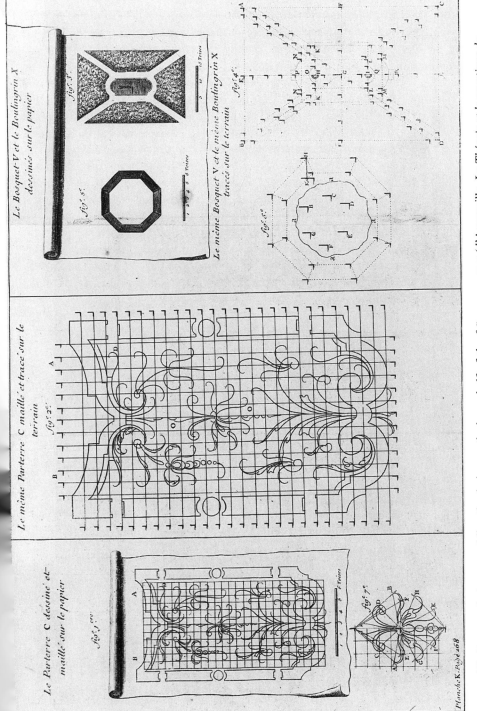

78. Parterre design resembling the design on the lower half of the *faïence porrager* (d'Argenville, *La Théorie et la practique du jardinage*).

parterre patterns in their illustrations. When the ceramics designers from Lille wanted new ideas for their plates and platters, these images were available to them. Perhaps because of the long-standing association of gardening with ceramics set by Bernard Palissy, the ceramicist who built garden decorations for parties given by Catherine de Medici, these *faïence* makers looked to garden books for inspiration. When they thought of gardens filled with flowers, they developed wonderful multi-color plates and platters, using the parterre designs. When they were inspired by the black and white patterns in garden books, they copied them almost directly to make their lovely blue and white china. These pieces seem covered with delicate lacework, but their decorations were not derived from lace patterns, but rather from garden designs. Whether this was intended or not, the result was a style of *faïence* to suit the fashions of the times. These northern manufacturers sitting near the borders of France so far from Versailles might have had trouble knowing how to tap the lucrative markets shaped by the tastes of the French court, but the published parterre designs made elements of court style immediately accessible to them. The effect in Lille was to turn this town into a producer of ceramics with distinctively French designs, ones that would please both the court and Colbert. Once again, the manufacture of commodities linked French taste, space, and politics, but this time the connection was explicitly and tantalizingly mediated through garden design.

The relations between state manufactures and French gardens did not end with the mutual borrowings between gardens and other areas of design. Artists and artisans from Gobelins provided decorative pieces that directly graced the gardens. Numerous urns, mostly of stone but often enough of lead, were spread throughout the *petit parc* (see plate 46). The ones by the Orangerie were filled with sumptuous bouquets of flowers; others on the terraces carried historical or mythological stories on their exteriors; toward the Allée Royale, some brandished images of the Sun King or sunflowers; and still others crawled with crayfish, lizards, and other animals or were encrusted with sea shells and precious stones. Many of the most stunning pieces were designed by Ballin, a master artist from the Gobelins, but he was not alone in decorating the gardens with artifacts from the *Manufactures Royales*. The gardens began to be filled with more decorative sculpture during the 1670s and early 1680s as Le Brun's tastes and the garden veered dramatically away from the Baroque. Le Brun's love of elaborate decoration that had already accounted for the exuberance, if not always beauty, of the château's walls and ceilings, now countered the austerity of Le Nôtre's formal gardens. The bosquets boasted more decoration and more elaborate fountain systems and architecture. Representations of garlands, shields and helmets, animals, and flower bouquets found form in stone and metal, making the *petit parc* more and more like the interior rooms of the château. When this period was over, vases and balustrades decorated the Bosquet des Domes; gilded candlesticks and shell-encrusted stone basins dominated the Salle de Bal; stone vases adorned the walls to the Orangerie, and marble buffets sat on either side of the Arc de Triomphe. All these elements linked the style of the garden to French decorative arts.[74]

Even inside the château of Versailles, elements of parterre design were echoed in decorative details. The ceiling to the lower aisles of the chapel at Versailles was adorned with radiating lacework patterns that were aesthetically comparable to the designs on the plates from Lille.[75] The floor for the main chapel was cut from different color marbles like many Italian palace and church floors, but the design was like a water parterre pattern by Mollet.[76] Parterre designs, since they were published in great numbers in the popular garden books of the period, were easily available for aesthetic borrowing. Moreover, by the end of the seventeenth century parterre designs were so identified and admired as French, that these forms had an authority in the French decorative arts. At Versailles, then, the lines between gardens and commodities, landscape and French taste, and the interior of the royal residence and the land beyond it were all blurred, helping to inscribe French culture in the earth and visibly marrying French territory to the state.[77]

French culture and the break with the Italian Baroque

Developing a distinctive French taste for Louis XIV's Versailles required not only the articulation of a new French aesthetic under Le Brun and Le Nôtre, but also a breaking down of the hold of the Italian baroque over the fine arts in Catholic Europe. Fashion might be swayed by Colbert's painstaking manipulations of industry and the king's power over his court's dress, but the Great Tradition was supposed to be autonomous. Greatness alone was meant to define art. Of course, there were rules about what constituted greatness. The classical Roman heritage had to be revered as the core to the European canon. Classical influence of some sort had to be sustained, but the authority to elaborate on the Great Tradition did not have to be left in the hand of Italian artists, giving disproportionate cultural power to Italy. Italian baroque architecture was indeed magnificently inspired by classical work. That is why the French court at first reveled in it and took advantage of the cultural authority it carried. But once the king and his advisors decided to cultivate the arts in France, the Baroque lost favor. Stories of two failed commissions from Louis XIV to Bernini can help to illustrate how French taste began to turn against the Italian Baroque.

The first commission offered to Bernini was for rebuilding the Louvre. Louis XIV finally agreed, after much urging from Colbert, to make this structure a proper palace. He was particularly taken with the idea of having the greatest living architect, the man who had rebuilt Rome into a monument to the Catholic Church, come to Paris to revive France's major city. In spite of some difficult negotiations with the pope, Bernini finally was given permission to travel to France, and arrived in 1665. The king was apparently impressed with the artist's presence as well as his art, and was delighted to ask Bernini to draw up plans for the project. Bernini accepted the commission, and after returning to Italy, sent the king his plans. The result was a scandal. Much to everyone's surprise, the *petite académie* rejected the drawings, and Colbert wrote to Bernini with suggestions for changes. Bernini was apparently furious. This renowned artist, so fawned over by Colbert and so celebrated in his own country, was being treated more like an artisan than an artist. Still, he developed a new design. But his second plan was sent back with even more complaints. It was too much. Bernini never made a third.[78]

The letters from Colbert to Bernini are fascinating in what they reveal of what went

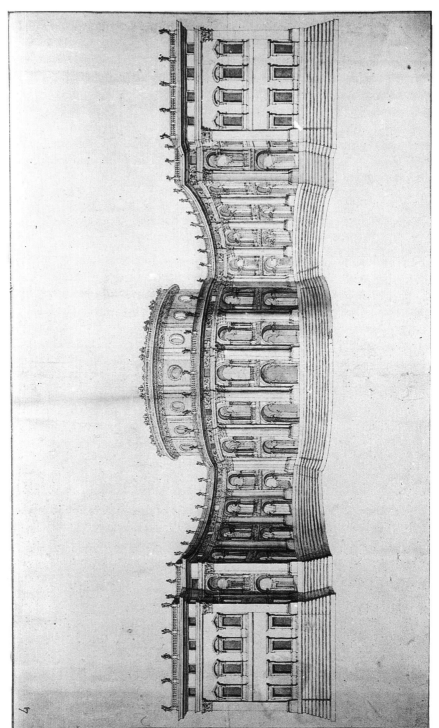

79. Bernini's plan for the Louvre.

wrong with this commission. Bernini's plans were not bad, Colbert assured him, but just not right for the French climate and court. Colbert argued, for example, that Bernini designed a large arcade around the building that was not appropriate for the rigors of the northern climate of Paris. The interior did not have the kind of entrance routinely expected for the French court. The plan was, simply put, not French enough. Colbert's painful and pained letters were filled with deference toward Bernini and his skill as an artist. He seemed to care very much that this famous man should not be too angry with the king. But his letters were also filled with a tone of dismay. How could it be that the artist, having visited France, had not anticipated beforehand the problems with French weather, and a French king's need for space? [79] But the Italian artist was not and could not be a creature of the French court. Bernini's final plan was indeed grand and was more than celebratory enough for a king, but it (like the first one) did not quite fit French court life.[80] Bernini, neither predisposed nor well positioned to articulate a new French culture, naturally failed to do so.[81]

In the end, the project was given to a French doctor from the Académie des Sciences, Claude Perrault, who built a celebrated hallmark of French classicism. He produced a kind of scientifically measured, long and stately colonnade that broke from the voluptuousness of the Italian Baroque. It was a design embedded in the very lively French battles between the Ancients and the Moderns. Perrault was one of the Moderns, who showcased in this piece of architecture his revision of Vitruvius' rules for creating pleasing proportions. Perrault used French intellectual currents to shape his French classicism, based on the ideas of the Ancients but going "beyond" them.[82]

The rejection of Bernini's plan was a scandal; the substitution of Perrault's plan was a monumental political gesture. It was not just that the French court had rejected an Italian palace and built a French one instead. Perrault derived his system of architecture explicitly from Roman precedent, and elaborated on the Great Tradition directly for himself. Classical influence no longer needed to be mediated through Italian tastes. Perhaps the power of Bernini's architecture would not be employed to glorify the French king, but it did not matter. The classical heritage was now in French hands. The Louvre with its colonnade even made Paris look a little like a new Rome. Rejecting the architecture of Bernini for the design by Perrault was certainly a grand gesture of cultural independence.[83]

There was an important lesson in these events for young French artists. The most advanced of them were well-positioned to learn it. They were already in Italy, finishing their education at the Académie Française à Rome. They lived in the Rome that Bernini had made magnificent, officially absorbing classical culture but presumably not blind to Bernini's grand style. If they had been tempted to follow his lead, now they knew better.[84] Already schooled in Le Brun's rigid aesthetic system, these students were trained in obedience as well as art. They were recruited as exponents and architects of French classicism, and embraced the project. They supplied many copies of classical works for French royal estates, particularly the gardens of Versailles.

The second and more successful commission given Bernini by Louis XIV was for an equestrian statue of the king. Louis XIV had asked Bernini, while he was in France, to create this sculpture for Versailles. For a variety of reasons, including the Louvre

80. Perrault's colonnade under construction at the Louvre.

fiasco, it was only shipped twenty years later. Even at that late date, the piece was eagerly awaited by the king, but he despised it when it arrived. It was a glorious sculpture, but baroque in style. The lively statue depicted Louis XIV in Roman armor on a grand horse whose mane was askew and whose rider sat astride a wild and marvelous beast. The rider was handsome, the horse was powerful, and the sculpture seemed to dance. Nonetheless, the king had it disguised as an historical piece, and banished it to the far reaches of the gardens, beyond the Lac des Suisses.[85] What went wrong? For one thing, by the time the statue arrived, French artists and patrons had abandoned the Baroque. Bernini's statue also violated the conventions for the now standardized equestrians that represented Louis XIV in many town squares across France – including Paris. In the French pieces, the king was placed on a huge but dignified horse. His body was erect and imposing. He exuded the solemn authority of physical power. His torso was held high like a dancer, and his countenance was still. All in all, he appeared solid, orderly and imposing. These very French statues of Louis XIV provided the sort of image of complete control appropriate to absolutism. They presented the king as an established fact, an historical figure, a finished act. Like the mechanical universe of the period, set in motion by God but now continuing on its own, this was a king who had been set in motion long ago, and was now continuing inevitably in his heavenly-inspired rounds.

The *académies* and French artwork

Bernini was not the only artist to feel the pinch of the political program inside the French artworld. Using *académies* and commissions for specific works, the state (at first, Colbert, the *petite académie*, and Le Brun, but increasingly Mansart) began to intervene routinely in the development of the arts. This effort did not just help to reduce the embrace of the Italian Baroque on French design but also codified some identifying characteristics of French taste. The pieces from French workshops began to display a quiet, sober, and measured look (some would say a boring solemnity) that matched the imperial ambitions of the king and the growing ritualized solemnity of court life.

The pressure toward classicism in French art surprisingly came in part from Colbert's vigilance about reducing French imports. The ambitious king wanted to fill his residences and gardens with classical sculpture, but Colbert was worried about losing too much French bullion by purchasing many pieces from Italy – even if appropriate work could be found there. The only alternative was to make classically inspired works in France or get copies of ancient pieces by French artists. While a small number of true antiques did indeed reach the gardens of Versailles from Italy, most sculptures were original works made in French workshops or copies by students at the Académie in Rome. Both kinds of works connected France to the Great Tradition, using standardized French techniques to fashion a distinctive style of art.[86]

Colbert's solution to the problem of supplying art for the court was surprisingly like the one he developed for manufactured goods: he persuaded local producers to imitate foreign pieces and impose a French style. The Académie de Peinture et Sculpture in

81. Bernini's equestrian statue of Louis XIV.

82. The equestrian statue by Bernini placed at the far end of the Pièce d'Eau des Suisses.

83. The equestrian statue of Louis XIV given pride of place in the front court of the château of Versailles.

Paris provided the system for instructing French artists in a distinguishable set of artistic conventions. They learned to embrace the Great Tradition as their own, and to use Le Brun's highly codified system of representational technique to connect with that tradition. Academy instruction emphasized drawing from live models and careful copying of classical pieces. These practices taught the students a sense of history and a commitment to representational accuracy which they could use to suggest that France was already the center of the next European empire.[87]

This solution for managing the arts was feasible because, when Colbert became minister, a weak academy system already existed in skeletal form in France. Colbert began reviving it with his first secret *petite académie* of advisors comprising Charles Perrault, Chapelain, Bourzéis and Abbé Cassagne. These men helped him refine his aesthetic judgments and sharpen his intellectual acumen so that he could effectively advise the king on cultural matters. This group met twice a week from February 3, 1663, and in these sessions helped to devise ways of celebrating the king and his reign. Colbert was apparently delighted with their help because he not only continued to rely on them, but expanded the academy system. He revived the Académie Française (from Mazarin's time) and established academies of arts and sciences (in the Italian mold) that would train and maintain standards for intellectual and artistic life in France. An Académie de Peinture et Sculpture already existed, but it was in conflict with the more powerful guild of painters in Paris. Colbert, who was in the midst of breaking down guild monopolies in French cities to aid his industrial enterprises, took this opportunity to undermine this powerful local institution. In 1656, Colbert gave the state academy a monopoly in educating young painters, centralizing art instruction for all of France and hence facilitating the articulation of a distinctive French approach to the visual arts.[88]

Le Brun was already first painter to the king when the Académie was reconfigured. He himself had studied in Rome, and brought the idiom of the Baroque back home to France. He knew how to play on classical themes about military might, heroism, and the power of the gods and use them to comment on contemporary politics in France. He knew that art could be a potent political tool because it had already proved to be so in Italy; he even seemed predisposed to seek and enhance political power in France. He wielded classical mythology like a weapon of war, just as Colbert used mercantilism in his battles, finding principles for both claiming and seeking to increase the stature of France. An identity for France was not the avowed purpose of either Colbert's economic reforms or Le Brun's arts program, but both helped to establish one under Louis XIV.[89]

Once in the service of the king, Le Brun constructed (with the guidance of Colbert's *petite académie*) the image of Louis XIV as the Sun King – the center of the heavens (Apollo with his chariot). He also depicted Louis XIV as Alexander, a great warrior, forging a new and massive empire. Le Brun's taste in artworks favored things overscale, historical, celebratory, dense with material excess, and filled with mythological references. Both in style and content, his work tied past to present. Historical writing was already being used in France, England, and elsewhere to legitimate state power by imbuing it with a sense of historical inevitability; Le Brun's paintings engaged in comparable politics, by claiming France as heir to the Great Tradition. This was France as it was displayed in the gardens of Versailles through its sculpture.[90]

The extent of Le Brun's contribution to French formal gardens has been downplayed by most garden histories because the artwork has been deemed simply trivial compared to Le Nôtre's grand designs. But this approach has obscured the centrality of decoration to the parks, and the role of Le Brun in giving it stylistic coherence. It was not just that Le Brun provided sketches for so much of the sculpture, and designed many of the decorative pieces set out for fêtes, but that he also oversaw the development of much of the permanent decorative artwork – from urns to grillwork. Le Brun supervised some of the pieces through the Gobelins; he even oversaw the production of much of the sculpture from the academies, the Louvre, and even the arsenal. His significance to French formal gardens cannot be adequately understood, however, simply by noting the number of pieces in the gardens with an aesthetic debt to him. A better measure of his influence must lie in an appreciation of the centrality of sculpture and decoration itself. French gardens, even royal ones, did not traditionally contain much sculpture before Le Brun.[91] The *parterres de broderie* of Boyceau and Mollet and the orchards of private estate gardens were not primarily or even usually sites for showing off statues. They were for growing things.[92] French gardeners had set out a number of marble statues in the Luxembourg gardens to please the Italian queen, Marie d'Medici, but classical sculpture was just too rare to be a requirement for French gardens. Not until the age of Louis XIV did garden statuary become obligatory in France. Under Le Brun's guidance, garden artwork began to be collected in astounding amounts, making French garden statuary more ubiquitous than garden sculpture in Italy. Parterres and bosquets were lined with busts and statues; the *tapis vert* was graced by a double line of statues and decorative urns from the Latona to the Apollo fountain (see plate 45). The Salle des Antiques was essentially an entire outdoor gallery (or bosquet) displaying classical busts. Gods and heroes from the past were set out along walkways throughout the park at Versailles as both witnesses to and exemplars of the glories of the French court. They both marked these parks as French, and located France as the proper center of a new Rome.

The king's publicist, Félibien, wrote that the gardens at Versailles were so beautiful because they contained a perfect marriage of nature and art.[93] He made clear that, to his contemporaries, the *combination* of artwork and the orderly landscape gave these gardens their distinction. Le Brun delivered the weight of Western history to these spaces with statues and monuments. In this way, he helped give physical France a cultural location through its art.[94]

The art of politics and the politics of place

The political identification of French territory with distinctive French tastes may have been gloriously cultivated in the gardens of Versailles, but this site was used ritually and mobilized to full effect only for a select group of aristocrats. How could it have had serious political effect? Perhaps the aristocracy at Versailles was recruited into a new political order through the articulation and celebration of French style, but how could

84. A row of statues marking the land as French. The images of the continents in
this series particularly draw attention to the depiction of land in statues. It also
shows the use of statues of land features to mark the landscape as a site of
politics.

a system of taste ever have affected the bulk of the French people? How, in particular,
could the association of France with luxury goods, fine taste, and elegant manners fight
regionalism in the lower ranks of society or help peasants to see themselves as part of
France? How could any of the material excess and consumer desire at Versailles mean
anything positive to a subsistence-level tenant farmer in Normandy or even an artisan
in Burgundy? Both the royal manufactures supervised by Le Brun and the economic
ventures started by Colbert during this period mostly manufactured expensive goods
for elite consumers. How could they help produce a cultural identity for the French
people?

Obviously, not all French men and women were tied into the world of fashion, court
life, or world of fine art, but many more experienced the shifts in the economy that were
shaping French taste. Craft production of textiles, the activity most central to Colbert's
enterprise, was not in the hands of aristocrats, but artisans. The trade that brought
items of fashion to the aristocracy was not managed by nobles but merchants. The
ships that carried statues from the academy in Rome to France were manned by simple
sailors or soldiers. The quarry workers who supplied French marbles for Le Brun's
artists were laborers, not gentlemen. The printed accounts of court life and mores,
which helped spread French fashions along with gossip, were printed by literati outside
court circles and studied by urban readers in many regions. Moreover, the broadsheets

and almanacs celebrating the reign also spread these messages to the semi-literate. Fountains and bosquets from Versailles were not only the subject of the commissioned engravings by Silvestre and Le Pautre but also appeared on the decorative borders of maps as wonders of the French countryside or the Paris region. Court culture was public culture, and this court had a publicity machine too, which made the performances at Versailles – and the technico-aesthetic feats of the gardens themselves – reverberate across the countryside. Images of the park of Versailles were made in such quantity that this space could never be construed as just the private hide-away of a petted nobility, but was instead a circulating image of what was unique to France.

Publicity in this context did not make the private world of the aristocracy more visible, but rather broadcast a culture that was already public. Noble life was traditionally filled with open spectacles: combats, dances, and processions through cities. Well before the seventeenth century, these activities were contributing to the formation of collective identities, particularly local ones. The bourgeoisie of Paris may have cherished privacy and exclusivity, but not the French nobility. They depended upon witnesses and rituals to reproduce their public standing. The king's park at Versailles constituted an open stage, where the monarch's power could be made manifest. Even the landscape was required to put on shows there. The fountains danced, rare trees bloomed, and fruits ripened out of season. The spectacles orchestrated there were made all the more wonderful because so many people participated in them. The great fêtes at Versailles required not only highly staged rituals and massively ambitious forms of entertainment, but also witnesses from Paris to stand on the terrace behind the château, and local peasants to sit in the trees and watch their king and court. The gardens may have seemed like private property, filled as they were with collections of rare statues, shells, and plants, but they were explicitly made open to the public. Peasants from nearby fields could enter the king's estate and find rest there. The political association of territorial France with a distinct style, material culture, and system of taste was thus more than just a matter of joining the nobility from different regions into a common system of fashion. It involved recruiting many kinds of French people to supply resources for, create, display, witness, and report on French style.[95]

This process incorporated a surprisingly wide array of people into a common political culture. Perhaps rural peasants from outside the Ile de France could not see or participate in the political ritual life of the court, but the urban artisans of Paris who supplied the elites with their costumes for fêtes certainly did; so did the merchants and financiers who supplied the cloth and jewels needed for court appearances; and so did the peasants who supplied the foodstuffs that made consumption at court so rich. The artisans in smaller cities and towns who were working in state-sanctioned businesses obviously participated both in the articulation of French style with their laces and silks, and helped to standardize these products in ways that made French style easier to identify. City fathers who commissioned the sober statues of Louis XIV for their squares not only bowed to the authority of the state, but also to the classicism that its authority partially rested upon. Colbert's effort to locate his new manufactures in areas where there were traditional skill bases in the population ended up distributing factories across all parts of France, and carrying French style with them. The *faïencerie* in Lille

– as much as the parterres at Versailles – tied people, land, and commodities into a single system of design, thereby building a new French style to associate with the new French state.[96] Peasants, too, would have seen some of the new material culture in the marketplace, even if they did not make, sell or buy French commodities. Novel goods would still have been apparent. Careful observation of the social world would have been routine in a culture in which dress was still often used to mark rank, and performance of duty or ritual was often more important than talk. Shifts in the material environment would not have been beyond the notice of most of those living on French territory.

The park at Versailles, to the extent that it contained images of abundance everywhere in the garden, not only made new twists in French style more publicly recognizable, but also celebrated the consumer desire on which it was built. The *Fountains of the Seasons* dripped with heaps of flowers, grapes, grains, and shellfish (see plate 62). The *coquillage* of the Salle de Bal was a study in excess (see plate 65). The myriad statues of Bacchus in the park pointed to the French love of drink. The hunting statues associated a kind of masculinity with the capture and consumption of meat. The miniature citrus trees with their colorful fruits, and the miniature pears that were also trundled out in silver tubs for ceremonial occasions, filled the gardens with more delicate images of material superfluity and desire. All the gilded statuary only added to the picture of excess, as did the great fountains when they were turned on. These decorations attested to the centrality of material desire to the politics of place. The park at Versailles embodied a tendency toward consumption and collection that not only exemplified French taste and style, but pointed to the world of desire on which the whole political culture was founded.

4

Techniques of material mobilization

The gardens at Versailles, seen through the eyes of Louis XIV and his entourage of court nobles, may have been notable for their natural orderliness, constrained classicism, and oblique militarism, but through the eyes of Colbert, Le Nôtre, La Quintinie, and the gardeners, engineers, and artisans who made and maintained them, these same sites were also a continual source of practical problems. New plants had to be coaxed into growing in spite of poor weather and soil; fruits needed to be forced to mature when the king wanted them; standing water required draining; fountains needed plumbing and repairs; and the entire property had to be expanded and reworked. Each new season brought new disasters to face and projects to realize for the king and court. Pipes froze, trees died, statues arrived late; parties were planned requiring new sculpted hedges and lath buildings in the garden; and the king developed tastes for fruits and vegetables which required their immediate cultivation. The land-management problems were astounding, and had to be effectively handled so the king could enter his gardens with utter assurance that they would testify to his power. No wonder Colbert's letters often sounded desperate as he tried to complete the myriad simple chores needed to keep the garden in good order, such as having the Intendant from Marseilles send enough bulbs from the Midi, or finding an artisan to fix the fountains damaged by winter ice.[1]

Gardens in this period were not just symbols and engineering feats, but the physical results of the work of ordinary people, exercising practical skills in manipulating and building on the land. Artisanal traditions, particularly but not exclusively in gardening, created a skill base in France that allowed men like Le Nôtre to dream about and work on formal parks. It is conventional to attribute the great gardens of the period to Le Nôtre's genius or the king's ambitions, but the parks did not spring Athena-like from the brows of these men. They were built stone by stone, ditch by ditch, seedling by seedling, tree by tree, using a vast range of expertise in cutting and fitting stone, casting metal, laying pipes, transplanting and transporting trees, collecting and shipping bulbs, wintering tender bushes and trees, and laying out rows of fruit trees and vegetables. Complex repertoires of land management and manipulation were used without fanfare in French formal gardens to engage in the land politics of the times.

Colbert, Le Nôtre and their collaborators had at their disposal for solving gardening

85. G. Marsy, *Faune jouant*, 1673–75. Trianon: a fountain in need of repair and cleaning.

problems knowledge accumulated in a variety of domains of French artisanal and entrepreneurial life. Many of the cultivation issues could be approached with estate-management practices that had been developing in France from the sixteenth century to increase the profitability of the land. Water supply limitations could be addressed using the experience of pump designers from the mines and engineers who worked on urban water systems. Transplanting could be accomplished using the techniques acquired by merchants who specialized in the sale of bulbs, seeds, and small trees. And fruits and vegetables could be nurtured and forced to ripen early using the skills of market gardeners.

Small-scale market activity seemed so far from the imperious gardens of Versailles that the two appeared unlikely at first blush to be connected. The court was indeed isolated from the day-to-day commerce of urban Paris, and the gardens seemed dedicated to elegant display or perhaps refined pleasure, certainly not craftwork or commercial life. But both depended on techniques of land and resource control.[2] Practical men, not the monarch, controlled the day-to-day working of the park, and they smuggled in techniques from other worlds of experience to make the gardens flourish – as though by magic or natural law.

Between city and country

The distinctive French culture of plants and the building trades that supported large-scale gardening emerged, surprisingly perhaps, from the city – mainly but not exclusively Paris. Although we tend to think of urban development as a process of replacing nature with artificial environments, increases in population density and the rising costs of land actually stimulated market gardening and the search for space-efficient techniques to create high quality produce. Staple grains could be brought into urban areas from quite a distance with little spoilage, but not fruits and vegetables. To have those fresh on city tables, gardeners needed to locate spaces between the city and the country where they could develop the commercial culture of plants.

The interaction of city with the immediate countryside was clearly not limited to market gardening, but gave rise to a range of experiments in engineering as well as plant culture that benefited the development of French formal gardens. Urban life with its increases in population required, for example, the development of elaborate water supply systems to deliver large amounts of potable water to a small area. This meant catching run-off from the plains around the city and tapping the river that ran through it into a system of supply. This project, however poorly executed or inadequate for Paris, nonetheless required the honing of skills and knowledge of hydraulic engineering that later helped shape the massive water system at Versailles. It was Denis Jolly, the engineer in charge of the Samaritaine pump in Paris, who was called upon by Colbert to build the first great pump and reservoir systems for the waterworks at Versailles. Similarly, population pressures stimulated new engineering to build upon land in the city previously seen as difficult or unhealthy to use. Draining and filling wetlands, setting up retaining walls on hillsides, laying pipes, and setting up pumps and spigots were all required for the job, and unintentionally provided a valuable skill-base for gardening in France. Even the surveying instruments and mathematical techniques of land measurement, which were applied to rebuilding urban wall-systems, turned out to be useful for laying out great gardens. So did many artisanal skills like metalworking, stone cutting, carpentry, and masonry, which were used extensively in Paris to build the great hôtels (or townhouses) of the sixteenth century. All these techniques were needed for decorating the gardens, and were supplied by the Parisian artisans most recognized in these areas.[3]

It is difficult to appreciate French formal gardens in the late seventeenth century without acknowledging them to be extremely complex practical accomplishments that required the mobilization of huge armies of artisans and massive displays of artistry and technical finesse. A broad range of specialists in art, crafts, cartography, and mathematics made them possible. Significantly, experts in these domains had already been installed in the galleries of the Louvre when André Le Nôtre came there as a young man to study painting.[4]

Thierry Mariage contends that Le Nôtre found in these urban techniques exactly the practical resources he needed for his gardens. More than being an aesthetic genius, Le Nôtre was a ingenious carrier and integrator of artisanal skills already present in France. He did not just draw on the aesthetic resources of art and architecture, as Boyceau recommended, but saw the possibilities for landscape architecture inherent in Parisian market gardening, land engineering, stone cutting, and water management. These areas of technique in particular allowed Le Nôtre to design gardens on a previously unimaginable scale.[5]

This debt of French formal gardening to urban artisanal skills in France fits nicely with Jack Goody's argument in his study of flower gardening. He argued that flower growing has arisen in many parts of the world as an offshoot of urban culture. It has not been some romantic response to the presence of flowers in the countryside, but more exactly, a response to the demands and wealth of the city imposed onto the near countryside.[6] Botanical gardens set out near universities like Padua in Italy, Leyden in the Netherlands, and Montpellier in France certainly took plants from the country and transplanted them to cities. Monasteries with their experimental gardens might have been mostly placed in rural areas, but they were established and often maintained with urban wealth. The great sixteenth- and seventeenth-century gardens of the Loire Valley and the parks set out on estates in the Ile de France (both of which preceded and influenced Le Nôtre's gardens) clearly owed a tremendous debt to the urban world of Paris. The wealth, power, taste, and technique of the city spread into the countryside through these estates. French gardens were not exceptional, then, in growing and flourishing in a surprisingly liminal space between city and country, where the meaning of the land, plants, bulbs, produce, flowers, earth, sun, water, and property could be questioned and restructured without the regulation of city life or the weight of rural traditions.

Market gardening grew in France most dramatically outside the city walls of Paris. Land prices there were low enough to allow entrepreneurs to set out orchards and fields for gardens. The restrictions on trade outside city walls were also minimal. Those gardeners who sold in Parisian markets (including one named Le Nôtre, who may have been André's grandfather) had to observe some regulations concerning the quality of their goods. But market gardening outside the city proper remained surprisingly open and experimental. Small differences in the quality of produce or timing of arrivals at the market could make a significant difference in profits, so there was incentive to try new methods of cultivation. Whatever the reasons, new techniques for heating and fertilizing the soil were explored. Intensive gardening methods were developed so that relatively small gardens could be productive enough to provide desired quantities of high quality produce for the city. New fruit trees or vegetable varieties brought through the plant trade to Paris were adapted to northern French soils and climate. And Parisians found new produce available for their tables.[7]

Gardening also flourished in new ways inside city walls as well. In the hôtels of wealthy families, some private gardens were established, using market-gardening techniques. La Quintinie, the celebrated head of the potager at Versailles, began his career as a gardener in one such hôtel. He had been in Paris as a young lawyer, working as the tutor to the son of Jean Tambonneau, président à la Cour des comptes. He was asked to take this young pupil on what was presumably an educational tour of Italy. La Quintinie returned from the trip fascinated with gardening, and gained the elder Tambonneau's permission to experiment with plants in a small garden at the hôtel. In due course, guests began to remark on the delicacies the young man was producing for the table. La Quintinie was so successful that he first was asked to go to Sceaux to counsel Colbert on his garden, then to Chantilly to do the same for the prince de Condé. Finally, he was lured to Vaux-le-Vicomte to build the potager for Fouquet, where Louis XIV discovered his abilities and brought La Quintinie to Versailles.[8]

As later commentators have emphasized, La Quintinie was an educated man, a lawyer, who knew ideas about gardening from the Ancients. This was perhaps what helped him appreciate the Italian gardens he visited, but it is not what made him a great innovator for his period. He was, more pertinently, an avid experimenter who educated himself in the latest techniques of market gardening from the Netherlands as well as France. La Quintinie immersed himself in the liminal world of land and labor culturally located between the urban and rural, between French soils and climate, on the one hand, and a cosmopolitan system of plant trading and acclimatizing. He was neither one of Paris' market gardeners, nor even from one of the families of royal gardeners clustered around the Tuileries. But he was one of the men who linked the urban worlds of artisans and practical gardeners to the burgeoning dreams and desires of elites, and he successfully used the combination to produce one of the great gardens of seventeenth-century France.[9]

The estate gardening tradition

The estates developed by Parisian gentlemen outside the city during the late sixteenth and early seventeenth century were, perhaps surprisingly, major vehicles carrying early techniques of gardening and land management to the countryside outside Paris. These great homes were intended to bring tastes, not skills, sharpened in the urban setting to what had been farmland. But the local artisans in the French countryside were not trained to provide what urban eyes yearned for. That is why aesthetically ambitious building projects ended up transferring techniques from the city into the landscape beyond the walls of Paris.[10]

Mariage contends that this cultural transfer was part of a process of re-feudalization. The rapid social mobility of the period resulted in a redistribution of real estate, and stimulated a building boom. Impoverished noble families, hit badly by inflation and without ways to profit from trade, sold their properties to improve their fortunes. At the same time, wealthy families from the city without noble heritage were in the market for estates and titles to elevate themselves socially and to protect their wealth from taxes. Many newly landed Parisians took up residence or at least built residences in the countryside of the Ile de France and other nearby regions. To make their holdings more extensive and to invest more of their wealth in the lands which provided them with tax-free incomes, they annexed contiguous properties when they could, and created larger landholdings. Land that had been subdivided for centuries into smaller and smaller parcels was now being reaccumulated into large properties, and used to reconstitute feudal patterns of landholding. This process reaffirmed the link between social rank and land, denying the social efficacy of the commercial world from which the new elite emerged, while also sanctifying the upward mobility of this group.[11]

The re-feudalized elites around Paris not only built large houses in the latest fashions, which they had already been able to do in Paris, but also celebrated their new footing in the land by surrounding their estate homes with fields and gardens that colonized the landscape. Their triumph was made visible through their invocation of new estate-management practices. They planted imported fruit trees and flower bulbs, and started to explore the commercial possibilities of better managing the forests. They leveled some areas, and drained others, turned fields into orchards, and made vegetable gardens that surpassed anything in luxury and variety that had been traditional to the area. They broke away from the old field systems and replaced the grain fields, which had fed the region, with decorative and market gardens that took land as a site for making and celebrating wealth.[12]

Even members of the nobility began to participate in the new approaches to estate development after the turn of the seventeenth century, when low rents were making their lands less profitable. Rather than experimenting with commercial field crops, such as woad, which extracted new wealth from the land by creating goods for a mass market (as the British started to do in the period),[13] French gentlemen – like Dutch businessmen – became interested in gardening with exotics. In the process, they placed the most exquisite forms of land stewardship in France in the center of elite culture. The garden became a site of noble cultivation and sensibility at the same time as it became commercially developed. This allowed the garden to be transformed into a meaningful site for articulating French greatness by the second half of the century.

As revolutionary as the techniques imported into the near-countryside were, they could not have been as momentous if they had not been used to transform the landscape and make it a source of new commodities. It took an urbanized sensibility to see the countryside less as a site of cereal production for feeding people and more as a place to feed specialized and potentially lucrative markets. The newly landed Parisian estate owners, accustomed to profiting from the marketplace, saw only advantage in looking for marketable commodities to extract from their newly acquired land. They had no immediate reason to mourn what was being lost until the famines at the turn of the eighteenth century made it clear that gardening skills and fertile soil did not ensure that the French would always be able to feed themselves. In the seventeenth century, even the cadre of urban artisans and gardeners who came with the new elites to the country had no more commitment to rural traditions of agriculture than their employers, and shared the more urbanized way of seeing land. Estate building in the period, then, not only brought a new aristocracy to the countryside, but also a new relation to land. The result was visible in the regional maps of the period, which showed the elaborate forms of estate gardens breaking radically with the meandering lines of old road systems, the unpredictable shapes of forests, and the odd geometries of traditionally cultivated fields. An estate was engineered to stand out from the surrounding countryside in order to make the estate owners stand out socially from others. No wonder the estate management tradition came to provide a useful technical platform from which French formal gardens could help France to stand out from the rest of Europe.[14]

Estate management and state management under Henri IV

Mariage argues that under Henri IV, estate management became a model of public policy. It was not only a fashionable enterprise for gentlemen in France but an ideal of stewardship that could be transferred to the state. As the king became convinced of the virtues of profitable land-use planning, he also embraced projects to develop both his own property and French land for public benefit. Many infrastructural projects of this period can be seen as direct extensions of the estate-management philosophy. The pump system on the Pont-Neuf, called *la pompe de la Samaritaine*, was erected under Henri IV to provide water to the Louvre and Tuileries. The palaces before this time had been consuming about half of all Paris' water supply. Improving these royal properties by giving them a separate water supply benefited the whole of Paris as well as the king. Good engineering served both public and private interests. (One could even argue that the king was the one to benefit least from this system, since the river water was of poor to questionable quality, but the pump did create a dramatic and reliable source of water.)[15]

Much like the estate surveyors of the period, who looked at the land for its potential uses and tried to realize these newly defined potentials through engineering (draining fens here or planting new crops there) Sully worked with Henri IV to improve the state with canals and roads. The Canal de Briare, which linked trade on the Seine with that on the Loire, treated the land as a medium for improvement, available for modifications to make it more productive. With this project, the extant practice of building irrigation and drainage canals on estates to increase the percentage of land under cultivation was both extended and eclipsed by the larger dream of joining major river systems with navigable canals. In this case, estate-management techniques were applied to state problems of trade. The result was to make France more productive, bringing goods more easily from the Loire river system into the markets of Paris, so the city

86. The Samaritaine pump bringing water to the Louvre in Paris.

could be better fed while the countryside was better served with large markets.[16] Much of Sully's economic policy rested on this kind of land-management approach to government. Roads were improved and manufactures begun. The land of France was indeed mobilized into a system of political power under Henri IV, albeit less successfully than it would be under Colbert. And the model for land mobilization may not have been as military as it would become under Louis XIV, but the political use of land was certainly apparent in the culture of the period. Since Louis XIV would find these earlier entrepreneurial relations to land abhorrent (while still profiting from them), the estate-management approach to landholding and improvement would be obscured in the late seventeenth century, but the debt of territorial politics of Louis XIV's period to the earlier estate-management tradition was nonetheless enormous.[17]

Thierry Mariage associates the political success of estate-management policies and the administrative practices under Henri IV with the ascendancy of Protestants in the political life of France (which may explain Louis XIV's rejection of it). No longer afraid of defining profit-making as a virtuous rather than a polluting activity, the Huguenot advisor to Henri IV, Barthélemy de Laffemas, advocated economic policies for enriching the country. He articulated a form of mercantilism that stressed French economic self-sufficiency, and fitted well with the estate-management ideas of the time. Significantly, Olivier de Serres, the best-known proponent of estate management was himself a Protestant, who tried to argue in his writings that landholding should contribute more to the wealth of France and *not just* provide a basis for determining social rank. When he contended that land ought to be organized for profit to enrich owners and improve the lives of the people, he was expressing a Protestant sentiment for the period.[18]

Serres' project for cultivating mulberry trees to raise silkworms was certainly an entrepreneurial venture as well, and one that Laffemas championed. French elites wanted to wear silk clothing, so there was a ready market for silk cloth. France could be made rich feeding this demand. With fine silks, France could be made more beautiful and rich at the same time. Henri IV had 15–20,000 square feet of royal gardens in Paris set out with mulberry trees, and built a facility for raising and processing the silk at the Tuileries. He also imported 60,000 mulberry trees from Languedoc to be planted by Parisians in their private gardens. Influential gentlemen were also urged to carry the tools and methods of sericulture to other parts of France to improve the local economy more rapidly and effectively. This project was built upon an entrepreneurial view of the countryside and its definition as the best route to a better France.[19]

It was in this context that Henri IV was positioned to lead his country as a gardener-king who realized his responsibility to his people in part through the rational development and use of land. Olivier de Serres taught him that gardening was a form of public good. The wealth of the people and the beauty of the land could be enhanced together. The garden could and should be a part of public life. No wonder that, in the late seventeenth century, the gardens at Versailles could take on a public character unheard of elsewhere in Europe. France was already conceivable as a garden capable of improvement for the public good.

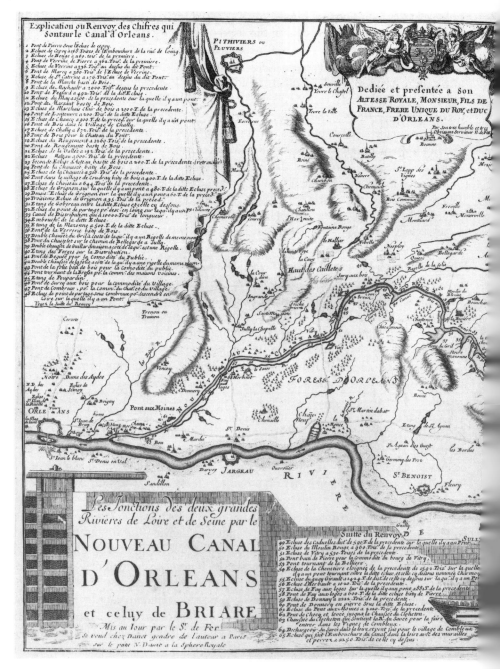

87. The canals of Orleans and Briare on a map by de Fer.

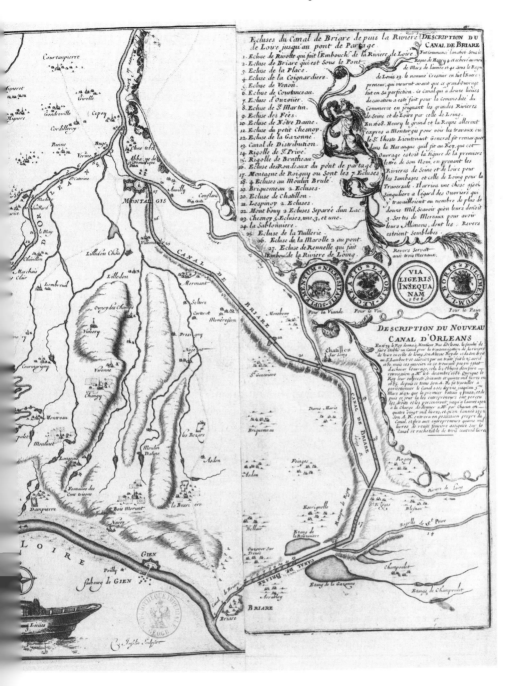

The estate-management tradition and gardening in France

Along with his utopian ideas about commercially oriented land stewardship, Olivier de Serres produced a practical farm guide that set out, among other things, some of the fundamental premises of French horticulture. His writings described methods for recognizing and exploiting the potentials of a piece of property by applying rational techniques of land stewardship and animal husbandry. Landholdings were to be divided into functional areas of activity, some being used for grain production, some being devoted to raising farm animals, some going to orchards, some being managed as forests, and some – the most important for our analysis – going into gardens of rare and delicate fruits and flowers.

Serres may have been most innovative as a gardener, but his book on estate management, the two-volume *Théâtre d'agriculture* (1611), began by outlining methods of traditional agricultural activity. Seemingly writing a primer for gentlemen who had never had an estate before, he began with the basics, trying to explain traditional agricultural methods as part of a system of rational land-use. He told how to cultivate basic cereal crops and raise farm animals; he carefully described how to store grain and use the products from the livestock; he even had a section devoted to raising poultry, explaining their diseases and their proper diets, housing and treatment. The point of good estate management was to integrate all farm activities within a larger rational system directed toward land improvement and profit.[20]

The techniques of modern gardening that Serres advocated had a privileged position in this larger scheme of estate rationalization. The most detailed part of the famous two-volume opus was devoted to the cultivation of flowers and produce. If the other parts of the book catalogued much that was common knowledge, this section went well beyond. Serres made public the wisdom he had acquired on his own estate in raising exotic varieties of fruits and vegetables. He wrote most voluminously about the newer species (various kinds of melons, for example) that were becoming available in France and that even experienced gardeners had trouble raising. He catalogued in detail the growing requirements of different fruit trees and the proper handling of the fruit. He explained how to set out an orchard and how to build a hotbed for starting seedlings of tender plants. Serres spoke soberly about the necessity of and dangers in the use of manure for different crops. He proclaimed the virtues of deep layers of mulch to protect tender imported plants in the cold, northern European gardens, and to force hardy plants to fruit sooner and grow stronger. He even described how to set glass bell-shaped jars over the most delicate and vulnerable varieties of garden crops to make mini-greenhouses for such desirable treats as melons and cucumbers.[21]

This practical information seemed to be just what many readers wanted. The book was a dry and systematic bit of writing, designed to be read for reference rather than pleasure, but it was enormously popular and early translated. No wonder. It contained a wealth of detailed, successfully tested information. The text assumed very little substantial prior knowledge (although anyone who knew practical estate management would have an easier time deciphering the directions). It was a practical bible for the literate, newly enriched gentlemen of France who sought to find comfort and profit in the countryside. It carried a new message about the commercial value of gardening, and promoted economic rationality in relation to land use. Serres pointed explicitly to the growing markets for rare or early fruits and vegetables, making a plea to include cultivation of these valuable commodities on rationally planned estates.[22]

Estate management in this vein projected a novel vision of spatial organization and land control onto the countryside that would influence later French gardens. The good estate manager was supposed to identify parts of the property appropriate for different uses, and to organize them into a system of spaces with identifiable functions and characteristics. Doing this well depended upon diagnosing the usable strengths of certain areas – for example, the warmth of southern slopes for grain fields, the sandiness of soil for crops with delicate roots, or the radiant heat stored in south-facing walls around orchards. Good land stewardship meant both exploiting and improving upon the natural characteristics of the land. Fields and orchards, for example, were supposed to be enclosed by banks of trees, stone walls or bushes to shelter the plants from wind and inclement weather. Where the properties of the land permitted it, Serres contended that the best way of organizing the estate was in relation to the house, putting the more beautiful and intensively cultivated areas like flower and vegetable gardens close to the residence where their beauty and sweet smells could provide pleasure to the owners. Orchards should ideally be set just beyond where they could be admired from the house without obstructing the view. Large fields and the forests would finally be set at a distance. This structure was meant to be practical as well as attractive, since the areas that needed closest supervision and attention were nearest to the estate owner.[23]

The resulting layout of the ideal estate, like the layout of the French formal garden later in the seventeenth century, displayed an overarching plan. It was made of distinct regions with different functions, carefully marked by boundaries made with either plants or stone. The land was developed in relation to the house, with smaller garden areas and orchards near the residence, and the large fields and forests at a distance. The increasing scale of land areas moving away from the house was not an intentional outcome of the system, designed to realize Renaissance ideas about proportions and perspective, but it was easy to justify later in those terms. The French heritage had, however, much more sturdy, practical roots. It broke with earlier rural property arrangements for reasons of efficiency. French estates had previously been organized around two areas: a square-shaped complex of buildings with a central courtyard near to but disconnected from a walled-off area of garden and orchard. Moving across these two distinct spaces was just not an efficient way to work. Serres and Mollet designed garden/estate lands that were integrated along a central *allée* to link the house to the other parts of the property. This system organized the two into a common, rational (often bilaterally symmetrical) order. Many elements of the measured formality in later French gardens were nascent in these forms.[24]

The design of parterres, described in most garden histories only in relation to pleasure gardens, were actually also part of the practical gardening system advocated by Serres. He recommended the use of complicated patterns for herb gardens because the differences in the colors of plants arranged this way would help keep the herbs separate and recognizable. His parterre designs were derived from patterns published by

Mollet for herb beds, flower gardens, grass knots, and water parterres. Serres claims that the knot structure of the herb garden was traditionally a material classificatory system for the plants. In Mollet's designs it seems that this form migrated into and out of pleasure gardening in late sixteenth- to early seventeenth-century France.[25]

One alternative to the knot garden for herbs suggested by Serres was a great mount with a spiral walk ascending it. Herbs were to be planted in a linear progression along the walk. This form played on the symbol of perfection, the circle, and ascended toward the sky. The mount itself, like the knot garden, had medieval origins, and the mount of sweet flowers was often used in cloister gardens.[26] The form both grew and changed in Renaissance Italy. The Villa Medici had a mount that was huge, and provided a site for viewing the gardens.[27] The top of this artificial hill was reached by a spiral walkway. Serres recommended this spiral-encased mount for a medicinal garden because, he argued, the space underneath the hill could be excavated to provide an inner sanctum for wintering tender plants. They could be kept in clay pots, dug up in winter, and placed in the warmth of the underground room. (Since the importance of light in plant growth was not yet recognized, the warmth of the room was the only aspect considered.) This made the mount a very efficient form for collecting the rare herbs from exotic places that were currently in demand for aristocratic gardens. The techniques of the collector's garden, and the close ties between plant trading and herb gardening were revealed in Serres' book.[28]

Estate management, as philosophy and technique, suffused many early seventeenth-century garden books – not only the works by Serres. Their intent was to increase the productivity of the land by draining fens, managing the forest, planting new kinds of fruits and vegetables, and keeping an eye on the market to know what kinds of crops to cultivate. Massive alterations to the landscape were required to change the culture of plants. It was not enough to add manure to the soil; landforms had to be reshaped and the arrangements of plants had to be carefully conceived to serve more effectively the requirements of the species and the desires of the landholders. A kind of feudal paternalism toward France and a commercial drive toward profit were oddly mixed in these conceptions of gardening, adding a patina of privileged missionary zeal to the practical job of subduing and exploiting nature.[29]

If the pragmatic relation to land and its manipulation set out by Serres and promoted by Henri IV was seen as Protestant, this may help explain why there has been so little explicit reference to this tradition in histories of French gardens. As Mariage suggests, most historians have assumed that French gardening began with Le Nôtre, who was supposed to be a lone genius. More sophisticated analysts point back to Boyceau, saying he provided a theory of gardening from which later French parks could grow. But even his artful arguments have usually been overlooked in French garden history – perhaps because Boyceau, too, was a Protestant. If this sophisticated philosopher of garden design was erased from most memories, no wonder Serres, with his hands in the soil and eyes twinkling with anticipation of profits, was never considered a fit entrant for the pantheon of French gardeners. Nonetheless, as Mariage makes clear, Serres was absolutely vital to the practical and aesthetic development of French gardening. Moreover, he may have helped to lay a foundation for territorial state politics by bringing land stewardship into the public realm.[30] The administration of the state as a measured and rationally managed piece of land remained at the heart of Colbert's economics, while French virtuosity in gardening remained a vital part of the political culture of land-based power in the court of Louis XIV. State territorial power under Louis XIV may have been carefully differentiated from commercial land management and organized primarily to subdue land through the art of war, but it was nonetheless deeply invested in a long-standing and Protestant vision of land stewardship.

Gardening as a literary enterprise

Like the new gardens, books on gardening were immensely popular throughout the seventeenth century, and were themselves a product of the cultural space between city and country, between Protestant urban culture and the culture of the Catholic landed aristocracy. They drew together the rural traditions of the old landed nobility and the experiments of re-feudalized estate owners. The books came from urban publishers but provided a program for the countryside that did not require such a high degree of learnedness that it might strain a newly literate nobleman. Most of the literature contained practical advice, and was far from the work of poets dreaming about the countryside. Writers described such prosaic skills as learning to recognize kinds and qualities of soil, how to improve them, and how to use them. They also described principles of design and aesthetics important to gardening – surely an urban conceit projected onto the countryside.[31]

There were two major kinds of books published on gardens in the sixteenth and early seventeenth centuries: those on horticulture alone, and those that emphasized garden design. There were also a few specialized books on waterworks and garden engineering (some repeating classical ideas about water systems), but they were rare in comparison to the plant-centered books. There was also a huge outpouring of botanical books, herbals mainly, that were important to gardening, but were not about gardening per se. All of these combined to provide access to an array of techniques for designing the landscape around houses, laying out gardens and orchards, choosing and finding appropriate plants for different sites and purposes, cultivating different plants in the garden, supplying them with water, filling the garden areas with elaborate water effects and decorative sculpture, and engineering terraces to sculpt the garden from the countryside.

The horticultural books were by far the most numerous and were extremely popular, going through multiple printings. Claude Estienne, Jean Laurent, Olivier de Serres, Nicolas de Bonnefons, and François Gentil, for example, explained not just common gardening practices but how to grow species and use techniques that were rare outside aristocratic estates. They described how and where to plant fruit trees of all sorts; how to prune and graft; how to improve soil for making a garden; how to grow plants in pots; how to make hothouses for tender plants; how to design orangeries to suit the trees in them; how and when to plant different kinds of bulbs; and how to lay out a vegetable garden or orchard. Some described different varieties of fruit and how they

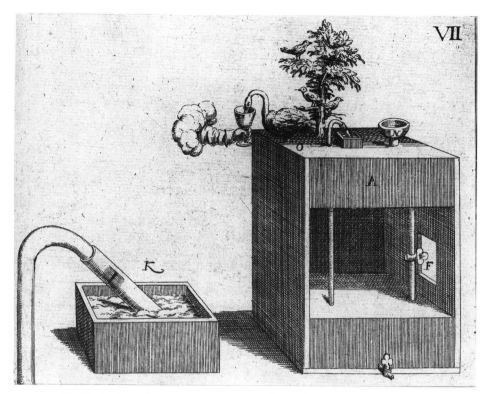

88. Illustration of a water-run automaton (Isaac de Caus, *New and Rare Inventions of Water-Works*, plate VII).

tasted and lasted on the trees. Others illustrated common gardening tools, and the appearance of the flowers of different bulbs so gardeners could know what to expect from them.[32]

Where the authors had connections with royalty, their words took on an extra authority that presumably served the ambitions of the upwardly mobile readers. Of course, there were less well-placed gardeners who wrote successful garden books in the period, too. Plant traders like Pierre Morin provided some horticultural knowledge about the species they sold, presumably as a way to promote their trade. Fountain and grotto designers like Palissy and de Caus also revealed some of the secrets of their trade. Some intellectual members of the gentry wrote on a variety of subjects, including gardening. Serres should perhaps be characterized as the most famous French example. But the vast majority of French garden writers of the seventeenth century gained authority for their ideas through their work for the nobility, and wrote about a tradition of pleasure and practical gardening that was centered on the world of these elites.[33]

The growth of the plant trade, through botanical, court, and market gardens, and the development of the astounding fad for tulips in the sixteenth and seventeenth centuries may well have stimulated demand for these horticultural books. With a new range of imported bulbs and plants to use in their gardens, gentlemen could not depend on local "folk" horticultural methods to guide them. Moreover, when they purchased extremely rare and expensive bulbs or exotic fruit trees, they did not want to risk killing them or ruining their investments by planting them inappropriately.[34] So practical knowledge of plant culture based on the experience of gardeners who worked with large plant collections became more valuable. And the French, with their estate-management tradition, became, along with the Netherlands, famous for horticulture.

European respect for French horticultural writing was heightened in 1706 when François Gentil's book, *The Retir'd Gard'ner,* was brought into print by two English market-gardeners, George London and Henry Wise. In this text, they provided their readers with translations of Gentil's French garden writings to explain the proper culture of plants. Self-servingly, they also counseled readers to procure plants and seeds from traders of high standing like themselves (explaining that even the best care would not keep unhealthy plants alive). And presumably they translated Gentil's advice on how to cultivate new species in Europe because they themselves traded in these plants. These men obviously had a stake in providing horticultural information to their customers so that the plants they sold would survive and their clients would be inclined to return to do business again. Admittedly, they prepared their book at the beginning of the eighteenth century when the commercial plant trade, particularly in England, was large enough to give them more standing as experts on gardening, but the information they provided readers came from seventeenth-century French books on horticulture, demonstrating that these texts already had commercial value.

Ten years later in 1717, these same two gardeners published La Quintinie's book as *The Complete Gard'ner: or Directions for Cultivating and Right Ordering of Fruit-Gardens and Kitchen Gardens.* They took the main body of the text from the earlier translation by Evelyn (La Quintinie 1693), and added his treatise on melons to the main text. Again they argued in the preface to the book about the importance of horticultural knowledge. They reiterated that by knowing about plants and their culture a gentleman would not waste his time and money on poor quality stock or improper care of healthy specimens. La Quintinie's extensive knowledge of espalier techniques and detailed directions for grafting fruit trees were added to the store of knowledge available to gardeners in England, where much of this information was news. Clearly, these traders had enormous respect for the horticultural experimentation that had taken place in France during the course of the seventeenth century. How much they thought English gentlemen could learn from this work was clear from the amount of text that was kept in La Quintinie's original form.[35]

Botanical writings were generally not intellectually related to books on horticulture, although appropriate horticultural practices were necessary for the botanical gardens of the period. The simple fact that botany books in this period continued to be in Latin, while horticultural books were not, helped to keep these domains of inquiry visibly and strategically separate. Botany was mostly devoted to locating and describing the medicinal properties of plants. On the surface, this simply required accurate identification and classification of species, not innovative plant culture. Much of the naming and depiction of plants from different parts of the world depended upon scientific voyages (long and short) that yielded books, not gardens. Not surprisingly, many of the famous botanists of early modern France were valued for their observations, not their gardening at home. But there were important exceptions. The botanists who were plant collectors brought home bulbs and seeds as well as drawings. Their efforts to keep their precious specimens alive forced them to acquire horticultural skills for which some of them became renowned. Carolus Clusius (Charles de L'Ecluse) went to Vienna for Emperor Maximillian II, for example, to set up the gardens there. He was able to provide the emperor with rare vegetables for his table because of his skills in acclimatizing plants. Pierre Richer de Belleval constructed a famous garden at Montpellier structured after the Italian botanical gardens he had seen in his travels. He encouraged the association of botanical research with gardening in France. Just around the turn of the seventeenth century, Jean Robin, *botaniste du Roy*, even built a small botanical garden for the faculty of medicine on the Ile Notre Dame in Paris. It must have been quite a small enterprise, since Paris was notoriously short on medicinal plants when Colbert set up the Jardin de Roi there. Nonetheless, Robin demonstrated once again that botany and gardening could and did go hand in hand in France.[36]

It is hard to assess how much horticultural knowledge botanists brought to France, since the writers of botany books themselves did not usually include their gardening practices in their writings. But this does not mean that they were not concerned with growing plants. Doctors needed a steady supply of species with recognized medicinal value. They could not easily replace ones brought to Europe from distant locales. Botany, particularly because of its links with medicine, then, needed to depend on horticulture as well as the plant trade. And as Serres made clear, private gardens gained medicinal plants as species were informally spread to the herbaria of estate gardens.[37]

The pleasure-gardening books of the sixteenth and seventeenth centuries in France formed another distinct genre of garden writing, but again one owing an enormous debt to the world of horticulture. They emphasized garden layouts, but they contained at least basic information on plant culture and uses. Their purpose was to elevate and elaborate pleasure gardening in France, and this required successful plant culture as well as good design. Of course, they defined their inheritance mainly with references to ancient gardens, particularly Pliny's loving descriptions of Roman gardens and their sensuous pleasures. They informed French readers, too, about some designs developed from Italian experiments in gardening, but adapted to gardening ideas and practices in France. Bernard Palissy, Salomon de Caus, Charles and Jean Mollet, and Charles Estienne, to name the most famous and influential, were all garden writers in the period who developed aspects of pleasure gardening in France.

These books were generally written by gardeners who worked for royalty. Some like de Caus and Palissy, specialized in hydraulic techniques and the design of fountains and grottoes. Others, such as Mollet, provided plans for entire gardens. Many like the Mollets and Boyceau, printed whole catalogues of parterre designs. All provided practical information for building pleasure gardens.[38] Some included very little horticultural knowledge in their texts, assuming it could and would be learned from other sources. Others included a great deal of it to make their works guides to the entire garden. Some assumed that elites would erect collectors' gardens, filled with both natural novelties like tulips or rare artworks like classical sculpture; the books often spoke in now familiar ways about how art could embellish nature. Some mused about the sciences and the garden as a representation of nature; others discussed engineering and the way art could be augmented by artifice; some elaborated the estate management tradition, while others gestured toward the Great Tradition with its abstract guides to design. These works asserted, each in its own way, that pleasure gardens were a proper element of aristocratic life. They advocated incorporating them into existing properties and using them to elevate the aesthetic and social value of the landscape.

Books on pleasure gardens spoke with most authority when they had well-placed authors. Since gardens were a matter of fashion as well as horticulture, an author who worked for the court was a more reliable source of information about the gardening tastes of the highest noble families. Some of the parterre designs published in Boyceau's book carefully indicated the great house or royal residence for which a particular parterre had been designed. This gesture cleverly associated the pattern with a socially elevated place. These books usually contained only basic horticultural information, but of course beautiful parterre designs had their own uses. These works were more attractive commodities to general readers than were the guides to horticulture (such as those by Serres). As we have seen, even commodity designers and embroiderers used these patterns for their work. Manufacturers, along with the re-feudalized property-owners dabbling in pleasure gardening, constituted the two poles of the broad readership for these texts.[39]

When Louis XIV started commissioning the reconstruction of the grounds around Versailles, France already had a reputation for gardening skills which was partly embedded in the vibrant and practical estate-management tradition, and partly associated with garden pattern books. The parterre designs in printed form added another level of self-consciousness to French gardening. The French were now not just exemplary caretakers of tender plants and nurturers of fine fruits and vegetables, but also intelligent and respected pleasure gardeners. A visitor from Italy like the priest Sebastiano Locatelli was impressed with the gardens at Fontainebleau, the Tuileries, the Luxembourg Palace, and Mazarin's palace even before Le Nôtre had transformed some of these great gardens because French gardening was already a complex and refined enterprise.[40]

Estate management and state power under Louis XIV

Surprisingly, the vital and varied traditions of French gardening that predated and prefigured the formal gardens of André Le Nôtre started to disappear rapidly from memory in France once formal gardening became established. Even before Louis XIV's leadership, the powerful French tradition of estate management waned visibly. Perhaps the Protestant roots of these practices were too troublesome, or French horticultural expertise was so well institutionalized that it started to be taken for granted. Perhaps French gardening techniques were simply eclipsed by the new Dutch work on the subject, or perhaps pleasure gardeners at the Catholic court found themselves at last able to focus on design and forget the embarrassing practical basis for their heritage once a range of successful gardening techniques was in place. Whatever the reasons, the earlier horticultural literature, based on rational estate development, lost its appeal, and French landscape design became a much more self-conscious activity. At first, Boyceau's intellectual approach to gardening submerged Serres' approach to estate planning, but soon even Boyceau's Renaissance-inspired intelligence seemed *passé*, too. Perhaps it was too Italianate for the ever more French world of Versailles. In any case, Le Nôtre's parks became defined as *the* true French gardens. Of course, the formality of their designs could only be achieved using the kind of interventionist approach to land management articulated by Serres and an intellectual view of garden design derived from Boyceau's program of aesthetic education for gardeners. Serres' utopian dreams of individual profits and material well-being for France may have been replaced by Boyceau's talk of science, the heavens, and the Ancients, but both were buried beneath Le Nôtre's monumental earthworks. Still, land management itself remained at the heart of French gardening. Military engineering may have added to the repertoire of land-control techniques that French gardeners had at their disposal, but there was nothing fundamentally new in France about moving earth, water, trees, and rocks to make a more desired landscape.

The estate-management tradition in the end may have been doomed because it tangled with the state-building program of Louis XIV and his ministers. Rational estate administration, after all, was meant to empower the aristocracy and the newly landed urban bourgeoisie. Since independently wealthy and powerful landowners were seen as a threat to the absolutist state, this scheme which supported their empowerment was unlikely to be welcomed by the king. Coming to the throne after the Fronde, the last thing that Louis XIV wanted to achieve was an increase in noble fortunes and political influence. Moreover, improving France through the initiatives of individual landed families, using Protestant practices, could only reduce the power, apparent goodness, and success of the state. The territorial state was the only estate to be legitimately cultivated in this regime.[41]

No wonder the descriptions of the gardens at Versailles written by Félibien make absolutely no mention of the cultivation skills used to build the great gardens. This official historian of the king's properties wrote glowingly about the grace and significance of the sculpture, fountains, and parterres. He even praised the collection of citruses at the Orangerie, and other rare plants imported from afar. But he did not find any reason to point out that French traditions of plant cultivation and estate management made all of this possible. Félibien had nothing to say about the design of the boxes used for holding citruses, or the practical techniques used to set out orchards and prepare the soil for garden beds. His job was to write pieces of political propaganda about the achievements of the reign. Anything practical inherited from the past was less of an accomplishment in the present.[42] So, French gardens were celebrated with their commercial roots hidden behind a thick layer of words about art, nature, and the king's greatness.

The reasons for this sleight of hand were simple enough. The commercial vitality of France was of concern to the king and his ministers *in so far* as it affected the treasury and the reputation of France as a world power, but the *skills* of those in the commercial world, like the tips given by Olivier de Serres about the culture of plants, were not to be accepted as virtues in the nobility under the absolutist state. Land-management methods were demoted to mere practices of support personnel, not the geopolitical techniques of the leaders of France. Land might be the identifying material marker of the aristocracy, but to enhance state absolutism, land had now to be celebrated for and through its domination and political mobilization, not for its productivity. Wealth and the search for it in nature was to be secondary to the search for new bases of power. Louis XIV wanted the plant trade to fill his gardens with wonders and his table with delicacies, but he did not want the trade itself apparent as a foundation for the glory the French state. That would have given too much importance to the financiers of Paris over the officers of the state. Acquiring the plants he wanted for the garden was important to Louis XIV for it made nature seem an obedient servant to the king.

Perhaps ironically, the seat of the court built by Louis XIV was (on one level at least) the most dramatic of the estates built around Paris in the seventeenth century. Serres might have been impressed by the size and scale of it, but he would not have found Versailles so alien to his notion of rational land-use. The reasons were clear enough. Vaux-le-Vicomte was both the model and nemesis for the king, and it was an estate for a newly landed Parisian gentleman. Vaux and Versailles were both built by the same skilled artisans and artists that Fouquet called from Paris, transferring urban skills and tastes to the nearby countryside. Both these properties were created by acquiring contiguous landholdings from traditional seigniorial estates. Versailles at one level seemed less the king's refuge from Paris than his re-feudalized country landholding. Did Louis XIV move his seat of power from Paris to Versailles because of the trauma of the Fronde, as so many commentators have suggested, or was he following the Parisian elite into the countryside? Did he build his estate with such grandeur that no wealthy Parisian could ever hope match it? Did Colbert usurp this bourgeois culture and use it to express French dominance over the landscape? These possibilities perhaps unveil new aspects of the garden at Versailles and the transformation of the French countryside during this reign.

The *jardin potager* under Louis XIV

The most visible and yet complex expression of the new system of land control developing under Louis XIV was located in the *jardin potager*. This scarcely modest kitchen garden was the one site at Versailles where the most advanced ideas from market gardening and some palpable remnants of the estate-management tradition were allowed to be visible. The *jardin potager* could boldly assert competence in commercial gardening technique in part because it physically belied this inheritance. It was structured like a miniature fortress. The fruits of commercial gardening (so to speak) were certainly there for all to see, but they were enclosed and protected by bastion walls, sheltered from the winds and warmed by retained heat in a stone structure that was built like a military enclave. The potager provided a nice metaphor for a France enjoying its natural abundance protected by the military power of the state and basking in the reflected glory of the Sun King.

89. The potager with its fruit trees.

Appropriately for a servant of the Sun King, La Quintinie made the sun's rays the centerpiece of his technical system of gardening. His espalier techniques opened up fruit trees so all their branches could feel the sun's rays. He used glass, radiant heat from the sun, and retained warmth in the stone walls of the potager to coddle and coax his vegetables and fruits into a glorious ripeness fit for the king.

Pruning fruit trees and vines, using glass for gardening with tender plants, improving the soil, regulating drainage and watering, and applying sources of external heat to force plants to grow earlier were all known elements of gardening when La Quintinie built his potager at Versailles. Market gardeners had long used hotbeds (made by placing raw manure under a layer of bedding soil) to bring vegetables to table earlier; the manure created a chemical reaction that gently heated up the soil and then provided the seedlings with nutrients when their roots began to grow longer. Some gardeners who worked with hotbeds in France also experimented with glass covers, either to retain heat in a hotbed or to protect and warm individual plants. As we have seen, Olivier de Serres had already advocated the use of glass cloches or bell-jars over hotbeds for growing melons and cucumbers.[43] The glass stimulated growth of these heat-loving species and protected them from pest invasions. La Quintinie simply pushed these techniques to a new level, and made bigger, better and earlier produce than anyone could expect in France.[44]

La Quintinie began his work with a terrible handicap. He had been ordered by the king to build the potager near the château in a swampy area with a pond that was entirely inappropriate for raising fruits and vegetables. Unable to talk his way out of this project, he was constrained to construct the potager as an entirely artificial environment, refashioning the land and its flora from the ground up. He first had to drain the area, and then fill it. The Lac des Suisses, that huge body of water beyond the Parterre de Midi, was the drainage pond for the project (see plate 82). The bed of the potager was raised with earth excavated from the mountain of Satory but this hard-packed earth was no medium for growing plants. La Quintinie built up the soil, adding richness to it. He then created raised beds specifically tailored to the produce he wanted to cultivate. A carefully constructed system of drains was installed around the beds to make sure that the swamp did not reclaim the garden, and a central pool was set out for watering. After providing the basic necessities for the garden, La Quintinie began to set out the plants. Delicate trees were put against the walls of the potager, and trimmed so they grew up in parallel lines of branches (see plate 75). Even the trees placed in the open were pruned into two-dimensional figures that looked like flat candelabra. In this way they made neat rows, and the trees did not shade one another too much (see plate 40). The orchards were kept highly pruned to produce a small number of large and sweet fruit. As a result, large numbers of each variety had to be planted. Many varieties were also put in the potager to ensure that fresh fruit would be ready for the royal household at different times of the year.[45]

La Quintinie did not stop even with this disciplined system of planting and pruning. He also experimented with using glass to manipulate the growing patterns of plants. He was able to employ a massive number of *serres* (glass frames) to cover long beds of the potager for vegetables. He also placed glass walls in front of some of the fruit trees planted along the potager walls, creating a kind of open greenhouse for these trees.[46]

La Quintinie's thinking on the use of glass in the garden may have been influenced by Dutch gardeners. By the mid-seventeenth century, the Dutch were experimenting with improved means of wintering trees and bushes. As the tulip fad died down, Dutch plant traders turned to a wider variety of species to raise and trade. Larger plants in particular raised vexing problems of wintering in northern Europe, forcing the Dutch to experiment with larger glass structures to protect their investments in the cold, dark months of the year. Orangeries were already common by the sixteenth century as sites for bringing plants indoors in winter, but they made no particular use of glass. Orangeries were often huge, and gardeners did not yet know that plants needed sunlight as well as heat, so they used glass sparingly. But in the Netherlands in the seventeenth century, Dutch gardeners began designing glass-faced hothouses for larger bushes and trees, using the sun's rays as a source of heat. These buildings had stair-shaped brick ledges for the potted greenery that absorbed the heat in the day and kept the plants warm at night. These structures were called stoves because they also contained areas under the ledges where the gardeners could light fires on extremely cold nights to heat the building and protect the plants.[47]

It is hard to know whether La Quintinie developed his system of raising plants under glass only from the French tradition of sheltering and heating tender plants with hotbeds, orangeries, *serres*, and cloches, or whether he was influenced by Dutch structures. Certainly, there were books at this time on Dutch gardening translated into French that spoke of using glass and mentioned stoves, but there is no evidence that La Quintinie read them.[48] Still, the potager was indeed given some version of a greenhouse. Walls of glass were erected in front of the stone garden walls, and a thin cloth was draped between the glass and stone to allow the rain in but to keep the insects out. Trees and vines were then trained behind the walls of glass, and held in a micro-climate more conducive to fruit production than the usual weather at Versailles. This technique combined with his radical espalier techniques for pruning fruit trees allowed La Quintinie to bring large and luscious pears to the king's table in February. This was the time of year when the poor were beginning to run low on food and fresh goods were hard to find. So, for the period, La Quintinie was making something of a miracle.[49]

La Quintinie's success was in part a result of the size of his budget. Unlike most gardeners of the period, he could get the money to cover fields of fruits and vegetables with *serres*. The extent of the conspicuous display in these techniques becomes clearer when we learn that, in the 1690s, the cost of a 1 meter square of glass was 225 livres – about one-tenth of La Quintinie's entire annual pension. Glass was a rare and difficult commodity, and La Quintinie commanded vast amounts of it so he could bring to the royal household fruits and vegetables *before* they were available commercially. The debt to commercial gardening for the techniques and skills that he developed and extended at the potager were hidden by his very success in surpassing what commercial gardeners could do, using the funds from the state treasury.[50]

The debts to commercial culture so palpable at the *jardin potager* were importantly and explicitly downplayed by La Quintinie, who denied any interest in commercial reward from his gardening. He specifically implored other gardeners managing *jardins potagers* to avoid selling excess produce to enrich themselves. The fact that he felt compelled to mention this suggests that many gardeners to the nobility did the opposite (as they clearly did in England). It also helps to explain the king's delight in his character; here was a man who took techniques from the culture of the market, while eschewing market values and promoting noble ones. At the king's orders, La Quintinie set up a stand to give away excess produce to the poor of Versailles, transforming the potential profit of the gardens into a means for a paternalistic exchange.[51]

However much the king denied the commercial and mundane meanings of the *jardin potager* at Versailles, ordinary gardeners saw the practical value in the innovations there. Jean Laurent, a notary from Laon, used many of the ideas regarding the culture of fruit espoused by La Quintinie, and dedicated his book on gardening to the head of the potager. La Quintinie responded that Laurent could (and perhaps should) have found a more powerful patron (as another garden writer, Dom Claude Estienne, had done when he dedicated a book on fruit culture to Le Nôtre, who was not in charge of the fruit garden).[52] But Laurent wanted to acknowledge how much gardeners in France recognized and appreciated what La Quintinie was doing as a gardener, and to what extent they equated his innovations with the experiments in gardening coming out of the estate-management and market-gardening traditions.[53]

The *jardin potager* at Versailles, then, remained a palpable influence in the world of market-oriented gardening, but was actively separated from it. The trees in the potager were pruned into an orderliness that was military in spirit, and they were trimmed to reach just to the top of the walls where the king and his guests would walk on promenades (see plate 40). From the battlements, the noblemen could survey the trees below set out like an assembled army. The gentlemen could look down on the wonders of nature spread out in the garden, and see the power of the king and state in the orderly lines of trees in his domain. The technical control in the garden was brashly flashed in the face of even jaded visitors to the potager by the sea of precious glass covering beds of vegetables and the surrounding masses of fruit trees. This conspicuous display of glass was probably as impressive as anything inside the château – including the Hall of Mirrors.

Collectors' gardens and the plant trade

Setting out great formal gardens required not only elements of design, horticulture, and land engineering; it also required plants. Bulbs, flowering annuals and perennials, bushes, vines, and trees were clearly needed to establish the bosquets and lay out the parterres of the great seventeenth-century gardens. Fruit trees were required to plant the orchards of the potager, and seeds and seedlings were needed to raise under glass the delicate fruits and vegetables favored for the table. Great elms for the *petit parc* may have been brought down from the forests of nearby hills and mountains, but many more exotic species like the ubiquitous citruses of Versailles had to be imported from more distant locations.

Clearly, the plant trade became necessary for the kind of collectors' gardens that started growing up in the estates around Paris in the seventeenth century. The urban world of trade and transport that made gardening on the scale of an estate possible at all also facilitated the amassing of unusual plants – not to mention the accumulation of exotic animals and classical art which would also express the reach and taste of the collector. Even by the sixteenth century, the plant trade had been serving the curiosity and ostentation of aristocratic collectors. Although early plant collecting is often described as mostly the province of botanists, in fact rare plants were often first imported by the nobility and wealthy gentlemen. Noble collectors not infrequently sent their gardeners on voyages to distant lands to locate new species for their collections. When they sponsored botanists' voyages, they often did this with the same spirit, expecting not just to advance science but to improve their collections. The differentiation of functions was clear enough between botanists associated with medical facilities and gardeners working for aristocrats in private pleasure gardens, but the world of collecting did not stay so neatly in those two camps. Collectors of both sorts routinely exchanged specimens, and filled both pleasure and botanical gardens of the sixteenth and seventeenth centuries. This trade without profit benefited its practitioners as a source of novelties.[54]

Amateur plant collecting had in this period powerful cultural lineages supporting it. The Renaissance culture of collection clearly influenced powerful men like Richelieu, Mazarin, Fouquet, and Colbert, and made collection a respected activity in France. The *cabinets de curiosité* set up by serious amateurs in the sixteenth and seventeenth centuries were expected to combine both artworks and specimens of natural history. The garden could serve as a comparable site, where botanical and art collections could be organized to fit this cultural constellation. Collectors' gardens might be outdoors rather than indoors, but they could combine statuary and rare plants and animals to constitute a similar array of exotics and beauties as that found in the *cabinets*. Libraries, the *cabinets*, and gardens all became standard sites for collection and displays of taste in the world of French elites. They linked the book trade, the plant trade, and trade in artworks and artifacts and were all used to refashion French elite culture.[55]

Collections were also important to gardening in the sixteenth and seventeenth centuries for exactly the same reason that dressing fashionably was vital to elites of the period. They were both status symbols. Men and women became collectors not just because they could suddenly get access to goods because of the expansion in trade (although that was prerequisite), but because collections of renown could mark them as persons of distinction. In this period of surprising social mobility, where taste was said to reveal the natural virtues of those of high rank, patterns of refined consumption like collecting or dressing exquisitely, just like good manners and fine body carriage, were important social resources. They were marks of an *honnête homme*. Great gardens were like fine clothing for the countryside; no wonder *parterres de broderie* became such a fashionable item in French formal gardens.[56]

The growth and elaboration of collections during the sixteenth and seventeenth centuries occurred, significantly, when capitalist trade was also butting up uncomfortably against traditional Christian values. The Church still officially defined profit-making as sinful. Accumulation of goods was certainly permitted – hoarding had for centuries been a necessary way of building up reserves of food and wealth during good times as a hedge against the bad. But the sale of goods to maximize profits was still not entirely sanctioned in this period. By the medieval policies of the Church, accruing more than a modest profit through trade was a sin,[57] yet trade was evidently present, powerful, and growing. New goods appeared in the marketplace. Fortunes were made. Seductive new ways of dressing, acting, and living were made possible through using new trade goods. How could these two cultures, feudal and capitalist, be breached? How was an elite but devout Christian to live? One answer was to trade in order to collect objects rather than to exchange goods for profit. Even those families that were made rich and powerful by the marketplace could become more virtuous and socially visible at the same time if they turned their money toward collecting and away from the search for profit. In this context, cultural capital amassed in taste and goods was a way to make economic capital socially more acceptable.[58] Renaissance Edenic gardens, devoted to spiritual purposes but filled with rare plants and ancient marble sculptures, were the perfect example of the beautiful results that could be achieved with money in the hands

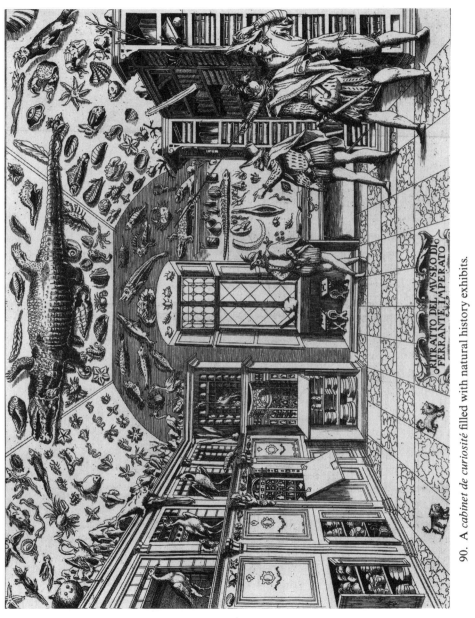

90. A *cabinet de curiosité* filled with natural history exhibits.

of a sponsor of exquisite taste and virtue. Collections, then, were an important link between the profits of trade and attempts to translate greed into sensibility. They (ironically perhaps) increased the range of trade goods from which merchants could profit.

The organization of the plant trade in the sixteenth and seventeenth centuries

The plant trade came into being in sixteenth- and seventeenth-century Europe within this complex interplay of consumer behavior and economic possibility. The Italians and Dutch were active in the early trade, being among the first to take gardening seriously. They both set out botanical and medicinal gardens. At the same time, the Italians were experimenting with pleasure gardening, and the Dutch were beginning their seminal experiments in market gardening.[59] By the end of the sixteenth century, elaborate plant collections were found in the kitchen and pleasure gardens of great houses in many wealthier parts of Europe. Collections of rare and interesting fruit trees were early favorites among the non-scholars. Trees were adaptable, and in their first few years, transplantable as saplings; they also provided pleasures for the table and potential for trade. Many of the early horticultural books emphasized orchard layouts and cultures of fruit trees precisely because there was so much interest in these items.[60]

Before the seventeenth century, the international trade in plants consisted mostly of the unorganized transport of seeds and cuttings by mariners, botanists, aristocratic travelers (or their servants), combined with exchanges among collectors along interpersonal networks. Ships' inventories did not usually include these items because they had no real market value. Where the spice trade was lucrative enough, herbs and seeds would be listed with the spices. And where the plant trade was motivated by scholarly interests, journal entries and botanical writings provided clues to their origins. But there remained few documents to help track the exact itineraries of many species. During the period of tulip mania, as we will see shortly, bulbs were valuable enough to be catalogued, but most trade in flowering plants was not so lucrative. Handfuls of seeds carried here by some sailors or a few bulbs carried there by unknown collectors were the source of novelties for many gardens in the sixteenth and seventeenth centuries.[61]

Amateur plant collectors, botanists, and men like Colbert, serving powerful patrons, used this modest plant trade very effectively. Even if their work was relatively casual and amateur, the consequences were quite visible in the gardens of Europe.[62] By the middle of the seventeenth century, this tradition of plant exchange helped to provide many species needed in setting out French formal gardens. During the reign of Louis XIV, many of the trees, bushes, and even bulbs that were acquired for Versailles by Colbert were dug out of the countryside or acquired in trades with amateurs, rather than bought on the open market. Colbert was loath to import what he could find in France.[63]

Nonetheless, there was a growing commercial culture of plants in France which gardeners increasingly turned to in the latter half of the seventeenth century. Just as monocultural plantations were stimulating a massive redistribution of species outside Europe, speculators in the plant trade encouraged a massive transplanting of plant species into and within Europe. Market gardening flourished, and collections in pleasure gardens were markedly enhanced.[64] The trade itself was not entirely commercial because informal exchange continued, particularly among amateur botanists. But by the late seventeenth century, the plant trade had become a lively, if not always thriving, field.

The commercial side of the plant trade was dramatically stimulated by a form of collection that exploded into fashion in the seventeenth century: namely, "tulipomania." Tulips in particular, but other bulbs as well to a lesser extent, were "the rage" among the gardeners of the period. They were relatively easy to ship and grow, and they yielded intensely colored and sometimes heavily scented flowers that usually lasted for a long time when cut. They were adored, and their popularity was expressed in the plethora of still life paintings from the period, often Dutch or French, that featured a vase of massed colors from the flowers of bulbs. Tulipomania as a term makes clear the primacy given tulips in this fashion, but it does not express the esteem for and fascination with bulbs of all sorts in this period.[65]

The popularity of these bulbs had important commercial consequences, even though the fad was in part supported by amateur trade. Demand for tulips was so great that there was a dramatic inflation of prices for them. Finding and importing new varieties was a lucrative enterprise, and helped to provide an economic basis for the expansion of market gardening.[66]

How a combination of commercial and amateur transfers supported innovation in plant culture in France can be assessed more closely by studying the career of Pierre Morin, a commercial florist who lived and worked on the outskirts of Paris (Saint-Germain). He seems to have built at least a reputation, if not a fortune, on the plant trade. We know a great deal about his plant collection because he published a well-known catalogue of flowering plants from his garden in 1651. He published it not just to attract prospective buyers but to exchange information with other collectors as well. During the period of tulip mania in Europe, he traded extensively in bulbs. In his catalogue, he described a vast collection of the flowering bulbs in his gardens, particularly tulips, irises, and ranunculi.[67] The catalogue is long, so the collection seems to have been enormous. The trade which brought him this immense variety of goods had to be extensive, and his knowledge of plant culture that allowed his garden to hold this massive inventory of goods must also have been quite impressive for the period.

What is curious, however, is the extent to which this man, who was self-described as a denizen of the commercial world, lived among garden amateurs as well as traders. To amass his garden's collection, he depended to a large extent on the informal trade in plants. In 1655, when he put out a revised catalogue of his flowering plants, he explained that, in the years since his original publication, he had received letters from flower collectors from all over the world, asking him about his collection and telling him about theirs. He traded with them for new plants, which he raised in his garden. These flowers, he claimed, had not been seen in France before, and were now on display in his garden for curious Parisians to see (he does not say buy). Pierre Morin was no botanist, and not a figure at court. He was a businessman who had amassed a huge plant collection, and lived off the trade in these specimens. Still, he could not conduct his work simply through commerce. He was in correspondence with those who saw collection as part of pleasure gardening, or at least he wrote for gardeners who loved finding and raising rare and beautiful plants. In his books, he categorized plants by their cultivation, and he catalogued his bulbs by the colors, sizes, and growth patterns of their flowers, the kind of information needed for flower gardening. He had nothing to say about garden design, yet he conducted exactly the kind of modest plant trade in showy rather than useful species that could make formal gardens so luscious in the period.[68]

It was this odd mix of commercial and amateur trade that supported gardening when the great French formal gardens were being built. The availability of plants and the possibilities for playing with novelties were well established in this system. The existence of commercial growers and importers made it easier to mass plantings of bulbs and bushes in parterres and bosquets. It is not entirely clear where in the Mediterranean Basin the plants imported to Versailles from the Midi came from. Many bulbs were probably dug from the countryside; others seemed to hail from the Levant. It is not clear whether there was some commercial flower bulb raising in this region during the late seventeenth century, although it is likely. The demand for bulbs from the Mediterranean region coupled with the existence of the botanical garden at Montpellier would have provided both means and motive for commercial gardening of flowering bulbs. The great flower markets of the Midi region were of later origin, but they may have had modest predecessors.[69] In any case, the means for expanding the garden at Versailles were in place when the king's ambitions drove Colbert to deliver multitudes of bulbs for the massive plantings in the *petit parc*.

Versailles and plant collection

The gardens at Versailles depended for their gloriousness, then, not just on the "genius" of Le Nôtre, but on the abundance of flowers, trees and bushes that gave life to his designs. The account books show that Colbert authorized huge annual purchases of sweet-smelling tuberoses, jonquils, and citruses from the Midi.[70] The collection of orange trees reached 3,000 plants in the Orangerie under Louis XIV. The king loved having flowering citruses not just in the garden but in the Hall of Mirrors and his private apartments, prodding the gardeners at Versailles to keep some citrus flowering at all times of the year. To this end, they assembled trees from distant parts of the world that naturally fruited and flowered at different times. They also used their skills to force some other citruses to flower during the times of the year when no natural blooms were possible. The cost of the collection and its maintenance was substantial. The treasury paid the duchesse de la Ferté 2,200 livres for only twenty citruses from her gardens.[71]

Not all plant transfers brought rare species to Versailles. In 1688, the royal treasury paid 16,949 livres for 25,000 trees brought to the gardens at Versailles from Compiègne, from Flanders, from the mountains of Dauphiné, and from the forests of Normandy, presumably to replace trees that had died in the winter.[72] Colbert's concern for the forests was palpable. In 1700, the state paid 1,500 livres for green trees to regenerate the bosquets in the gardens. Just the year before, the king had ordered 1,000 small trees (some 4–5 feet tall) and 200 fully grown trees to be taken from the forests at Marly and other locations.[73] The importance of flourishing forests and abundant tree collections created a huge demand for trade and transfers of these garden staples.

Colbert's letters make clear that the treasury paid dearly for the plants at Versailles, but not all the purchases were clearly from commercial plant traders or market gardeners. The palms and citrus trees that adorned the Parterre de Midi came mostly from the Intendant at Marseilles whose sources for the bulbs and citruses are not named. The tuberoses probably came on ships from Italy, where they were native. Many more plants came to Marseilles from the Levant. Sailors at Toulon were said to carry bulbs and seeds with them to supplement their incomes. So the Intendant may have tapped a wide range of sources to meet Colbert's demands.[74]

Delicate flowers and trees brought to Versailles could adorn the gardens in part because of technical innovations in their storage and care on board ships. We may not know specifically where the plants from Marseilles came from, but we do know that they were shipped to Versailles either on merchant vessels or military ones, using techniques for shipboard transport that commercial traders developed to protect their cargoes. A cascade of innovations were developed for boxing, shipping, and cultivating tender plants, mostly in the seventeenth century. They were developed first by the European botanists, estate gardeners, and the explorers who sought out plant species from continents beyond Europe. They were then refined by commercial traders trying to protect valuable cargoes of bulbs and saplings for both colonial and European markets. Long-distance plant transfers became so frequent that the movements of trees and bulbs from the Mediterranean to the gardens at Versailles became technically routine during the construction of the park.[75]

Colbert not only orchestrated these transfers, but may well have been the inspiration behind the plant collection at Versailles. Interestingly, he was one of France's most avid collectors of not only books, but oddities from nature as well. Probably inspired by the collections of his early mentor, Mazarin, Colbert set up a distinctive *cabinet de curiosité*. Many foreign visitors making a tour of France called on M. Colbert to see his collections. Because of Fouquet's imprisonment, Colbert seems to have been appropriately worried by the notice given to his collections, so he persuaded the king to use his books as the basis of a new royal library.[76] From this point on, he did most of his collecting in the name of France. In the name of the king, he both helped to produce and collect medals commemorating the achievements of the reign; he purchased series of tapestries from the Gobelins that made glorious additions to the king's residences. But Colbert's main interests lay in books, plants, and animals.[77]

Colbert set up the Jardin du Roi in Paris to collect medicinal herbs, make them available to the city, and provide a site for training Parisian doctors in their culture and use. The botanical garden of Montpellier in the south of France had been the center for French botany and had amassed a fabulous collection of plants. But it was too far away to serve this growing metropolis and was in a part of the king's domain that had been attacked for housing dissidents. Paris was too important to go without adequate medical supplies, and medicine was too important to leave unregulated by the state. In Paris, Colbert began overseeing the collection of botanical plants for the state and

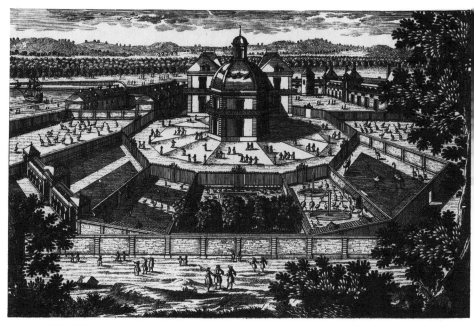

91. Silvestre, *Ménagerie*.

crown, while building up goodwill in the city by making medicine available to the populace.[78]

Colbert also took great interest in the Ménagerie at Versailles. He apparently enjoyed collecting rare species of animals and birds. In its heyday, the Ménagerie housed pelicans, deer, ostriches, flamingoes, humming birds, camels, parrots, lorikeets, cockatoos, birds of paradise, bears, lions, pigeons, chickens, turkeys, swans, peacocks, herons, Egyptian ducks, wolves, foxes, gazelles, cows from Flanders and Holland, horses, a crocodile, and an elephant.[79] This array was appropriately astounding and clearly a match for the collections of artwork and rare plants in the garden.

While Colbert took a relatively scientific interest in plants, animals, and gardening, Louis XIV was more concerned with making the gardens at Versailles a source of glory. This impulse, too, had an effect on plant culture. French gardens had to be as good as those in Italy, and this meant, at the very least, that they had to contain all the desirable Mediterranean plants. In Italy, these plants were mostly native to the Mediterranean so they could be cultivated with relative ease, but in Versailles, this was not the case. Just making Italianate gardens with citruses and pomegranates grow in the outskirts of Paris, where the skies were so often gray and the winds frequently cold, required enormous gardening ingenuity. Importing species from the south necessarily helped to make French royal gardens sites of elaborate experiments in plant collecting, acclimatizing, forcing, and transplanting. In addition, the gardens at Versailles had, of course, to surpass Italian precedents, and this meant, among other things, containing exotics from even more distant parts of the world. Only such efforts could ever hope to make the parterres and bosquets at Versailles more astoundingly wonderful than those in Italy. The potager was not immune from this competitive plant trading and cultivation. La Quintinie had to raise peas like those in Italy, bringing them to table earlier than they could be imported, despite the northern French climate.[80]

Dutch influences on the plant culture in French gardens were also palpable. Dutch merchants were among the most aggressive and successful plant traders, and were certainly the ones who profited most from the tulipomania that swept Europe in the early seventeenth century. Although there is no evidence that Colbert used Dutch suppliers for the gardens, French plant traders were heavily involved with their Dutch counterparts, and so bulbs with origins beyond the Mediterranean trading area were likely to have arrived through the Dutch plant trade. Louis XIV was as smitten by the fashion for bulbs early in his reign as many other European collectors of his period. Even though he walked almost daily in the gardens or elsewhere in the countryside, he appreciated having bulbs planted near the château so he could see them from the window. In warm periods he could also smell their fragrances from the château. These pleasures were probably partially provided by French trade in the Mediterranean, but many bulbs could only have come from Dutch sources.

Other rare and coveted plants were brought to Versailles from outside France. In 1672, Colbert wrote to the director of the West India Company asking for his people to bring back unusual fruits and flowers for the royal gardens; he was regularly asked for plants to be brought from Portugal and the Near and Far East.[81] Some of these went to set up the botanical garden in Paris, but many others went to Versailles, the Trianon, and, later, Marly – all of which had elaborate gardens in which the king took great pride and pleasure.

Later in his life, Louis XIV's allergies were said to have turned his attention away from flowers in the gardens at Versailles but this did not prevent him from collecting. He concentrated on citruses, whose wonderful scent did not bother him. He liked to have citruses in pots in his section of the château at Versailles, as well as in the Parterre de Midi, outside the Orangerie. The palm collection for this parterre was also growing, as palms became more fashionable.[82]

This movement toward potted trees in the gardens did not mean that flowers disappeared from the parterres. On the contrary, the turnover in plants there became greater in this period. Only the number of scented flowers was limited. Using Olivier de Serres' techniques for keeping plants in ceramic pots for easy transplanting, gardeners regularly dug up and replaced the flowers in the parterres at night to make the blooms as colorful and fresh as possible when the king arose in the morning. The extensive nursery for young plants, the *pepinière*, provided the steady supply of new plants needed for this purpose.[83]

Simply controlling nature – importing, acclimatizing, transplanting, and forcing plants to make a garden to please the king– was certainly part of the significance of gardening to the king and court, but the political significance of the plant collections went well beyond that. The trees of the Parterre de Midi in particular were vital political assets. The oranges, palms, and other tender species primarily from the south of France were rare treasures, whose collection was meant to glorify the Sun King. These

92. Palms inside the Orangerie at Versailles.

specimens, which had been successfully brought to court from the far reaches of the kingdom, consisted of plants which could not winter outdoors at Versailles. It required a great deal of gardening skill simply to sustain these flora of the Mediterranean basin.[84] But the parterre did not just exude a vision of horticultural expertise; it provided a metaphor for the state's political reach. There was a vast cultural and historical divide between the northern and southern regions of France that was underscored by the ecological differences between north and south. Containing and controlling the plants from the Mediterranean in the vast Orangerie obliquely pointed to the ability of the French state to overcome the difficulties of distance and history, and govern this part of its territory. Calling the garden beds the Parterre de Midi made clear the geopolitical meaning of the collection, since the Midi was a specific southern region of France. The parterre could have simply been called the Mediterranean garden, referring to the geographical source of the plants without using the language of social regionalism, but it would have lost its specific and politically rich association. By blurring the distinction between the natural and political, this collection of plants helped to work against any attempt to naturalize the regionalism that threatened the state. Nature and art both contributed to the definition of a unified, French culture of plants.

The collections in the garden at Versailles, then, became both a living map and cultural inventory, marking the capacity of the French state to manipulate the natural resources within its boundaries, enrich them with bounties from abroad, and unify them into a single world of nature. The plants helped define France as an integrated political territory with a distinctive and complex plant culture. The gardens both presumed and lived off the commercial world of trade, but used plant exchanges as a means for decorating, and defining political geography. The *petit parc* at Versailles testified to the *singularity* of France under Louis XIV, and the contents of collections made manifest its political reach. The long and strong networks of people and things connected to Versailles helped make this court a powerful political center.[85]

Water systems and land management

The water system in the *petit parc* at Versailles was an astounding sight, and a vital element in the display of power and nature in these gardens. Part of this attention to water was derived from the Italian gardening heritage. Simon Schama argues that water themes were very important to the Renaissance landscape and to gardening in sixteenth-century Italy because spiritual powers were thought to be invested in this precious liquid. The transformative and lively qualities of water made it seem miraculous. That is why water was so often engineered in Italian gardens to perform tricks and be as animated as this culture suggested it should be. The newly elaborated technologies derived from Roman precedents for the gardens were harnessed to realize those effects. At the same time, these techniques themselves forged a self-conscious connection between Renaissance gardens and the classical tradition. Waterworks were already culturally loaded elements of gardening before Louis XIV began to demand new gardens for Versailles.[86]

During the seventeenth century, circulatory systems had become central to science, adding a new layer of significance to garden water systems and stimulating even more work on hydraulic engineering. Harvey's famous research on the blood had opened up inquiries into natural patterns in the movements of fluids, and increased interest in the techniques by which liquids could be made to move. In this context, a water system was not simply a way to cool areas of a garden or an opportunity to make dramatic shows of natural resources. It was a way to elaborate on the forces of nature, increasing the grandeur of a site through aesthetically seductive but also technically powerful engineering. Water was used simultaneously to mark the royal park as a place where the powers of the earth and heavens were visible, and to claim French superiority over Italian gardening technique.[87]

A vast repertoire of skills developed and exercised in France was needed to make the water system at Versailles first possible and then appropriately astounding. The *petit parc* actually contained only a minute part of the water engineering that went into the development of this royal garden, even though it contained most of the fountains. The huge central canal and extraordinary fountains were (and remain) quite impressive, but they were nothing compared to the vast system of canals, reservoirs, aqueducts, pumps, water towers and windmills that brought water to the gardens. When Louis XIII built his hunting lodge at Versailles, and even when Louis XIV first started going there as a young king, a small stream in the valley and a marshy area to the northeast of the property were enough to provide water for the few reflecting pools set out there. But the construction of the first axis of parterres to the north and south of the château with their

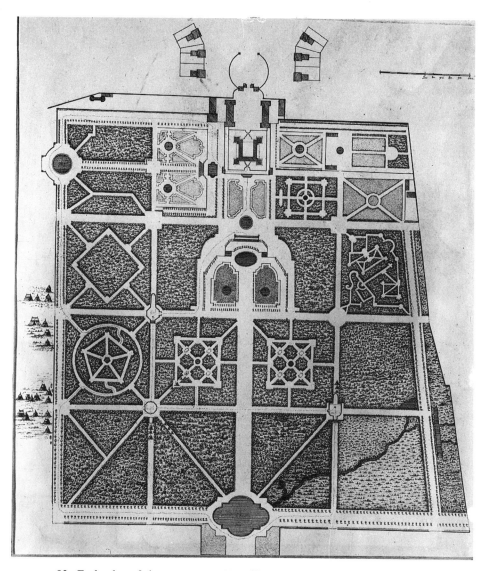

93. Early plan of the *petit parc* at Versailles, showing small fountain ponds (darker circular forms) arrayed primarily along the two main north–south and east–west axes.

Italianate attachment to fountains initiated a demand for more water that would not end until the close of Louis XIV's reign.

The whole story of French engineering and state power could be told through the history of this water system. Its whole rationale was to glorify the center of French political power, and make the château at Versailles the kind of seat of court that Louis XIV wanted for France. The search for water required, however, a movement away from Versailles, a taming of the countryside that went farther and farther into the landscape as the demands at the center grew in scale. The relationship between the two was negotiated not so much through personal influence or imposition of authority as through engineering. Of course the engineering was possible in part because the king had the authority to make the countryside suit his intentions, but it would only do so when the land could be engineered to serve his glory. Both the French countryside and king were co-constructed materially in the process.[88]

The technology for the water system, much like the techniques for gardening, grew from that space between city and country where urban expansion placed pressures on the countryside to force nature into serving human needs and desires. Cities needed improved water supplies and reticulation in order to grow. For many years Paris had experienced problems in maintaining an adequate water supply. At the beginning of the seventeenth century, the water for Paris was still brought to the city in ancient aqueducts. The *aqueduc d'Arcueil* was rebuilt under Catherine de Medici to serve the Luxembourg gardens with water primarily from the springs at Rungis and nearby areas. This indirectly provided some relief to the parched Left Bank, since the royal family gave its excess water to the urban supply system. Water engineering in this case clearly linked the search for sources for royal gardens to the urban water supply. The vast demands in both systems set cultural and engineering precedents for Versailles.[89]

The technical difficulties of providing *potable* water for city-dwellers and water for pleasure garden fountains were in principle different from providing water for fountains (which could and often did have the high bacteria counts of stagnant water), but the techniques for delivering the water were much the same. Moreover, since public fountains were often the source of potable water in cities, using good water in even purely decorative fountains was deemed desirable, if not always possible.[90]

The technologies for water systems were not always derived from the city itself, but they were often drawn from worlds of commerce where market demands were transforming the countryside. The pumps used to supply garden fountains had their origins in the mines, where excavation depths had been limited by inflows of water. Pumping systems were designed to dispose of the seepage, and hence made mines more efficient suppliers of the ores and minerals required for war and manufactures. Windmills, used mostly for grinding grain, had already been attached to pumps and been used for raising water in canals and land areas where flooding was a problem.[91] The waterwheels used to supply Versailles also came from the machines for milling that had been adapted to raising water (as in the *Samaritaine* in Paris). Canals, too, had commercial roots. Many small canals had been built to increase the agricultural yield of estates by allowing more land to be put into cultivation. (The canals in Le Nôtre's gardens were, perhaps not surprisingly, often set in low areas to drain boggy sections of the parks to make them usable.) Clearly, the water management methods that had been developed for mining, transportation, urban development, and agricultural improvement all had commercial roots, and now took on particular significance for building the gardens at Versailles.

What may be more surprising were the strong links between military and commercial uses of these technologies. Obviously, the more complex techniques of canal building were developed either to enhance military barricades around the perimeter of France or to link river-based trading systems. Less obviously, military installations also needed water supplies, and soldiers contributed to the development of water supply systems for cities as well as royal residences. François de Francine, one of the Francini brothers hired to construct the fountains at Versailles, clearly combined water management and military concerns in his own life. He was trained in hydraulics by his father, who was *Intendant général des eaux et fontaines de France*, but François began his independent career in the military. He was hired to police and provision the soldiers. When his father died, he was put in charge of the Paris water system, and in that city combined water engineering with local policework. In both phases of his life, control of people and control of water were continuous interests. Even the two major initiatives he pushed in Paris linked military to social engineering. First, he advocated for Paris the creation of an encircling canal, like a fortress's moat, that he said could transport water around the city for public benefit. Comparable projects were being tried in Germany with good effect. But this plan was never realized. More successfully, he convinced the king to restore and improve the ancient aqueduct bringing water from Rungis to the city, in part because it was a great monument to Roman military engineering and also because it could improve the Parisian water system.[92]

The demand to outdo Italian gardens in French designs created the other great pressure to introduce innovations in fountain engineering in the *petit parc* at Versailles. The point was once again to bring the power of the classical past to France. This meant that French gardeners could not just make larger pools with finer statues than those found in Italy, but had to develop more complex engineering to make the water spouts reach higher, do more tricks, and appear in more diverse parts of the garden. The Italians might have had the technology of the Ancients close at hand to imitate, but this could not guarantee their ongoing superiority in water engineering. The French wanted to be (and by some accounts became) more successful in producing breathtaking fountains for their gardens. Ellis Veryard put it this way:

The Water-works [at Versailles], far exceed those of *Frescati* and *Tivoli*, so much boasted in *Italy*, for as the *Italians* have been happy in their Inventions, so the *French* have been prosperous in promoting and perfecting them: Tho' in reality whole *Europe* has, in some measure, contributed toward the beautifying of this Master-piece of Art, by the most expert and famous Artificers that have been cal'd from all parts, and are daily employ'd in this stupendous Work. (Veryard 1701, p. 68)

The king and his ministers could not have commissioned praise that would have pleased them more. Veryard raised France to the rightful center of a new European culture. The French were now able to make best use of classical precedents in the arts and engineering, rallying all the aesthetic and technical forces in Europe to surpass the accomplishments of the Italians. Fountains, with their combination of aesthetic and engineering requirements, were perfect exemplars of France's achievements. No wonder they were so central to the gardens at Versailles. The problem was supplying the necessary water to the fountains. This was no small engineering feat – as became abundantly clear at Versailles.

To summarize what was in fact a long and complicated history, there were three important, if not necessarily sequential, stages for engineering the water supply at Versailles. One involved efforts to use more efficiently the water already flowing through the valley. The second exploited the plateaux around the valley, using different techniques for capturing the water there and routing it into the existing supply system. The third concentrated on raising river water and transporting it to the king's lands.

The early efforts to make the gardens at Versailles sparkle with fountains for Louis XIV tapped extant valley waters. Denis Jolly, an engineer who had been put in charge of the Samaritaine pumping station in Paris and who constructed a second pumping station for the city at the Notre Dame bridge, used dams and an ingenious system of pumps and reservoirs for the job. At first, he dammed the stream at Clagny, and used it and some Bièvre river water to supply the gardens. In 1642, he built the first small pump to run the system. Jolly added a second pump in 1664 for the Ménagerie. The latter system could only supply the fountains for half a day, but it still made the Ménagerie enchanting for that period. The king, however, was not happy with the meager water spouts, so the plumbers and engineers carried out additional work on the system and made the Ménagerie satisfactory by the time Louis XIV visited it two years later.[93]

In 1666, the first major effort to build a truly glorious water system was initiated to serve the set of fountains being built near the château at Versailles. At this time, Le Nôtre was developing the north–south axis of the garden by the royal residence, installing Italianate elements in the decorations of the park. Vivid but subtle waterworks were part of the package. Denis Jolly was contracted to build the circulatory system that would send water through it. He designed a great pump to raise water from the reservoir at Clagny into a holding tank on the top of a great tower. From there, the water would fall using gravity through a linked series of fountains. The pump was operated with two horses, turning large gears in separate rooms on either side of the tower. The pump house was designed by Le Vau in brick and stone like the Louis XIII section of the château, and stood just outside the northern parterres by the Etang (lake or mere) de Clagny.[94]

The problem with the system was that it had very little water to call upon. The reservoir on top of the tower was very small, and produced quite disappointing jets in the fountains. The situation was improved with the addition of new holding tanks: first, one on top of the grotto, and then, three additional ceramic-lined pools in a three-storey high wall along the northeast side of the property. A second pump was added to return the water that reached the Bassin des Cygnes (later the Apollo fountain). This pump sent the water back to the upper reservoirs to be used again, diminishing the demand for new supplies of water. It was an amazingly well-designed system, but it still lost much water through evaporation, spray, and leaks. This left the water supply barely adequate.[95]

Soon afterwards, Le Nôtre started reworking the area directly behind the château. This work presented the most vexing problems for the water engineers because this terrace was at the highest point in the garden, and stood above even the elevated reservoirs built into the garden walls. Water for the terrace had to have its own system of

94. Perelle, *Veue et perspective du Chasteau et la Grotte de Versailles* . Note the evidence of the pump tower to the left of the grotto, and the walls in front of it which may already have held the early ceramic reservoirs. The top of the grotto was itself a reservoir.

supply. Three underground reservoirs were dug under this part of the garden by the Francini brothers, the two official fountain-designers for Versailles. These subterranean tanks would feed the Parterre d'Eau, using the original pump. A new and grander pump was added to the park's water system in 1674, and a number of windmills at Clagny helped raise the water to the reservoirs. But with all these improvements, the fountains still seemed too puny for the ambitious king. Worse, they had to be turned on and off in sequence for promenades because there was not enough water to run them all at once. Even used selectively, they could not run continuously. In spite of the effectiveness of the return pump, water was lost into the system so rapidly that the supplies dwindled away in only a few hours. The water available in the valley was simply not enough for the growing garden.[96]

Already by 1668, a small reservoir set on the south side of the garden held water from the Bièvre. This was the source feeding the lower part of the *petit parc* that could not be attached to the system from Clagny. Eventually it became a linchpin in the most successful part of the water system for Versailles: the linked set of reservoirs bringing water from the plateau of Satory. The valley at Versailles was edged on two sides by plateaux. There was a small but accessible one on the Clagny side of the garden, whose water table was relatively easy to tap – and not too difficult to tie into the existing water system. On the other side of the valley, by contrast, far from the extant main pumps for the garden, there was the expansive plateau of Satory, carrying abundant water and covering a large and often difficult terrain.[97]

The second wave of engineering experiments, aimed at bringing water to Versailles, began tapping these plateaux, taking advantage of the surveying and engineering skills of scientists from the Observatory as well as the muscle and canal-building experience of military personnel. The projects drained groundwater from these areas by tapping streams and damming hillsides to create reservoirs with run-off from the hills. The resulting accumulations were taken through canals to the valley at Versailles. First the engineers experimented on the plateau between Marly and Versailles, filling the nearby lake at Clagny. But now the water that could be stored there was much less than the garden demanded. A new storage system as well as more water sources started to be developed toward Satory. A series of much larger reservoirs were built by damming the deep canyons that came down from the hillsides. These were linked with canals, pipes, and smaller holding reservoirs, using windmills to raise the water over elevations on the plateau where necessary. The whole system was expanded over the years until it stretched from Rambouillet in one direction to Vauballan in the other.[98]

The use of soldiers to dig the canals and build dams for this project seems to follow the Roman practice of using soldiers in peacetime for great "works." The fact that French soldiers were engaged in water engineering only added to this sense of historical continuity. Reservoirs were an ancient means of collecting water both for agriculture and urban use. Damming up streams in narrow valleys was a familiar activity to the Romans. Water accumulated in this way – providing it came from a healthy source – could provide large quantities of even potable water. That is why this kind of water engineering had already been used for supplying growing cities like Paris in the seventeenth century.[99]

Canals and aqueducts for water delivery were also of ancient origin. By the late seventeenth century in France, canal building had become again a domain of military engineers like Vauban, but was now serving new commercial and military needs. Vauban helped in the development of the Canal de Midi, which linked the Atlantic and Mediterranean via a network of river systems. Colbert called upon him to help with the project because he was confident that Vauban would ensure that it was done properly. Although the avowed purpose of the canal was to stimulate trade by breaking down commercial regionalism, Vauban was interested in it because he wanted a water route through French territory between the Mediterranean and Atlantic that would be large enough to carry naval vessels. Pirates were so plentiful in the Mediterranean that French ships were not always able to reach the Atlantic quickly when they were needed. In peacetime, this was a worry. In war, it could be a disaster. A canal through France seemed the perfect solution, although technically this grand scheme proved too much for French engineers. Nonetheless, vital technical experience was acquired on this project which Vauban brought to the water system of Versailles. While Denis Jolly used his Parisian experience with water pumps, Vauban used his fortress and canal engineering experience to help with the reservoir system and its massive array of dams, canals, and pipes.[100]

The third set of experiments for supplying water to the gardens involved efforts to pump river water to Versailles. This began with a proposal from the engineer who had built the Canal de Midi, Pierre Riquet, for taking water from the Loire by canal to

Vüe et Perspective du Château de Versailles et d'une

Dedi

Dessiné et Gravé d'après le Naturel par P. Menant.

Par son tres humble tres obeissar

95. P. Menant, *Vue et Perspective du Château de Versailles et d'une partie de la Ville et de la* Clagny. Here the lake abuts the garden, and is seen close to the walls to the north of th

partie de la Ville et de la Paroisse du côté de l'Étang.
Au Roy

et tres fidele serviteur et sujet   P.Menant.   *Se vend à Paris chez Demortain pont N.Dame C.P.R.*

l'éstang . The éstang de Clagny would later be incorporated into the garden for the château at
g the early reservoirs.

96. The walls that once held the reservoirs.

Versailles. When Abbé Picard from the Académie des Sciences did a survey of the area, he concluded that the château at Versailles was higher than the river, so the project was abandoned, but the dream of tapping river water was not.[101]

Next, there was an ill-fated effort to bring water from the Eure River to Versailles. Vauban was put in charge of the project in 1685. The trouble was that this required first pumping water from the river at one site, and then making it recross the Eure Valley itself at a higher elevation near Maintenon. Pumping it to such a height was one problem. The more intractable obstacle, it turned out, was building a gigantic aqueduct 5,047 meters long and more than 73 meters high to cross the valley. It required three storeys of arches, stacked in diminishing sizes one on top of another. Vauban brought a huge force of soldiers to the valley in 1686 to begin erecting the great edifice. In the end, 30,000 men had worked there before the project was abandoned in 1688. The valley was wet and cold, the work was hard and dangerous, and thousands of men got sick. An epidemic spread through the encamped army, many soldiers died, and the work had to be frequently stopped because too few men were well enough to continue. The whole design for the water system seemed increasingly illogical, as the difficulties of realizing it became clearer, but no one could stop it while the king was committed to the project. Finally, France went to war again, and the king found more pressing uses for his soldiers. French fighting forces never returned to the Eure aqueduct because the treasury was depleted by military expenses after the war, and the futility of the project seemed more obvious by then. Still, the system of reservoirs that had been

97. Pierre Van der Aa, *La Grande Piece d'Eau à Versailles* .The windmills which also helped to bring water to the gardens at Versailles can be seen in the background.

designed to hold water from the Eure aqueduct was connected up to the Satory reservoir system, and helped carry water to Versailles.[102]

Finally, one river project succeeded. At the edge of the Seine, the "machine de Marly" was able to raise river water to an aqueduct and reservoirs serving both Versailles and the king's retreat at Marly. The "machine de Marly" was a dramatically impressive, if elephantine, spin-off of the pump systems built on the bridges in Paris. It used the river current to run the pumps that raised the water up the steep hills of the river banks. The pumps themselves were not very efficient. They were wooden and had to be made rather leaky so the pressures would not build up and break them. Nonetheless, they worked, and since there were so many of them, the machine could raise large quantities of water. This project turned out to have little effect on the gardens at Versailles, not because it failed technically, but because the reservoir system came on line shortly after the machine was finished. This meant that Versailles was sufficiently well served with water and the machine could be devoted almost exclusively to the king's now favorite retreat of Marly.[103]

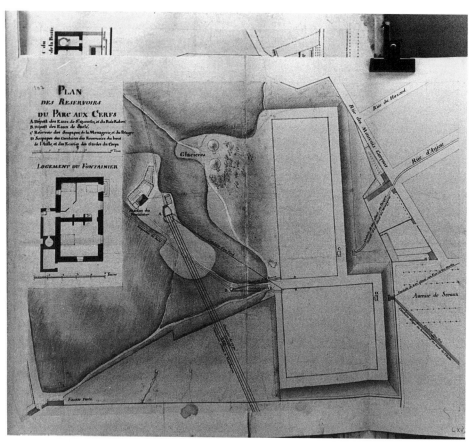

98. Plan for the water supply from the southern plateaux, showing their connection
through pipes to the garden at Versailles.

Throughout this period, the water sources tapped for Versailles had to come from
greater distances and were carried in an ever larger network of canals, pipes, and aqueducts. Wind-powered pumps were placed to raise the water over hills and push it across
flat areas of countryside. Gravity carried water down slopes in canals and aqueducts.
All these systems drew lines across the countryside for everyone to see, making French
engineering and the king's power visible upon the land itself. Great reservoirs filled
valleys and drained hillsides, changing the landscape to make it serve the king's desires.
The more sources were tapped for the increasingly ambitious projects in hydraulic engineering, the more the power of Versailles was etched across the countryside. The water
system carried messages of royal power both within and beyond the walls of the park.

Mlle Scudéry in her description of a promenade through the gardens mentioned the
great circulatory system that had been invented there. She celebrated the new pumping
system which had been designed by Jolly and which had brought such wonderful water
effects to the gardens. This pump was visible from the garden for those who cared to
peek beyond the walls. Locke, in his trip through France, made note of the gardens and

was also enthralled by the water system; he took notes, trying to explain the engineering. Nonetheless, the hydraulic engineering of Versailles, particularly after it moved into the plateaux and river catchment areas away from the garden, was for most people and for most purposes kept "backstage"– outside the main garden or camouflaged within it.[104] Local peasants digging the ditches saw more of it than the gentlemen touring Europe. Nonetheless, the waterworks in bosquets and parterres, and the major fountains on the king's itineraries were deeply indebted to the windmills and water towers, reservoirs, and aqueducts, plumbing and drainage ditches that brought water from a vast area of the landscape to allow them to sparkle against the sky.

It is odd in a way that the water system did not get emphasized at court, given its classical roots. French water systems in general owed an enormous debt to Roman engineering, and the king's propagandists often tried to claim that he was building the new Rome. Hydraulic engineering was also an active area of scientific and technological inquiry in seventeenth-century France. But while it gave garden designers a powerful body of knowledge and a range of practical skills to use in and for the garden, it was not highlighted in the gardens. Still, the water system testified to a technological cleverness in France. Water was a precious and difficult resource to contain, and the fact that the water system succeeded in placing it in the garden in such great abundance was a measure of French power. Nonetheless, this technology tended to be associated with other practical aspects of gardening so it was generally hidden within, while being essential to, the garden at Versailles.

When the Fountain of Latona was bathed in water and the parterres around her were filled with delicate plantings of exotic flowers, Versailles took on a breathtaking beauty and grandeur. But it could only achieve that magical quality because of the nervous efforts by the cranky Colbert to get things done on time and done well, and because of Louvois' more stubborn and persistent determination to extend the project until it worked. It took Denis Jolly to build the first pumps at Versailles, and M. Arnouil, the Intendant from Marseilles, to find enough new bulbs for each season. It required Le Nôtre's consummate skill in drawing across the landscape, not just to play with vision or to work out themes about the Sun King, but to harness the countryside for political ends in ways reminiscent of Olivier de Serres. The garden of Versailles was built with skills that were honed by masons, carpenters, pipe-fitters, and even ditch diggers. It was built by soldiers who gave their lives in the Eure Valley and not the battlefield, exercising the fundamental techniques of siege warfare: digging and laying stones. All the glory of the garden was built with ordinary acts combined in extraordinary ways to make a marvel intended to remain for all times. It stood out from the countryside and yet was deeply embedded in it, arising from the liminal world between urban wealth and rural tradition, where a new France could be constructed.

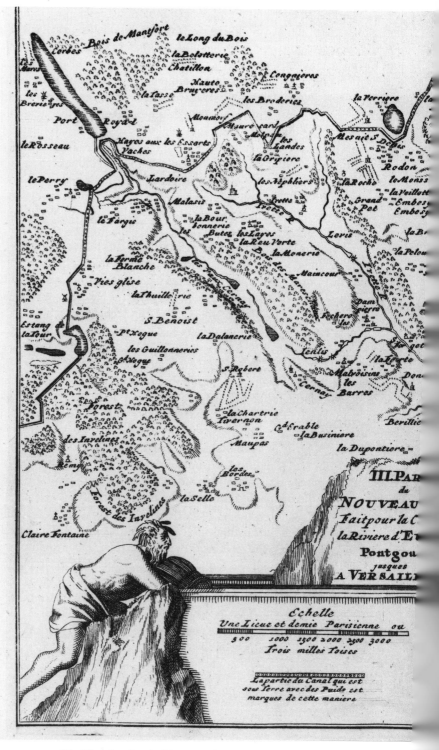

99. The plan for the Eure canal, nearest the garden (upper right), show

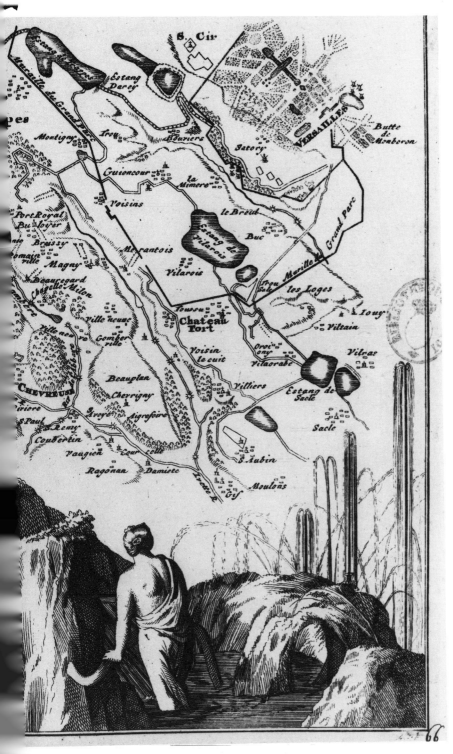

of pools which the canal was supposed to connect.

100. The "Machine de Marly."

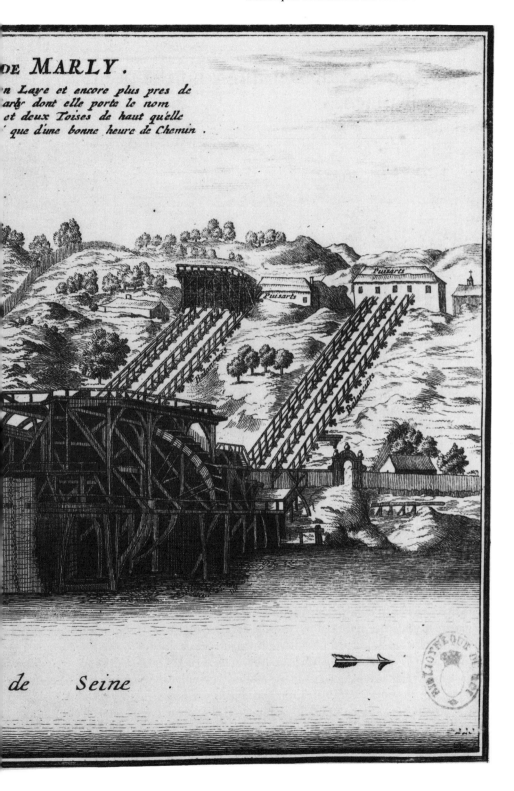

DE **MARLY**.

n Laye et encore plus pres de
arly dont elle porte le nom
et deux Toises de haut qu'elle
que d'une bonne heure de Chemin.

Puisarts

Puisarts

Balanciers

de Seine.

5

Social choreography and the politics of place

The gardens at Versailles may have been, on one level, a cold, inanimate structure in which military power was flaunted, bloodless collections displayed, and daunting waterworks devised – all for the celebration of power; but it was also a stage on which the court played and tried to glitter so brightly that the glory of France would be visible throughout Europe and beyond. Breathless chroniclers were appropriately enrapt by the scale of the king's festivities, the lavishness of the nobles' dress, the formality of the decorum, the sumptuousness of the food, the exoticism of the fruits and candies, and the attention to detail and choreography that made possible the elegance and apparent ease of the court's ritual life.[1]

Stories also began circulating about the dissipation at the heart of this world: the king's public pursuit of his mistresses, the intrigues among courtiers to gain favor and wealth, the blatant homosexuality and cross-dressing of the king's brother and his friends, the excessive gambling in the evenings for jewelry and signs of the king's favor, the exorbitant feasting by the king that was publicly witnessed rather than enjoyed by the nobles, and the parties lasting for days filled with music, fireworks, plays, and pageantry beyond belief. As if such self-indulgence had to be marked by God as moral depravity, we are told that members of the nobility had strange deformities (which later scholars have attributed to inbreeding, not moral lapses).[2]

In both the idyllic and the grotesque renderings of court life at Versailles, the elements of appearance and performance were always in the spotlight. There is good reason for this. At Versailles in the late seventeenth century, to play, act, dance, or attend parties was no casual affair. These things were part of a politics of performance that celebrated the monarchy, signified submission to absolutism, kept the nobility under surveillance, and used the royal residences and their gardens as sites for public display of state power. Nobles did not verbally claim loyalty to the French crown in this period as much as they expressed it through their attendance at court, their adherence to French-led fashion, their use of finely tuned gestures and forms of etiquette blessed by the court, and their loyal participation in any festivities the king wished to see. Whether enjoying parties or watching the king's ritual awakening in the morning, aristocratic participation signified the authority of the king through physical gestures. Gentlemen and ladies at court had little need or opportunity to speak; at most, they whispered to the king for favors after the most solemn events, or (in less formal settings) they used wit to please both king and court with that most trivial and supposedly apolitical form of speech. They were not at court to bring new political voices into the state, but to act out their subservience to this emerging system of power.[3]

It might seem to contemporary readers that titled gentlemen at the birth of the modern French state would or should have acted more like modern French citizens, speaking out for themselves, if not yet for the people, but even that was not the case. The citizen, that self-consciously political actor, whose major weapon in politics has been the word, that product and creator of nationalist sentiment, may have been nascent somewhere in the French cities or countryside, waiting for the French Revolution, but was surely invisible in the court of Louis XIV.[4] During this reign, the nobles who were potentially powerful enough to threaten the king were drawn tightly into the swirl of social activities surrounding the monarch, made economically and socially dependent on the court through conspicuous waste of their wealth and the need to buy offices, and tied into the system of performed obedience to royal absolutism in which only the king's voice was of any political consequence. Censorship was tight; exile from court meant social death for an aristocrat; and the ministers who spoke for the state were careful to speak through the king's authority.[5]

In this context, the garden at Versailles was a public space, but one strange by modern standards. It was open to the public, but it had no speaker's corner or public arena for political debate; it was surely not a site for a nascent bourgeois public sphere or a throwback to the Roman Republic, where gentlemen could speak their minds. Rather, it was a place where the nobility practised a form of "politics by other means," a politics of things and bodies, not ideology.[6] The events that went on in the garden were filled with costumes, predetermined roles, and choreographed ritual, rendering a politics of simulation, gesture and indirection that was an outgrowth of earlier (sometimes church-based) ways of celebrating and marking power.[7]

Public performance and traditions of power

From the Middle Ages, public ritual had been an important part of the expression of political relations in Europe, an enactment of deference through pageantry and processions. Church authority had its highest expression in the mass, where the glory of God, power of the Church, and dependence of the people were made manifest in ritualized movements and chanting. God's word was presented to the people in Latin, a language most did not understand, but could hear as a voice beyond their comprehension that gained its meaning through the Church. Simulation was in that ritual as well. Christ's sacrifice for sinners was enacted in the mass (just as his anointment was reproduced in the rituals for installing the king). The fundamental relations between God and man were made manifest in these ritual moments when human silence made way for God's word.

Rituals increasingly became part of court as well as church life in the Renaissance and baroque periods. The seventeenth-century promenades through the gardens at Versailles were heir to traditions of witnessed performance derived from both Spanish and Italian court formalities from the sixteenth and seventeenth centuries. Routines of the monarch's daily life in Spain and the movements of Italian princes from place to place were both punctuated by ritual. All changes of status or location needed to be solemnized and socially acknowledged. The French court was not immune to these forms prior to the reign of Louis XIV. The migration of the French court along a string of royal residences scattered across the kingdom constituted steps in the "king's progress," part of the purpose of which was periodic regional submission to and celebration of the king. The reception given to the sovereign along the route was meant to be a measure of respect accorded to him, a gesture with real political consequences.[8]

Parties or festivals were also important political vehicles in France, and had been from the reign of Henri II. *Mascarades* were the early favorites. These precursors to court ballets were not so much large costume dances, as the English word suggests today, but rather relatively small-scale parties in which nobles paraded, danced, sang, and recited poetry, using verses and songs given to them in written form; through their words and movements, they enacted a scripted, central narrative. During the sixteenth century, Catherine de Medici helped to import into France the Italian *mascherata*, a more elaborately staged and costumed type of performance that employed allegories for political effect, and helped to explode the scale and consequences of political ritual. New costuming, elaborate horse-drawn vehicles, and larger processions were grafted onto older court ceremonies and began to associate Valois rulers with Roman emperors or other figures from past periods of glory. Catherine de Medici also brought an Italian penchant for outdoor revelry to France, binding the garden and urban spaces more robustly to court ritual and politics. Theaters, triumphal arches, and obelisks were raised in Paris to create fictional spaces in which the king could stand simultaneously as heir to the Trojan line and contemporary ruler; the Tuileries gardens were transformed into stage sets for enacting genealogies of virtue and potency. With costumes and sets, past and present could collide and be fused in elaborate spectacles of power.[9]

The most developed theatrical devices were employed by Catherine de Medici and her son, Charles IX, as they faced daunting religious strife in France. In 1564, for example, Catherine held a set of jousts, *mascarades*, and fêtes at Fontainebleau, all organized around a timely theme: religious conflict undermining the power and moral authority of France. She tried to engender a spirit of religious tolerance in constructing as well as thematizing the parties; she had the famous Huguenot potter and garden designer Bernard Palissy, for example, construct many of the sets for her parties, including a glorious ceramic island he built at the Tuileries. His religious beliefs were not flaunted, but his position was known, and thus his work was (among other things) a way to make manifest the cultural value of Protestants in France. Unfortunately, Catherine de Medici lost her reputation as a religious peacemaker when Protestants accused her of plotting the St Bartholomew Day's Massacre and setting it off with an anti-Huguenot party. It is certainly true that her *Paradis d'amour*, performed August 20, 1572, presented a politically volatile theme: the nymphs of paradise being assaulted by knights who represented the Huguenots. A *carrousel* held the next day, which pitted Huguenot knights against their enemies in a series of military contests, symbolically brought the religious struggle that had only been danced the evening before closer to actual fighting. The combat of the *carrousel* was claimed to be organized to defuse tensions by transferring the extant political conflicts to a symbolic level, where they could be played out bloodlessly, but the results seem to have been disastrous. Three days later anti-Huguenot passions went out of control in the bloody massacre. Whatever the intentions of Catherine de Medici or the entertainments she organized, the belief that these spectacles were politically potent enough to cause the rioting demonstrates quite clearly how accepted these rituals were as political vehicles.[10]

Under Henri III, the ballet became a particularly elaborate medium for enacting and embodying a complex of cultural themes. Musical forms, traditions of religious and secular pageantry, *mascarades*, "momeries," and forms of ballets from earlier in the century were combined in the *ballet de cour* and helped to set this performative genre in the center of French cultural and political life. The *Ballet comique de la reine* that Henri III had mounted in 1581 contained not only political messages, but made political use of astrological and Platonic beliefs about the power of numbers and music as a means of creating human harmony and peace. It also expressed the struggle between reason and passion ubiquitous in classical and medieval stories, and conveyed these themes through a story pitting man against nature. All these cultural repertoires for linking human powers to superhuman ones had some standing in this event and helped to locate the *ballet de cour* as a serious and complex site for political reflection and expression.[11]

The scale and importance of court pageantry may have declined with the death of Henri III and the growth of Protestant influence in French court culture,[12] but the *ballet de cour* survived into the next century. Marie de Medici and Louis XIII both revived and restructured the form, re-establishing its position in the center of court cultural life. In this period, the dramatic, narrative elements of the ballet became secondary to the symbolic and decorative ones; movements were choreographed to set out *tableaux vivants* and other formal arrangements of bodies with symbolic significance. The techniques used in developing and decoding the ballets changed; ribbons were sometimes used to join together dancers so their movements would help to constitute geometrical figures with numerological significance. Audiences were given programs to help them recognize the meanings of the forms. Songs and recitations punctuated the dancing, coordinating the voice with the music and ritualized movements of the body. Even the point of viewing these events changed: the audience was supposed to gain moral and psychological value from considering the symbolism, rather than derive overt political messages from it. Through all these changes, however, the *ballets de cour* – these public displays of aristocratic vitality and excess – shored up the political hierarchy; the costumed dances with their elaborate meanings embedded the nobility in a world of action quite different from that of ordinary French men and women.[13]

Henri IV and Marie de Medici were also instrumental in restoring to the repertoire of court entertainments the *carrousels*, or feudal equestrian games, that had been common a century before. These contests became so stylized and highly costumed in the seventeenth century – with the performers taking on personas from literary sources, acting out stories of combat, and doing so using music, dancing and recitations – that

101. Le Bal Royal au Louvre de Louis XIII.

they, too, seemed much like *ballets de cour*. They blurred the line between dance movements and military practices in an interesting way, giving greater authority to the aristocratic culture that cherished both. Louis XIII, that devoted military man, became an aficionado of the ballet and seems to have taken pleasure in shaping his reputation through public performance. He even staged ballets regularly for the people of Paris – though the amount of public access was always limited. In spite of his playing to public tastes and audiences, however, the lines of power remained clearly drawn in these ballets; the events provided enough ceremonial pomp and elaborate production to separate the world of nobles and monarchical power from that of ordinary Parisians. The dances displayed the healthiest of noble bodies, too, shaped by good diet, dancing, and military exercise, which moved very differently from the bodies of most French women and men, whose carriage was shaped more by the trials of labor.[14]

It was against this cultural backdrop that the fêtes and *divertissements* of Louis XIV's reign were devised and the performance politics of the period took shape in the gardens of Versailles. It was clearly not the case that the king or his household were original in placing great emphasis on the use of parties, rituals, and performance at court for political purposes. Louis XIV had, as a young man, gained quite a reputation as a dancer in court ballets, and was quite vain about it; he certainly knew the pleasures of dance and had already detected the political significance of their elegance and symbolism.[15] It was also not the case that this was the first regime to place these performance forms in the garden to link social location to physical location. It was not the first time that elite bodies were trained to realize physical as well as social ideals of social superiority. What changed in this period was the character of the political goals at stake and the effectiveness with which these cultural possibilities were used politically. Promenades, rituals of daily life, parties, ballets, concerts, and processions became standard techniques for pursuing absolutism during the reign of Louis XIV; they helped to naturalize the shift in power to the state through placing rituals of social order in the highly ordered formal garden, which made the imposition of order itself seem natural; and they relegated the nobility to secondary support positions within French constellations of power by scripting them that way, thereby serving the process of transferring power to the state by visibly undercutting the autonomy of the nobility.[16]

The politics of pleasure under Louis XIV

The fêtes and *divertissements* at Versailles in the late seventeenth century were excellent examples of "politics by other means": the use of cultural forms to transfer issues of power to a symbolic plane where they could be played out, while decontextualized from ordinary political life.[17] In the baroque parties that predated and prefigured the early fêtes at Versailles, noble actors enacted traditional narratives that reaffirmed their power. As they engaged in the entertainments, participants were dressed and named as classical figures, medieval heroes, or elements of nature, taking on new but importantly elevated identities. These parties created what Alfred Schutz called a non-ordinary reality: a fictive world in which noble party-goers could enact their social superiority

102. Almanac depiction of a "bal" in the court of Louis XIV.

REX
ROMANORUM IMPERATOR.

103. Louis XIV as the Roman Emperor in the *Grand Carrousel* of 1662 (I. Silvestre).

where pleasure and politics could be elided.[18] Members of the nobility simultaneously escaped their everyday lives and entered a domain of manifest potency. They became (for the moment) makers of history, the forces of the world, or powerful heroes of the past. The fictive worlds of fêtes were meticulously constructed with stage sets as well as costumes and scripts. Complex mechanical devices, water-run automata, and scenery drawn using linear perspective helped to transform the gardens and halls of power into fanciful worlds in which the narratives for the parties could be realized. These literary-inspired concoctions tied the elites to greatness not just by asking them to take on appropriate costumes and to learn their lines, but by demanding that they *re-enact* heroic narratives of high rank, natural virtue, and social efficacy. This was serious play which demanded that aristocrats both appear to others and see themselves as social actors of consequence.[19]

During the first great fête in the gardens of Versailles from May 7 to May 14, 1664, when Louis XIV brought the elites of France to play his games and follow scripts written to please him, he enticed them to participate in an event that was ostensibly in this tradition, and apparently meant to consecrate the social significance of the nobility while amusing their senses. Nothing seemed to be lacking. Premier Gentilhomme de la Chambre, comte de Saint-Aignan, had assembled all the music, dance, costuming, food, stage sets, fireworks, and candlelight needed for a baroque spectacle. *Les Plaisirs de l'Isle enchantée* was appropriately made up of a number of discrete plays, dances, games and musical interludes which were roughly organized around a literary theme derived from a medieval romance that was easily wedded to classical themes. The story, taken from Ariosto's *Orlando Furioso*, described the enchantment and subsequent restoration to power of a warrior-hero, Roger. In this tale, Alcina, a magician, temporarily captures Roger on her island of delights. Her powers are great, and she holds him helpless in her spell, but in the end, his military virtues overcome her seductions. He defeats her allies and escapes, but (luckily for the party-goers) there is plenty of seductive pleasure to be had before this occurs.[20] There are equestrian games, music, dancing, feasting, theater, and finally, the fireworks that bring an end to Alcina's spell over Roger and her island. What better theme for an aristocratic party than a story of power! What better premise for a baroque party than magical enchantment!

In typical fashion for the period, the story of Roger's capture and escape from the spell of the sorceress was brought to life by members of the court, using elaborate stage sets, employing classical and fanciful costumes, and following pre-determined scripts. Bodies and voices, not just minds, were used to create the ritualized entertainment. With choreographed gestures and speeches often set in verse, nobles realized a dream world designed to please the king, delineating a space in which his powers could be felt.[21]

The relation of play and space in the event was of crucial importance. The fête took place in the newly refurbished gardens at Versailles, where Le Nôtre was already beginning to resculpt the contours of the landscape and organize elements of the natural world to make the king's territorial ambitions manifest. In this already enchanting site, theatrically sophisticated backdrops to the fantasy were constructed: a *carrousel* for the tournaments near the château, stages at the intersection of garden walkways for

Molière's plays, and even a set of rocky islands built behind and into the round pool at the end of the *petit parc* to serve as Alcina's island domain. For this fête, the arts and nature were joined to supply sites in which the court could enact narratives of power, covering the earth's surface with palaces and public stages on which the military strength and potential glory of France could be heralded. In the trees and walkways behind the château at Versailles, during this fête and long afterwards, workmen hammered, shoveled, planted, and otherwise tailored land to fit the political aspirations of the architects of the new France, setting out for public view some nascent dreams about the territorial possibilities of the state.[22]

The 600 or so aristocrats who attended *Les Plaisirs* began to arrive at Versailles on May 5, 1664. The château was still a small hunting lodge, and accommodation was in short supply, so most guests tried to find housing (not a simple or satisfactory process in this small town) and recover from their journeys before the festivities began. *Les Plaisirs de l'Isle enchantée* itself began on the evening of May 7 around 6.00 p.m. Directly beneath the château, where the Latona fountain now stands, a circle of combat (or list) was set out, and the official audience was seated before it. As curious onlookers from Paris stood and witnessed from the terrace, the king, dressed in Greek military gear and representing Roger, entered this circle on a breathtakingly beautiful and powerful horse. He was preceded by his page, the duc de Saint-Aignan, representing Guidon le Sauvage, and he was followed by the duc de Noailles, dressed as Oger le Danois, the duc de Guise as Aquilant le Noir, the comte d'Armagnac as Griffon le Blanc, the duc de Foix as Renaud, and others who arrived in order, representing different heroes. Their characters were made known to the assembled guests with a booklet, containing short verses describing the attributes of these figures. The commentaries included sometimes serious and sometimes humorous allusions to the nobles in costume, which amused as well as informed the witnesses to the events. The parade of warriors was followed by the arrival of a giant chariot, carrying Apollo with the Four Ages at his feet. The Age of Gold was played by Mme Molière, the Age of Silver by Hubert, the Age of Bronze by Mlle de Brie, and the Age of Iron by Du Croisy. The chariot was followed by other members of the court representing the twelve hours, and twelve signs of the zodiac. This great entrance was the start of medieval contests, known as *courses de bagues* and *courses de têtes*, which were played before and judged by Apollo. The marquis de La Vallière, the brother of the king's mistress, won the contest.[23]

When it was dark, the circle was lighted with candles, and Lully's musicians played while the Hours and Signs of the Zodiac danced. Then a procession of the four Seasons entered with the first season, Spring (Mlle du Parc), mounted on a Spanish horse, Summer (Sieur du Parc), placed on an elephant, Autumn (Sieur de la Thorillière) on a camel, and Winter (Sieur Béjard) on a bear. Finally, Diana and Pan (Molière) appeared, reciting verses for the Queen of France written by the playwright. The forces of nature and its creatures were thus paraded before the assemblage, summoning up the natural world to bestow its powers on the guests and royal family. Finally, the circus-like procession of exotic animals called the guests to a collation (of delicate foods and drink) set out for their indulgence.[24]

Marche du Roy, et de sa chevaliers avec toutes
leurs suitte au tour du Camp, de la course de

Première Journée.

bague representant Roger, et les autres chevaliers
enchantez dans l'Isle d'Alcine

104. The king enters as Roger on a great chariot to open up the games at the first fête (*L'Isle enchantée*) given at Versailles by Louis XIV (I. Silvestre, *Première Journée, Marche de Roy ... 1664*).

Premiere Iournée.

Comparse des quatre saisons, avec leury suite de confortans, et porteurs
de presens, et de la machine de Pan, et de Diane, avec leur suite de
Seruiteurs, dont Juihz et et.

Concertans, et de bergere portaus les plats pendant le recit des vers
et, des autres duuant le Roy, et les Reyns.

Dan Proal. 99a.

105. The parade of animals and servants after the carrousel, on the first day of the fête. (I. Silvestre, *Première Journée, Comparse de quatre saisons . . . 1664*).

The next night, a stage was set at an intersection of walkways in the garden, farther from the château. Tapestries were hung from a lath structure around the stage to keep the wind from blowing out the candles that provided lighting for the spectacle. Lully's music constituted the elaborate *intermezzos* commenting between acts on the characters in the play. The *Princesse d'Elide* was performed there with Molière himself in the role of Moron, the facilitator for the princess' education in love. In this *comédie-ballet,* the young princess Elide begins the play immune to the advances of young men interested in her, more enticed by hunting than erotic pursuits. She is inflamed into passion, however, by a young man whose coldness intrigues her. By artfully using her own techniques for shunning others, the young man is able to interest her in trying to seduce him. As she plots to win his favor, she finds herself falling in love. Love is presented in this story as a kind of natural truth, lying behind all the illusions and self-delusions of the players. It breaks down the barriers that stop appropriate mates from finding one another, and realizing their happiness.[25]

It is easy to see this light-hearted play as an allegory, legitimating the king's love for his mistress. The play celebrated love as a natural truth that ought not be denied. It even depicted the heroine as an avid hunter just like La Vallière. It certainly was meant, like Molière's other *comédie-ballets*, to contrast the clarity of love against the illusions of elite seductions and intrigues, but it was not just a legitimation of the king's passion. There was more political significance to it. The freedom to love was equated in this play (as elsewhere in Molière's work) with natural order. Lovers, according to Molière, necessarily eschewed unnatural tyranny but embraced legitimate obligations, freely accepted.

No wonder these comedy-ballets, assuming that the social order was natural, inevitable, and sanctioned by higher powers, were popular for fêtes where ritual expressions of noble power were physically installed into the natural world of the garden. Most of what was portrayed as natural in Molière's work suited the aristocratic audiences at fêtes. Only socially appropriate alliances were realized in these stories; nobles found true love in other nobles; and servants were drawn to the servants of their master's or mistress' love. Without hesitation, those of lower rank accepted their inferiority and facilitated the welfare of their "betters," while nobles were free to charm and be charmed by their peers of the opposite sex. Court audiences, whose social relations and positions were assumed in these stories, were not surprisingly charmed by the *comédie-ballets*. At the same time, they were seduced into believing that freely accepted affection was the opposite of tyranny.[26]

On the third evening of *Les Plaisirs*, another stage was constructed at the end of the Allée Royale at the far rim of the pond that would later be the site of the Apollo fountain. This became the enchanted lake and Alcina's magical island. The set must have been quite stunning. Vigarani, the Italian designer, who was particularly known for his technical effects, built a massive chain of rocky islands and a strange palace on and around which the narrative could progress. The evening's entertainment began with a concert played before the pool by Lully and his court musicians, and then Alcina arrived on a barge on the lake. To show her powers, she addressed the queen and queen mother in poetry, and with a wave of her hand (and the techniques of Vigarani) the lights went on in the enchanted palace. The demons, dwarfs and giants of her domain danced a ballet until Roger (no longer played by the king) arrived with his knights, stormed the castle, and initiated the final, great battle. Alcina's demons fought back, but Roger had a magic ring, and could not lose. The palace of Alcina was finally destroyed in a brilliant fireworks display planned by Vigarani. With this spectacle, the story of enchantment ended and Roger returned to his life as a warrior. The powers of war triumphed as the night sky was filled with dazzling, decorative, explosive charges.[27]

The traditional military power of noblemen was ratified both by the mock combat of the *courses de bague* and *courses de tête* and by the eventual success of the hero over Alcina. At the same time, the power of noble women was also proclaimed through the representation of Alcina as a seductress who could stop even great heroes in their tracks. The sorceress may have been overcome by Roger's powers in the end, but her magic was potent enough to control most of the narrative.

In spite of the elaborate staging and costuming efforts, this most famous fête was actually quite a hastily constructed extravaganza, and was never thoroughly contained within the story chosen as the theme. After three days, the tale of Roger was over, but the party had barely begun. The festivities tumbled out of the confines of the narrative, and an array of thematically unconnected sensual attractions and ritualized entertainments took over the party. The new events were less baroque confections, scripted by traditional narratives, than activities strategically and directly under the king's control. Roger triumphed in spirit as well as in the story of this fête, as social control overcame playful magic in the entertainments. The logistical skills and discipline that would come to dominate French political life made their way into this first great fête at Versailles.[28]

On the fourth evening, for example, another *carrousel* was set in the dry moat of the old château. This time the feudal contests had no god from Olympus to judge the games nor story from the past to legitimate the sport. Warrior skills were tested and rewarded unadorned by parades or scripts. The results were still meaningful. The high rank of the nobility remained linked by memory, if not deeds, to feudal knighthood. Acting as brave soldiers was enough pleasure and playing feudal games was enough expression of prowess to make the activity delightful, particularly in the afterglow of Roger's fictive victory.

The king won the contests at first, but graciously left the prize for others to pursue. After some time, the duc de Coislin finally defeated his other competitors, receiving a diamond from the queen's hand. The prize of jewelry put the exercise on the pragmatic plane of power and wealth which would soon become typical at Versailles. Once the court was permanently installed in this residence, the nobility was more thoroughly trained to play the king's games to win comparable prizes. Gambling would become an obsession of all-too-many courtiers, as their worlds of action were narrowed to Versailles. On this evening, in a prescient manner, the nobility gaily fought one another for royal rewards, while the king remained the only true winner. The fact that the victory for the duc de Coislin was gained only after the king declined the prize merely underscored the monarch's primacy and exemplified how noble successes could become dependent both on his victories and graciousness.[29]

Rupture du Palais et des enchantemens de l'Isle.   Troisieme Journée.   d'Alcine representé par un feu d'artifice.

I. mat. Silvestre, del, et ex.   Cum Privilegio Regis.

106. The fireworks on the third day of the fête, which destroyed Alcina's enchanted island, but did not end the party (I. Silvestre,
    Rupture du Palais et du enchantemens de l'Isle d'Alcine, 1664).

On the afternoon of the fifth day, the king led a promenade to the Ménagerie, the site of the king's collection of animals, which was particularly rich in exotic birds (see plate 92). An assemblage of elaborately dressed and elegantly mannered aristocrats, just as decorative as any of the feathered rarities at the Ménagerie, was routed through the gardens, past the *petit parc*, and to the octagonal structure where the captured exotics were housed. Members of this human entourage were taken to a second-storey balcony on the Ménagerie where they could view the creatures below. The octagonal shape of the structure gave it an oddly military form. Octagons, like pentagons, were common fortress shapes. This walled compound, however, was designed to hold its creatures inside, not keep enemies out, so it was made with thin stone walls, not bastions. In this, it was much like the emerging social world of Versailles, which kept the French aristocracy enclosed within a society that made their rare attributes visible to the world but kept them from exercising their powers.

Arrayed around the central building were eight walled compounds in which the animals lived. The decorative animals were kept there on permanent display. The visitors to the Ménagerie were encouraged to view the collection from the balcony, providing a model of panopticism that would later fascinate Foucault. The Ménagerie was not, however, just a means of surveillance of animals by their social superiors, but a place in which natural order was represented. The compounds separated different kinds of animals, and the central building set up a hierarchy of supervision. The medieval social hierarchy, which was assumed by the aristocracy to be still in force, had been founded on hierarchical relations between God and men and was supposed to be mirrored in the relations between men and the creatures. The Ménagerie seemed designed to evoke this whole structure of relations and meanings, providing a social lesson along with a pleasant view of exotic wildlife.[30]

The evening after this promenade, Molière and his troupe performed *Les Fâcheux*: one of the first *comédie-ballets* written by Molière. It had been part of the entertainment originally produced for the ill-fated fête at Vaux-le-Vicomte. The dramatic form itself, the combination of narrative comedy and short ballets, was the sort of novelty that Fouquet liked to patronize; it was light, pleasing, but also innovative. Using this piece for the first great fête at Versailles was an interesting choice. Natural order was once again central to the play, so it was continuous in theme and tone with Molière's *La Princesse d'Elide*. This play was less about love and more about the victory of pleasing behavior over willfulness. Although the *fâcheux* in this piece tormented the hero Eraste, even they regained stature in the end because of the beauty of their dancing. Submission to discipline, Molière was perhaps suggesting, could redeem even the most annoying of characters. This moral could have been an interesting elaboration of the message conveyed through the story of Roger and Alcina.[31]

In the afternoon of the sixth day, there was a lottery for the ladies. Gifts were awarded arbitrarily among those present. Being there could make the ladies potential recipients of the king's beneficence, but it was not enough to ensure it. This was the fundamental rule for nobles at Versailles, when the court was permanently seated there. Being at court was a necessary prerequisite to any favor, but it never did assure it. The rules of internal French politics under absolutism were visible on this day of the fête, not wrapped in some allegorical form, but directly enacted.[32]

That evening, Molière and his troupe performed *Tartuffe*. The play, still not in its final form, was nonetheless already quite unrelentingly critical of those of high social rank. It was a comedy, but it was not full of fun. The story line was serious and never punctuated with the dances and musical recitations of the comedy-ballets. This meant that problematic characters could never become endearing through their performance skills. Worst of all, the play raised the most threatening question haunting the nobility since the massive upward mobility of the last century. What was the basis for the social superiority of aristocrats? If birth was no longer the only source of high rank, if some positions could be bought by rich financiers, then how could high rank remain a legitimate form of social superiority?

The problem was presented in the play by having despicable and weak characters claim and seek high social rank. How were those who claimed natural virtue to be treated? Were they to be accepted as natural elites? Should aristocrats who were swayed by false piety continue to be treated as better than their servants who could see through it? How could proper social (or theatrical) order be restored when hierarchy was confused? The problems of rank were carried in period performances through a misalignment of voices and manners. In this social period, men of high standing were meant to have high voices to mark their rank.[33] In *Tartuffe*, the disreputable characters were disconcertingly given high-pitched voices. Worse, the bases for distinguishing truly superior persons were never convincingly established.

Unlike the baroque allegories that ratified the superiority of the aristocracy, this play made the power of elites problematic. It seemed an unlikely theme for a royal party. The king seems to have liked the play, perhaps because it suggested the necessity of absolutism to govern an aristocracy filled with more pretension than superiority. But he also agreed to ban its production since it so clearly undermined the credibility of nobles.[34]

Finally, on the seventh evening, the guests saw Molière's *Mariage forcé*. This was one of the most successful of Molière's comedy-ballets, integrating narrative, music and dance in a much more thorough manner than in the earlier pieces. It also explored much more systematically issues of deception, love, and natural order. A unifying theme for the piece was the suspect character of speech. All the major characters talked past each other. The resulting less-than-systematic misunderstandings gave the play its humor. The audience always knew more than the characters, simply because they listened to what they were saying. The laughter, however, contained a serious commentary on human communication: it pointed to the duplicitous possibilities of language, and the way egoism could prevent characters from wanting to hear or respond to the words of the others. Once again actions said more than words, and proper performance was heralded as a virtue. In the end, love triumphed against obstacles and freed hearts from the tyranny of others. To love and respect the truth of love, to reject talk as a site of deceptions and pretense, to dance and follow the body's wisdom, and to laugh at the follies of self and others were all themes of this play that made it a happy antidote to the seriousness of *Tartuffe*. It was a fine ending to a very long party.[35]

Molière's comedy-ballets kept the tone of these last days of the fête light and full of laughter, but nonetheless placed these delights more proximate to French contemporary life than the fictive space of Roland's *Isle enchantée*. Molière depicted French men and women in his writings, not gods and heroes. In *Tartuffe* he even showed familiar elites as potentially deceived or despicable hypocrites, and raised quite a row in doing so. But mostly he introduced characters in the ballets who were entertainingly weightless, close enough to songs on the evening breeze or gestures in empty conversation that they could be easily naturalized or forgotten. In Molière's fictional worlds, the seductive immediacy of the present may indeed have begun to overshadow the allure of the literary past, allowing some reflection on the political details of elite life, but the characters found in the comedy-ballets were trivialized by layers of baroque illusion. With the mixture of voice, dance, music, gesture, stagecraft, and posturing necessary for the form, the superficiality of the characters and artificiality of their actions seemed to make sense. The ritual formality of the *ballet de cour* and the serious social commentary of Molière's dramatic comedies could be forgotten in these moments. The comedy-ballets were above all designed to please the king and court by diverting them with spectacle and presenting a tamed social present in which magic, illusion, and power could coexist on the stage.[36]

Still, this fête sent the attendees away from Versailles carrying many important social lessons, some conveyed through Molière's works. They were certainly cautioned to act properly to avoid the kind of ridicule that was so devastatingly employed in Molière's plays. They were invited in this way to adhere willingly to a code of conduct that would help naturalize the social order and legitimate their high status in it. The fête also introduced the French aristocracy to a model of social etiquette for the court of Louis XIV. They were given prizes and pleasures in return for acting as obedient performers in the king's social rituals. They were trained already in a model of bodily discipline that had its roots in feudal military skills and traditional *ballet de cour*. They were now enjoined to enact their social superiority through similar kinds of body-based court rituals, and not cultivate their voices and political ideas. Happily for the king and his ministers, this system of discipline in the context of seventeenth-century France kept nobles at court and restrained them from seeking autonomous bases of power.

In seven days, then, a social script for the nobility was written for this reign. On the eighth day, the court left for Fontainebleau.[37]

Seduction at the gardens of Versailles

One can see these festivities in the gardens at Versailles just as they were portrayed in the press of the period: as pleasant relief from warfare and politics. The *Fête de l'Isle enchantée* was produced by and for a young king, who had surprised the nobility with his willingness to fight in war, stunned his ministers with his insistence on ruling France himself, and was gaining some political legitimacy because of his early successes in leading the French army on the battlefield. This young monarch, in taking the reins of power so authoritatively, seemed to be trying to bring power back to the nobility in France after a long period in which real power had been wielded primarily by two churchmen, Cardinals Richelieu and Mazarin.[38] For all his seriousness, the monarch was nonetheless young, and was a man of appetites, seemingly capable of thoroughly enjoying his diversions. Wanting to throw a good party for the nobility, whom he seemed ready to champion, was perfectly in character for this saucy monarch, an innocent extension of his love for his position, his mistress, and his hunting lodge.

According to most narrators of the French past, the *Fête de l'Isle enchantée* was not about politics at all, but about passion and betrayal. This party was nominally in honor of the queen and queen mother, but was really for Louise de La Vallière, the king's mistress. Contained within the usual narrative about Louis XIV's reign, which follows Saint-Simon in highlighting the passion and intrigue at court, La Vallière was the real enchantress, not Alcina, whose power was made so manifest in the gardens in May, 1664. This sensuous celebration was about sexual seduction and deceit, or (the positive version) lusty sensuality and appetite. From this perspective, the fête was a means of managing the king's love life, playing erotically on his position of power and his desires. Admittedly, this king was unbridled in his passions and breathtakingly extravagant in his gestures, but it is still hard to believe that a full week of collations, processions, plays, dances, and military contests was only a delicious seduction for one woman. Louis XIV had after all held a *carrousel* in the courtyard of the Tuileries in honor of La Vallière in 1662; she was already his mistress. Although he was certainly pleased by her, the fête at Versailles seemed more a play within a play within a play. A tribute to the queen and queen mother was pretext for the seduction of La Vallière, and the enchantment of (and by) the king's mistress was part of a larger seduction of the aristocracy by a politically as well as sexually passionate young king. La Vallière's story pointed to the deception structured into the event, but it also diverted attention from the manipulation of the nobility – their enchantment for Roger's glory.[39]

Allusion to and diversion from the political aspects of the spectacle at hand were written into the script for the fête itself. When the first *carrousel* was about to start, Apollo addressed the queen with the following lines:

> Contre tant de grandeur, contre tant de vertu,
> Tous les monstres d'Enfer vnis pour ta deffense
> Ne feroient qu'vne foible et vaine resistance:
> L'Vniuers opprimé de ton joug rigoureux,
> Va gouster par ta fuite vn destin plus heureux:
> Il est temps de ceder à la Loy souueraine
> Que t'imposent les voeux de cette auguste Reyne;
> Il est temps de ceder aux trauaux glorieux
> D'vn Roy fauorisé de la Terre et des Cieux:
> Mais icy trop long-temps ce different m'arreste,
> A de plus doux combats cette Lice s'apreste,
> Allons faire ouurir, et ployons des Lauriers,
> Pour couronner le front de nos fameux Guerriers.40

[Against this assembled company filled with virtue and grandeur, the monsters of Hell, even if united, would offer only feeble and vain resistance. The universe, crushed by its bondage, now has a happier future to anticipate. It is time to obey the sovereign law, and realize the prayers of this great queen. It is time to give oneself over to the glorious works of a king who is favored by the earth and the heavens. For too long I have been held back from preparing myself for combat in the list. Let us open the games and make way for the laurels to crown the forehead of our famous warriors.]

This monologue makes clear that politics was not abandoned in this fête. The king's right to power was both the reason why this assembly of nobles was sanctioned and why the queen has to be the formal addressee of all the activities. It was her dreams, her prayers for France, that constituted the underlying justification for this show of power – both in the list on this day and in the other events to come. The queen represented the political passion for French glory at work in this event.

If the real enchanted island was Versailles (as Molière himself suggested) and the fête was an opportunity for Louis XIV to capture the aristocracy through pleasure,[41] it seems odd that the theme underlying the occasion would alert the nobility to the dangers of submission. Roger fought off his enchantment. But there was no reason for the nobility in that moment to fear the spell of Versailles. They were, after all, enjoying the allegories of love, and gossiping about the king's feelings for La Vallière. Even though they had been essentially *summoned* to appear at Versailles when they received invitations to the fête, the nobles were not reluctant to come. The occasion was clearly going to be a delight, a confection of large proportions; it was also going to be interesting to see how the king could salute simultaneously his mother, wife, and mistress. Those who were to take part in the processions, games and plays, putting on costumes and playing roles, were not frightened as much as honored by their selection. If the king and his island enraptured the nobility and made it temporarily subservient, what could it matter? Even Roger would free himself in the end. The aristocracy could have had no sense of how prescient the story of enchantment would have been.[42]

The progression of events at Versailles in early May of 1664, the limits and possibilities of the literary technologies and techniques of the body that unfolded through the week, only gestured toward the complicated and politically charged tale of power that was beginning to unfold in France at this time. As the events of *Les Plaisirs* transpired, there were hints of the political stakes being wagered: themes of obedience and social order began in the second half of the events to undermine the theme of noble potency suggested by the story of Alcina and Roger. The nobles who came to the fête, play-acting, costuming, reading lines written for them, and sitting, fighting, walking, and eating according to prescribed patterns, no doubt enjoyed themselves but also unwittingly participated in rituals of their submission. The structured entertainments seemed at the time only means for having a bit of fun, but eventually these very activities would help contain the power of the nobility and keep this group effectively outside of French political life, serving state absolutism.

Not just in this one fête but throughout the reign, the spectacles of power moved from baroque playfulness to disciplinary seriousness – from the extraordinary to the ordinary, from allegorical dramas to carefully choreographed rituals of daily life, from realms of the fictive to political regimen, from mythology to history, where the enactment of power could be rawly presented.[43] In 1668 and 1674, two great *divertissements* were held at Versailles – both to mark military victories. The themes for these events

107. A concert during the *Divertissement* of 1674, showing the use of garlands, potted plants, and more decorative elements in the gardens (Le Pautre).

were recent heroic military action and geographical expansion of French territory by contemporary soldiers. They were not stories of past heroism by medieval or classical warriors. The participants may have donned antique costumes to invoke the image of France as the new Rome, but narratives from ancient times were not to be celebrated here. The story of France's contemporary greatness was told through an evocation of the gods and heroes of the past, who pointed to the grandeur of France and the glory of the king. The park at Versailles was transformed for these parties into a fairy-land of abundant delights – not to transport the participants to other times and places, but to present contemporary France as rich in natural resources, cosmopolitan tastes, and cultural sophistication. In 1668, pear, orange, and other fruit trees were set out along the walkways in the garden, filled with fruit and placed in silver vessels made in Gobelins style; even the excessive food for the occasion was made symbolically more potent here. A tableau of figures was fashioned from the foods set out for a collation. It was playfully (but intentionally) demolished by the guests after they had satisfied their hunger and the king had left the area.[44] In 1674, the level of consumption and display increased, and the celebration of France as a military power was more central to the event.There was theater, dancing, and an abundance of music in the program that showed off French work in these media. The classical allusions in the events were plentiful enough, but without a narrative structure organizing the diverse events, one could say that this *divertissement* had abandoned the impulse in fêtes to enact a dream-world of power. But there was, nonetheless, a fictional aspect to the *divertissement*. It projected an imagined and desired France; it used the magic of the fête to locate France through its military might, classical inheritance, territorial control, and cultural grace. The ritual enactment of French greatness did not, of course, bring to life an imagined community, a French nation, but it nonetheless conjured up a culturally defined place of power. This France was naturally abundant, divinely blessed, militarily potent, aesthetically cultivated, socially superior, and materially located in the landscape. It was a France appropriate to the territorial state. The *divertissements* made the line between fact and fiction more slippery, and made the fête a much more directly political event. Even the reasons for the *divertissement* were pragmatically political. The king wanted to provide relief and rewards for the nobles who had been fighting for the state too long. They had missed the pleasures of Carnival season in winter because of the war. Now that it was summer, they needed some pleasure. With victory at hand, a party was appropriate and possible. No wonder the party that was thrown celebrated a victorious, elegant, and magically powerful France.[45]

One could downplay the political importance of the second *divertissement* (1674). It was designed for pleasure of the king's second mistress, the elegant and discreet Mme de Montespan, and had the subtlety, grace, and lack of passion for which she was known (and admired). But the king had never been adverse to aligning his sexual and political powers, and giving Mme Montespan's tastes a public stage at Versailles was not a politically inconsequential act. This event more than any other helped to bring French *taste* to the forefront of French politics. On the fifth day of the fête, the most elaborately staged and fantastically designed ritual took place. M. de Gourville, in the name of the prince de Condé, presented to the king 107 flags taken from the enemy at Seneffe. The court then entered carriages and took a tour of the gardens, surveying this piece of France's land. They attended a fabulous collation, which was followed by a play. At the end of this evening of extravagance, where militarism merged with French taste, there was a huge display of fireworks over the grand canal.[46]

The *divertissements* were formally dedicated to French military victories, but informally also expressed French cultural prowess through massive displays of goods. The nobles were required to attend this party in costume, dressed as Olympian gods. They did not have to engage in any staged narrative of power in this guise. The point was not to create an allegory, but to show off French nobles in a fantastic display of wealth, taste, and learning. Symbolically, the costuming could elevate the French nobility to the status of godlike figures on the European stage. More concretely, the clothes marked their bearers as the rightful leaders of European fashion. Perhaps the expense of outfitting themselves for these celebrations contributed to what Elias described as the impoverishment and political marginalization of the French aristocracy, but this was hardly the message of the event. It was probably not even what participants thought was important about it. As the guests showed off their glittering attire, they ratified their cultural power along with the state's new configuration of political power. They connected French possibilities of empire with the luxuries from French manufactures, adding to the political complexity of this *divertissement*.[47]

André Félibien, official historian of the king's buildings, said in his *Relation de la Feste de Versailles* in 1674 that a Roman once claimed that it took a great man to create

108. Collation in the park of Versailles during the *Divertissement* of 1674, show
culture were displayed. Once again garlands are conspicuous, helping to de

ks, candelabras, vases, decorative plates, elaborate costumes, and other items of French
ents as celebrations of military valor (Le Pautre, *Festin donné dans le petit Parc de Versailles*, 1678).

a great festival for his friends, just as it took a great man to defeat his enemies. Félibien obsequiously maintained that the festival of victory of 1674 showed the king's capacity for both. The manifest point of the *divertissements* for Félibien was to show the king to be as heroic and worthy of a great empire as any ancient emperor or warrior. France was destined to be the new Rome, carrier of the Great Tradition, and the next center of leadership for all Europe.[48] The *divertissements* made this ambition clear. They were staged in some bosquets that had been recently refurbished by Le Nôtre, where French taste and power could be seen invested in the landscape. A glorious *arc de triomphe* was placed in a bosquet at Versailles facing a new statue representing France. Nature and art made this corner of the garden a tribute to both the art and military power of France. At this site, during the *divertissements*, newly acquired territories were ritually given to the king by the prince de Condé.[49]

Thousands attended these events; accounts like the one by Félibien and prints engraved by Jean Le Pautre carried the story of these evenings farther. France as a military and cultural powerhouse was depicted in the propaganda campaigns of the period to make France's achievements seem even more impressive than they were.[50]

The nobles who participated in these court festivities gave their bodies (and not just avowed political allegiance) over to France, its monarch, and its territorial power. Whatever their personal or political feelings about the king (which seem to have been more often edgy or hostile than not), they engaged in whatever events he deemed necessary for the glory of France. They took to their horses for feudal games when the king told them to, they danced when he requested it, they sang, they acted out parts in pageants, they recited poetry, and they took on the roles (both political and fictive) that he and his ministers assigned to them. They performed a political function in all these cases merely through their obedience. In exchange for the right to participate, they gave up their political voice. It is not that they said nothing in their daily lives. They wrote and talked endlessly. They tried to influence the king or his ministers. But they had no standing to speak outside the context of the king's will. Moreover, what they spoke publicly was often scripted by state authority. They learned lines in plays, sang songs composed by others, and recited poetry handed to them by the king's literary advisors. They taught themselves to value new attributes in themselves, new markers of their true nobility. Books of etiquette were written for the noble man of France, an "honest man" or *honnête homme*, whose "natural virtue" became apparent when he developed pleasing ways of speaking and the physical grace to make an attractive presence at court. (The relationship of this image to women at court is not so clear. Was this "man" generic or gendered?) What is clear is that this man was to be honest, but not in the modern bourgeois sense of that term: someone who tells the truth. This man did not really have to speak at all – or at least not think up his own lines. He was supposed to be an unaffected actor like Molière, who could seem perfectly real and know exactly how to act within prescribed social roles and specific situations. Improvising or rendering appropriate lines with simple grace in a way that would please everyone constituted the height of *honnêteté*. This honest actor was a person with manners, who could follow fashions, and make ritual life proceed successfully along its scripted course. This was a socially mobilized body whose voice was made useful to power by being trained to please.[51]

The underlings at court also participated in this ritual life, although not within the cult of *honnêteté*. They, too, took on costumes and played out roles, only doing so while engaging in other jobs. Servants brought food to table in the gardens and musicians played for the entertainment of king and court while dressed to add to the atmosphere of the event. Some rituals required some hidden efforts of the staff as well. A few underlings, for example, had to come into the gardens during the night in the middle of a fête, after the nobility had left, to construct the stages for the next day's plays or concerts. But the support personnel was surprisingly integrated into the fantasy worlds of royal parties, performing in costume, and carrying their burdens with a ritualized choreography that added greatly to the pomp at court. This performative culture of power was socially more inclusive than exclusive, even while it celebrated hierarchy. At the early fêtes, people from Paris came to watch the festivities from the terrace behind the château, and peasants from the area were set in the trees to witness the grandeur of the king and his court. Their mute presence added to the construction of a public space without voice, filled with ritual and music and carefully scripted speech. The sweeping political dramas of noble superiority and efficacy could only carry their messages when other people were willing to watch, and the court could only make its claim to be the center of French life if other French men and women ratified the rituals and cared about their meanings. The gardens at Versailles, were made public so the political relations there could be witnessed, not hidden. The gardens were both a stage set and political ally, not a retreat, so the rituals of submission and obedience that took place there would make visible and dramatic the new form of state-based politics and the authority of the king as its head.[52]

Casting the nobility in the play of power

The resulting performative politics of the late seventeenth century may seem odd to contemporary eyes, if we take the public sphere – an image of political equals discussing ideology – as our model of politics.[53] If we take for granted (as social scientists often do) that ideology shapes consciousness, and collective political behaviors result from belief, and if we imagine political realities to be woven primarily through words, then, of course, politics by performance seems to be hardly a kind of politics at all. But as anyone from the theater can testify, realities (political or otherwise) can be created through gestures as well as words. And the seventeenth-century French court with its comedies of manners was a fine site for a kind of politics of manners, in which political realities were projected and embodied through collective performance.

If the dramaturgical school of social theory is to be believed, performative forms may actually be more common than we think in social life – even in politics. Much face-to-face interaction is self-consciously performed behavior, planned and sometimes even rehearsed for specific audiences and occasions. Politics is much the same – just with more pretense. Political groups in the twentieth century often hold demonstrations to show the ties of members to political positions and to make visible the size of their membership. The speeches ubiquitous to demonstrations are often less powerful political statements than the size and energy of the crowds, for example, the embodied commitment of participants to the events themselves.[54]

Group life in general, according to Erving Goffman, emerges from mutually chore-ographed performances. We use performative forms to signal our intentions and expec-tations of others; we use tie-signs such as touching and mutual glances to make visible social bonds; we use stares and grimaces to tell others on the road or on the sports field what we are going to do next.[55] This gestural level of social interaction may not seem politically important unless we realize how often diplomats look for signs and gestures behind statements in order to determine the "real" political relations behind the expressed positions among nations. Signs of friendship are sought in the meetings among heads of state; arms build-ups in one country are read as communicative acts that influence military policy in others. This is not to say that political ideology and position statements have no authority in politics, but it makes the point that politics has been and remains in part a domain of performance, and hence the performative politics of the seventeenth century was not quite so strange a part of our political ancestry as it might appear at first blush.[56]

The turn toward territorial politics in seventeenth-century France gave performance new significance in that historical period. The marking of territories, and the mobi-lization of spaces as political tools could not be entirely accomplished through lan-guage and voice. One could claim control of some land in public statements, as when Louis XIV claimed the right of succession to the Spanish throne, but that could not and did not end the story; it only started it. The words could have little standing if the speaker did not have the resources to act on them, or could not do so effectively. The capacity to control the land itself always had to be demonstrable behind the claim to power, and in the case of the Spanish succession, could not be produced by France.[57] Just as military parades in the present are used to claim a fighting capacity to enforce political will, the military games, processions, and allusions in French ritual life of the seventeenth century were some of the means (short of warfare itself) for communicat-ing comparable strength to a political world dealing in territorial power.[58]

The French aristocracy was used as a vital and elegant political medium for the pursuit of state-based absolutism. Nobles were made effectively and subtly into a kind of local social resource for the new political system; their cooperation with the regime was part of what could make France in this period into a force on the European stage. Through their cultivation as courtiers, nobles demonstrated that they, like French ter-ritory, now belonged to France, its political system, and the crown. Using Goffman's language, this aristocracy presented itself as a politically rehearsed team, aligned behind the king and state, using a specialized language of gestures (etiquette) and an aesthetic of performance (both of costume and choreography) that conveyed publicly their ties to France.[59] Nobles with their court-based ways of life were making them-selves just as French as the statues in the gardens. They acted less like cosmopolitan elites from other states or regional political leaders with provincial interests, and more like members of a French society and culture. Nobles who changed their residences to Versailles allowed themselves to be "items" collected by the king and shown off to foreign visitors. They became like the rare orange trees or the birds of the Ménagerie.

There they participated in the social life of this complex court, and through their obedience to its social forms, constituted Versailles as the central showplace for displaying the absolutist state's power over the land, people, and politics of France.

We can learn more about the training of the nobility for their role in the construction of French "greatness" from a short play by Molière, "L'Impromptu de Versailles."[60] In it, some actors, supposed ladies and gentlemen of the court, were preparing to perform for the king. While the "Impromptu" was apparently just describing preparations for a fête, the lessons about aristocratic performance and court life went well beyond this. Molière, as always, found important political patterns in the private lives of elite French men and women. The "Impromptu" reveals a backstage behind the court of Louis XIV, where the playwright, having stripped away the smooth surface of the court's performance culture, has laid bare its skeleton. The audience, instead of being greeted by a glittering, finished extravaganza showing the brilliance of the playwright and the perfection of court entertainment, finds actors in disarray fearing imminent failure.

As the story opens, the actors are at a rehearsal, starting to read the text for a new play by Molière. It is not clear that the writer has even completed his script; he is distracted and suffering from some stinging criticism received from fellow playwrights. The actors have clearly just begun to look at their lines, and Molière has not yet had time to go over their parts with them. The problem is that the king is expected soon; the actors are beginning to get desperate; Molière is ready to improvise, but finds his players less than sanguine about this possibility.

> BRIE: What would you have us do? We don't know our Parts, and I think you have a Mind to make us Mad, to oblige us to play thus.
> MOL: O what strange Creatures to be governed are Actors![61]

The problem that Molière faces in the play is *government*, getting actors to do what they should before the king. The desperate actors want directing, some social regulation to retrieve order from disorder and self-assurance from confusion. The actors are more than ready to give up autonomy to achieve this goal; they are clearly not prepared to improvise or act on their own; they claim they will go mad without being fed their lines. Molière tries to calm them down by pointing out how they can indeed improvise; they are supposed to play social types that are all familiar to them, so they ought to be able to craft their parts by evoking what they have repeatedly seen around them. They can play off of one another, using the rules of social decorum to guide them. He sees the project as simple, but this is not what the actors feel. They complain that they need to be *told what to say and how to say it.* They want more than social rank to tell them how to act; they want *lines* to tell them what to say. Molière explains that what they really need to do is please the king. He says:

Kings love nothing so much as a ready Obedience, and hate to meet with Obstacles. Things are never good but just when they desire them, and to defer their Diversion, is to deprive it of all the Agreeableness with Respect to them. They'd have Pleasures which may not make 'em wait, and what is least prepared, is always most pleasing to them. We ought never to regard our own Conveniency in what they desire of us; all our Business is to please, and when they lay any

Commands on us, 'tis our Duty to improve with speed what they Desire. We had better acquit our selves soon enough; and if we have the shame of not succeeding, we have however the Glory of a quick Obedience.[62]

The problem of pleasing the king is transformed. He wants ready obedience, so they must comply no matter how awkward that makes them feel. The players want to be well prepared, but if the king desires performances to be delivered on time rather than to be well polished, then they will try to meet his expectations. No personal expression of discontent or point of view is pleasing to the king, so it is not what they should indulge in now. The players are stirred to action, and the rehearsal begins.

In rehearsal, Molière teaches his actors less about the lines they must speak than about effective social performance: the *politesse* of *honnêteté*. Molière reveals indirectly the aesthetics of proper courtly grace: artifice made pleasing through feigning authenticity. In admiring the work of one player he says, "Do you see how natural and passionate this is? Admire the smiling Countenance which she preserves in the greatest Afflictions."[63] An apparently funny contradiction between behavior which appears to be natural and what the audience and players know is entirely artificial carries a more-than-serious message about life at court. If a good performance is a pleasing one, then a "natural" performer will be pleasing even under the greatest afflictions. The highest achievement of a truly superior actor is a role that is well-played even when it goes against the feelings of the player. The individual must therefore have and seek no personal voice. The only hope is to achieve a graceful style within the given lines. Style alone can make the actor stand out. Choreography and song replace voice; both are modes of pleasing using physical discipline to achieve graceful performance. Rehearsal is necessary not so much for learning what lines mean, but for realizing a pleasing style that could make a performance at court both a delight and tribute to the king. The desire to please is the proper countenance of a courtier or courtesan and at the heart of good etiquette, on stage and off.

As in many of his other plays, Molière points to the problematic nature of social standing in this time and place. Social mobility, enhanced by the disempowerment of the nobility, is making proper performance and dignified behavior a problem even for those of high rank. "The Marquis now is the Jest of the Comedy. And as in all the ancient Plays, there was a Buffoon Servant, that made the Audience laugh; so now in all our Pieces there must be a ridiculous Marquis to divert the company."[64] Social types who would have been too important to laugh at before are now fair game for comedy, making clear enough that ridicule and exile from polite society are the threatened consequence of improper performance. Ridicule is the police power of the performer's life; it is the critic's voice that associates virtue with a well-made illusion. This critical culture, focused on gesture and decorum, turns the attention of participants away from politics to style, from the exercise and expression of political will to the niceties of performance. Molière indicates in an off-handed manner how vacuous this cultural system could be, but he also makes visible how terrifyingly important it was to participants. Saint-Simon would later indicate in his diary how much this anxious world of performance at court, organized around disdain and laughter, came to fill up the days of the courtiers at Versailles.[65]

Molière in the "Impromptu" also shows how surprisingly impersonal this system could be. He claimed explicitly that the secret of the comedy of manners was to get the audience to laugh at the foibles of the people of the age, not individuals. And while we know that he was indeed using his position as playwright to make fun of specific enemies, he did this by trying to construct a social type that would contain their weaknesses.

[M. Molière claimed] that all the Personages he represents are random Characters, and Phantoms which he dresses as he pleases, to delight his Spectators. That he shou'd be sorry if he had mark'd any body in them; and if any thing was capable of disgusting him against writing Plays, 'twas the Resemblance which People are always pretending to find in 'em ... As the Business of a Play is to represent in general all the Faults of Men, and principally of those of our Age, 'tis impossible for Molière to make any Character but what may hit somebody in the World; and if he must be accus'd of aiming at all the Persons who are guilty of the Faults he describes, he must certainly leave off writing plays.[66]

Individuals in his plays tend to make themselves ridiculous through social gaffes that were familiar enough to typify this age of social mobility: poor manners, inappropriate clothing, and unpleasant speech. We know that when Molière described specific persons in his plays, he was using laughter (like any other courtier) as a weapon in the social jockeying for position in the court.[67] This feigning of impersonality to mask social manipulation was just like the feigning of proper emotions that Molière praised in his actors. It was a technique of those who made appearance at court into a way of life. The fawning characters described and ridiculed in his comedy of manners were equally clay for the playwright's fantasies and for the king's performances of power: dolls to be dressed, inhabitants of named social positions, keepers and breakers of manners, and measures of human weakness in the face of power. They were, in sum, courtiers: phantom actors, social markers, who embodied pleasing forms of action, caught within the net of court etiquette.

At the end of the "Impromptu," an emissary of the king comes to announce the sovereign's approach long before the rehearsing has been satisfactorily completed. The ladies refuse to play, the male actors are confused, and all seems lost, but the king defers the performance until they are ready. Molière claims to have found new life in the king's kindness, and exits to go and thank the monarch for his goodness. The moral of the story is revealed in all its complexity: all depends on the king's goodness and so performers must make his goodness evident to the world.[68]

In the ritually elaborate late court of Louis XIV, the need for good actors, manners, and rehearsal was everywhere. The smallest moves in the king's day were inscribed through elaborately choreographed displays. Nobles in these events could not be spontaneous; they had routes to follow and roles to play. To seek some power or favor, they had to wait through ritual moments for the opportune time to whisper to the king some request for self, family, or friend. They appeared on cue; they bowed; they whispered; the king spoke. Molière's comments on performance, the need for rehearsal, self-control, courtesy, decorum, and the like were not just issues for his fictional actors waiting to come on stage, but – particularly late in this regime – essential modes of social discipline within the French aristocracy.

The routinization of political spectacle

It was in May of 1682 that state policy made Versailles into the permanent seat of the French court. Public life there took on the scripted character of fêtes – but without all the baroque fantasy or fun. There were stately processions, scripted promenades, contests, plays, music, gambling, and costumed dances – all of which had contributed to the delights of *Les Plaisirs*. There was even an increase in masked balls after Marie Adelaide (the future dauphine, duchesse de Bourgogne) came to Versailles. Some of the elaborate costuming and decorous wildness of the early fêtes were reproduced for the delight of this young adventuress, but, for the most part, entertainments were routinized in the 1680s. Solemn rituals surrounding the sovereign's body provided a rhythm and a vacuous content to much of court life. Seductions, intrigues, and gambling might have broken the monotony at Versailles for some courtiers, but they only bored others. The land of France was stabilized, and so was the terrain of ritual and even sensuality on which the social stabilization of power was built.[69]

Why did the nobles succumb to this regimentation, particularly when it meant a degradation of their lives, autonomy, and social importance? Why did they put up with their cramped quarters in this cold and damp valley? There was little else they could do. With state-based absolutism in place, they had to be at court to be socially vital persons, and this required obedience. They had lost the means to rebel. They could not requisition soldiers on their own account but only for the state, so they had lost their independent military power. They could only engage in business – provided, of course, that they were given special dispensation by the state; otherwise, if they tried to profit from trade, they lost their tax exemption. They could get monies from the state, if they were obedient to the king, but this undermined their independence. The privileged aristocratic families moved to Versailles, and those who were left out begged to be included. Elite power and well-being were now intertwined with state power, so all those who could came to Versailles where they could pursue their new constrained interests.[70]

This political mobilization of the aristocracy for the state required their exclusion from political power. The king did not want important nobles in important positions in the state, since they could challenge his authority, if they gained too much power. So nobles at court were given no serious administrative tasks to perform, and little diplomatic work. They had temporary assignments or military roles to play but the important posts in the central council were held by bourgeoise or impoverished nobles who were "ever-so-grateful" to the king. For the apparently pampered but isolated nobility at Versailles, the boredom of their impotence was unspeakable. Any little change, any sign of favor from the king, any chance to take part in another ritual, or any possibility of dressing up and acting as someone else was a relief from the tedium. Aristocrats developed what Molière described as the desire to be governed just like actors, not so much because they lost the will to speak for themselves and thirsted to be given lines; rather, they wanted to be given parts so they could move, so they could act at all, even if they were play-acting or engaging in ritualized motions.[71]

The gardens at Versailles must be understood as sites for this formulaic order of sim-

ulation if they are to be comprehended as a means of doing politics. They helped to
constitute a politically potent public space – not one where political voices could be
put in conversation with one another, but one through which coached bodies moved
and empty eyes monitored their mutual coordination. This was a site for choreography, not ideology, or perhaps more accurately, choreography as ideology. Like the
king's progress, rituals mobilized space and bodies at the same time, coordinating them
to dream into existence a new France. Body politics was a politics of enactment of
scripts for courtly behavior. It was a highly skilled regulatory practice that built worlds
of power from public coordination.

As much as the king was part-orchestrator of this regime of spectacle, he was also
caught in it. The monarch of a great absolutist state had to be absolutely great. The
strain was enormous, as we can tell from the diaries of his physician. The fears, psy-
chosomatic pain, exhaustion, and physical stresses of his life made the king particularly fond in later life of his medicines containing his *opiat* of soothing herbs. The
robotic life of power in the temple of the Sun King could only be faced, it seemed,
through a slightly drugged haze. An astoundingly routine set of solemnities, so elaborate that even the word "baroque" does not begin to contain it all, replaced the occa-
sional fête or *divertissement* at Versailles and provided the contours for the days of the
Sun King. Every morning, Louis XIV was wakened at 7.30 a.m. by his *valet de chambre*
and took his beloved morning medicine. From the moment, soon after, when the cur-
tains around his bed were pulled aside and the "princes of the blood" and grand officers
of the crown were let into his chamber, the king's movements were ceremonially ritualized. Louis XIV assumed his mantle of power and enacted his absolute authority
with the discipline of the seasoned dancer that he was. There was no more room in his
day for personal concerns – any more than there was for his noble entourage. He might
rant and rail in his negotiations with other leaders in Europe; he might be horrifyingly
demanding and narcissistic in his command of servants, family members, and
courtiers; but his absolute authority caught him in a painful web of demands as well.
Perhaps it served him right. Nonetheless, every part of even his rising and dressing was
ritually witnessed by members of the court.[72]

At 8.00 a.m. the first *levée* began in front of the small group of intimates mentioned
above. Louis XIV washed his face and hands and heard a mass even before he left his
bed. He then would rise, and, while washing, choosing a wig, and shaving himself,
allowed members of the inner circle to approach him with their problems. As he sat on
his toilet chair, he listened to their entreaties, and prepared for the second *levée*: his
entrance into public life. Courtiers who had been chosen for the second *levée* were
allowed to enter the chamber, where they could watch and assist the king with his
breakfast of broth, water, or watered-wine and bread. Then the king took off his night-
shirt and robe, and his son or a comparable member of the royal family would supply
him with his shirt for the day. Finally, his servants would bring the rest of his clothing.
Once dressed, Louis XIV would be touched with holy water and begin his morning
prayers. These completed, he held his first council of the day and began his morning
of work.[73]

The favor shown to courtiers by being invited to the second part of the *levée* was so great that even the rather contemptuous Saint-Simon speaks solemnly and respectfully about the few occasions on which he was able to attend. These intimate rituals provided access to the king, a place to speak with him privately perhaps, or at least to be near him and witness his glory. These were times to be treasured by those rarely invited and to be dreaded by the many required to attend day after day and year after year.[74]

While the king was working, the other members of the court would begin assembling in the Galerie, waiting, as usual, for something to happen. There they would show their deference to the king as he would pass on the way to the chapel to hear morning mass with the queen and other members of the royal family. He returned by the same route, and then made himself available to those who wanted to talk to him or present him with petitions. The king would then spend some time with the court before sitting down for his midday meal.[75]

Even though this midday meal was usually *petit couvert* (a small but formal event), he and perhaps the queen were still the only ones fed there. The rest of the participants, the few courtesans and family members invited into his chamber, were there to facilitate in the ritual or to watch. Close members of his family, namely his brother or son, would serve him at table. There was certainly plenty for the guests to watch. The scale of these meals can be better appreciated by learning that 498 servants were employed just to serve the king's table. The scale of food consumption that the king was able to manage (to show his prowess in this as well as other areas of physical activity?) is almost impossible to believe. For one lunch, after the soups, the king was presented with *entrées* consisting of twenty-eight pounds of veal and twelve pigeons. These were followed with *petites entrées*, including three partridges, six meat pies, two turkeys, and three chickens. For the roast course, he was served two capons, nine chickens, nine pigeons, two baby chickens, six partridges, and four meat pies. (The comparable supper had only two capons, twelve pigeons, one partridge in cheese, four pigeons prepared in another fashion, six chickens, eight pounds of veal, three fat chickens, one pheasant, three partridges, two *poulendes*, four baby chickens, nine full-sized chickens, eight pigeons, and four meat pies. In his old age, when he was suffering painful digestive problems, he was put on a strict regimen that reduced his supper to merely one carp, 100 crayfish, one milk-based soup, two turtles, one herb broth, one sole, a ragoût, a grilled brochette, two medium soles, one perch, two more soles prepared differently, 100 oysters, and a medium salmon served with six soles.)[76] These courses were enormous, but they were not all. These menus did not mention the fruit that the king was told to eat after meals to aid his digestion or the vegetables that he was served from the spectacular *jardin potager* as a delicacy.[77]

The king's afternoon would begin generally with a walk, hunt, or carriage ride into the countryside; alternately the king spent time studying his collections.[78] If there was no pressing business of state, the entire afternoon would be taken up with these pleasures.

Early in the evenings, the entertainment began for the members of the court. The king believed in using pleasant distractions to keep members of the aristocracy in line. Boredom was, in his mind, a threat to the system of power. The nobility had to live scripted lives and adhere to a regimen that would keep them in order, and pleasure was the central means of social control used for this purpose. So aristocrats were regaled with comedies three times a week, balls on Saturdays, and music, dancing, and gambling on Monday, Wednesday, and Friday evenings in *les appartements* or informal evenings with the king (see plate 111 below). The *appartements* took place in a suite of chambers near the chapel, and, although they were informal, these were required activities for members of the court. The king's sister-in-law, an avid hunter and woman with little interest in the gossip, gambling, and sexual intrigues of the court, found these evenings deadly dull, but they had many attractions. The room for the collation was filled with glittering lights, abundant drink, and the delicate foods that courtiers could take as they wished. Another room was set up with card tables, where musicians also played to entertain the gamblers. Still another room had a billiard table, where the king often played. And there was a room for dancing as well. The king appeared as a less formal host on these occasions, and made himself available to the *invités* – so much so that foreign visitors saw these evenings as quite gay and intimate. As most court activities paled in excess, the gambling during these *appartements* still retained an attraction to many members of the nobility. Some courtiers claimed to make a living from their winnings; others lost enough on these evenings to keep them so dependent on the monarch that they had to appear again at the tables only to lose another night. In all these activities, consuming and witnessing, moving and waiting, were the elements of the choreography of political life at Versailles. As the ritual life at court was solidified, it was moved indoors, away from the play and life of the gardens. All the lessons of power from the *L'Isle enchantée* remained, but there were no more warriors at Versailles capable of breaking the enchantment.[79]

Aristocratic costumes and the play of power

Costuming was an essential accompaniment to all the posturing of the leisure-filled days and night at Versailles; it made the public events richer, more colorful, and more indicative of noble submission. The late-night balls, beginning at midnight and going on till dawn, were particularly opulent events. The *mascarade*, which required the monarch to supply costumes for the court, was replaced by the masquerade ball, in which participants came in costumes provided by themselves. Often they dressed as culturally exotic "others" – Turks, Moors, Persians, Indians, and Chinese, or characters from the theater. The point was to choose a character that would allow the costumed noble to wear the most exotic and richest clothing and to play a role with "natural" affectation. Not only was the certainty of fashion and clothing made an object of play in these events, but so was the whole problem of affectation and social identity.[80]

Norbert Elias has argued that the sumptuousness of the court life at Versailles, particularly the exorbitant display of expensive clothing entailing horrific costs, was not, as some have assumed, a marker of the dissipation of the aristocracy (or callous disregard for the poverty of ordinary French people in the early and late years of the reign), but rather a powerful weapon for disciplining French nobles and bringing them under the control of king and state. The expense of staying in fashion, combined with the burden of buying commissions or offices, undermined the economic independence of the nobility. Moreover, required participation in courtly events kept this group too distracted to seek political autonomy.[81] In this system of noble regulation and impoverishment, the following of fashion, then, rather than being a silly form of obsessiveness and sign of personal wealth and taste, was a visible display of loyalty required by court etiquette that also disposed of exorbitant amounts of money.

Fashionable dress, as defined by king and court, also became an important way of inscribing French taste on French bodies. Those who inhabited the French court were coerced by pressures of taste into costuming themselves as French political subjects. The fashion system, which had for some centuries linked cosmopolitan elites loosely within a central model of taste in fashion, was used self-consciously within the French court to locate a distinct French taste in dress to serve as a model for Europe.[82] This move was surprisingly successful in part because the fashion system was already active as a means of trying to claim social power.

From the fourteenth century, newly enriched merchants and financiers in Europe began to adopt aristocratic styles of dress in order to claim a higher status to match their wealth. The system of fashionable change began (roughly) in the Burgundian principality. In the fourteenth century this court, which was set along the major north–south European trade route, found itself rapidly enriched by commerce and immersed in a cosmopolitan world of goods. In the fifteenth century, fashion moved to Italy, as the Mediterranean trade brought wealth to that region, and the city-states of Italy became hotbeds of cultural innovation. With the growth of the Habsburg Empire and the opening of the Atlantic trade in the sixteenth century, the focus of fashion moved to Spain. During the early seventeenth century, as this empire fell apart, fashion was bifurcated and shaped by both Italy and Holland. The innovative manufacturing in Holland and that country's efficient system of trade made Dutch goods an attractive source of new items for fashion. At the same time, the classical artwork in Italy was making that area a strong influence on European aesthetics. This split in fashion was enhanced by the division of Europe into separate Protestant and Catholic social worlds, centered around Amsterdam and Rome. As if this were not enough, the traditional separation of the Atlantic and the Mediterranean trading systems allowed the development of two loci of business and wealth, one in Holland and the other in Italy. But for the reasons described earlier, neither area was strong or culturally central enough to unify European style around it. During the reign of Louis XIV, however, fashion in Europe was once again given a common center – this time in France.[83]

Dressing in the French court, from this point on, was hardly a casual business. Pleasing the king – and being quite French in doing so – required careful costuming. Members of the aristocracy had opportunities to shape fashion in all of Europe, if they developed styles that first pleased the king and then caught hold in the court. And this happened with some regularity. The chronicler Saint-Simon claimed that whenever the king made a positive remark about a choice of fabric or cut of clothing made by one of the courtiers, others quickly followed that lead, rushing to stay up-to-date.[84] But innovation of this sort was risky since failed attempts would surely bring ridicule. So the system of fashion kept the nobles at Versailles all-the-more attentive to style and to one another as sources of cultural competition. They spent ever more time and money on dress. All this, Elias has argued, diminished the nobles' capacity to develop political interests or autonomy in defiance of the world and wishes of the king.

The clothing worn by the king and his court showcased French manufactures as well as tastes. As we have already seen, the figured silks and laces coming from the manufactures set up by Colbert were central items in the dress displayed at the French court. As these fabrics began to be worn regularly, the economic success of France was made visible on the backs of members of the country's highest social ranks. Ironically, this very conspicuous display of dress at court began impoverishing noble families. The elaborate costumes were taking up the shrinking incomes from their estates while they were also presenting to the rest of Europe's elites a vision of French economic well-being that further enhanced the king's standing.[85]

The interesting thing about this costuming was that, while it was highly regulated, it was not used to mark the particular office of the bearer, as medieval clothes had often done. Instead, court clothing was worn to show taste, political alliance and social influence, not social role or responsibility. *Political* location was elevated in French fashion above all other social meanings of dress, and hence made clothing a more potent weapon in state-based politics.

Fashionable clothes, as we have seen, were wielded in the French court to stake out political identities. In this sense, they were much like military uniforms that were designed to locate quickly the political identity of the bearer. But court attire, unlike the military uniform, was a creative fashionable change. Those outside France could and did imitate French clothing. This encouraged the development of new styles in France to make those at the center of French social life still distinguishable from others. Through the cultivation of small differences, fashionable clothes could continue to distinguish friends from foes, insiders from outsiders, in spite of the spread of styles. The attempts at imitating French fashions outside France itself carried another kind of message about the power of the French court. Italy was visibly losing the war for European culture. Just as the use of French military uniforms in the army made French military power more apparent on the battlefield and in the streets of the border cities that French forces had won, so the use of French costume by other aristocrats testified to the power of France over European culture.

Power *within* the court of Louis XIV was marked most clearly by a type of clothing that was partly a uniform and partly an item of prestige and fashion: the *justaucorps à brevet*. This outfit was mentioned earlier because of its golden garlands, draped over the shoulders. In the 1660s, Louis XIV decided to develop an identifying garment for the *Gardes de la Porte*, a group of honorary guards charged with holding the keys to the château. These were not ordinary soldiers or guards but rather an elite of trusted men specifically named by him. The garment itself was a special coat (playing off the current fashion for coats at that time) which was made in blue, lined in scarlet, worn with a waistcoat, and embroidered in gold and silver with a special pattern. Only the king, members of the royal family, princes of the blood and fifty listed men could wear the coat. It was called a warrant coat because it could only be worn by those who had warrant to do so. Those chosen for this honor were given special privileges, highest of which was that they were allowed to accompany the king to Saint-Germain and

109. The costume of one of the king's Swiss guards. Notice the parterre-like lace in
the collar, the ribbons with inside decorations, and the use of the sash and high
heels in this costume. This was a model of military masculinity (N. Bonnart,
Suisse du Roi, 1678).

Habit d'Esté

Ruban. large
tabize ou —
brode auec
de la frange

Iuste au Corps
destamine Couleur de
Prince.

La Veste aussy longue que
le Iuste au Corps de toile
blanche garnie de —
dentelle ou point.
tour de manche —
double.
Les gans garnis de —
dentelle.
Le Baudrier a fons —
blanc et des grans —
fleurons brodes de la —
Couleur de l'habit.

B.R

110. Habit d'Esté, 1680s. This fashionable attire for a gentleman has many
elements in common with the military uniforms, and shows how the
rank of "gentleman" was encoded in the costume.

Versailles without specific invitation. Those who wanted coats but were not part of the
original fifty had to wait for someone with the *justaucorps à brevet* to die before they
could be considered for this status. The limits of membership in this group made
belonging a particularly valuable sign of the king's favor, and one that many courtiers
wanted very badly.[86]

When the dauphin came of age, he too had a warrant coat, this one made in brown
rather than blue fabric. He was able to appoint his friends to this honorary group, but
with the enthusiasm (or generosity) of youth, made the group too large to suit the king,
and had to stop this practice. The king also revived the Order of St. Michel, an honorary order for 100 Catholic men, which had its own uniform.[87]

For women, the restrictions on dress were not tied so tightly to uniforms and honorary group membership, but the king did insist upon a fundamental uniformity in French fashion for women. Ladies at court had to abandon their taste for the loose (and comfortable) *manteaux*, which the king did not like, and take on instead the *grand habit* with its tight lacing, bare shoulders and elaborate embroidery. This style held the women's bodies erect and appropriately disciplined for this formal court. This outfit was not, however, immune to changes in fashion, with the shape of the skirt being periodically altered. Lots of ongoing changes in ornamentation made staying fashionable at court enough of a problem to be interesting. Furthermore, the fundamental uniformity in this style of dress made French fashion for women more codified and thus easier to export, and yet the details of dress design could be altered enough to sustain cosmopolitan attention. More kingdoms and principalities followed or developed variations on these fashions as French forms were codified. [88]

Dress in the court at Versailles was not just a matter of fashion but also a means of costuming for the performances of power that occurred daily. Wearing costumes was a way of pleasing and taking on a public identity. Fashion was historically an art of pretense. The fashion system in Europe began when wealthy merchants used clothing to *pretend* to be the equal of the nobility. Through costume and politics, they took on a new social identity.[89] Dress at Versailles was similarly filled with pretense and politics. Nobles at court used extraordinarily elaborate and up-to-date clothing to pretend to be powerful Frenchmen, thereby making themselves French and simultaneously making France more powerful.

Slippery relationships between dress and social location were so ubiquitous to the period that they became a common theme in plays and operas of the sixteenth and seventeenth centuries. Many dramas pointed to outrageous or pitiful forms of overdressing, the odd possibilities of cross-dressing, or the mobility of social identities through fashion. Molière was clearly among the dramatists who pursued this line in his comedies, where the clown-like qualities of low-level aristocrats were made all the more vibrant through their hideous forms of overdressing.

Cross-dressing (or using clothing associated with the opposite sex) was a surprisingly common part of this court's culture of dress. It was a typical part of costume balls, a common practice among the gay men there, and a device used in narratives for complicating and advancing plots. Overdressing and cross-dressing were obviously related, one stepping over status lines and the other transgressing gender boundaries. Both provided narrative opportunities for deception and laughter in a world in which pretense was taken for granted but always carefully monitored. What is interesting is that the two forms of category violation through dress did not have comparable meanings in the culture of the period. Cross-dressing was much less condemned in France than overdressing. One could argue (with some basis) that the ubiquity of cross-dressing in late seventeenth-century France was a response to the presence of a powerful contingent of gay men in court culture. Certainly, the king's esteem for his gay brother led to at least a superficial diminishing of homophobia (particularly in contrast to the fears present in much of the rest of Counter-Reformation Catholic Europe). It is also true that the strict disciplining of the aristocracy in so many areas of court life did not extend to the regulation of sexuality, so that dress that spoke to gender was not as

111. The *grand habit* of the ladies of the period is illustrated in this picture of the informal evenings (*appartemens*) at Versailles (André Trouvain, *Seconde Chambre des Apartemens*, 1694).

importantly controlled as might have been expected (or as much as dress that conveyed rank).⁹⁰

This difference in the social meanings of dress and identity was important to the plays and operas of the period. In these stories, overdressing was stunningly visible to most characters (and often an object of much discussion among them), while cross-dressing was often not even noticed. In many dramatic narratives, for example, a lover would use cross-dressing to learn the true feelings of his or her love; the cross-dresser would become a same-sex stranger to the object of his or her affection; he or she would gain the confidence of the love and press to learn about the prospects for the relationship. This kind of play with sexual identity through costuming was treated as virtuous in the narrative arts of the time; it could promote love and hence serve the natural order of things. In the end, men and women found each other as partners, and heterosexuality would be triumphant, but the possibilities of other kinds of coupling were played upon by these stories.

Pleasures of the senses were surprisingly permissible in this otherwise very socially regimented French court. It was not just that the French aristocracy had become dissipated and corrupted. It seems that erotic pursuits became one of the few compensatory rewards for an aristocracy that was being denied the pleasures of power. As long as people knew their places and did not make fools of themselves by wanting to rise beyond their social rank (overdressing, for example), they could find their sexual place in the world through the paths of passion, without hindrance from the codes of courtly etiquette. Cross-dressing was simply one route for doing this, and one that did not disturb the careful marking of social rank and political identity through clothing.⁹¹

In spite of this interesting point of social relaxation, the court at Versailles depended upon a strict enforcement of etiquette and fashion. Etiquette kept the aristocracy gracefully voiceless, at the expense of their political power, and the enforced fashions of the court helped both to impoverish the French aristocracy and mold a French identity around the state. The laughter in Molière's plays directed at those who visibly over-dressed or acted without the grace of a true courtier, without apparently natural *politesse*, pointed to the stakes at risk for aristocrats and would-be aristocrats who failed to recognize and take appropriate note of the system of social regulation in the French court. There was nothing to do at Versailles except to please the king. The resulting uniformities in dress added to the military look of this court, and expressed clearly the trained commitment of the nobility to serve the king and state. The exemption of cross-dressing from the disciplinary regulation of this social world reveals not a break in the enforcement system as much as a technique of power: political control over aristocratic behavior was traded for a kind of sexual license in court. The space left for pleasure was only a condition for the regulation of the rest of one's life at Versailles, including most matters of dress and decorum.

It might seem that interest in dress and identity would not have been important to the gardens at Versailles. Most of the statues were nude, or nearly so. But gender ambiguity was there – albeit in subtle ways – and it was sometimes associated with dress. The Achilles statue at the end of the *tapis vert* depicted him in disguise as a woman. According to myth, his mother tried to hide him this way so he would not be recruited into fighting, and die from his vulnerable heel. At the gardens of Versailles, he appeared as a very beautiful young man, whose identity was signaled by drawers of clothing, which drew attention to his means of disguise. There was no other so explicit representation of cross-dressing, but male pairs were visible. The Castor and Pollux group by Coysevox (1685–1712) may have referred to brothers from classical mythology, but they were depicted as two beautiful naked youths with their arms draped about each other. This statue was more suggestive than innocent. Even the statue of Ganymede and the Eagle (1682) by Laviron is about disguised relations between men. The eagle represented Jupiter, and indirectly pointed to an intimate relation between an older man and a beautiful boy.

Much of the sense of sexual possibility in the park was presented more diffusely. The gardens were filled with statues showing Pan with a lurid smile or Satyrs with desirous looks. Bacchus was repeatedly depicted in the garden, and he, of course, stood for Dionysian excesses of pleasure, including sexual delight. Even the sensual statues of women in the park pointed to a kind of acceptance of sexuality in the court. Martin Lister, when he visited the gardens from England, was careful in his memoirs to suggest that the statues at Versailles were naked not just to titillate spectators, but because classical statues studied the proportions of the human form. What he failed to appreciate was that nudes could have both meanings. As Peter Berger has pointed out, nude images of women in Western art, while explicitly about the beauty of the female form, have also been means for elite men to surround themselves with objects of sexual fantasy. Clearly the gardens at Versailles provided many opportunities for sexual revelry, both for homosexuals and heterosexuals.[92]

The cultivation of political bodies

The world of the seventeenth-century French aristocracy was essentially organized around the body: its obedience, sexuality, gestural grace, and physical stature. Etiquette was a matter of choreography and self-control. As Elias has pointed out, the feudal knights of earlier times were made into courtiers as they learned to keep their fighting equipment, swords and large knives away from the table. They learned to use utensils designed specifically for meals. The design of the implements themselves would distinguish between knives for hunting and fighting, and those used for eating in polite society. They also learned new ways to hold knives at table to underscore their civility. These "manners" were embodied actions that both shaped social intercourse, and gave birth to the gestural and physical presence of civilized elites. This aristocracy was trained to please and became distinguishable both from their social inferiors and their own historical predecessors by the ways they bowed, engaged in rituals, spoke their lines, and remained confined within the proper clothing. The extent of the body discipline required at the French court was made painfully apparent in one incident reported by Saint-Simon. The king caused a miscarriage to one of his family favorites (his granddaughter) because he demanded that she accompany him – in formal dress while eight months pregnant – on a long carriage ride to one of his distant residences. He liked the company of certain women on these long journeys, and he refused to make

112. *Castor and Pollux.*

concessions of dress to women who were pregnant. The corseting as well as the rigors of the carriage ride were too much for mother and baby, and shortly after the journey was over, the pregnancy ended. Even the king's current wife/mistress and his doctor objected to his proposal for the trip, but Louis (according to Saint-Simon) was adamant about having his wishes fulfilled. He even apparently showed little remorse after his actions proved disastrous. This story tells us much about the vanity and tyrannical nature of the king, but even more about the system of political performance in which this unfortunate woman was stuck. Obedience to the king was a physical matter, and she had no choice but to succumb to his wishes.[93]

The men at court may not have had to suffer from tight lacing, but they too were expected to make their bodies please the king. In fact, their very posture and carriage was meant to convey their high birth and masculine nature. Their physical presence was formed by the combination of ballet dancing and military training that Louis XIII had delighted in, and which produced distinctively French male aristocratic body contours and styles of movement. It is well known that Louis XIV was a dancer in his youth, and particularly proud of his successes in this realm. He danced the role of Apollo to great acclaim long before he became known as the Sun King.[94]

The importance of ballet to this culture of the courtier under Louis XIV cannot be overestimated. The king appointed a court ballet-master to ensure that the nobles had dancing lessons, and he elevated the dance as an art form by setting up an Academy of Dance. The results were palpable. Many of the prints depicting gentlemen of the period, whether they showed men standing in the garden or engaging in war, presented them in ballet positions with their toes pointed out and their hands held in a graceful line.[95] The elegance of the French court was often associated with the refined movements courtiers would use in executing the smallest details of everyday life, including the rituals of the king's day. To be noble and French, then, came not only with a costume but a style of body carriage, and the good manners to use them in and out of court.

Peter Wollen has argued that the equestrian skills expected of military men in that period, ones that also made Louis XIV a passionate hunter, also placed emphasis on balance, leaps, and posture, just like ballet.[96] An elaborate system of surveillance and control of the aristocracy, according to Wollen, centered on a culture of the body. Aristocratic men fill their days with physical activities that would render them good soldiers, graceful courtiers and elegant dancers. These physical attributes were taken as marks of their "natural" virtue and social superiority. These codified forms of body control helped to produce a distinctive posture, movement, and set of gestures identified with the French aristocracy.

In Foucault's *Discipline and Punish*, in which he describes the growth of disciplinary activity, particularly in the French military, Foucault begins by describing a seventeenth-century soldier's body.[97] This body is straight, tall and strong. It is the model of the soldier that will be sought through training in the eighteenth century. Where did this seventeenth-century soldier come from? His body is presented by Foucault as a fact, almost natural, in contrast to the constructed body of the eighteenth-century soldier. But this seventeenth-century soldier's physique was likely just the noble

113. Louis XIV as Apollo, in the costume for a ballet he performed before becoming king.

114. The gentleman in Mallet's book on military technique is often shown in ballet position (Mallet, *Les Travaux de Mars* , 1684, p. 189).

115. The king in ballet position for his famous portrait by Rigaud.

masculine body, trimmed by dance, tall because of a good diet, and strong from military exercise and hunting on horseback. This is the physicalized aristocratic body that would lose much of its strength in the eighteenth century, as the professional soldier gained power and took over this stature. The Saint-Simons and other intellectuals would help make the aristocracy more learned, and change the body characteristics of the elites to a softened, bored, leisured look. The earlier aristocratic soldier's body would be eclipsed by the emphasis on physical passivity. But the body as a site of politics would not be entirely lost. Grace and gesture remained a memory of this earlier physical regime of power.

Although required military training may seem an expected discipline for soldiers in any period, those nobles born in the early seventeenth century grew up in a world of feudal masculinity in which birth rather than training was expected to be the origin of true warriors. Learning to march and obey orders was a novelty of this reign and one of the offenses that most distressed Saint-Simon about Louis XIV.[98] True enough, feudal noblemen were supposed to learn equestrian skills by hunting and jousting, not enduring formal kinds of training. Under Louis XIV, learning military discipline was a prerequisite to participation in the army, and one means by which nobles learned to make themselves subservient to the king. The application of this training to the nobility seemed an affront to Saint-Simon because it denied the "natural" right of nobles to their traditional social role. It made clear that nobles were no longer military men by birth, but had to make their bodies into vehicles of state power and sites of political identity if they wanted to sustain the illusion of belonging to a warrior caste.

Dance and military training once again made the nobility of France physically distinguishable, and standardized the look and carriage of members of this group. At the same time, these disciplines also taught them to to coordinate their movements with one another to serve collective ends. Books on military strategy and their counterparts on dance from the period showed readers how to fight or dance *together*. The dancers or soldiers were not supposed to be just trained individuals, but formed members of a group that could act as a political force, whether showing grace in a public ballet or prowess in battle. They submitted themselves to common formations, ways of moving, and relations to one another. The dances and military formations depicted in books of the period, significantly enough, presented generic turns for dances, marching formations, ballet positions for the feet and hands, or ways of holding weapons. These strategies/choreographies ordered the bodies of aristocratic men into politically meaningful forms; these techniques yielded French aristocratic men who were visible and subservient members of court society and military life.[99]

Inside the court, those who excelled in these forms of body discipline were socially rewarded. Individuals who were outstanding in horsemanship or dance were praised and pointed to as models for the rest of the court. They were thought to embody a physical grace and elegance as pleasing to the eye as wit was to the ear. Their very posture conveyed a desire to please and became the physical equivalent of *honnêteté*. Given Louis XIV's love of dance, these movements were indeed ones that could and did please the monarch.[100] As a result, the pursuit of these skills became a point of

116. A gentleman's hands as well as his feet had well-codified positions that were presented in books on dance, etiquette, and war (Mallet, *Les Travaux de Mars*, 1684, p. 42).

competition among the courtiers. The result was that the aristocracy in the French court voluntarily struggled to acquire the most disciplined bodies.

The importance of bodies and grace during this reign also helps to explain the centrality of music to Louis XIV's court. The cultivation of new and distinctively French music clearly contributed to the distinctiveness of French culture, and was used to help disentangle French style from Italian precedents. But music also aided the production of bodies and relations to space that was recognizably French. Lully's orchestration of the fêtes and *divertissements* at Versailles, as well as his ballets, provided a rhythm for the ritual and festive aspects of court life. Lully's music increasingly took on a slower pace and formality that matched the rhythms of the ritual and promenade of the French court. Gone was the ecstatic sexuality of Italian baroque music, the rising tones and agitated rhythms overflowing the bounds of the form. Musical elements became more contained, carefully paced, and delicately placed. This was a music of gestures in which instrumental and vocal ornamentation was essential to performance to express a natural grace and elegance. This was also a music that was so often tied to ballet or processions that it structured relations between body and space as well. The musical measure and measures of space were linked in a different way when musicians paraded in costumes during fêtes or marked out the pace for ballet dancers. Even during outdoor concerts, the bosquets at Versailles were animated with music and mobilized by sounds that took over the night air.[101]

The promenade, that mixture of parade and dance, was the ultimate expression of this culture of body and land. Legs, fingers, and hands marked, measured, gestured, and moved as they did in a dance or while playing instruments. They made manifest the significance of the space as they moved through it. More than other forms of body work, the promenade joined land and body, France and French nobles, in the ultimate dance of social and geographical place. This was a dance choreographed by the king himself to demonstrate his political power.[102]

The French aristocracy, well and truly caught in this system of political choreography, became part of a system for enacting social order and connecting it to natural order. They took on the role of nature deities, and filled the gardens with their disciplined bodies and scripted voices.[103] The participants contributed their own submission to the growth of state absolutism by trying to develop the body skills as warriors and dancers that would make them seem worthy members of the court. They learned to value the qualities of the *honnête homme* who could submerge his feelings to social demands, and do it with charm and grace. Courtiers became like the cultivated and potted plants in the garden, who could be clipped to fantastic shapes and still manage to grow. Not surprisingly, their social character was best seen and displayed in the garden where the continuities between social discipline and land control were obvious, where silent obedience was the norm of daily life, and where the power of the king over both his territory and French elites could be made manifest to the world as a single system of politics.

6

Naturalizing power in the new state

While many chroniclers of the reign mentioned the stunning effects produced in the gardens for the social spectacles at Versailles, it remains something of a mystery why the French court under Louis XIV so frequently used the park for events ranging from the *Plaisirs de l'Isle enchantée* to the more ubiquitous promenades. After the Italianate influences of the sixteenth century waned, most of the *ballets de cour* and carrousels were set in palace halls and courtyards, not royal gardens. Nonetheless, in the late seventeenth century, the garden once again became a central theater of power. Why? There are clearly multiple answers to the question, some addressed in earlier chapters. The garden was a place where military engineering could be showcased and French style could be displayed. It was also a site where the disciplining of the aristocracy could be made public enough to underscore the power of the absolutist state. All these contributed to the garden's political saliency for this time and place. But one other element was just as important: the garden could embody and convey natural forces. It was a site where the relations between political power and natural order could be asserted or assessed. Jacques Boyceau, in his theory of gardening (1638), suggested explicitly that a great park ought to make manifest the orderliness of nature known to science. And both Félibien (1672) and Scudéry (1979) claimed that what made the park at Versailles such a tribute to the king was its embellishment of nature with art.[1] In this polysemic place, many forces of nature were symbolically accumulated close to the seat of French power, and were held together by a formal structure that championed natural orderliness above all else. Nature was at the heart of the garden, and its presentation was central both to its beauty and its political usefulness during the reign of Louis XIV.

To the extent that French formal gardens contained and conveyed nature, they portrayed a reality that required no arguments to legitimate or disputes to defend. Gardens *depicted* a reality rather than made any argument about the real. The formal parks, for all their artifice, could be considered natural because they were made of plants, animals, and minerals from the earth; and with their artifice, they structured an experience of the natural world that would pleasingly reproduce what the gardeners understood to be true of nature. In this way, the gardens did not assert truths but assumed and circulated them. As the popular science writer, Fontenelle, suggested, "Only the truth can persuade, and it needs to bring no array of proof with it. Truth enters the

117. Du Goulon, *Vase de Soleil*; a vase in the garden, showing Louis XIV as the Sun King surrounded by laurels and sunflowers.

mind so naturally that learning it for the first time seems like merely remembering it."[2] The formal gardens of the period conveyed truths by making aspects of nature enter consciousness with just this facility. The fact that much of the labor and most of the technique used to build the parks were hidden helped to make these spaces seem to speak directly about nature itself. Certainly, the geometrically aligned parterres and bosquets looked nothing like the untended forests of northern France, where nature could seem so wild and chaotic, but they still persuasively represented nature in a politically useful way. They naturalized the image of the world as orderly. Growing things seemed to flourish effortlessly in the carefully structured garden beds and forest rooms of the *petit parc* at Versailles, so they appeared to belong in such a structure. (Perhaps, by extension, the French people were meant to prosper in a similarly structured system of political order.) By careful management, these formal garden plots near the château were able to convey a vision of natural order triumphing over the forces of natural dis-array. Diverse garden areas were joined in an aesthetically triumphant fashion, demon-strating the possibilities of territorial integration through the imposition of order – presumably under state absolutism.[3]

Where the social order could be equated with the natural order in these parks, the garden became a laboratory of political pedagogy. To the extent that the land of France could be equated with the garden (now that land was being given new weight in the political system), depictions of the forces of nature invested in the land became useful for portraying the potential power of the state. In the gardens of Versailles, no one needed to provide evidence for the state's power; no one had to persuade foreign dig-nitaries about the grandeur of French accomplishments. The glory of France was a truth presented in the landscape itself in a way that permitted it to enter "the mind so naturally that learning it for the first time seem[ed] like merely remembering it."[4]

There was much in the natural philosophy of the period useful for crafting political imagery for the gardens. This new science described the cosmos as a single, encom-passing, and material system that included the earth as well as the heavens. It was pleas-ingly easy to equate this centrally ordered world with the absolutist, territorial state. Natural philosophers were abandoning the classical notion that glass spheres divided the heavens from the earth, separating the forces of nature into completely different systems of order. The Christian-based division of the world into heaven and earth was also being set aside by this science, although for most natural philosophers, the Christian God remained in evidence. There was only *one* perfectly ordered system, cen-trally and materialy controlled: the world of Creation. This whole and limitless system was an attractive image of absolutism.[5]

The system of nature was also a material and measurable one. Its properties were revealed to the human intellect through simple, mathematical relations. The *pré carré* that Vauban so wanted for France was a comparable model of mathematical simplic-ity for the political domain, a measured space whose properties and relations could be revealed through surveys, and achieved through war. The state, the garden, and the uni-verse could be mutually understood using the same systems of measurement, and the measured order created by each could be treated as equally natural.[6]

Of course, there were controversies in the new science that gave gardeners (and the artists supplying them with artworks) a complex cultural palate to bring to their work. Many natural philosophers still believed that the universe was composed (as Aristotle suggested) of four elements: earth, air, fire, and water. These four elements were repre-sented in human form in garden statuary, and three of them (earth, air, and water) were clearly visible building blocks of the gardens. The fourth element was intentionally added to the park during fêtes, when bursts of fireworks were rocketed over the canal, illuminating the earth, water, and air already in the gardens. In these moments, the park at Versailles was transformed into a dramatic showplace for the fundamental forces of the Aristotelian natural world.[7]

The great water system at Versailles also gained interest because of scientific work on circulatory systems. Those who believed Descartes' notion that the universe was floating in a great system of invisible circulating fluids, or those familiar with Harvey's landmark work on the circulation of the blood, were fascinated with how fluids moved. Hydraulic engineering was developing rapidly in the period too, both influencing the construction of the water system at Versailles and drawing public attention to the circulation of water there. The water supply for Versailles grew to unprecedented proportions, and filled with abundant fountains a valley that had always had an extremely limited natural water supply. If fluids linked heaven and earth, as Descartes suggested, no wonder Versailles was given such a massive water system to circulate through and around the court of the Sun King.[8]

The garden at Versailles may also have alluded to and benefited from one of the most touchy and dangerous ideas from the science of the period: the heliocentric model of the universe. To the extent that anyone dared to entertain Copernican ideas about the universe, there was obvious political capital to be made for the Sun King.[9] The gardens at Versailles clearly revolved thematically around the *Roi Soleil*. The Apollo fountain was also placed near the physical and aesthetic center of the park: at the intersection between the *petit parc* and the canal. The statues of gods and heroes arrayed around the Apollo fountain were set in a semi-circle – satellites of the central figure. And the entire *petit parc* was littered with urns decorated with suns, sunflowers, and images showing Louis XIV with rays of light emanating from his head, all alluding to this favored image of the monarch.

Perhaps intentionally, the designers of the royal parks saved themselves from conflicts with the Church on heliocentrism by presenting the Sun King and his powers in the language of classical mythology. This move sidestepped conflicts between the new science and theology, by equating Louis XIV with Apollo and making the Sun King part of an ancient cosmology. The Apollo depicted in Tuby's famous fountain, showed the deity emerging from the underworld with his chariot of fire, starting to carry the sun across the heavens. There was no Copernican heresy in this story of Apollo, so the Church had no cause to fear or hate it. Nonetheless, the Sun King symbol, which had been used by French monarchs without much comment before, took on new stature in the seventeenth century, just when the Copernican system was suggesting that the sun might be the stable point in the skies around which the Earth revolved.

If the new sciences were importantly shaping the art of gardening in seventeenth-century France, an important question remains unanswered. Why would esoteric and even dangerous ideas from natural philosophy find form in the gardens of Versailles? Why would they be used to glorify a king who had no love for the sciences and was seemingly empowered by traditional theology, not these new secular systems of thought? Why would his advisors want to surround him with potentially heretical notions – particularly ideas that he probably knew little about? Certainly, one member of Colbert' most respected of advisors, the doctor Claude Perrault, was both a scientist and one of the most vocal "Moderns," who saw science raising the contemporary world above that of the Ancients. Colbert himself was an avid collector and advocate of the sciences, who would have had great sympathy for gardens alluding to science. But Colbert was first and foremost unwaveringly subservient to the king.[10] He cared more about the king's public stature than his personal passions. So Colbert and his entourage would not have threatened the welfare of the king to suit their intellectual

118. *Le Loiret* by Thomas Regnaudin, in the Parterre d'Eau.

agendas. A more fundamental problem must have moved them to place the king in the natural world, and equate him with a force of nature.

Nature as a source of political legitimacy

Nature provided a touchstone of truth that was of particular value at the end of the seventeenth century. Peter Burke (1992) claims that even while state absolutism was putting more power in the hands of Louis XIV and his ministers, the political *legitimacy* of the reign was being undermined by the transfer of powers to the state. The movement of political authority into a secular institution detached politics from its earlier theological roots in the Divine Right of kings. The king's will had previously been seen as an extension of God's will on earth. But if France was ruled in the king's name but not always through his direction, how could political authority be understood? Giving power to ministers was already a political liability in France. A string of regencies had allowed first Richelieu and then Mazarin to rule France in the name of the monarchy – much to the chagrin of French nobles of the blood. The nobility had been so distressed by Mazarin's political power that many had joined with powerful Parisians to destabilize the government and force the minister to leave the country (at least temporarily). Louis XIV vigorously claimed his personal right to rule at the beginning of his reign, asserting his role as the final political voice in France, but as the bureaucracy grew more powerful, even his government looked increasingly impersonal. Since placing new authority in the hands of ministers was a politically risky business, it had to be handled carefully. New ways of understanding the monarch's authority and right to rule had to be (and were) fabricated to legitimate state absolutism.[11]

The equation of political order with natural order began to become commonplace in the propaganda of the regime. The image of Louis XIV as Apollo, or the Sun King, quickly became ubiquitous. The Sun King was, of course, the natural center of political life and a guiding light over his land. He was of the heavens, but had his effects on Earth. Other objects of Creation revolved around him or tried to follow his trajectory through the heavens, just like the state bureaucracy tried to follow the will of the king. This placement of the king in the natural order of the heavens maintained a connection between the king and higher powers. Calling him Apollo even described him as a deity. But the equation of the king with the sun also located him in a secular system of motion and order. The king may have derived his powers from God (by riding a chariot of light that had already been created), but he was part of a larger system (like the state). To the extent that some problems surrounding the legitimacy of the regime could be diffused by this kind of metaphorical placement of the king in the natural order, these images became political assets.

The problems of legitimacy for the political regime were also related to more general theological problems raised by secularization of social life in Europe. For example, new secular theories of the universe came in conflict with theological assertions about the true meaning of the heavens. Some moves toward secularization often yielded destructive and bitter fights, as Galileo's trial and censure had made clear.[12] The political

119. *Air*, a needlepoint in the style of Le Brun. Louis XIV is here depicted as Jupiter and surrounded by laurels and garlands, with parterre-like designs on either side of the Sun King emblem.

problem facing the French state was to allow some secularization of politics without undermining what was left of the traditional sacred sources of monarchical rule. Making explicit arguments about the king's authority was risky, since it could highlight the problems of legitimacy. The alternative was to locate a new source of power. The earth became such a site. If sacred and secular claims to knowledge of the heavens provided a point of contest in the period, claims to the earth provided, so to speak, some common ground. Natural philosophers had already begun to argue (with mixed success and in different ways) that God's will could be learned not just through study of the Bible (his Word), but through empirical study of God's works (nature, creation). To study nature was not a desecration, then, but an act of worship, particularly when it revealed the abundance of God's creatures and the perfection of his grand design. Gassendi, among others, claimed that natural philosophy provided evidence of God himself by showing the orderliness of Creation. Descartes might have objected to the doctrine of works, but he still argued that nature had patterns accessible to human reason because God's creation had set those laws in motion.[13]

On Earth, God's works could meet the works of men. If the bureaucratic authority of the modern state could not be legitimated as an extension of God's will, the authority for territorial politics could be derived from the doctrine of works. To improve on God's works was a legitimate activity, and making French territory a tribute to its maker was an activity befitting a great Catholic king with dreams of empire like Louis XIV. The *pré carré* was part God's work and part Vauban's project, and easy to see as the legitimate site of French politics, directed by the king. Formal gardens were effective political vehicles because they embodied this politics of works. French royal parks were designed first to make manifest the diversity and orderliness of nature, and then to embellish God's works with art to glorify and empower the land. Both sacred and secular ways of depicting nature could be joined in these spaces, demonstrating the practical virtues and sacred significance of state territorial development.

The meeting of sacred and secular worlds in the gardens at Versailles was most evident at the canal. This great cross-shaped water feature was a visible mark of God's will on the king's lands. The canal also structurally set up a kind of Cartesian coordinate system for the garden's design, constituting the center of a measured and geometrically ordered terrain. In fact, the canal is often discussed in art histories as part of a system of axes used to structure the park that developed slowly over its history. The first axis was built using the north–south series of fountains that cut across the terrace behind the château, intersecting the terminus of the Allée Royale. This first T-shaped structure for the *petit parc* lasted through all the subsequent alterations of the gardens. It was finally repeated (or reiterated) on a larger scale with the crossing of the canal. To the extent that these axes provided a central geometrical structure for the park – differentiating, measuring, and organizing the different areas of gardens – they made this site seem rigorously rational. But Descartes' own theological reflections, equating God's existence with mathematical order in the natural world, made it quite easy to associate this structure with God and the cross, too. The canal became a surprisingly polysemic site, which could provide a meeting point for religious and scientific imagery.[14]

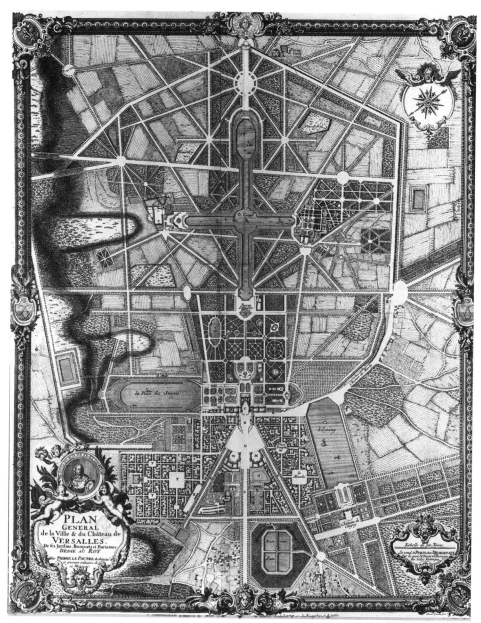

120. Plan of the town and park of Versailles indicating the cross-shaped canal at the center of the park. The plan shows a portrait of Louis XV, but illustrates the garden as it existed at the end of the reign of Louis XIV (Pierre Le Pautre, *Plan Général de la Ville et du Château du Versailles*).

To the extent that the garden was also filled with artifacts that glorified the king, it placed the monarch's "works" in the context of God's works. The territory of France itself could be seen as one of the king's "works": something ordained *and* a human accomplishment. No wonder in the gardens at Versailles, France was both personified in statues as a female figure and represented as land, using plants and flowers. Set out this way, France was both a separate, artificial entity, and a natural form growing out of and coherent with God's works.

Peter Burke argues that the diminishing of political legitimacy during this reign was both countered and made visible by a massive growth of propaganda.[15] Censorship was rampant to reduce the cacophony of voices in the political domain. Official sources of information (from the printed work of the *Imprimerie Royale* to the journalism of the *Mercure Galante*) provided the regime's authoritative political voice. Each new victory on the battlefield was recorded in accounts of the events, printed on propaganda sheets, and celebrated at great parties that were described in journalistic detail for the literate elites who could not attend. The positive spin placed on these stories for the French media was balanced by their critical counterparts in English sources, where scathing remarks were made about the brutality of French soldiers and the vanity and depravity of the king as their leader. A war of words and images surrounded the regime, as propagandists fought over its position in history through languages of power.[16] Clearly the word was not abandoned in the pursuit of works, but material manipulations became a means of sidestepping the conflicts of representation by founding the legitimacy of this regime in demonstrations of efficacy in the world of things.

At the gardens at Versailles, a visible and aesthetically refined system of political reality construction was at work, one that manipulated the look of France rather than its assessment in words, and one that placed the legitimacy of the new state not in ideas, but in the natural world. The French capacity to measure, know, and govern its own territory through the state apparatus was not a matter of debate in the garden, but of demonstration. The look of the land, the representations of nature in statuary, the uses of water, and the correspondences drawn between heaven and earth were showcased. Engineering and art were used together to construct and defend the territorial state.

Habermas has argued that legitimation crises of modern states have never been adequately addressed with ideology or propaganda, although this has been tried. The legitimacy of states has come to depend on the capacity of these institutions to solve technical infrastructural problems. Governments have only turned to propaganda to cover up technical failings.[17] Certainly, the French state in the seventeenth century sought and to some extent found legitimacy in engineering, in the technical manipulation of the land for political ends. Winning battles to gain more land, draining areas to make more of it useful, joining different regions with canals, and building a better road system were all technical solutions of this sort. These efforts both *legitimated* and *defined* state power first by locating it as a relation to land. The interdependence of technoscience and the state that we have usually taken as a twentieth-century phenomenon was essential to *the very construction* of state power in seventeenth-century France, when political authority began to be associated with the powers of the natural world.[18]

Following Weber[19] (with theoretical roots firmly in the late nineteenth century), we do not expect to find serious political legitimation in the world of things – much less in the engineering of landscapes; we expect language to be the heart of politics. We are not as well prepared either to see or analyze the political implications of material culture. Nonetheless, no matter how disquieting, garden designers of the seventeenth century like Boyceau made their gardens renderings of nature's orderliness, as they understood it. They materially defined the category, nature, while using the landscape to tell a morality tale about power. The sense of discomfort we may have today with the idea that interventions into the environment could comment on and work out relations of nature and power stems from a new political significance of language that has developed from the late nineteenth through to the twentieth century.[20] The rise of literacy and the increased education of elites have made this possible. Still during the reign of Louis XIV, however, in a period when the monarch's learning was not extensive, material strategies for claiming and gaining power made sense, and the garden was an appropriate locale for addressing problems of legitimacy.[21] There was certainly plenty of praise for the king written by his admirers in the period, mostly paid memorializers but also friendly journalists and essayists. But what was most striking about the "fabrication" of Louis XIV described by Burke was the importance of art works, artifacts, and infrastructural (public works) projects to the constitution of his greatness.[22]

The outdoors and landscape took on particular importance in establishing the legitimacy of the regime because these sites were where political works could meet the works of God, demonstrating their continuity. The garden was a creation built in Creation itself. The plantings, architectural features, and artworks in the park at Versailles all testified to the glory of the king because, no matter who crafted the actual pieces, they were easily treated as expressions of the king's will. Similarly with the state, no matter who was administering any of the policies of the government, political processes could be seen as expressions of sovereign power. This helped to make the state seem to be a legitimate embodiment of political authority.[23]

Not surprisingly, the park at Versailles turned out to be a finely tuned technical demonstration of domination, a record of human (sovereign) will. The very artificiality of the gardens (that would make them bothersome to subsequent gardeners) helped to make them visibly human works. The measured proportions and geometrical shapes might have been derived from gardening theories about the fundamental order in nature, but they also marked the land as belonging to human culture. To the extent that these works were seen as deriving from the sovereign, they were continuous with God's will. They were part of the king's rightful exercise of his earthly power. This relationship of creation to Creation, if not immediately obvious in the overall design of the garden, was certainly made visible in the artwork. The garden was full of statues of the seasons, times of day, and other elements of Creation, all rendered in human form. These were not mirrors of Creation, but representations of unseeable forces made by men to look human. The manicured lawns, clipped trees, espalier fences of fruit trees, and fabulous water system of the garden at Versailles all showcased in their formality techniques of domination. They presented human culture controlling nature in ways continuous with God's imposition of order over the natural world.

Science as a resource for the territorial state

The problem of legitimacy for the absolutist state may have revolved primarily around the king's right to rule and the growth of bureaucratic management, but it also involved the territoriality of the new state. The so-called centralization of power in the modern state depended not just upon rationalized oversight of state functions, but also on the political integration of diverse parts of the country. There was plenty of regional opposition to the authority of Versailles, which thereby created a second face to the problem of state legitimacy. If there was no traditional basis for increased state intervention into local political and economic life, then how could this kind of authority gain legitimacy?

Vauban's answer, as we have seen, was to naturalize the *pré carré*, that square French territory carved from the European continent. France, as a land-based political entity, was a construct of both nature and art. The oceans and the Pyrenees mountains, which marked most of France's borders, gave it a fundamentally natural form. The geometrical shape of this territory underscored France's place in a larger, natural order. According to this perspective, the actions of the military along the northern and eastern borders of France simply filled out the form, and gave the country its rightful shape. The state of France governed a territory, then, that was formed in large part by Creation and only needed some "works" by the monarch for its completion.[24]

The sciences – particularly astronomy, mathematics, and cartography – were of great use in making the *pré carré* come to life as both a symbol and site of French political life. Early in the reign Colbert noticed that he could not obtain an accurate map of France. This was a problem for a man who liked good inventories of his resources and good planning tools for administering the bureaucracy. He wanted maps for his forestry work as well as for planning economic and infrastructural projects. Vauban and his engineering counterparts, too, needed maps and *plans-relief* for their military projects. There was plenty of reason, then, for Louis XIV's ministers to encourage map-related scientific research in France to serve state power through territorial measurement and control.[25]

Of course, there were many non-cartographic reasons why Colbert and his *petite académie* encouraged scientific research in France. To be a center of European civilization to rival or even eclipse Italy, France needed to be a leader in the sciences as well as the arts. A French system of academies, based on Italian precedents but better funded and organized, seemed the best way to surpass the Italians.[26] Under Colbert's supervision, there was a proliferation of scientific institutions and increased state patronage for research in the early part of the reign of Louis XIV. The Académie Royale des Sciences, the botanical garden in Paris known as the Jardin du Roi, and the Observatoire all were institutions of science set up or augmented by Colbert.

The broad political and cultural ambition of the regime certainly increased the urgency of this institutionalization of science in France, but it did not reduce government need for better maps. Even Louis XIV came to support the Académie Royale des Sciences in large part so that improvements in astronomy and mathematics could increase the cartographic knowledge of his kingdom. While the Jardin du Roi may have been intended primarily to provide medicines for the doctors of Paris, rather than

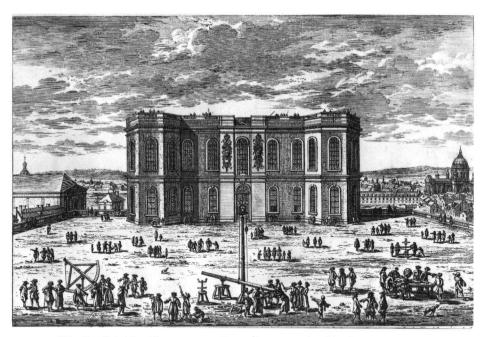

121. Perelle's *The Observatory in Paris*: the text under this picture states that this
beautiful building is shown surrounded by the instruments used by the
scientists, and is made so imposing that it looks from the distance like a citadel.

create an image of France, it still, in its own way, provided a map of France's position
as a trading nation by documenting the extent of its trade in plants. The depth of the
geopolitical interests at work in the science of the period was illustrated, surprisingly
perhaps, by a suggestion made at the Académie Royale des Sciences that the scientists
who were working with Perrault on a large-scale natural history project should study
only French native plants. This restriction was officially accepted by the scientists, but
never put into practice. Knowing a broader spectrum of plants and animals seemed
more of a tribute to French science and scientists. Nonetheless, the policy made clear
that political geography was not an issue completely sidestepped by those interested in
the life sciences.[27]

Physical scientists of the Observatory and Academy, in contrast, were more overt
and systematic in linking major research agendas explicitly to problems of territoriality.[28] Even though the French government set up the Observatory ostensibly to promote
astronomy in France, the astronomical observations and techniques of survey geometry cultivated in these institutions gave French scientists a greater lead in cartography
than astronomy. Louis XIV first invited two important foreign scientists to work at the
Observatory whose work was relevant to the most pressing problem in cartography:
measuring longitude. Giovanni Cassini and Christian Huygens were internationally
known mathematicians and astronomers who had both done work salient to this
problem. Cassini was (not incidentally) also a skilled surveyor and designer of fortifi-

cations, but he was best known as an expert on the movements of the moons of Jupiter. Galileo had argued that the complicated movements of these moons could make it possible to measure longitude, using the time of their appearance on the horizon and their configuration at that moment. Cassini's careful observations (unlike Galileo's) were accurate enough to make this possible. In France, Abbé Picard had already developed methods for measuring latitude that were quite precise. What French cartographers needed now was a good measure of longitude. Cassini's expertise was a valuable place to start.[29]

Christian Huygens was supposed to help with the problem too. He was not only known for his mathematics, but for his famous pendulum clock. In principle, his invention could make mechanical time-keeping precise enough to be used for measuring longitude. Because of the Earth's rotation, different longitudes experienced different times of day. A change in longitudinal location thus changed the position of an observer in time as well as space. An exact marine chronometer, which kept good time even in the roughest seas, could provide a record of the time at the prime meridian and allow a navigator to compare local time with the time on the chronometer. The difference could then be used to determine the longitude.[30]

The work done at the Observatory, linking astronomy to cartography, jettisoned entirely any remnant of the earlier belief in a dual system of nature, in which the laws of the heavens and those of the earth were fundamentally disconnected. Now, measuring the king's territory and studying the stars had become one continuous activity. Science helped link God's works in heaven to the king's works on Earth, forging a connection with as much political as scientific value. When Abbé Picard made his measurements to determine the precise shape of the Earth, he not only developed a more accurate scientific description of it, but produced an image of the Earth by "shooting" the sun.[31] He co-constructed the land of the Sun King and the centrality of the sun as a means of knowing and using the Earth.

Much was learned in the process of these experiments with land measurement, and the state was able to commission more exact maps to use for political projects. Although it is not usually proclaimed in books on science in the period, Cassini routinely worked with Vauban to improve the surveys done by army engineers in France, helping to transfer ideas about fortress design and survey techniques from Italy to France. The vast majority of the surveyors for the state, of course, were not well-known scientists but students of their work. If the men of the Observatory made measurements of land more accurate, military surveyors made them a more strategic resource for the pursuit of state power. Vast numbers of maps, globes, and models of cities and fortresses were made in this period to administer the work of common foot-soldiers, to fill the imaginations of noblemen, and to tie France's warrior elites to the emerging system of geopolitics.[32]

As we have seen, Colbert's reform of French forests also depended on surveys. The minister not only wanted to know what timber reserves were available to build French ships to compete with the English and Dutch, but wanted more reliable information about the size and state of the royal forests. Small groups of modestly trained surveyors invaded different forests of France to measure the perimeters of royal landholdings,

122. The king's supposed visit to the Academy of Science in Paris (Le Clerc, *Visite de Louis XIV*).

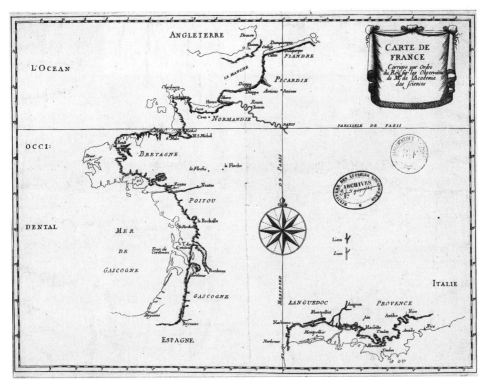

123. The corrected map of France, compiled from new surveys.

and study the quality of privately held timber reserves. These surveyors were not the great mathematicians and cartographers of the period, but they, too, used their techniques in the name of science for the state.

In sum, there was a massive amount of state-supported surveying, map-making, improvement in survey geometry, and astronomical calculation applied to cartographic problems in seventeenth-century France. These efforts yielded images of French territory that represented it as a natural unit. Scientist-surveyors presented France, using a language of mathematics developed for describing natural phenomena and employing it to delineate the natural contours of the French countryside. These images naturalized France as a territorial entity, while providing cartographic tools for facilitating civil engineering, military planning, and economic development. The political culture of state power was not highlighted in these studies, but it was the reason for them. At the end of the reign, the Cassini family began a great national survey – the first of its kind – based on an exacting system of measurement applied systematically throughout the whole domain. It was the crowning achievement of French cartography, and a project that finally depicted France as a singular and natural location.[33]

The politics of measurement

This geometrical reduction of the Earth's surface to a single system of geographical measurement has been described by commentators such as Proctor and Koyré as part of a cultural flattening in early modern science of human relations to nature.[34] As scientists translated physical and biological processes into the language of mathematics, the characteristics of creatures and things that could *not* be quantified were lost. The result was a preference for quantitative thinking over other ways of knowing.

While quantification may well have had this effect in the long run, at first, at least in France, it was not the immediate consequence of the new sciences. For example, superstition and the search for spiritual truths were not immediately and irrevocably excluded from the realm of science because they could not be measured. In fact, the perfect geometrical orderliness of nature was taken by Galileo, Descartes, Gassendi, and Samuel Hartlib (among others) as evidence of God as the power behind Creation. And numerology was among the most prevalent "superstitions" of the period. In seventeenth-century France, there was a surprising amount of interpenetration of spiritual and mechanistic conceptions of the natural world, and the language of mathematics often provided a point of translation between the two. Numerology was used routinely as a means for seeing the play of spiritual forces in the world. The four elements of Aristotle were matched by the four seasons, and four times of day. There were seven wonders of the world, and seven planets in the heavens.[35] These older uses of quantity were revived, not suppressed in seventeenth-century France. The measured approach only seemed to enhance other forms of significance related to numbers.

Mathematical thinking did not so much create a loss of diversity in relations to the natural world, then, but rather provided a way of connecting different sets of languages about nature. For example, John Dee made maps with accurate cartographic images in the center, and then surrounded them with borders containing spiritual power symbols that often included some numerology. Dee could use the power of quantity to craft both kinds of images of the natural world. In the maps, he recorded observable characteristics of nature, and in the borders, he pointed to the hidden forces within it. Numbers were used in both projects. The French and Dutch cartographers often decorated their maps in much the same way. Their elaborate borders indicated the importance or power of the Earth being depicted in the center. Sr. de Fer, cartographer to the dauphin, even used images of the great fountains and bosquets at Versailles in this way to decorate his maps. In these pieces, the lines between scientific measurements of land, engineering accomplishments, and symbolic representations of natural powers were not carefully drawn. Yet measured landscapes were shown in both the maps and their borders.

The turn toward measurement also did not assure the rationality of science or suppress the imaginations of scientists. Descartes claimed that the celestial bodies, which were moving in the sky in such mathematically precise ways, were actually floating on giant vortices of invisible liquid. Later in the century, Fontenelle argued for the existence of extraterrestrials, and urged others to think about what life on other planets must be like. This kind of science, like numerology, tried to grasp the vast powers of the universe through conjecture. The scientists who developed these theories were not fools, but serious men, attempting to conceive of natural forces or beings that were potentially knowable, but beyond immediate human perception. They explicitly wanted to use the language of mathematics to go beyond just description of perceived objects. But this led them to develop a surprising array of images to connect nature and number. Rather than being a cause of reduction, mathematics in this moment expanded the range of truths to be found in nature.[36]

Geometry in seventeenth-century France was used to join an amazingly diverse range of domains of human life. Sébastian Le Clerc, in his book translated as *Practical Geometry or a New and Easy Method of Treating that Art*, began a section on "The usefulness of geometry" by saying:

Geometry is not only useful, but in several cases necessary. 'Tis owing to this, that Astronomers are put into a way of making the observations, coming at the knowledge of the extent of the heavens, duration of time, motions of the heavenly bodies, measures of seasons, of years, and of ages.

'Tis by the assistance of this science that Geographers present to our view at once, the magnitude of the whole earth, the vast extent of the seas, the divisions of Empires, Kingdoms, and Provinces.

'Tis from this that Architects take their just measures for the structure of public buildings, as well as private houses.

By its help Engineers conduct all their works, take the Situation and Plan of places, measure their distances from one another, and carry their measure into places that are only accessible by the eye.

Persons of Quality, whose birth engages them to take the field [of battle], are oblig'd to apply themselves to this science. It not only serves as an introduction into the art of Fortification, which teaches how to raise proper bastions for the defense of places, and to raise and manage machines, that may serve to overturn or make breaches into those of the enemy; but also brings them to get skill and dexterity in the art of war, in forming an army in order for battle, in encamping, dividing the ground for quartering the army, taking maps of counties, plans of towns, forts and castles; measuring all sorts of dimensions both accessible and inaccessible, and in forming designs; finally to recommend them as much for their skill and address, as for their strength and courage.

All such as possess the Art of Designing, ought to know something of Geometry, seeing that without it they can't make themselves masters of Architecture, nor Perspective, which are two parts absolutely necessary to their art.[37]

Scientific knowledge, land control, art, engineering, and military power could all find common ground in geometry because they manipulated or measured relations within spaces. Geometry could be used to generate an orderliness in the world through art, engineering and war, or it could be used to reveal the extant orderliness in the cosmos itself. If this was a reduction, it was an ambitious one. Mathematics was, after all, the language of the universe and a tool for finding its underlying harmonies. With geometry, the connections between the heavens and the earth, God's works and the king's enterprises, artworks and the arts of war, could all be made evident. Many of the forces of nature and the arts of men were realized in the divinely written language of mathematics.

Natural order and the formal garden

More than any other garden area, the *petit parc* at Versailles, with all of its formality, naturalized mathematical order and made it continuous with the king's land. It located powers in nature, and showed them to be part of a rational and measured space. To the extent that state politics required legitimation, this site provided it. Diverse areas of the *petit parc* were both carefully delineated with hedges, trees, and topiaries, and also integrated into a single and dramatic design. This model of territorial integration could naturalize a comparable system of regional control. The visible order in the landscape was easy to equate with the lawful authority of the government. Mlle de Scudéry, in describing Versailles, slipped easily from praising the structure of the gardens to proclaiming this site as the birthplace for the king's military adventures that brought glory to France. French military achievement and natural order were artfully aligned by her prose just as they were in Le Nôtre's grading system.[38] Even the bureaucratic order, that system of power so suspect in the period, could be identified with the *petit parc* and its compartmentalized spaces organized according to formal, impersonal measures. The impersonality, the lawlike order, and the measured extension of the gardens made them also assimilable to the mechanical versions of natural philosophy. Truth, power, and social order were all aligned on the land.

Although the formality of French gardens in the seventeenth century has frequently been described as Cartesian and certainly had the geometrical orderliness to be called that, the point of French gardening was not to advocate or articulate a position in natural philosophy, but to present nature's diversity and orderliness as a model for human life. To what extent, then, should the formal gardens be called Cartesian?

At one level, it seems odd even to pose the question since Louis XIV officially rejected Descartes' work, and declared that the university should not teach Cartesian ideas. At the same time, the equation of the king with the sun was specifically associated with particular *virtues* of that heavenly body, not its role in a mechanical universe. It was the perfection of the sun that made it so much like Louis XIV. Such thoughts would have been anathema to Descartes. Yet the association of Le Nôtre's gardens with Cartesian thought has been undiminished by these historical inconsistencies. There is something about the formality, materialism, and impersonality of Cartesian thought and French formal gardens that makes them seem part of a contiguous, if not the same, cultural system.[39]

There are some elements of the *petit parc* that seem to fit well with Descartes' ideas – particularly the simple geometries of the overall designs. The careful proportions used to organize the complex spaces of this most formal area at Versailles seem derived from Cartesian principles. Descartes contended that truths about nature were found in simple principles, and could be recognized as true by their reducibility to mathematical formulations. He felt that the universe was fundamentally orderly and measurable. The human mind, having been created by God, was prepared to recognize the order of nature through examination of its measured relations. A well-founded natural philosophy, by his account, would describe the universe in terms of extension, proportion, and movement.[40] Since these were the fundamental organizing principles of French formal garden designs (with their huge scale, measured spatial relations, and active water system) one could rightfully call them Cartesian.

Still, in many ways the gardens of the *petit parc* were not at all Cartesian. For example, the parterres were so complex (even with Le Nôtre's simplified designs) that they undermined the Cartesian search for simple fundamental principles. Descartes did not just want to contain the complexity of nature within his formal system; he wanted to eliminate distracting details entirely from his philosophy. The surface of nature, with its jumble of features, was an active problem for his thought, not just a source of analytic complexity and intellectual challenge. These were exactly the elements of nature that made the foundation of science on true knowledge so difficult. He insisted that the distractions of sense perceptions had to be swept away.[41] But French gardens could not be so austere and lacking in sensual pleasures. If they had been that purely intellectual, they would not have seemed either French or so beautiful. As pleasure gardens, they had to engage the senses and be delightfully distracting. In fact, French gardens relied for their beauty on the *contrast* between distraction and abstraction, abundance and order, elaborate parterres and simple structures, glorious displays of flowers and unadorned walkways. Moreover, they depended for their fascination on the visual tricks set up by the complex grading system and the strategic uses of plantings. There was plenty of austere elegance in the gardens to call Cartesian, but it was relieved by the playful, complex, hierarchical, sensual, and abundant qualities of the gardens – the distractions of nature in all their glory.

The formal part of Versailles' gardens also had social uses that placed them at odds with Cartesian thinking. Descartes militated against hierarchical views of the natural world,[42] but formal gardens were filled with terraced hillsides, and images of natural superiority. Nobles had their high rank ratified in the gardens, and the king had his position as a semi-deity reiterated in the Apollo statuary as well. The Labyrinthe (as we will see in more detail later) was filled with sculptures of animals that described their relations as naturally hierarchical. Many classical statues in the *petit parc* were of heroes and gods, who embodied and conveyed natural superiority. The Sun King himself was a liaison between the Earth and the heavens. Worst of all (for a Cartesian), the gardens were inhabited by nature gods, fauns, and satyrs that brought superstition and mythology into this haven of rational order. Even alchemical symbolism seeped into this seemingly controlled space, diversifying the powers of nature in the king's gardens but clearly undermining any Cartesian effort at purifying the natural world. All these presences would have been anathema to Descartes who wanted to rid philosophy of superstition and of belief in a hierarchical universe. The resulting garden, then, was not so Cartesian. It did indeed carry a measured rationality into the landscape, but combined it with a complex image of nature as both mechanical and spiritual, simultaneously impersonally ordered and filled with supernatural forces.[43]

So, should one say, in the end, that the formal gardens of the *petit parc* were decidedly *not* Cartesian? That would probably be a mistake as well, since what made the gardens so politically valuable was largely derived from a central tenet of Cartesian thought: that nature itself was orderly. God had made it that way. Although Descartes has mostly been celebrated for championing formalism – the abstraction of

124. This engraving shows the complex details of the *Parterre de Sud* and *Parterre de Midi* that undermined the strict rationality of the geometrical structure (Perelle, *L'Orangérie de Versailles*).

thought and cultivation of mathematical reasoning – he placed orderliness in Creation itself, and presented abstract reasoning as a means of recognizing it. Descartes' interest in mathematics and thought were based on his concern about how to find the fundamental order in the natural world. And it was a cultivation of order in nature itself that was so central to French formal gardening and its political uses. The orderliness of the gardens themselves and their presentation of French land as part of a naturally lawful universe provided probably the most powerful political possibilities in the gardens. The geometrical reduction of complexity into a singular system of order was a wonderful model of state power that naturalized precisely what was being challenged by traditional notions of legitimacy: the impersonal and systematic exercise of power and expression of order in a territorial space. The formal gardens revealed in nature a model of order that sanctioned the impersonality of state absolutism and located its authority in the arrangement of land areas. Their measured artificiality was what made the gardens so politically important. They seemed to grow from natural systems, yet they clearly expressed the possibilities of systematic, rational domination.

Le Nôtre and the problem of natural order

In the end, the French formal garden was not an *argument* about nature derived from any theory of science, but a *display* of natural powers, forces, and possibilities, some presented in the argot of the new sciences and some not. Perhaps the gardens could seem like demonstrations of Cartesian orderliness to those hoping to find such patterns in them, but Le Nôtre was probably not promoting Cartesianism. If anything, he was following Boyceau's quite vague instructions to make gardens manifest the patterns of nature known to science. Beyond extrapolations from Le Nôtre's gardens themselves, and some rudimentary evidence about his life and character, there is very little evidence about Le Nôtre's interests in or explicit knowledge of the sciences.

To those familiar with Saint-Simon's descriptions of Le Nôtre's personal simplicity and modesty, the idea that he would have been constructing any model of the natural world or allusion to political philosophy in his gardens might seem absurd. But simplicity was one of the most respected affectations of the period, and Le Nôtre was smart enough to cultivate this virtue along with aesthetic ones. Le Nôtre may have been simple enough to adore Louis XIV and modest enough to ask that his family's crest have a cabbage in the middle of it, but he was no common man of the earth or bumpkin from the country. He was an educated man who studied optics, geometry, and architecture as well as the art of gardening. He lived most of his life at the Tuileries gardens in a court milieu, where his father had pushed him to study broadly, apparently believing Boyceau that royal gardeners should use intellectual rigor. He was raised in a community of royal gardeners whose families had held their positions for generations, and whose members had been instrumental in developing the distinctive French tradition of gardening. He would certainly have been exposed early in his worklife to Boyceau's idea that gardens should reflect the order and diversity of nature. Le Nôtre may have sustained a kind of social innocence through his life because of his apparently tranquil personality, but he was an articulate, interesting, and educated man, who lived in a social world where science and art frequently met.

But Le Nôtre showed no particularly propensity for science. He put together a curiosity cabinet late in his life that was famous enough that some foreign visitors came to see it on their tours. They said it contained mostly medals, stamps, and artworks, but not one item of natural history. It demonstrated that Le Nôtre had a lively intellectual side, yet no obvious fascination with science. Of course, natural history was the kind of science least respected by Descartes, so a true Cartesian would have resisted this kind of scientific collection. The apparent lack of interest in natural history, then, did not demonstrate a total lack of interest in science per se on the part of Le Nôtre, but did make it more difficult to establish in any authoritative way if and when he was using the new sciences in his gardens.

The biggest hindrence to analyzing Le Nôtre's thoughts on gardens, of course, is the almost complete lack of letters, drawings, sketches, plans, and theoretical writings on the subject. The few extant plans for bosquets in Versailles contain very detailed measurements of garden proportions and show very developed information about how the plumbing and planting were executed. They do indeed indicate the careful structuring of these designs and are interesting for the details inserted by Le Nôtre. Still, it is hard to use these sheets to evaluate Le Nôtre's way of working, since Mariage argues that he made these drawings after the gardening projects were complete.[44]

Many scholars have wondered why such a brilliant and educated man would have written so little and left so few records of his plans and practices. His silence on the theory and practice of gardening was so deafening that it has become in itself a curious piece of evidence about the man. While an artist in the post-Renaissance world was expected to claim his own creations and allow others to celebrate his genius, Le Nôtre seems to have been reluctant to do this. Perhaps he was just modest, as Saint-Simon said, but it may have been that he was just a consummate politician carefully negotiating a socially dangerous terrain. He was not shy about telling the king his opinions about gardening. He was certainly forthcoming when he did not like the addition of Mansart's Colonnade to the *petit parc* at Versailles. He seemed possessive of the park, and assertive about his tastes. But he did not interfere with the king's claims to the gardens. He seemed too politically astute for that. Perhaps he even realized that if the gardens at Versailles were treated as indicators of his personal genius, they would have ceased being so clearly works of the king set in Creation. If, on the other hand, the formal gardens of Versailles' *petit parc* were seen as evidence of higher powers at work in nature, then they could speak more effectively to the legitimacy of the reign. If Le Nôtre kept silent about his part in the designs, the park at Versailles could be more easily seen as evidence of the will of the sovereign furthering the will of God.

Le Nôtre seems to have cultivated his reputation as a garden designer primarily around his work at the Tuileries. Martin Lister and John Evelyn, both visiting France at different times from England, praised the beauty of his gardens in Paris, yet said not one word about his contributions to Versailles. Perhaps because he lived in Paris, Le Nôtre was able to take visitors through the Tuilleries and discuss his work there.[45] But it may also have been simply more prudent for the gardener to build his reputation

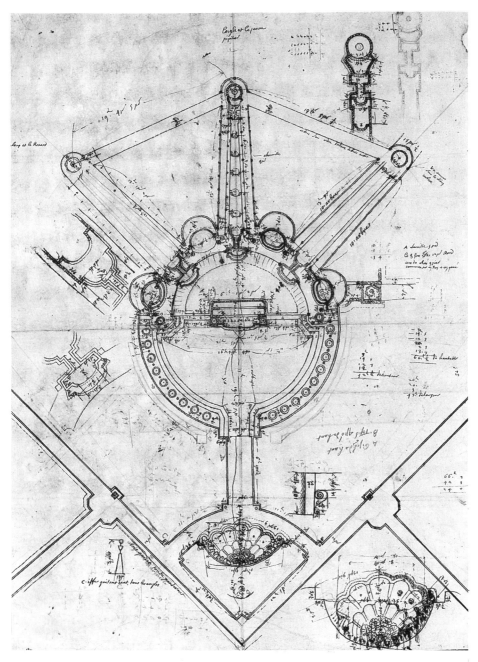

125. *Théâtre d'Eau*: one of the few sketches of a bosquet at Versailles attributed to Le Nôtre.

around a public space developed at a distance from the king. If the king's "works" at Versailles were so important politically, there was reason for Le Nôtre to remain modest about his work there.

The park at Versailles was seen (as intended) as a reflection of the king. Madeleine de Scudéry's fictional stranger, who in the *Promenade* came to take a tour of Versailles, explicitly said that she was moved to visit this site because it was the residence of such an important prince. During this tour, her group of friends discussed at length what constituted better records of a political leader's greatness: chronicles or monuments like the garden. They uttered not one word about the artists who did the writing or built the monuments. Louis XIV was supposed to manifest *his* greatness, not the efforts of others, both on the battlefield and in his building projects at Versailles. In keeping silent about his work on the gardens at Versailles, Le Nôtre was perhaps being less a modest man than a knowing courtier with a highly refined sense of political etiquette. The designer of such ambitious and yet delicate gardens certainly had the sensibility for such political finesse.

In the end, the gardens at Versailles became part of an elaborate system of reality construction in which both the natural world and the political order were constructed in reference to each other. The king was made into Apollo; the universe was presented as a model of impersonal order; animals symbolized particular virtues and vices; France was a woman-warrior; and both flowerbeds and golden statues represented natural abundance and the wealth of France.

Nature, representation, and the problem of authority

The gardens at Versailles were constructed using two importantly different modes or media: artworks and plantings. Statues in the *petit parc* could represent natural phenomena such as the Aristotelian elements, times of day, the continents, the seasons, and the stages of life. They could also stand for French rivers and military victories. Both the Trianon and Ménagerie also contained paintings of the animals and plants that reproduced and refashioned the look of creatures living in the gardens just outside these buildings. Much of this artwork anthropomorphized natural and political forces, but even the works that did not (like the paintings) still idealized and fixed aspects of nature and images of power.

The representations in art were matched by plantings that provided, through the structure of the gardens, another vision of the natural world and French territorial control. When Boyceau said formal gardens should represent nature, he meant the plantings, not artwork. So, although the most literal references to nature were in the names of statues and paintings, the garden beds and forest rooms were still explicit representations of a cognitively and aesthetically known natural world.

Both the arrangements of flora and of statuary in the gardens were intentional and artificial. Neither one was meant to provide simple mirrors of perception. Rather, they were meant to represent qualities of nature not immediately available to the senses. They made nature look the way it was *supposed* to look, with its inner, true structures revealed. In this, they were like science. As Fontenelle suggested, the problems of visibility and invisibility were at the heart of studying nature for science.

"All philosophy," I told [my student], "is based on two things only: curiosity and poor eyesight; if you had better eyesight you could see perfectly well whether or not these stars are solar systems, and if you were less curious you wouldn't care about knowing, which amounts to the same thing ... So true philosophers spend a lifetime not believing what they do see, and theorizing on what they don't see."[46]

Great gardeners, like true philosophers, cared about revealing what was not immediately apparent in nature, and tantalizing visitors with the unseen. They may not have cared about the niceties of natural philosophical debates, and may not have maintained a pure position about the structure of the natural world, but they did share this interest in revelation. For French gardeners like Le Nôtre, revelation was importantly connected to illusion. He played with both these elements in the grading of the gardens and in the rhythms of visibility and invisibility in the structure of walkways. For visitors to the parks, not believing what they could see and guessing what they could not see were sources of the pleasures of French formal gardens.

The strains between visibility and invisibility were centrally problematic for the sciences of the period. Descartes founded his notion of truth in science on images of natural systems that were felt with such clarity that they could not be denied by reason. In holding this position, he was caught in a debate with Gassendi about the foundations of mechanical philosophy. Gassendi located scientific truths in sense impressions, representations directly from observation, while Descartes, saw those as sources of deception. A clearly constructed *image* of underlying truths was his touchstone for science. The problems of truth and perception were forefronted by these debates and raised questions about the propriety and limitations of representations.[47]

Many elites in France were suspicious of natural philosophy and found it unfashionable, so they would not have cared whose natural philosophy (if any) appeared in their gardens. But they were fascinated like natural philosophers with the creation and deconstruction of illusions. That is one reason they were entertained by Molière's plays and the visual surprises in French gardens.

The popular science writer, Fontenelle, trying to make science more attractive and accessible to these elites, appealed to just this appetite for artifice in French elite culture:

I have always thought that nature is very much like an opera house. From where you are at the opera you don't see the stages exactly as they are; they're arranged to give the most pleasing effect from a distance, and the wheels and counter-weights that make everything move are hidden out of sight. You don't worry, either, about how they work. Only some engineer in the pit, perhaps, may be struck by some extraordinary effect and be determined to figure out for himself how it was done. That engineer is like the philosophers. But what makes it harder for the philosophers is that, in the machinery that Nature shows us, the wires are better hidden – so well, in fact, that they've been guessing for a long time what causes the movements of the universe.[48]

If nature was a kind of spectacle to please the eye and trick the mind, it was also like a great royal garden, with its elaborate water effects, visual surprises, and mythological allusions. Both made visible some of the hidden machinery of nature, and allowed people to contemplate the tricks and truths of the world. One could learn from the garden while enjoying its pleasures.[49] And one could learn political as well as scientific lessons, where natural order and the political system were merged in the garden's designs.

What could one learn about nature in these gardens? The two modalities for representing it provided a basic lesson: there was more than one nature in European culture. One nature, *natura integra*, was the pure system of Creation that existed with the Garden of Eden. The other nature, *natura lapsa*, was the spoiled nature that appeared after the Fall. Nature was both perfect and flawed, both orderly and filled with conflict and decay. The two modes of representation in the garden helped to underscore this difference. The statuary and paintings were perfect forms unchanged by time. They were (according to the ideal of French classicism) gracefully structured and well balanced. They also highlighted the process of representation itself by anthropomorphizing natural phenomena. The body of America, with its Indian headdress, was not a representation of the continent as a geographical shape or even a set of unique plants and animals. It stood for something natural (a continent) through the use of a natural form (a human body), but the relation between the two was symbolic.

In contrast, the parterres of formal gardens were made of bushes and flowers whose beauties were fragile and fleeting. The shape of a parterre might be highly artificial, and symbolize an orderly nature that was meant to endure, but the abundance of flowers was subject to decay. The underlying structure of nature might be made visible in the symmetries of the parterre designs, but was set out in low-growing bushes that lost their color, if not all their leaves, in the wintertime. Nature was depicted as both fleeting and enduring in the parterres.

The resulting parterres were not in any way more natural than a statue. Marble was, after all, as much derived from the earth as any bush. But plantings and artwork could point to the two Christian natural realities: perfect and flawed nature.

These images of nature were also connected to some popular visions of the natural world. The wild nature of natural histories (and more and more of political philosophy) seemed heir to that powerful, female presence described by Carolyn Merchant as part of European popular culture. This nature fused pagan traditions and the Christian view of nature after the Fall, imbuing the world with sexuality and violence, fecundity and danger. Wild nature did not stay outside the world of modern science, as both critics and proponents of the "Scientific Revolution" have suggested. Pascal, Mersenne, and Hobbes all posited a natural world of conflict, in which both truth and harmony were hard to find, and decay and death could be seen. The theories of Descartes and Galileo may have conveyed the purity of *natura integra*, even though they argued in different ways for a harmony, rationality, and perfection in nature, but they had to struggle against a deceptive and difficult surface-of-things to find this degree of natural order. Both wild and perfect nature were fundamental to the science of the period and held a wide range of possibilities for gardening and for political reality construction.[50]

The different and conflicting images of nature helped to amplify the problems of knowledge in science and politics. If there were so many ways to see some aspect of the natural or political world, on what basis could some be preferred to others? How could anyone establish a foundation for authoritative knowledge? For science as for politics, legitimacy depended on authority, and this meant distinguishing illusions from truth.

126. Girardon's *L'Enlèvement de Proserpine par Pluton*, 1677–99: a rape statue in the center of the very orderly Colonnade.

Both science and politics addressed and questioned the relationship between representation and authority. The point for scientists was to try to create representations of nature that would be based on firm foundations for knowledge. The point for Colbert, Le Nôtre, Le Brun, and the king's other advisors was to establish a conception of France and the monarch that would give French state-based power firm foundations.[51]

Marin argues that in the seventeenth century in France, there was a powerful interest in representations of the sovereign that affected the growth of state absolutism. The point was not so much to create propaganda for the regime, using the patronage system to craft an intentionally false image of the sovereign, but to create symbols of the sovereign that, like representations of the heavens, could reveal fundamental truths. Seeming distortions in the images of the king were less to distract the viewer than to make visible truths about the sovereign that were not immediately visible to the human senses.[52]

Rigaud's portrait of Louis XIV provided a case in point (see plate 115). This odd but stately portrait of the king placed his aging face on top of the youthful and healthy body of a dancer. It probably appealed to the king by giving him the physical stature he had once had in his youth. He was supposedly quite vain about his legs, and Rigaud's image had him flaunting muscular, lean legs all-too-much like a Las Vegas showgirl. The portrait was easy to discard as just another flattering artwork or a piece of political propaganda that projected a healthiness in the monarch that was simply false. The portrait was certainly deceptive rather than realistic, if verisimilitude was the issue. But, Marin says, it was not.[53]

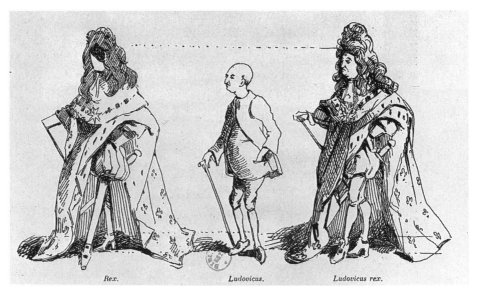

Rex.   *Ludovicus.*   *Ludovicus rex.*

127. Thackery's cartoon depiction of Louis XIV. Compare this with Rigaud's
portrait of the king (plate 115 above).

The portrait by Rigaud was hung in the room at Versailles where the king held his
public audiences. Whenever courtiers came near the monarch, they were required to
bow to their sovereign. This was not so surprising. But when Louis XIV was away from
Versailles, they were nonetheless required to bow to the Rigaud portrait. The representation of the king could be treated in this way, according to Marin, because it represented not the actual king but the power of the king, the notion of monarchy itself.
Courtiers were never bowing to the man, Louis XIV, but always to the abstract principle of monarchical authority. In his absence, the portrait embodied that authority.[54]

The distinction between the aging man who was king of France, and the idea of
monarchy had its counterpart in natural philosophy where neo-Platonic thought was
gaining interest. To Descartes, for example, the natural world was full of deceptive
appearances, complex surface features of a natural world in which birth and death,
changes of the seasons, and the times of day were examples. These were the transitory
features of nature that could distract the philosopher from the enduring truths of
nature. A flower might come into bloom and then fade, but the truth of the mechanistic processes by which this occurred would be enduring. This was the fundamental law
of science and the true principle of natural law.[55]

Marin argues that the representation of the king became in this period not just a
reflection of the king's form but a source and definition of absolutism itself. He contends there were two culturally identifiable bodies of the king – a mortal one that was
supposed to exercise power on earth, and a symbolic/represented one that was eternal
(existing even after an individual king had died). The second, the ideal monarch,
helped to define, locate, create, and legitimate the power of the monarchy. The distinc-

tion between the two bodies of the king, according to Marin, became a crucial ingredient in Louis XIV's pursuit of absolute power. If the true monarch had no limits, having been placed on earth to rule in God's name, then the ruler could and should exercise absolute power. This is how Louis XIV could legitimate his power to rule absolutely, when his predecessors had failed to find such a foundation for their ambitions.[56]

Representations of Louis XIV, for this reason, presented him as unbounded in his power, as an immortal force, a classical deity like Apollo or a timeless hero like Alexander. The king was symbolically located in the heavens in murals on the ceiling and fountains that pointed to the skies, suggesting the king's special relationship to God. The power of the king was not merely mirrored but constructed in these artworks and in writings of the period that described the king's body. Even Saint-Simon, who was not afraid to criticize the king's character, often praised his body and described in him a physical stamina greater than ordinary mortals. This is how he was projected in court ritual, too. Flatterers like Félibien could hardly contain their praise for the spectacle he presented publicly. The moral for French politics was clear. There was a superhuman element to monarchical authority that was enduring, and was projected equally onto the body of Louis XIV and the Rigaud portrait.[57]

Marin focused in his analysis on images of the king, but something comparable could be said about representations of the territorial state that appeared in the gardens of Versailles. The statues standing for France or French rivers, and the garden areas standing for French landmasses (sometimes even marked with French coats of arms) all pointed to an enduring principle of land-based state power that was intended to survive any change in regime. The political bureaucracy governing France might change, and the boundaries of the state might move through warfare, but the existence of France as a territorial site of political power was enduring.

The tensions between enduring and transitory elements of the natural world, and their relationship to political symbolism, were perhaps surprisingly explored at the Trianon. According to the historian Lenotre, this was the place where, late in his reign, Louis XIV could go to conduct his family life beyond the constraints of court formalities. At first, it was a small way-station near the hunting forests in the park of Versailles, used alternately for sexual encounters and resting after a hunt. Late in the reign, the king had it remodeled for housing Mme de Maintenon, the king's mistress who became his secret second wife. This became the place where confidants of the king, his family, hunting partners, princes of the blood, and those temporarily in favor could have more personal contact with Louis XIV. The human scale of the architecture, the intimacy of the gardens, and the proximity to the hunting park and distance from the main château all gave the Trianon an air of relaxation quite unlike that to be found elsewhere in the park.[58]

The Trianon was most importantly a place where the king did not have to represent himself as the monarch. While his portrait by Rigaud stood in for him at Versailles, the king was free to be a man, not the sovereign. At the château of Versailles, both king and courtiers might be caught in a permanent system of etiquette, but at the Trianon, this formal system of performances could be dropped, and the king could become a

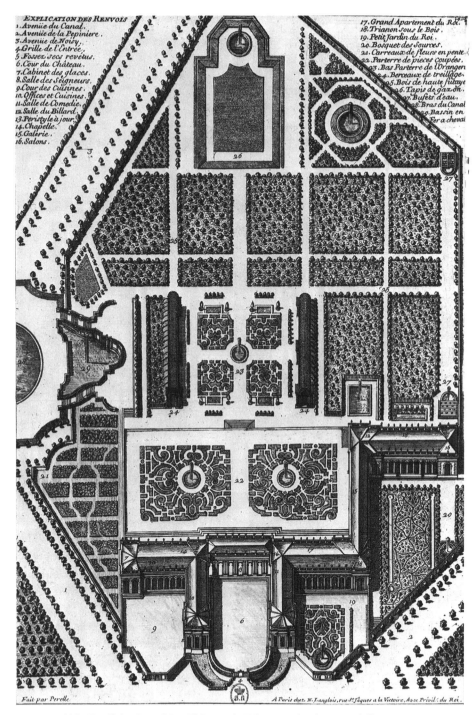

Fait par Perelle.   A Paris chez N. Langlois, rue St Jaques a la Victoire, Avec Privil. du Roi.

128. Perelle's plan of Le Château de Trianon, after its remodeling.

member of his family.[59] The Trianon provided not just respite from the representational structure, but a place to contemplate it from a distance. The château was dedicated to Spring, and was filled and surrounded with images of children and spring flowers. These sweet creatures never aged, and never died. For the aging king, they offered either memories or solace.

The most remarkable thing about the new Trianon was the way it worked out its theme of springtime. It juxtaposed interior murals of spring gardens to exterior views of actual plantings. The walls were covered with representations of bosquets at Versailles not just rendered in elegant detail, but filled with a colorful profusion of flowers, excessive sprays of waterworks, and skies full of putti and images of a young Apollo on his chariot. Beyond the windows were the gardens outside, never quite able to reach this level of perfection. The fading flowers of the parterres were replaced with new ones in the night, so that they would seem fresh again in the morning, but even these efforts could not really disrupt the cycles of changing seasons. Falling leaves outside would eventually set up a contrast with the unmoving, painted vistas of spring in the interior. Representations of gardens could somehow hold the eternal beauties and charms of nature against the forces of death. Significantly, Louis XIV frequented the Trianon in his old age, when the growing gap between the waning powers of his body and the idealized representations of monarchical power seemed (from his doctor's diaries) to have been burdensome for him. The Trianon paintings of the bosquets at Versailles provided an opportunity for contemplating a meeting of art and nature, where the effects of time could almost be arrested. Just when the portrait of the king was being used to provide a permanent presence for the monarch at Versailles, the Trianon created a permanent presence of the gardens at Versailles, perhaps suggesting that even the landscape with its natural cycles could be made a permanent feature of European political and cultural environment, providing an aging king's dream of an undying France, held always in its youth.[60]

Natural hierarchy and the problem of social stratification

Even if the territorial state gained new legitimacy from its relationship with the land, and the bureaucracy found new foundation in an impersonal and abstract order of things, there were still unsolved problems of legitimacy in late seventeenth-century France. The government could not be stable without some agreement about who should have the right to rule. The English Civil War had shown the potential vulnerability of European monarchs. If the sacred authority of the anointed sovereign could be called into question, then on what basis could the monarchy be sustained? The social mobility over the preceding century in France had made it particularly hard for people there to believe that noble families were naturally better suited to govern than others. Those who were upwardly mobile and *bought* their new positions could not point to differences in blood to distinguish themselves from the rest of the population. Nobles were no longer a special breed. If there was no obvious natural or spiritual reason for their political status, why should nobles rule over France? The answer, developed in this period, was "natural virtue."

129. Jean Cotelle's *Bassin de Neptune*: one of the paintings of the gardens at Versailles on the walls of the Trianon.

By the natural virtue tradition, some people, whatever their parentage, seemed to contain personal qualities that made them visibly superior to others; they had manners, learning, taste, a sense of place, and a strength of moral character that made them rise above the rest.[61] They were naturally superior in the sense that their good character was innate – they were born with it. Others could try to cultivate learning and taste, but only those with natural virtue could make use of this kind of education. The absurd new rich, so powerfully ridiculed by Molière, were the perfect negative case; they aped learning and taste only to look ridiculous because they could not comprehend the subtleties of elite culture.[62] The naturally virtuous could not only develop personal elegance, but had a moral superiority as well. Their stature may have been in their natures, but it had a sprirital component as well.

The notion of natural virtue provided a flexibility in French social life that allowed some social mobility while still restricting access to power. Men like Colbert, Vauban, Le Nôtre, and La Quintinie were naturally virtuous men, whom the king admired precisely because they were modest, tasteful, and had a clear sense of place. They could be given powers to transform France because they had the virtue to do it well. Their capacities to excel allowed them to be distinguished from others of their background, but, importantly, their successes were not interpreted as a result of personal effort but rather as an expression of natural endowments. This new group of naturally virtuous, upwardly mobile men had particularly useful political attributes. The king could trust them with power because, unlike nobles of the blood, they could not take control of the government without him. As a result, they brought new blood to French government, where Louis XIV could keep both his ministers and the state under his control.[63]

The natural virtue tradition also gave the nobility something to do with their time at court. The increased demands on those who wanted to sustain high social standing distracted elites with new kinds of learning. If they were to demonstrate their high rank through grace and wit, they had to cultivate themselves. Aristocrats studied ballet, manners, and even the classics so they could mark themselves as "naturally" better than those of lower rank.[64] Not surprisingly, the dauphin was much more carefully and strictly educated than Louis XIV, and took to his studies quite seriously.[65] Just as predictably, the French formal gardens in this period were filled with images of natural virtue and natural hierarchy to help shore up this system by equating it with God's larger design.

The natural virtue tradition developed in France in a period when the relations of people to animals were undergoing change. Keith Thomas argues that the move toward scientific thinking in Europe interrupted relations to the creatures based on Christian doctrine. At the moment of Creation, Adam had been given dominion over animals and plants. Powerful hierarchical relations between man and animals were needed because animals had no souls. They suffered no spiritual pain, and could never be as close to God as humans, who were made in his image. People of lower social rank were often seen as bestial, and more like animals than their soul-filled social betters. Social hierarchy was legitimated by this natural hierarchy, which was derived from Creation.[66]

The growth of science began to undermine the firm underpinning of these beliefs. The growth of mechanical philosophy and its application to living creatures put new emphasis on the physical attributes of plants and animals. (Perrault 's natural history project for the Académie des Sciences was based on these principles.) For the majority of Cartesian scientists, animals' placement in a hierarchy was no longer an issue. Still, the debate over animal souls continued, with many philosophers still asking whether there were fundamental spiritual differences among the creatures that ranked them.[67]

The natural virtue tradition developed in this context, bringing comparable ambivalences about the salience and sources of social hierarchy. Proponents of the idea of natural virtue assumed that there were innate hierarchies among men, but that virtue was visible in behavior. It was a perfect transitional theory in a world where ascribed social station could no longer be assumed and the achievement of social rank (unfettered social mobility) was unthinkable as a basis for legitimate social rank. The natural virtue tradition maintained elements of traditional notions of rank (God made natural differences) and yet added possibilities for changes in rank through behavior.

The images of animals in statues throughout the *petit parc* and the live animals in the Ménagerie at Versailles provided opportunities for exploring these themes and working out problems of social rank. The creatures at the Ménagerie brought to Versailles evidence of a wild nature that was at once hierarchical and chaotic (see plate 91). This was a world of beasts in which violence produced domination, creating hierarchies that were both natural and yet so brutal that they justified the forceful subjugation of all animals to humans. The building itself was a panopticon, a site for centralized suveillance of the animals. The creatures were enclosed in a series of walled outdoor compounds. The yards provided a disciplinary structure built by "man" to contain "nature," and they also sorted the animals into groups, just as a natural history book might do. The site ended up functioning as a kind of living *cabinet de curiosité*, where scientific classification based on natural differences produced a display of order.[68] This attention to classification in the structure of the Ménagerie was reproduced in the scientific uses to which these animals were subjected. Specimens from the Ménagerie were used by scientists in Paris for dissections in the Académie Royale des Sciences. In both Versailles and Paris, then, animals were contained in a humanly designed system of order intended to replace one order of nature based on bestiality with another order of nature derived from science.[69]

In the Ménagerie, animals of the same species enjoyed an egalitarian existence within their own compartment in the building, but they were strictly separated from other species with whom they might vie for power. Moreover, the whole collection of beasts was carefully segregated from other parts of the garden, drawing a sharp distinction between the plants and animals in the park. In the natural history work being done in that period, researchers were particularly interested in investigating variations in sexuality and aggressiveness. Many scholars were arguing that while animals were sexual creatures, plants were not. Seeds, they maintained, were fundamentally hermaphroditic, so plants reproduced asexually. This lack of sexuality or bestiality in plants was taken as the reason why plants were so peaceful and apparently orderly. Predatory animals were the ultimate expressions of violent, sexual, and wild Nature, while plants embodied an Edenic innocence. No wonder, then, that the Ménagerie so carefully segregated animals from the rest of the garden.[70]

The most varied and explicit social lessons about natural hierarchies and virtue were to be found in the Labyrinthe. This part of the garden was a clear pedagogical tool. The dauphin even received part of his education by learning the versions of Aesop's fables inscribed by the fountains there.[71] The reason why this charming bosquet was used for education is simple enough. The stories described relationships among animals that were thinly veiled social lessons. The morals to the stories might have emerged from nature but they were applicable to French noble life. In the story of the tortoise and the hare, for example, the silly hare was too confident of his superiority, and lost the race to the slower tortoise. Foolish creatures did not accept or understand their positions, and wise ones flourished because they knew their place. This was surely a lesson for courtiers who were daily learning about the dangers of overconfidence and the proprieties of place.[72]

Physically, the Labyrinthe consisted of narrow, meandering walkways with forty small fountains set along the paths at corners, intersections, and open areas. Each fountain illustrated one of Aesop's fables, and was accompanied by a quatrain of poetry to relate the story. This was a reader's garden and a charming pedagogical tool, but it was not a child's playground. In the labyrinth, the meandering paths broke with the geometrical orderliness of the rest of the garden, and identified this site as one where animals could find their true nature.[73] The structures of the human world seem to fade away – in strong contrast to the Ménagerie. Still, the arrangement of pathways was simple enough so that no one would find themselves lost for long. Compared to medieval mazes, this one was easy to learn. But the labyrinthine form was a reminder of the complexity of the world. One could get lost in life. Creatures who did not learn their place and master their natures put themselves in danger.[74]

The meandering paths of the Labyrinthe were interestingly like a patched-together sample of parterre designs. They formed partial geometrical figures organized with a complex yet somehow organic system of curved lines. Fountains were set at most of the intersections of the maze, associating moments of choice with the morality tales of the sculptures. The paths were narrow and constrained the vision of those who walked there, but were arranged to allow visitors to see (on most occasions) the next fountain from where they stood. The differences among the fountains helped to provide strollers with evidence of where they were and where they could go next. It was as though this maze suggested that, through the confusion of pathways (or life), the fountains (or moral lessons in the fables) could guide the nobility to safety.

What lessons could courtiers learn from these renderings of Aesop's fables? One cannot answer this question directly from the fables themselves, since their presentations in the Labyrinthe were not always consistent with written versions of the fables published today. But Charles Perrault wrote a description of the *Labyrinthe* that describes each of the fountains, its quatrain, and the fable from which it was drawn. This "reading" of Aesop's stories best expresses what contemporaries of Perrault assumed the Labyrinthe to convey.[75]

Two fountains were given the most prominent positions in the bosquet. One, near the entrance to the Labyrinthe, was "The Owl and the Birds" (*Le Duc et les Oiseaux*). The other, "The Battle of the Animals" (*Le Combat des Animaux*), was placed at the

130. Le Clerc's plan of the Labyrinthe at Versailles, from Charles Perrault's book, *Le Labyrinthe de Versailles*, describing and illustrating this bosquet.

center of the bosquet. Their fables carried a frightening message: namely, that nature excluded unworthy animals. This was a territble threat at Versailles where access to the king and court was a prerequisite for gaining social importance. In these fables, animals who were ugly, ungainly, or traitors to their own species were no longer permitted to see the light of the sun; they were made nocturnal. In the court of the Sun King, this message must have been bone-chilling.

Inappropriate social ambition was also a central theme in many of the fables. In one, a monkey, trying to rise above his station, pretended to be a man. When his ruse was pierced, he was eaten. Characters like this monkey could be shamelessly brutalized in the stories because, in the world of wild nature, violence was a major determinant of natural order. Fighting against or trying to evade natural hierarchies was both foolish and dangerous – certainly for the animals, but by extension, also the French aristocracy.

Some subtle measures of natural virtue were presented in a fountain that told the story of the Peacock and the Magpie, *Le Paon et la Pie*. The peacock was chosen as king of the birds on the basis of his beauty, but the magpie challenged his elevation, asking whether it was better to be beautiful or virtuous. (The word for magpie, *pie*, is also the French word for piety or good works, which makes clearer the differentiation of good looks from good works.) In most of the stories, the superior animals were presented as the most beautiful, but in this one, the importance of virtue was both disentangled from good looks and singled out as the highest mark of distinction.

There were lots of fables, too, about natural enemies. A little mouse was counseled by her mother (in *La Souris, le Chat, et le Petit Coc*) that a nice looking cat, even though she liked it better than a small rooster, was actually her real enemy. In another story (*Le Coc et le Renard*), a fox lying to a rooster claimed that peace had been established between their two species, but the smart rooster knew better than to believe an enemy, and stayed away from the fox. The point of these stories was to show that random social mixing was dangerous and that care had to be taken to recognize even disguised enemies

Finally, many fables associated nobility with a sense of social place and gratitude toward allies and helpful superiors. They also preached avoidance of the ungrateful, and respect for rightful authority. A porcupine who was taken home by a snake, threw the snake out when the latter complained about the quills. The porcupine was clearly an unmannerly sort to be avoided. Similarly, a wolf who had a bone removed from his throat by a bird, then ate the bird for dinner. These were naturally contemptible animals without manners and with low moral character, who were dangerous to noble animals and should be avoided. The Labyrinthe also spoke to the legitimacy of kings. The story of the monkey king and the peacock king, demonstrated that while a false ruler could be elevated temporarily, his natural limits would lead either to questioning of regal authority or the downfall of the unfit king himself.

Recognizing natural differences, knowing how to distinguish the animals of better character from those of lower quality, seeing through the disguises and good looks of some and recognizing the ruses of others, were the social lessons to be taken from these stories. They spoke to a world of nobles concerned with the definition and location of natural virtue, and provided models for acquiring that virtue, displaying it, and avoiding those without it. The Labyrinthe as a whole presented these lessons as a guide through the confusions and twists of life, and naturalized them by displacing the tales into the world of animals.

The animal stories of the Labyrinthe not only conveyed natural hierarchy, but depicted a natural world full of conflict, ambition, uncontrolled desire, and aggression. This wild nature was the condition for the establishment of the hierarchy of creatures. Domination was a result of conflict among the animals. Only the rightful exercise of

131. *Le Cigne et La Grüe.* The Swan and the Crane fountain from the Labyrinthe.

power by human beings could restore order and peace. The struggles in the natural world were a central issue to the political philosophy of the period. They were taken as a model of the aggressiveness and jealousy of people that created a conflict-filled state of nature for humans as well as animals. The exercise of force by the king was justified by some philosophers as the only virtuous means for ending the struggles. Given the political potency of these arguments and their particular attractions for absolutism, it makes sense that images of the violent conflicts among animals were arrayed in many sites of the gardens at Versailles.[76]

Hierarchy was also naturalized in other parts of the garden, where no animals were present. Water features, such as the *Cascades* and the *Bosquet des trois fontaines*, for example, placed water on step-like structures and let it find its own level. The cascades were not just noisy waterworks or lovely sights to see, but embodied a lesson about the order of things: natural phenomena trying to rise above their level would only fall to the bottom again. Cascades in French gardens became a separate kind of water feature from regular fountains, ranking and animating the slopes of hillsides without the assistance of statuary. The cascades had no gods or heroes to elevate like Italian fountains did, and spoke only to earthly hierarchies with their structures. That is why they seemed connected to the attempts to naturalize hierarchies through depictions of animals.

The organization of the garden around different grades and terracing, which regulated who could see what, also spoke to the relation of rank and vision. The battlement walls that helped to distinguish gardens levels, also seemed to guard these differences.

132. The cascade in the *Obélisque* fountain.

There were many ways in which the formal orderliness of the gardens was achieved through regulation of hierarchies. These did not have to be directly applied to the social world to be meaningful in naturalizing social hierarchy. By making grades in nature seem important and inevitable, they contributed to the sense of natural order that then reappeared in the Labyrinthe, where social and natural orders were clearly linked.

One area of the park stood for wild nature itself, uncontained and uncontrolled. It was the ultimate site of violence and desire: the hunting forests. At the opposite arm of the canal from the château and across from the orderly world of the *petit parc*, the landscape scaled slowly up the hillside toward the hunting forests beyond. The land rose gently without the steplike grading (the hierarchical landings) so abundantly evident in the *petit parc*. While elsewhere in the park, all the views ended with a gate, statue or other boundary object, in this direction there was an infinite horizon, where the grand plan of the universe could melt into another kind of nature. This was the direction of the hunting forests, an enclave of wildness, where the infinite, chaotic, corporate, and sexualized nature could be sustained. Aggression and predatory impulses could be indulged here and could replace the measured control of the rest of life at Versailles. Its very wildness made this forest the opposite of the ordered world of the *petit parc*. The fact that they faced each other across the canal added to this contrast. If the *petit parc* displayed the order of Creation, this part of the park pointed to the effects of "the Fall." Faced with the uncontrolled world of the hunting forest as the alternative to the rightful exercise of human power, the issue was only how to impose

133. The hundred steps by the Orangerie.

order, not whether to impose it. Hierarchy was both natural and necessary, given the fall from grace.

The explicit lessons in natural virtue in the Labyrinthe, the threat of disorder in the hunting forests and the Ménagerie, and the formal explorations of systems of hierarchy in cascades and graded terraces all made the French formal garden a kind of primer in social stratification for this period and place. The message was fundamentally conservative. The garden's orderly world suggested that there was no real point in trying to reverse natural rankings because such reversals, like water pumped to the top of a cascade, would only be temporary. Everything in nature would eventually find its own level, and rightful rulers would be given their power.

This message was quite explicitly presented in the fountain of the slave, *L'Encelade*. This fountain was designed to illustrate the classical story of a giant who wanted to raise himself out of his bondage in the earth, where in fact he belonged. In the fountain statuary, his huge hands were used to illustrate his physical strength and his contorted face made clear his desire for freedom, but he was not able to leave his assigned position. The fountain manifested the giant's desire, rage, and will with a central water jet that seemed to scream from his mouth toward the sky. His angry countenance spoke to the natural but dangerous forces of the world, which were always struggling against natural order. His ill-fated battle to free himself in the end demonstrated the power of the natural order to keep creatures in their place, in spite of the subterranean, potent, and violent forces in nature. The moral of the story was that, although some creatures

134. G. Marsy, *L'Encelade*, 1675–77: the central statue in the fountain.

might try to use this kind of natural but illegitimate power to rise above their station, they would fail. Even if they were as powerful as a giant, they could not fundamentally change the established order of things. They could cry to the heavens, but their cries would simply fall to the earth like water from the fountain. The natural world of social hierarchy would necessarily triumph.

Investing power in the land of France

Making gardens into models of the natural world and using them to make statements about natural order was not an innovation found first in French gardens. Pleasure gardens in Renaissance Italy, for example, had constituted Edenic nature, using the materials of Creation itself. Within these Edens, Europeans could be restored temporarily to a form of garden that had been lost after the Fall. In seventeenth-century France, such a theologically invested park would have been too controversial to construct. Playing with Christian imagery after the Counter-Rreformation was a dangerous business, and filling a symbolic Eden with decadent elitist pleasures would have been an unimaginable heresy. No wonder French gardens could not and did not simply reproduce Italian gardens. Still, they did bring to life a natural world. If it was not heaven on earth (Eden), it was at least a version of earth invested with powers from the heavens and from the world of nature itself.

The absolute power of Creation, the eternal forces of Nature, and the untrammeled

135. The canal as a mirror, bringing heavenly reflections to the earth below.

truths of Science were revealed on the earth and invested in the land of France in the gardens at Versailles. They marked the center of the French court as a power center in a world of natural order. At the end of the *petit parc* and the actual, if not aesthetic, center of Le Nôtre's design for the gardens at Versailles, the great canal cut an "X" into the French landscape. This giant cross-shaped body of water lay along the surface of this valley, reaching with its long arms toward the formal gardens near the château, the Ménagerie, the Trianon, and the hunting forests of the larger park beyond. This giant reflecting pool obviously joined four diverse regions of the garden, but at the same time (and more importantly) it used subterranean forces of nature to capture an image of the sky. It was fed with water that seeped up from underground and then acted as a mirror, drawing the heavens down to the earth. It integrated a range of social and spiritual forces and spread them out onto the soil of France.

This imposing water feature was as central to the social life of the garden as it was to the layout of the park; it was where miniaturized naval vessels were launched to fight mock battles on social occasions; on other evenings, it carried courtiers on gondolas, who were lulled by late-night concerts as they defied the division of day from night and waited for the dawn; it was the king's favorite route to the Trianon, where his last mistress was installed and his family life solidified; it was the mirror for fireworks set off to symbolize the power of the state and the meeting of the four Aristotelian elements – earth, air, fire, and water; but most of all it was a peaceful sliver of water drawn through the French countryside in which carp grew and from which mists rose on cool mornings. It was, in short, a culturally loaded but nonetheless organic piece of France. In the canal, the lights of the heavens and the riches of the earth were joined in a cross at the seat of the French court. Visible but unspoken powers were united on the human plane where French state power was being fashioned and legitimated on the land.

What was the purpose of this liquid cross at the heart of the royal garden? It certainly could have alluded to Louis XIV's claim to be the great Catholic king of Europe, heir to the Habsburg Empire and the true defender of the Counter-Reformation Church. This was a man who proved his "devotion" to the Church by expelling the Protestants from France with the revocation of the Edict of Nantes (in a devastating move of religious intolerance that permanently undermined the French economy).[77] No Christian of that period could have dismissed the shape of the canal as insignificant, but then the canal was never touted as the marker of Divine will nor surrounded by statues filled with religious symbolism, which would have stabilized this vision of it. In fact, the canal at Versailles provided a striking contrast to many of the reflecting pools in Italian gardens, which not only mirrored the heavens but routinely contained small water jets to spout toward the sky or abutted architectural features that pointed upward, alluding to the connection of heaven and earth. In contrast, the horizontal surface of the canal at Versailles was uninterrupted by sprays of water. At the shore, the canal merged into broad expanses of lawn that continued the horizontal line away from the water for many yards until it reached the trees. This cross-shaped pool seemed designed to pull the heavens *earthward*, rather than turn the viewer's eyes toward the sky. It *embedded* God's power in the natural world and located his will in Creation rather than in a domain far above the level of human perception and action. God's presence was signified in this part of the garden with water, rock, and earth – the same materials used in Creation, but now being employed to mark the territory of France.

Even though Le Nôtre often produced gardens organized around central intersections and cross-shaped walkways, he did not make any other canals with this form in his gardens. Vaux-le-Vicomte had a straight canal that cut across the main pathway that led away from the château. The canal at Sceaux was similarly linear but had a large square pool projecting to one side of the main canal itself. Chantilly had two water systems, one near the château that meandered and served partially as a moat, and the other, a bent, linear canal. The latter had a side channel approaching the form used for Versailles' cross, but it was never developed to the same geometrical perfection. Each seemed like a truncated or imperfect version of what was finally realized at Versailles: a canal that formed a huge, discrete, and recognizable cross. The idealized form of the canal located

Versailles' gardens as a center, a site that united land areas in all four directions, simultaneously reflecting the heavens and taking the measure of the earth. It could speak at once to science, religion, and politics.[78] It was a place where legitimacy could be transferred from heaven to earth because the sky merged with the landscape. It was a place where water found its level, and the orderliness of the natural world found forms. It was a silent carrier of the central political messages of the garden. It presented a natural reality that entered "the mind so naturally" that it did not need to be spoken.

The system of fountains and pools scattered through the gardens similarly drew attention to the surface of the earth. For reasons not well explained by art historians, fountains in late seventeenth-century French formal gardens tended not to be constructed in the typical Italianate way with a central statue elevated over a series of ranked catch basins. The Pyramid fountain by Girardon set along the north–south axis of the *petit parc* had a comparable structure, even though it reversed the relation of statuary to the basins. The basins were held aloft by sculpted figures, not vice-versa. Still, it was one of the few manifestations of Italian baroque hierarchical fountain design at Versailles. Most of the fountains used no tiered basins at all, and simply placed the statuary at the surface of a reflecting pool, which was embedded in the land itself. Even the sculpture of Latona and her children, set in the famous fountain near the château, was at first placed on a simple mirrored surface. Only later was this family elevated to the top of a wedding-cake structure, where in triumphant fashion the group could be bathed in a riot of water jets and dominate a mountain of cascading water.[79]

The design shift that placed the Fountains of the Seasons, the Apollo fountain, the Dragon fountain, and other prominent pieces at ground level visually restructured the relation between the heaven and earth in the park. In these pools, just as with the canal, reflected images of the heavens were made part of the earth. Fountain statuary, too, located gods and heroes not on pedestals that would hold them closer to the heavens, but at ground level where French nobles walked. This plane of social action was not detached from spiritual forces, even though it was pulled down from the heavens. It was invested with spiritual powers. Classical nature gods – even unruly and provocative beings, like Bacchus, water nymphs, and satyrs – inhabited the landscape. These creatures of the earth, forests, seas and rivers appeared in many sculptures, and on the inside and outside of fountains, and brought a sense of spirituality and possibility to the ordered world of the *petit parc* (see plates 62, 63 and 118).

Water nymphs joined the gods representing the rivers of France in the Parterre d'Eau. They, like other nature spirits at Versailles, animated the natural world with spiritual forces. In this case, they addressed nature's sensuality and abundance as seemingly benign forces. The glistening figures, barely clothed, were reclined in a sensually inviting manner, not in erotic poses, of course, but something much more subtle and relaxed. They were surrounded, too, by flowers, childlike figures, and edible sea creatures that could indicate their re-productivity. The rivers were represented half by male figures and half by female figures, an arrangement appropriate for a heterosexualized universe. At the same time, the water nymphs were female and identified this sexualized natural world as fundamentally female, just like the nature in European popular culture described by Carolyn Merchant.

Interestingly, the chaotic and dark qualities of nature were placed just across the terrace from the Parterre d'Eau in the Fountains of the Animals with their violent hunting scenes. These animals were predators engaged in tests of strength, where their muscularity could be made most visible and their desire to kill most manifest. The great beasts were set to the side of the water jets that pointed to the heavens, but the jets also rose considerably higher than those in the main water parterre, suggesting the scale of the power invested in this wild element of nature.

Farther into the *petit parc* and helping to structure it on either side of the *tapis vert* were set the four Fountains of the Seasons. Bacchus, Ceres, Neptune and Flora, representing the seasons, were cast in lead and gilded to glisten in the sun. Around them were piles of nature's bounties: flowers for the spring, grains for the summer, grapes for the autumn, and seafood for the winter (plates 41 and 62). If the Fountains of the Animals highlighted the violent and wild in nature and the river gods revealed its sensual side, these statues displayed the almost magical productivity that followed the seasons of the year. These golden deities presented a nature full of riches that could realize human dreams, and pointed to an abundance that was of and in the world. These magical and spiritual beings were placed almost near enough to touch in their pools, and built close enough to human scale that they seemed almost a part of the social world around them. Yet they embodied forces well beyond human control. Provocatively, these specific classical deities were those that aristocrats often impersonated at fêtes, blurring the social and spiritual definitions of natural superiority.

Classical deities, unlike the Christian God, had two aspects that made them useful to politics. In early Greek theology, they were primarily nature gods who inhabited specific parts of the earth or heavens, and carried powers appropriate to their placements. Later, these gods were given Mt. Olympus, a heavenly kingdom to retire into, where they could live but still return to the earth. They may have held onto some of their attributes as nature gods or stayed in the parts of the universe where they had first found their powers. For example, Neptune did not leave his watery realm. Still, most classical deities took to the heavens, returning to earth when it pleased them but finding their meaning in their spiritual superiority to men.[80]

For the seventeenth century, the superiority of the gods (in the heavens) remained important, but the fact that some classical deities could be represented as nature gods, set into the forests or located beneath the sea, was absolutely essential to their uses in the gardens. Fountain statuary in particular put these figures squarely down on the earth again, where their sacred powers could merge with natural ones. Most of the classical statues in French formal gardens *not* associated with fountains – the figures which guarded the parterres and filled the bosquets – were elevated on pedestals, standing above the world of mortals. These pieces were a mix of antique and French classical pieces, and remained consistant with the style of old Roman works. Nonetheless, these statues depicted elements of nature as often as they did ancient gods and heroes, helping to continue the equation of the sacred and the natural in French gardens. In the end, there was no corner of the *petit parc* without classical figures to fill this natural realm with powers and instill the sacred into the terrain. The land of France was inhabited with these deities who blessed and empowered it with their presence, mixing the sacred and secular, wild and orderly, and putting it all at the disposal of state power.

It might be easy to explain this classical artwork as a means for claiming the Great Tradition for France, using antique statues and their copies to locate France as next in line for Rome's glory. Yet there remained surprisingly little real interest in using these figures to convey classical stories in full detail, or even to show off a mastery of classical culture in France. Certainly, in many propaganda campaigns, Paris was presented as the New Rome, and Louis XIV was shown as a great general in the Roman mold. But the cultural link between past and present, Ancient and Modern, was actually quite problematic to French intellectuals, who were arguing about who had the superior knowledge. Perrault, after all, claimed that the Ancients were in many ways not as good as contemporary writers and scientists. They did not eschew learning from the Ancients and finding inspiration in their work, but they did not see any absolute superiority in classical knowledge. That is why it would not be appropriate to argue that classical statuary in the gardens at Versailles was there just to make the past visible in the present. The past was much more a way to construct the glory of the present, using emblems from the past.

In his book on the statues at Versailles, Francastel raised the question of why Apollo was presented in his fountain sitting in his chariot; classical heroes did not sit in chariots, but rode them standing, as both Ancient and recent Italian statues had made clear (see plate 44). Why the change at Versailles? Were the nobles and artists of seventeenth-century France simply so ignorant of classical life that they made an error? If the point of this and other classical deities in the garden was to link France seriously to the classical past, why would it have been done with so little care?[81] These questions were probably just not relevant to men like Le Brun, who were using this imagery to fashion a contemporary political image for Louis XIV.[82] When Apollo was placed sitting in his chariot, he was located closer to the earth, where he could appear more stable and a more earthly power (like the king). Apollo might have been, in his mythological context, supposed to be hauling the sun toward the sky, but as the Sun King, he was already on the plane of his power. He had no reason to stand up and reach vertically with his body. Seated, this Apollo was made part of nature, and shown bringing his light to the earth, not trying to illuminate the sky.

Statues and waterworks not only brought heavenly powers to the earth, but raised subterranean forces and riches to the surface of the landscape where they could be admired and used. In a move that both drew on and conflicted the popular animistic view of nature, which abhorred mining as a violation of Mother Earth, the gardens at Versailles were built with materials quarried from the earth. Sculpted nature deities were made from gold and marble, and were often surrounded with rare shells, precious stones and other riches from the earth. Underground treasures not surprisingly lined the walls of the grotto, which was meant to represent the underground resting place of Apollo. But the Labyrinthe fountains and the cascades of the Salle de Bal also showcased these treasures, as did the Fountains of the Seasons (see plates 62, 65, and 66).

The Salle de Bal did not just contain these treasures from the subterranean world but arrayed them artfully across a wall of cascades that was open for all to see.

Churning water flowed over and between a vast collection of shells and apparently precious rocks set out on steps that stirred up the water to make it gurgle and sing. There was no shame in this display. Carved imitations of stalactites were made to hang from the cascade walls, taking even this feature of caves and setting it out as a visible miracle rather than a hidden one. Even when Versailles' grotto was destroyed to enlarge the château, the Salle de Bal remained.[83] On the surface of the earth, these riches joined nature gods, cavorting across the land, carrying grapes and game, flowers and wheat, shellfish and other bounties of nature. They all pointed to the procreative and productive qualities of the natural world that made it a site of spiritual as well as material power.

Néraudau argues that even alchemical references were part of the symbolic world of power embedded in the gardens at Versailles. The abundance of nature included a multitude of planes of power, some of which could be tapped and marked symbolically. The obelisk fountain not only provided the garden with a beautiful and geometrically controlled giant plume of water, but also marked the garden as a power center. The parterre for the Arc de Triomphe was similarly endowed with spiritualist symbols. The arch itself was flanked by obelisks, and farther down the grove were two pyramids. Moreover, the whole bosquet was filled with waterspouts. Temporary obelisks were also constructed at the extremities of the canal during one of the fêtes there. The cross and obelisk forms were merged during these celebrations of French power, and manifest in the reflections on the water of the canal. The symbolism of water itself as a source of life helped to give a spiritual undertone to the north–south axis of the gardens with its linked fountains. So did the theme of the sun that dominated statues and decorations along the east–west axis of the garden. The park at Versailles, then, was made in many ways a carrier of arcane symbolism and an intersection of diverse powers in nature.[84]

Along the pathways and bosquets of the *petit parc* at Versailles, there were also more explicit images of the material and spiritual strengths of the land of France embodied in the myriad statues of gods and goddesses who populated these gardens. These were the ever-present witnesses to the rituals of power enacted here. They were the idealized models for the nobility of France: Diana, Hercules, Bacchus, and Apollo. Bacchus, god of wine, was a fine symbol of France's thriving wine industry and the productivity and pleasures that could be derived from the land. Diana and Hercules were powerful hunters and warriors who clearly represented the military strength of France, carrying their bows and swords and projecting their serious demeanor over anyone who might pass by.

France herself, that female figure embodying a powerful unity and coherence of the land, was represented in the garden as a great marble statue, elevated on a hefty pedestal and sitting firmly upon on it. The great states and empires of Europe were also presented as female figures on some of the great pillars holding up the gates to the château and marking the end of the Parterre de Midi. They also stood for territorial regimes, embedded in nature, and expressing female power. The female warrior was perhaps the figure that best fits this new territorial state, embodying the wildness, power and unity of nature, while making these qualities visible as military resources of the state.

136. This image of the lights set up around the canal shows the obelisks erected for the fête of 1674 at Versailles (Le Pautre, *Sixième Journée*, 1676).

Demonstrations of power

While the focus on representation earlier in this chapter might seem to suggest that the park at Versailles was in some ways just the physical realization on the earth of an ideal of nature linked to an enduring vision of state power, this would be a poor description of the gardens at Versailles. The ideals of nature and state legitimacy were sought and realized in the land itself. The parterres and bosquets were dug into the earth before they were analyzed on paper by Félibien or Scudéry. Even Le Nôtre seems to have built his ambitious landscapes by designing on the earth itself, using the techniques developed by fortress engineers to set their projects into the local topography. He had sketches made of new garden areas only *after* the work was completed.[85] Even promenades did not highlight the symbolic structures of the gardens. What garden areas and statues represented was secondary to what could be measured and demonstrated there: a controlled natural world organized to serve a political order. The naturalization of power and order in the gardens was not so much an *idea* promoted by the gardens as a *characteristic* of the gardens – built with picks and shovels, and then projected by publicists on paper as an idealized form.[86]

Given the theoretical biases of seventeenth-century French science toward ideal models and abstract representations of natural systems, it is easy to assume that the nature realized in the gardens at Versailles was developed from theory. But nature was less represented there by imposing the beliefs on the earth than built from the ground up, using techniques from art, science, and engineering. Even the basic geometrical structure of the gardens was not developed from paper and pencil techniques to fulfill Cartesian theory, but was accreted over time, beginning with an original structure of the *petit parc* from Louis XIII's period. The geometries became increasingly more encompassing, simple, and related to survey practices as the park was expanded and the gardens elaborated. The simplicity advocated by Cartesian theory was invested in the land, but it probably came to the gardens indirectly through survey geometry and surveying practices in France. Cartesian theory did not need to enter the consciousness of Le Nôtre or any other gardener in France to make the design of French formal gardens more geometrically refined as long as the techniques of surveying were part of gardening practice. This does not mean that no ideals were at stake in the designs, or that no symbols were developed in the gardens. Clearly that was not the case. Le Nôtre systematically pursued an ideal of territorial order (geometrical, almost symmetrical order around a central axis) in all his gardens. It did not matter if he was inspired by military surveying, applied optics, or architectural trends that emphasized mathematical proportions. The practice of gardening required measuring the earth and giving it pleasing proportions. This purpose helped to impose a surface geometry on the gardens of Versailles.

This argument might seem at odds with Marin's ideas about the centrality of representation in this period. Marin argued that the disjuncture between the monarch-as-ideal and the man himself was central to the political pursuit of absolutism. Representations provided a way to reconstitute a cultural category and could open up or close down possibilities for human action and political power. That does not mean that representations would have to be (as Marin suggested) opposed to their material instantiations. France, for example, did not have to be disentangled from the landscape of the region for the political pursuit of territorial politics. France as the *pré carré* was a demonstration of France idealized in material form. This kind of demonstration had many of the same powers as a representation.

Demonstrations and representations were in fact intimately connected in seventeenth-century France.[87] The image of Louis XIV as monarch was crafted first on the body of the king himself as a demonstration of his stature as monarch. The rituals of court life organized around the king's physical being helped to transform his living form into a demonstration of monarchical power. Only after the daily cycles of rituals developed at Versailles clearly distinguished the monarch's physical form from that of ordinary men did Rigaud paint his idealized portrait of the king. The location of monarchial authority in the physical presence of the king was not an odd or new phenomenon. When Louis XIV was first anointed king, his body was made different from all other bodies. The will of God was now located on earth *through* the physical presence of the king. The massively ritualized world of Versailles only secularized and reaffirmed daily this assertion of difference. The king's power as a physical presence was not lost, but naturalized. It was part of the movement of his bowels, and the act of his eating. It was part of his walks in the countryside, and his dancing at parties. The final separation of the "image of monarch" from the king's physical presence in the Rigaud portrait simply confirmed that monarchical power lay in a world of physically embodied performances. Rigaud's painting would have had no meaning without the ritual life at Versailles around the corpus of the king himself. It was simply a representation around which to organize the daily demonstration of monarchical authority at Versailles.

France as a territorial power was similarly demonstrated more than represented. It was a physical space to be won by wars, and ordered through infrastructural projects. Its existence and improvements had to be marked on maps, but it was not developed as an ideal through representations on maps. It was developed as a *pré carré* by Vauban. Even the gardens of Versailles were a more powerful political tool than any garden print could be because of their physical presence. They showed what the French could *do* with land, not just what they thought about it. Only when the gardens at Versailles were in the process of being built did their political possibilities begin to be exploited through the dissemination of prints by Silvestre, Le Pautre, and Le Clerc. The new bosquets and parterres of Le Nôtre were only documented after the fact, and his style of gardening was only codified (quite badly, in fact) by d'Argenville, who tried to idealize elements of existing gardens.[88] The king, French gardens, and the state were all first manifested physically before they were reduced to representations. It was demonstration rather than representation that opened up political possibilities for naturalizing state power.

In the end, the gardens at Versailles did not so much promote theories about nature or politics as show political order as an extension of natural order. Even before the scientists at the Observatory were able to represent France on their scientific maps, and even while the soldiers of the state were reshaping the boundaries of this domain, Le

Nôtre was building his microcosm of French territory to show how wonderful this land could be. He demonstrated how powers of nature, drawn from the heavens and the earth, could be assembled to create a heaven on earth. The gardens at Versailles may have been filled with hierarchical features and may have called upon subterranean and heavenly forces of nature, but they were worked out on the surface of the landscape: the plane of human action. Only on the earth could man enhance God's works with his own – only here could art embellish nature. Building a great garden into an abundant and orderly environment for human life was a heavenly task brought to earth by the designers of French gardens, and politically mobilized by dreamers of French empire.

7

A history of material power

Histories of gardens are not usually thought to be hefty enough to carry important stories of our heritage. As supposed realms of pleasure rather than power, gardens are generally seen as sites for aesthetes and amateurs, women and lovers, not men of power, arbiters of our past, or guide posts to the history of power. It is quite extraordinary how completely most people have accepted this opposition of pleasure and power. Garden historians have certainly reflected both on the uses of gardens by the powerful, and the investment of potent and resonant symbols in garden designs and statuary.[1] But in most formulations, gardens are (at the most) expressions of the power of social elites, never a source for or laboratory of that power. But as Marshall Sahlins[2] suggested some years ago, gardens are sites where cultures meet the natural world and try to find sustenance in it. They are locales of cultural creation, where the natural world is remade to suit human needs, and human cultures are enriched both physically and symbolically. The self-conscious fashioning of garden plots is an act of human faith and will, making a small part of the material world into an element of human social and cultural life. Gardens are not, then, as we often think, an Edenic place to *escape* from everyday culture, but a constituting site for the *development of culture*.

Social theory is certainly not without resources for materialist analysis which should, in principle, help us understand how cultures and political economies are co-constructed on the land. Marx recognized the fundamental importance of the material transformation of nature, and saw it as a concrete activity in the moment of production. He was a materialist in his vision as well as his theory of history. But in Western Marxist theory, this fundamental moment in human life seems to have been lost. For many theorists, materialist analysis was simply a way to understand exploitative social relations. The world of things was of no consequence outside its role in structuring relations of domination. Once a commodity was manufactured, its alienation from the worker was achieved, and labor power was transformed into commodity relations, there was no longer interest in the object. The trash heaps of old commodities had no role in the theory. We heard about fetishizing commodities as a degradation of the human spirit, but not how these objects themselves transformed the relations between the built and unbuilt environment.

Marxist materialism was so concerned with the *social consequences* of relations to

300

137. The road and ditch to the north of the Apollo fountain at Versailles. Trees, soil,
grass, and gravel are transformed into roadways, walkways, lawns, ditches, and
stands of trees.

nature that it ignored many cultural and material ones. Yet economic processes depend
on cultural meanings associated with things and includes the conversion of countryside into commodities. Consumption is as much a cultural and physical act as an economic one. You cannot make economically successful commodities that have no
cultural meaning to people. Social relations of production necessarily depend upon
cultural processes that make sense of the goods produced. This insight encouraged
neo-Marxists, particularly in Britain but also in the United States, to explore the role
of culture industries in creating demand for commodities. But this work has focused
increasingly on consumption's role in the manufacture of political consent, and has
turned away from the world of things. Neo-Marxist cultural studies gave more attention to the hegemonic processes stabilizing exploitative economic relations, as this issue
became more pressing to the weakening political left. The result was that the focus of
analysis turned once again to social relations of domination, and left out the cultural
meanings of things.[3]

Modern economies not only use labor power to extract wealth through social relations of domination; they are structured with material *culture* and create built environments from unbuilt ones. Since the eighteenth century in the West, factories have
deployed technology and human effort to produce goods, and have left landscapes
ravaged by use. The separation of economic activity from cultural ones in our analytic

languages and thinking has been so successful that it has militated against the articulation of a good social theory that includes this kind of cultural transformation of the material world as part of social process. But as more people ask questions about environmental degradation and begin to think about how human life is embedded in the physical world we live in, this traditional separation seems a hindrance rather than a help.

Even if a new theory is needed, what good does it do to turn to gardens, as I do, to ask questions about material culture in human social life? Gardens in Western culture have become associated with leisure and pleasure, not serious sociocultural issues. Even the sturdy vegetable garden, with its enduring role in feeding rural families, has been reduced to a weekend hobby, not a vital element of household economies. If pleasure is forgettable and amateur activity is not serious, then why look at gardens? The answer is that wherever the unbuilt environment is mobilized for human culture and is rebuilt to serve the needs and desires of members of a culture, something very fundamental and important about human life is at stake. Even flower gardening is not, as Jack Goody points out, just a matter of sentiment and beauty, but part of a world of vital symbolic politics and material transformation. We may naturalize our responses to flowers by saying we like them for their scent and beauty, but that does not make them any less parts of culture when they are recruited into human social life. We do, after all, relegate some flowers to the category of weed.

Members of cultures frequently transform both their environment and the world of creatures living around them. It is certainly true that many human cultures require their members to tread lightly on the landscape, and make few and impermanent marks on the world around them. But there are many other social communities where the human hand and human will are vividly and actively shaping the world – even the countryside. The rolling green fields of England and Ireland are the products of a history of active and insistent deforestation. They may not seem as artificial as New York City, Los Angeles, Beijing, or Buenos Aires, but they are physical manifestations of a social period in which timber was readily sacrificed to serve British sea power. Even demographic patterns have been affected by the way people have transformed the landscape. The population of southern California was increased enormously when the agricultural disaster known as the dust bowl, created by drought and inappropriate cultivation, stimulated mass migration from the lower midwest. Both the landscapes in which people live and the demographics of human settlements are shaped by the relations of the built to the unbuilt environment, so social theory needs better accounts of this subject. Garden history provides a surprising but useful way in.[4]

Political culture, cultural studies, and cultural history have all become fashionable topics in recent decades. Material culture studies seem as though they should be compatible and not really so important addenda to these fields. But is this kind of analysis really so continuous? Much work in cultural studies moves all too rapidly away from the world of things into a domain of abstractions and the politics of linguistic relations. Scholars in the various schools of cultural studies have become fascinated with the techniques for constituting collective meanings. How does music carry its own history? How can violence gain aesthetic standing? How do bodies become variously racially and sexually coded? How are meanings sucked out of human lives to be replaced by commodities? These are questions of culture that assume that human understanding and clarity are embedded not in the built environment and actions around and within it, but in language categories and language-like signs systems.

A taste (perhaps exaggerated) of this kind of analysis should make clear how cultural approaches can easily let go of the material world. Linguistic transformations within culture (we are told) can open up new possibilities for human action. The "nation" can be constructed with signifiers, and that (in political history) can make all the difference. Alternately, tags and labels heaped onto people or strewn across the cultural landscape can weigh human beings down, and distort communities' features. In much of culture theory, barely recognizably human forms seem to dance and hop about inside an imaginary landscape held up and set out with categories. The figures moving in it seem to be tripping over the nets of meanings or plucking at them, trying to produce sounds. Material objects may appear and disappear in this imaginary landscape, but the treacherous lines of linguistic control remain. Things can arrive in this space as commodities, but they dissolve into categories or desires. They become simulacra. The material world vanishes as virtual realities spring Athena-like from human heads filled with language and imagination. The world does not stay close to the earth with its soil, seeds, and water, so the possibilities for wonder and terror grow; meanings are not fixed yet categories remain constraining; everything floats but nothing is free.

These images may be too spare and dark to accurately represent much current cultural analysis, but it remains the case that Cultural Studies often conjures up brilliant dystopias; no wonder cultural analysis is so inviting. But the built and unbuilt environments have no real standing in these linguistically-based approaches to human meaning except as instantiation of categories. The smartest theorists in cultural studies know this, and try to confront the problem, but with mixed results. If the assumptions of cultural analysis make it hard to hold onto the world of things, should we then simply forget these objects? Should we turn our backs on human constructions like battlement walls and the wars fought from them? Should we only privilege the articulation of political boundaries and not their physical embodiment or the struggles over their placement? Should we forget about the cannon forged at arsenals or the soldiers killed from their fire?

One great beauty of cultural studies is that it can yield and has produced so many new conversations among disciplines and so many hybrid forms of analysis that it can indeed provide ways into the analysis of the world of things. Art historians are increasingly looking at the connections among science, technology, and art that are the backbone of modern material transformations. People in science studies bring together linguistics, cultural studies, ethnography, and philosophy to explain how the materiality of nature is converted by scientists into the ephemera of knowledge, allowing us to pretend that nature has categories and laws more than weight and presence. The work of Simon Schama, that great chronicler of Western materialism, sometimes describes the empire of things and sometimes presents the landscape as a repository for human memories. Schama simply is better at describing how the natural world has become *necessary* to Western culture than how it has become *transformed* to enter into social life more fully.[5] But that analytic oversight only turns our attention again to gardens and their construction.

We all know that human life depends on a garden of some sort – some way of supplying food and other material needs. That is why lots of origin myths, including the Christian one, are set in gardens (or their productive counterpart, the sea). Human beings recognize their need for food and other sustenance. We all understand at some level that we must grow, kill or gather our food, not from our words and customs, but from something beyond us and of which we are a part. We grow in and from nature both symbolically and practically.

We also know that our relation with nature does not begin and end with food. We have much too complicated cultural structures for that. Minimally, we find aesthetic and spiritual pleasures and analytic delights in watching trees, flowers, and insects. We forge common analytic approaches to nature, trying to account for their forms. We revel easily enough in the sounds of birds or in the look of falling leaves marking changes in the seasons. We can write poetry about the reflections in ponds, or philosophy about the life in and around the ponds themselves. But that's not all.

Humans are generally not content simply to admire and reflect upon stones, trees, water, birds, insects, and clay without moving them around. We end up constructing a humanly modified world in which to live. This building impulse is seen closest to nature in the garden, where the human hand is visibly at work, but plant life must cooperate for the garden to be culturally recognizable. The garden is socially significant in large part because the building impulse in some sense starts there where nature's role in the built environment is most obvious. But it certainly does not stop there. The same tendency to move things around to give the world aesthetically or economically satisfying form can also end up producing cities, buses, elegantly dressed people or even something as complex as the Arc de Triomphe in the middle of a traffic-ridden circle in Paris.

All the efforts to find food, to experience beauty, and to build are at the heart of human cultures, and they are similarly at the heart of the construction of gardens. The garden is a site where members of a culture can play with these possibilities, figure out how to balance them, look at the result, and reconfigure them to suit better the requirements of that particular time and place.

Seventeenth-century French gardens and state-formation

The French formal garden was a vital political resource for state-formation in its time and place. It was a laboratory for the techniques of land control used to construct the territorial state. The very elements that went into building the garden were the ones necessary for rebuilding the landscape to make it a politically marked and fortified territory that both enhanced and defined state power. Each chapter of this book has, without being explicit about it, brought to the forefront elements of state-formation that a number of theories have taken as more-or-less central to the development of the modern French state. They simultaneously explain the formal garden and the articulation of a territorially based state, and help make visible the state as a *material* accomplishment.

138. Desjardins' *Le Soir*, 1680. Diana, representing evening, and the Fountain of the Animals together show nature as a source of food, natural order, and art.

139. Tubi, Coysevox, and Prou, *La France Triomphant*, 1682–83, from the bosquet near the Arc de Triomphe.

One obvious site for the development of the modern state was the growth of the professional military. The stripping of feudal rights and responsibilities for military power was a basic prerequisite for the relocation of powers inside the state. To the extent that the state was a machine for gathering taxes to support warfare, the modern state had to have a strong and independent military. That is why France was so often depicted in statuary as a woman in military garb, associating the state with both a collective life and military power.

It is clear enough that the military in France was not just a means for relocating power in the state, but also for embedding state power in the land. French military life was not innovative solely in the separation of soldiers from an independent nobility, but also in the engineering managed by Vauban and his successors. The land of France was made into a territorial state in large part through the construction of fortresses, which dug the geometries of French territory into the French landscape. The gardens at Versailles reflected and interacted with these efforts. They too were built using military engineering, decorated with military symbols, filled with evidence of the growing success of French forges, lined with healthy specimens from the French forests, and used for celebrations of successes on the battlefield.

For the people living in France, the garrisons, fortresses, ports, and forges built to serve the military were material testimonies to the power of the state. They constituted the authority of the central state in local communities. French accumulation of state power, to the extent that we can talk about such a thing, was a diffuse and material construction. The military installations placed this power well beyond the sphere of the court, helping to show the peasants of the countryside that they, too, were part of the French state.

The professionalization of the army at the same time helped convince many soldiers and the communities they came from that there was indeed a powerful and militarily ambitious French state. They were salaried by the government, housed in garrisons, put to work in fortresses and ports, mobilized for war, or used to build the king's gardens. They were made actors in a political world that was being claimed as potent by the king and his ministers. They helped to make this world real to themselves and others. Their uniforms marked them as Frenchmen, and helped to identify them as part of a social system organized around the state of France.

Colbert's economic policies contributed to this new political identity by providing a repertoire of tastes and commodities that came to be seen as distinctively French. The French court had its style of dress and decorum that was both recognized and imitated across Europe. The products of French industries were similarly identifiable as French, and made the distribution of those goods across households in France another locating marker. If the French could not yet think of themselves as a people (a nation), they could come to recognize one another as sharing common tastes and objects. The state could have a cultural identity connecting place and taste, even if it could not yet project a convincing coherence to the French people.

This sharing of materially defined political identity had a limit. Most of the French peasants had no need or opportunity to use objects from the Gobelins. The products cultivated by Colbert, except for some exports, tended to be products for the elites who were the major consumers of the period. This meant that the land of France was more marked culturally by the dress, consumption patterns, and decorum of aristocrats and financiers. On the other hand, the material culture of France was created by workers and traded by merchants who all contributed to its forms and uses. They learned to cultivate exactly the tastes that they thought would appeal to elites. They were prohibited from making traditional regional goods, and disciplined carefully by Colbert to manufacture objects seen as more healthy for the French economy. Their regimentation was clearly a marker of state power felt in the far reaches of the countryside, but it was less obviously and more importantly a means by which the local material culture became distinctively French. So in spite of the elite bias of the manufactures in the period, the French economy yielded a more generally shared material culture which passed through the hands of French men and women of many regions and ranks. French fabrics appeared in clothing across France. The *faïence* took on new patterns that helped to mark it as French. And both the decorative cloth produced in France and many other consumer goods brought to the French aristocracy were modeled on parterre patterns. In French formal gardens, these confections made with bushes and flowers were set out alongside the marble statues, which were now taking on qualities of French classicism. Together they adorned the land of France itself with distinctively French designs. In the end, the new state politics was a politics of place, and this state-administered and state-developed material culture provided a way to mark France culturally as a singular political force, using French taste in material objects.

France was made French through the cultivation of its people as well. This did not mean all the ordinary people, merely the visible ones: members of Louis XIV's court. The aristocracy, if it wanted to participate in the benefits of state power in France had to attend to the king and the rules of his court. This meant that they had to discipline themselves to be players in the larger narratives of political life. In the ordinary rituals of the court, nobles were trained to become actors rather than speakers for the new regime. They dressed themselves properly, and learned to feign authenticity to become the ultimate tool and construct of state power: the *honnête homme*. This courtier was the precursor of the modern politician who speaks to please, not to tell the truth, in order to take part in the system of power.

The great parties and rituals set in the gardens of Versailles repositioned the aristocracy within the new regime of power. There was no balance of power in France that allowed the state to take over. Nobles and financiers alike had independent powers stripped from them instead. Social discipline was used in rituals of obedience to produce a model of political control for the rest of France. The land was peopled with subjects obedient to the king. Fashions, uniforms, and even costumes marked these subjects as French, making them politically identifiable, and showing their subservience to a larger system of power. The orderly formal gardens in which so many ritual moments took place only seemed to ratify this lawlike order, making it seem natural because it worked so beautifully on plants and animals.

The shift of power into the state raised problems of legitimacy for the king and state that once again made references to natural order in the garden a valuable political resource. Nature had lawlike powers that could be transferred to the state, and nature had wild forces working to disrupt peaceful order, which ratified the imposition of law by force. But what gave the state its greatest legitimacy was its territorial dimensions. State power was not only natural, but the state itself was a part of the natural world, too. When Vauban advocated transforming France into a *pré carré,* he wanted to make its form simultaneously orderly and natural. The territory of France in this configuration could be seen more clearly as an extension of Creation itself. It was at once a naturally delineated part of the continent and a vision of lawlike orderliness.

The land of France might be the easiest element of the absolutist state to naturalize, but it was not the only one. The king's rule over this land was similarly naturalized when the monarch was portrayed as Apollo, a nature god. He was not only a deity, but a force of nature, the necessary power for moving the sun through the heavens. As the Sun King, he was meant to bring light to the world, and be the center of history. Perhaps more surprising, even state administration could be naturalized too. It was, after all, an impersonal order, just like the order of the universe itself. The state bureaucracy viewed in this light was not corrupting the expression of Divine will on earth by undermining direct rule by the monarch, but rather functioned as a form of power continuous with God's plan for the universe. Forces naturalized this way were difficult to oppose because they were portrayed as a fundamental part of God's Creation. Nature and politics found a common home in state territory, and state power was made good by equating it with proper administration of God's lands.

The gardens at Versailles were instrumental in developing and exploring these themes. They were clearly a site where nature and culture could meet. They were also part of the permanent residence of the French court. Attempts to naturalize the king's power or to legitimate state-based politics, using images of nature, were tried outside the garden. Images of Apollo, for example, were painted on the château's ceiling, woven into Gobelins tapestries, and printed in almanacs, but the search for ways of grounding the absolutist state in nature was most rigorously and effectively located in the great park at Versailles.

Of course, the state was less a natural political arrangement than a carefully managed part of the European continent. To make land into a controlled and useful territory, the French had at their disposal a tradition of estate management and state-based rational land-use policies to employ for political ends. From the period of Henri IV and Sully, the land of France had been equated with the property on an estate. A good administration used it well for the good of all. Canals were built to stimulate trade and break down regionalism; manufactures were distributed to use natural resources and skills to best effect. These policies were designed to use and unify the land more efficiently. Improvements in ports, rationalized forests, and state-administered manufacturing projects in the period of Louis XIV were all rooted in this earlier era of administration, and derived in practice – if not in propaganda – from the estate-management tradition in France. The roots of this heritage, with their Protestant look, were well hidden, but lay closest to the surface in French formal gardens. The parks depended visibly on the practical skills derived from this world, and were designed using principles from this tradition of practice. Perhaps it was bad taste in the aristocracy to see the French qualities of formal gardens as indebted to this earlier approach to land management, but it was indeed part of what made these gardens seem so different from their Italian predecessors, and what invested politics in land management itself.

In spite of the theories of state-formation which deny this element of politics, the state of France was constructed not so much through rational bureaucratic centralization, but through material manipulation of the land. France was made as a *place* of power. The territorial state was a geographical reality as well as a political one, and its power lay in part in its new relationship to land.[6] No wonder military action and engineering were privileged in the state politics of the period. And no wonder the French state was represented at court by a great garden that could demonstrate French territorial integrity and techniques of land control in a lavish and seductive way.

The methodologies of state history and the problem of state power

If the material aspects of state power were so important historically to this period, how could it be that so many scholars, devoting so much energy to studying the early French state, could have missed it? Does it seem reasonable to believe that over the whole of the twentieth century, when social science has been so visibly shaped by Marxist materialism, everyone could have overlooked the material bases of state power? (It

140. Courtiers posing by the Bains d'Apollon (P. Martin, *Les Bains d'Apollon*).

141. Naturalizing the lines superimposed on the landscape.

clearly seems more reasonable to believe that anyone foolhardy enough to approach political history through the story of gardens would be in error about the importance of territoriality and engineering to state power.)[7]

Of course, not all scholars have overlooked the material aspects of state power, even though they may not have drawn enough analytic attention to them. William McNeil has been particularly interested in military, cultural, and even microbial relations as part of world political history. Foucault in a quite different way pointed to the materialization of cultural categories in French architecture and bodies in the seventeenth and eighteenth centuries. Many French historians like Braudel have pointed to the centrality of political geography and environment to the political identities and lives of people in France. Some *Annales* historians have even written about the growth of territorial thinking in French life. In addition, the myriad British and American scholars who have written about technology and economic development in early modern Europe, associating changing balances of power with technique, have also made this aspect of power more visible. But this has not made *territoriality* a common part of theories of the state – except perhaps in France where this aspect of the history of modern state has just been too vivid to ignore completely.[8]

142.   Water pump on the Pont Notre Dame in Paris (Genty, *Vue de Paris*).

The work done by historical sociologists in the 1970s and 1980s, trying to wrest some "semi-autonomy" for the state might have supported a move toward a more territorial conception of state power. This would have made sense given the ties of some state theorists, mainly Immanuel Wallerstein, to Braudel and his school of historical analysis. But in fact, the opposite was the case. The state was defined as semi-autonomous from the economic system and the structures of power derived from it. The state in this context was treated more as a *counter* to material forces than an embodiment of them. Since cultural analysis was early deemed unnecessary or superfluous to this brand of political history, there was little incentive to pursue questions of land and identity. In the end, the point was not to determine what cultural factors kept the state together, but to show what social factors made it fall apart for the Revolution. The result was that this new and powerful semi-autonomous state of social theory, when described as developing in seventeenth-century France, was not a territorial state etched onto the landscape of the European continent.[9]

Corrigan and Sayer came closer to an understanding of the material culture of state power with their cultural theory of state-formation in England. First of all, and to their great credit, these scholars gave culture some credence as an historical force – even though they explicitly limited their notion of cultural power to its ideational or ideological function. More importantly, the authors inadvertently but significantly pointed to elements of the material transformation of place necessary to English state power when they described the importance of enclosures and land reform in the politics of the period after 1688. Again, without making much of it, Corrigan and Sayer also pointed to the oddly performative aspects of English political culture. Perhaps ironically, many material activities constituting a territorial state in England ended up being delineated in loving detail by the authors, but were never made explicitly central to the culture of state power. The problem of legitimacy remained for these scholars one of collective conscience or moral regulation rather than material culture.[10]

If theories of the state provided one reason to ignore the materiality of state power, methodological considerations added another. To the extent that records of the political bureaucracy have constituted the major source of data for the state, the documents have favored the view of the state as a centralized, bureaucratic phenomenon. What you see is what you get. But this does not mean that the state did not have other aspects. Charles Tilly pointed to this problem from the start in the introduction to *The Formation of National States in Western Europe* (1975). For Tilly, state archives created severe limitations from the scholars' point of view. They provided a top-down vision of the state's development and excluded the perspectives from the bottom. He did not question, however, the reduction of state power in these records to bureaucratic problems: legal rulings, political moves, resource management, regulation of manufacture, and funding. He just wanted to know more about how these policies were met by the people. He never considered that something else might be *entirely* left out. But the material basis of state power, so easy to tease out of the records but seemingly so immaterial in account books, was masked even from Tilly's critical eyes by the flux of administrative rulings and actions.

Bureaucratic documents in fact have always provided rich evidence of territorial engineering, if you know what to look for. Vauban's fortresses appeared in the accounts as expenses of the military and some of the many building projects approved by the king. What the documents did not and could not show is that they were physical intrusions into the countryside. Only where formal complaints were lodged about the construction projects by local authorities because of their destructive effects on local fields or woods, which were being sacrificed for new wall systems, did Vauban's projects become problems of sociocultural engineering. Natural features of the landscape were clearly being erased as Vauban's new fortresses were erected. Nonetheless, a reader in the archives predisposed to ignore the built environment could easily reduce these complaints to problems of local elites facing centralized authorities, rather than evidence of the material engineering of territorial power. Canal projects similarly appeared in bureaucratic records, but as administrative problems requiring surveying and funding, and serving military and economic needs. They were not heralded as new works in the French tradition of estate management and the material improvement of France. Even though we read that Colbert worried about the details of their construction, he still did not comment on the origin of the survey techniques or engineering systems being considered for the project. He just wanted to make sure it would work. As a result, the relationship of this canal project with those from the period of Henri IV, or the importance of land stewardship to the political culture of France, could not be highlighted in his assessment of the projects. Nonetheless, French experience in canal engineering and surveying did indeed serve the bureaucracy well. In sum, while the territoriality of the early modern French state was not achieved without leaving traces in the record books, it was primarily documented in the built environment itself – the new landscape engineered in the name of the state. No wonder efforts to study the state through its bureaucratic documents have made the role of engineering and land management less visible than it should have been. But that does not mean that building was any less significant to state-based politics. Much of what ministers did in the bureaucracy was to simultaneously feed the king's passion for building and war and turn it into a source of French power.

In spite of this tunnel vision on the part of researchers, the relative neglect of construction projects as sources of French state-formation is somewhat surprising given that material records have been touted for years as a necessary part of French historical analysis. They were recovered as methodological tools by the *Annales* school precisely to get away from the historical distortions of written accounts. If those people at the bottom of the social ladder were not literate, their lives and contributions to history could not be adequately explained using bureaucratic records. Written accounts would always be structured through the eyes of literate elites, whereas material culture could provide less biased evidence of the lives of ordinary Frenchmen. This tool of historical equalization made the world of things interesting to historians, but more to those studying peasant life than those studying the state. Just as bureaucratic records were supposed to show the view from the top, the built environment and material culture were meant to show the view from the bottom. This tradition in historiography made the world of goods and engineering projects less obviously a resource for studying the *state* and territorial power.[11]

143. An almanac depiction of Louis XIV's ministers surrounded by their "works." It shows how bureaucratic achievement was measured in this period by material accomplishments.

Another methodological problem inhibiting analysis of state power in material terms has been a lack of analytic techniques for approaching the world of things. While there has been no absence of evidence of statues depicting Louis XIV, for example, being erected in French towns during his reign, there has until recent decades been a disturbing lack of tools for analyzing them as sites of politics. Art historians could provide means for their aesthetic analysis, but not ways of assessing their political significance. Happily, a recent proliferation of interdisciplinary work in the histories of art, science, and political ritual has yielded many new analytic strategies that can help make sense of material objects. Scholars such as Michael Baxandall, Roy Strong, Simon Schama, Svetlana Alpers, Bruno Latour, Donna Haraway, Peter Burke, Arjun Appadurai, and Martin Kemp have all presented models for dissecting cultural objects as potent parts of political, social, and cultural processes.[12]

In spite of these pioneering efforts, most social scientists and historians still insist that written records have to be deployed to make sense of images and other meaningful forms as sources of historical information. They argue that "readings" of the works not derived from the period are necessarily suspect, so scholars must find period texts for interpreting images. But these practices raise vexing historical questions themselves. If Martin Jay, Frances Yates, Michael Baxandall, Svetlana Alpers, Jean-Christophe Agnew, and Roy Strong[13] are correct, the culture of sixteenth- and seventeenth-century Europe emphasized vision and ritual over words – particularly in politics. Performance was so central to the exercise and representation of power that it is hard to say what role language had in the period for decoding visual information. Of course, there was a flurry of publications in the seventeenth century on emblems and their meanings, translating images into words. And these certainly can be used to make sense of images from the period. Still, the interpretations of symbols presented in different emblem books often conflicted with one another, suggesting that there was no authoritative visual language at stake. Perhaps there was no easy way, even in the seventeenth century, to read contemporary symbolism authoritatively, so different authors of emblem books were actually struggling with mixed success to *stabilize* meanings by setting out their books of symbols.

If this was possibly the case, how can we now legitimately assert that we can *only* make sense of images if we can indeed read them like a text or find texts with which to read them? Can we be sure that this attention to text-like features of the cultural environment is not just the projection of the assumptions from modern semiotics onto a pre-modern world? Perhaps some scholars and artists in the seventeenth century saw objects this way, but it is unlikely that most aristocrats or local elites would have shared such a scholarly point of view. Francastel argues, for example, that most noble visitors to Versailles were probably not familiar with all the classical allusions in the garden statuary, but still could recognize the garden as a tribute to the king and his power. They could be introduced to the equation of Louis XIV with Apollo and see the theme of power woven throughout the garden. That was enough. If Saint-Simon is correct, Louis XIV was woefully ignorant of classical culture, but this did not dampen his interest in collecting and displaying classical statuary in his gardens. He only cared that visitors to Versailles saw French wealth, taste, and power in the context of the Great

144. Almanac picture celebrating the erection of an equestrian statue of Louis XIV in Paris.

Tradition at his seat of court. How different visitors would respond to the park's particular features would depend on their education. Some would know Fontenelle's writings on science, and see the references to nature most clearly. Others might know some
classical mythology and recognize some of the themes in the statues. The point was that
the park had to be meaningful to all of them, but not *all* parts of it had to be meaningful to them. The very multivocality of the artworks probably made them easier to
deploy as political resources in the seventeenth-century world of power where elites
had such various backgrounds, interests, and educations. As Michael Baxandall has
pointed out, one can study *patterns of intention* in works of art and engineering instead
of studying iconography, and reconstruct pieces as part of social projects. People in the
seventeenth century, who could see the built environment changing along with the
political reconstruction of the French state, were certainly primed to do that, too. As
long as they could understand what an equestrian statue of Louis XIV in a town square
was doing there, they did not need to "read" its meaning as a text.

Contemporary scholars who want to pin objects down as *statements* on the times in
which they were made may find themselves in trouble – particularly if these objects
were never made to be "statements." Certainly, the statue in a seventeenth-century
French town square was never just a symbolic object to be decoded, but part of the life
of the city. Sculptures like this constituted an element in the political negotiations
between local elites and Versailles. The social intentions of these projects were what
counted, and these were never made visible just in the statues themselves.

Vauban's fortresses, which were designed and used so effectively in France, were not
just good symbols of the power of the state derived from ideal city plans, but effective
fortresses, too. These artifacts were meaningful as part of a system of military action.
They gained significance as markers of power because they were used effectively as
means to power. Similarly, the image of Louis XIV in a town square, which worked to
keep the king in the consciousness of his subjects, was a political tool not because it
represented monarchical authority like a text, but because it worked to instantiate it
locally. It was a demonstration of power, not just a representation of it.

Peter Burke (1992) has argued that a variety of media were self-consciously used
during this regime to fabricate a glorious and successful Louis XIV. The political propaganda of Henri IV was nothing in comparison. Great crews of historians, designers,
writers, and sculptors were used to make Louis XIV monumental. His critics could
cynically say that this vast enterprise was needed to make him appear even vaguely
appealing, since to his enemies he was a scourge and a scoundrel. But this was not the
point. Fabrication was at the heart of French state policy in the period. France and the
king were manufactured together on the battlefield, in the world of fashion, in scholarly debates between Ancients and Moderns, and in the Observatory where the
problem of locating France cartographically were discussed. This whole material
approach to power was more than a matter of propaganda. It was a political strategy
with multiple sites and myriad local consequences.

State-making was not just a matter of political alignment in the seventeenth century.
The pursuit of state-based absolutism involved a physical mobilization of people and
things that included manufactured goods and artworks, fortresses and rituals. Citadels

and fashionable garments alike began distinguishing France from the rest of Europe. Both warfare and exports were material means for conveying state power and territorial ambition. Creating a great civilization, engineered into the countryside and displayed across the land, was part of a drive toward establishing a new political identity for France and making visible to the rest of Europe France's bid for political leadership of the continent. The state of France was not so much a bureaucracy, then, but a territorial political force that developed bureaucratic structures in large part to manage and mobilize the land for power.

States and the centering/decentering of power

Acknowledging the material aspects of state power and looking at the politics of place in seventeenth-century France makes clear that we cannot talk about state-building (as we often have in the past) as just a matter of political centralization, rationalization, and bureaucratization. The territorial state may have centralized the social institutions of power, formalizing, if not rationalizing them, but it also diffused power across the landscape. It made space a container for social life that simultaneously anchored and spread it geographically. The problem of talking about centralization in this period becomes all the more vivid when you look at the cartographic shift in the period. Images of Europe now changed, making the continent less a collection of power centers in a landscape than continental spaces divided into territories with clear political boundaries. Just in the period when historians and sociologists talk about state centralization, the maps of Europe displayed power as less centralized than marked by borders. What could this mean?

State centralization is usually equated with the unification of multiple principalities into a single state. How could this process be described as anything but a centralization of power? Incorporating new lands into the state, however, required a tightening of the grip on the outside boundaries of the political territory. As boundaries changed by incorporating new areas, their locations were made both more problematic and crucial to claims to power. The result was that new problems of centralization were essential to the modern state. Soldiers had to go from Versailles to border citadels, and Intendants had to be situated in cities far from the court to create a presence for state power in the peripheries. This did not make the state a centralized system, but a diffuse system of power, trying to manage the decentering tendencies of the expanding state. It was the loss of the possibility of centralized authority that made bureaucratic efforts to keep tabs on the peripheries seem all the more important.

The exact features of this historical shift in political geography is actually easier to think about using garden history. Just as the city-state in late sixteenth-century Italy was a much more centered political configuration than France in the late seventeenth century, the Mannerist garden in Italy developed a highly centralized design focusing on the house (the source of power). These configurations yielded what were called, appropriately enough, power houses (the equivalent of power centers). In contrast, French formal gardens so extended the boundaries of the land which they were meant to integrate that their centers migrated away from the château. In the garden at

Versailles, the main axis might have reached from the house through the garden to the canal and beyond, but it did not make the house the center of the design. The different parts of the garden were joined at the canal, where the powers of nature were united and identified with the land itself. It was French *land* that held the system together, not the house, and land was known more by its boundaries than its center.

Political centralization itself, the growth of the bureaucracy at Versailles, also had decentering properties. Before this time, Intendants had acted as itinerant emissaries of the monarch, but in the period of Louis XIV, they were becoming permanently assigned to particular provincial towns or regions. In this situation, they stood as permanent reminders of state interests in local affairs, but they also helped constitute local centers of power away from Versailles, speaking in the voice of the state. Both territorial integration and regionalism were enhanced by the growth of this system. Similarly, state-based academies, industries, tax codes, fashions, and legal regulations all helped to make visible the regional traditions they were set up to undermine. Regional dress, habits, foods, political traditions, and the like all became more salient as they were placed under assault by these "centralizing" forces. No wonder the physical boundaries of the state took on such importance in the period. The geographical lines that incorporated all the land of France and held the countryside inside these boundaries as a seamless whole became increasingly politically salient. They provided a "natural" unity when social unity was difficult to see or define. This physical territory could always be manipulated and developed, and the results associated with a singular state.

With regard to seventeenth-century French territoriality and its relation to the state bureaucracy, any attempt at describing state formation in simple terms becomes rather more difficult. It is so economical to describe the process as centralization, but that term only points to the institutional development of the bureaucracy, not the mobilization of land. Power derived from the control and use of territory required and created an odd combination of centralization and decentralization. But how can we talk about it analytically?

It has been chic since the writings of Foucault to describe a decentralization of power through *language* as a counter to the reification of power in some clear "center." The idea has been that speech is so diffuse that governmental organizations could never keep language entirely under the control of political or social elites. The Académie Française has certainly tried, but has always failed to some extent. The result is that efforts at ideological control have necessarily been partial. But this does not mean that language has constituted an alternative domain of freedom. On the contrary, language categories define fundamental cultural constructs, and hence necessarily constrain the possibilities for human thought and action. The power of language may be diffuse, but this does not make it any less coercive. It just shows how decentered politics can be, and how little discussions about centralization of power can reveal about modern systems of social control.[14]

The coercive qualities of language are, of course, only the result of the fact that growing up in a language community is only rarely a matter of choice. To belong to a speech community requires participating in a language-based structuring of the world of experience and action. Language provides an external means of social control that

145. Almanac picture of territorial unification, showing uses of maps to connect
peripheral territories to the political center of the court.

is easily internalized and reproduced. That is why it cannot be captured or located, and yet why it can be so powerful in shaping human thought and action.

In contrast, there is a different kind of decentralization of power in the material world of state politics that does not seem to be in such clear contradiction to notions of centralization of power. State territory is clearly a diffuse phenomenon that can carry political constraints across space. At the same time, state buildings, offices, garrisons, and the like are used not only to mark state boundaries but to house a bureaucracy that is treated as a "center." The diffused constraints on citizens of a territorial state are not unlike the decentered constraints imposed through language. Being part of the population of the state, for example, is also often not a matter of choice, and certainly was not to people in seventeenth-century France. Their taxes and their military duties were not choices but matters that faced them because of where they lived. They were part of France without being part of its "center." Only a select few families were allowed to take residence at Versailles, and even though they might have been housed at the center of the court, they were usually kept from exercising power through the bureaucracy, so they were not able to act from the political "center" of the state. Most other French men and women had no illusion of being at any power "center," but this did not make them any freer to stop being French. They still had to buy the goods at the market that Colbert's economic policies allowed to be there. They still had to contribute men or money to the military. They even internalized tastes and ways of life that made them French, even when they felt only hatred toward the government. Just as they were "carriers" of their language, they were "carriers" of a geographically defined political location. In the end, their actions, just like their speech, could never quite be held within the direct control of state authorities unless they were soldiers under orders. But they were no more free of their political location than they were free of the coercion of language.

The centering and decentering of politics achieved through territorial manipulations in seventeenth-century France was based upon a link between land and bureaucracy. French territory was managed as a unit. The system of control was indeed centralized, although the fact of territorial control always had to be local. The image of French territory itself as a measured and marked part of the European continent was pursued by members of a centralized, state scientific academy, but also yielded a view of France described by boundaries, not the center. French soldiers went to war because people at Versailles told them to do it, but they fought the wars in sites far removed from this court. French lace was a pet project of Colbert, but it, too, was made locally by artisans, following in their own way Colbert's directives for their work. There is reason to see both centralization and decentralization as part of all these material activities used to achieve and assert state power.

One essential requirement for accumulating material power in the state was the reduction of physical impediments between the bureaucracy and the sites where its directives were realized (or not). The territorial boundaries between France and its neighbors were ideally the only places where the movement of people and things was to be disrupted. That is why Vauban not only built large numbers of border fortresses, but also razed many citadels that stood in the interior of the country. These interior sites were particularly dangerous to the state because they could be used as alternative centers of power. The citadels were first to go in areas of the country where the loyalty of the subjects was questionable. Political pacification was in these places engineered like one of Vauban's sieges. The result was a countryside in which the king's emissaries and soldiers could move without hindrance, shrinking the distance between the political center and the boundaries of its defining territory.

The construction of barracks by the army was used in a similar fashion to pacify suspect populations and reduce the potential hold of local towns on the military. With barracks, soldiers were no longer housed by local citizens. This not only reduced the resentment of local families, but also minimized the potential recruitment of soldiers to local causes. Again these barracks smoothed the roads between the court and the countryside.

Versailles, in this context, was like Latour's center of calculation.[15] It provided the management and measurement systems by which the territory was known and engineered, but it had no powers beyond those invested in the land itself. It provided means of circulating resources and regulations across French territory. The land supplied the valuables on which power was built: soil, waterways, minerals, and the edifices built with them (like military strongholds). The center used surveys, maps, censuses, and tax plans to transform places and resources into inscriptions that political leaders could carry, point to, and use to claim power. Maps were vital tools for reshaping the land located on it; they were used in France to plan wars, dig canals, dredge harbors, rebuild fortresses, increase tax collection, and rationalize military recruitment in order to empower the state. Then these projects were realized locally, through the efforts of both regional populations and representatives of the state.

What was produced through this exchange between diffuse locations across France and the center of calculation was a state territory; it was not natural and it was not just locally known and used. It was an order of things, not in Foucault's sense of language-based categorization of the natural world, but a political order realized on the land. It was made with the aqueducts running across fields. It was embodied in the border fortress cities designed by Vauban that told the ordinary traveler where the land changed political hands. It was dug into the canals that linked major rivers in France, and was felt by all those whose lives were transformed for good and bad by the new trade running along them. This material order structured a social order that was felt everywhere, and nonetheless had a center where the engineering was being managed through the institution of the state.

The France that was produced this way was not a political concept, a title for a regime, or the product of an imagined history. It was a place. It lay in the land and the peculiarities of its ordering. It was in battlements, botanical collections, tapestries from the Gobelins factory, the Canal d'Orleans, the Canal de Midi, the water system of Paris, and the fashionable dresses of the French court being imitated by ladies and gentlemen all across Europe. It was equally in the espalier trees, ground-hugging fountains, topiary hedges, green lawns, glass-covered hotbeds, windmills and water pumps, statues of Louis XIV, and thick trees of French formal gardens. It was a product of engineering and material innovation, the same kind of intervention in nature celebrated at the gardens of Versailles.

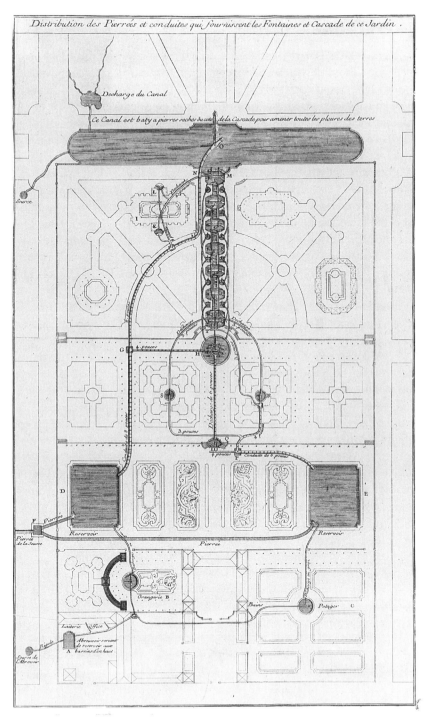

146. Dezallier d'Argenville's plan for a water system, illustrating how formal gardens depended for their style on technique.

Material culture and knowledge

The cultural materialism in this analysis and the way it locates meanings in objects may seem to exclude all possibility of studying ideas as historical forces in state formation. We are taught in our society to see the creation of material culture as the manifestation of an idea – a realization of a prior mental representation. As a result, we tend to think that we cannot study the formative qualities of thought in social life by looking at things. We have to find the ideas behind the things. But this is not a necessary analytic move. The Russian philosopher, Ilyenkov, has argued that thinking is a fundamentally social activity that occurs less in individual minds than in action in the world (Bakhurst 1991). Thought is not meaningful unless it is shared with others, since meaning is necessarily social. Even the claim that something *is* a thought depends on its social status. Language provides one very powerful system for making thought social and constituting collective meanings, but it is not the only one. Meanings are also developed with the construction of monuments, clothing, or any other item of material culture. The crafting of the built environment is itself the locus of a kind of conversation. People look at the material results of their productive activities, and learn to see things in common. They reflect on their work and achieve the kind of cognitive reflexivity associated with language acquisition and writing systems. Making things, according to Ilyenkov, is not a poor substitute for language use, but just the same kind of cultural construction. We often do not know what we think until we try to do something with our thoughts – write a paper, design a building, speak a phrase, or even organize a political movement. In viewing what we have done, we can see our actions as socially meaningful and so decide what to do next. The multiplication of equestrian statues of Louis XIV, the spread of formal gardens in France, and the proliferation of Vauban's fortresses can best be explained in these terms. They were all on-going experiments in thinking about power not through language but through material action. Most observers assume gardens to be pre-designed objects: physical projections of prior mental images. But we know that Le Nôtre made sketches and plans of garden areas usually *after* the work was completed. He learned to make great formal gardens by building them, not drawing plans for them or theorizing on paper about them. Louis XIV, Colbert, Louvois, and others did much the same thing with the state.

People clearly experiment with plants, soil, stone, and sometimes metal when they construct gardens. They certainly do not know what they will get from the earth until they start digging and planting. As the growing season progresses, the garden will change with variations in weather and attacks of insects. There is no end moment in the growth of a garden, only an ongoing project that lives until it is removed or dies. Each day requires working with the results of previous actions. The garden is therefore a perfect site for seeing the kind of material thinking Ilyenkov describes. Making a garden is always an act of coordination with the material world that gains meaning from its social uses; it cannot exist only in the individual mind; it cannot even be entirely preconceptualized. In this, it is like most built environments. Cities are not preconceptualized, built to specifications, and then left inviolate. They are sites of continual material experimentation; they decay so they cannot even be sustained intact without being actively worked upon. Even the virtual worlds of fiction share some of these properties. Writers, who would seem to have their stories under control in their minds, talk frequently about how characters in their fictions can take on lives of their own. Once parts of the story and elements of character are set down on paper, the writer must interact with them as part of their exterior environment. Even sculptors working with marble, not a very plastic or forgiving material, find lines in a particular stone and characteristics of the way it breaks influencing how their work develops; they interact with the material to make the results. What they produce is not, then, just a tribute to art history or creative genius, where the mind imprints its vision on the world, but another example of how human action and thought emerge from action on the material world. Activities like building a state that require extensive interaction with huge numbers of people are even more unpredictable than gardens during a growing season. The outcomes of even the most carefully constructed plans can vary enormously, when people with their different skills, practices, and interests must work together. Group life is always filled with surprises, and group dynamics are even more loaded when they are materialized in institutional structures and engineered landscapes.

The state-building in late seventeenth-century France could not be the kind of rational or inevitable social development that it sometimes seems in histories, since it was very much a material activity and was improvised as it went along. Obviously, Louis XIV and Colbert did not develop a mental model of the state, and get others to make it appear just the way they wanted it. They did not seem to have a firm conception of what they wanted at the start. They sometimes lost wars; the treasury was often not as full as they wanted. These great "architects" of the state were not even the ones to do most of the state building. This political shift was very much a material accomplishment of practical actors: laborers who dug bulbs into the garden, soldiers who manned fortresses, surveyors who made maps of the land, and tax collectors raising revenues. They improvised, studying what they had already done, and trying something else. (The king did much the same thing geopolitically as we can see from the reflections in his *Mémoires*.) All these improvisations, in coordination with myriad others and embodied in the material world, produced what we call "the state." This state was a collective and material construct, but not one that inevitably appeared from the distributed interactions of groups manipulating the world in concert to seek material advantage; it was not always clear in this fluid situation where advantages for any group might lie. Reactions of groups to state-building changed as the process progressed. That is why legitimacy was a different kind of problem at the beginning than at the end of Louis XIV's reign.

In a comparable way, the gardens at Versailles developed not just as a simple transfer of the Italian garden from the hill to the plain, but a series of expansions and revisions. When Le Nôtre and his colleagues turned toward the land behind the château at Versailles, they had no clear conception of the garden they would eventually make; they kept changing the elements for particular parties or remodels of the château, keeping those they liked and rejecting those that did not satisfy them, working to find ever better ways of organizing the valley and decorating its surface. To build the

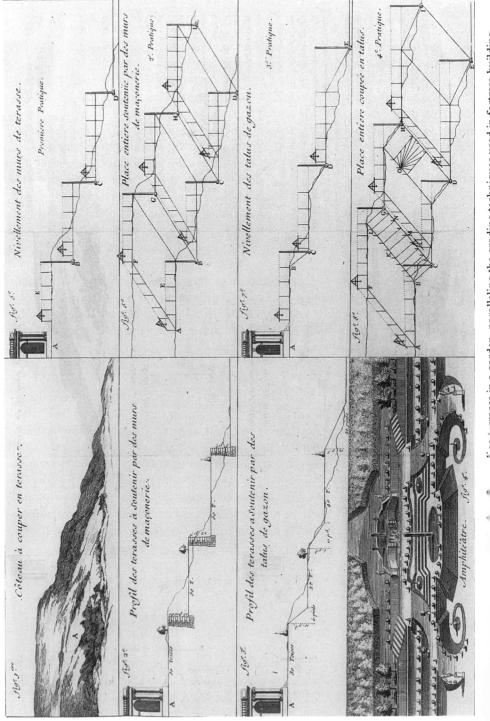

148. The south walkway from the Apollo fountain: a model of natural order and land control.

149. The military presence at the entrance of the château is matched by the

he landscape behind it (*Vue du Château et du Jardin de Versailles*).

gardens at Versailles, thousands of workers terraced hillsides, built new outbuildings, laid down water pipes, built retaining walls, imported trees, cut down others, and dug a canal, while Colbert commissioned statues and collected rare plants and animals. This huge population transformed the grounds of the château, and through ongoing experimentation and manipulation, made the most renowned of French formal gardens.

Similarly, state-makers engaged in a complex of changing and often material activities provided what we now refer to as an immutable form: the modern French state. From a myriad of routine actions like digging trenches and erecting walls, the king, his ministers, and thousands of unnamed accomplices created meanings probably well beyond their dreams. They made a state not through some sweeping gesture of political architecture, but by fighting wars, drawing maps, setting up factories, organizing artists and scientists, counting the population, expanding the château at Versailles, appointing new tax men, giving new powers to Intendants, and making a professional army. They organized a system of people and things through mutual coordination that articulated the territorial state of France.

The political culture of modern life is so deeply invested in the territoriality already becoming visible in seventeenth-century France that we cannot easily see how land entered our systems of power. We usually do not begin conversations about the future of the nation-state with consideration of territorial control. We think that the real contemporary problem for politics is nationalism and ethnic conflict, where political identities and state power do and do not connect. We forget the fact that groups that consider themselves nations are often willing to fight for land in which to found a state. For much of the world, territoriality and nationalism grew together, so it is easy to see the two as a natural pair, and think that modern politics had only one cultural foundation: political/national identity. But in France, almost a century separated the politics of state-formation from the growth of nationalist politics. In the period before the French Revolution, the militarized, aestheticized territoriality of the modern state was laid bare in France. The French case therefore can help reveal how Western societies took nature as a touchstone for political empowerment and military development, and transformed the earth into a foundation for modern geopolitics.

The key to state territoriality and state building can be seen most readily in the formal park behind the château at Versailles. No wonder Louis XIV wrote itineraries for walks in the garden, where the power of engineering the landscape for political effect was being explored continually. In the garden, a new relationship between land and social life was always under construction. The new configuration of state power was not so much symbolized as explored in the park. The massive water system developed at Versailles resulted from the most ambitious set of engineering schemes in France. However flawed the projects, they taught French surveyors and engineers more than a little about topography, geology, and hydraulics. They gave the French state new tools of power to apply elsewhere. And no matter how imperfect the water delivery in its early stages, the end result was a tribute to French power and was used in the massive fountains of the garden to celebrate the glory of the reign. The military engineering in the garden may not have advanced technique in the same way that the waterworks did,

150. N. de l'Armessin, *Habit de Jardinier*.

but it did help associate French military might with state power just as the military was being professionalized under the state. When the nobility walked the ramparts of the garden adorned in fancy dress or costumes, the alienation of French military authority from noble family life was made almost palpable.

Even the massive consumption at Versailles and the overbearing sumptuousness of the château and grounds constituted an experiment in material politics. It not only contributed to the subjugation of the aristocracy, as Elias has made clear, but also projected a vision of French cultural leadership that was meant to serve French political ambition. France was supposedly rich; France was beautiful; the French had taste; the French had staggering military skills; so France was clearly meant to be the new Rome. A few steps into the great formal garden at Versailles provided all that anyone needed to know about the natural authority of the king, the state, and the land of France.

Notes

1 The culture of land and the territorial state

1 Saint-Simon 1958. "My child, you are about to become a great King. Do not imitate my love
of building nor my liking for war, but try, on the contrary, to live at peace with your neighbors. Render to God all that you owe Him; recognize your duty toward Him; see that He is
honoured by your subjects. Always follow good counsellors; try to comfort your people,
which it grieves me that I was unable to do . . ." (pp. 241–42). Saint-Simon soon reflected on
the character of Louis XIV and said that he loved flattery and this made him seek glory in
war and nothing but adulation in his life. "Flattery fed the desire for military glory that sometimes tore him from his loves, which was how Louvois so easily involved him in major wars
. . ." (p. 248). "Pride and vanity, which tend always to increase, and with which he was fed
continually without even his perceiving it, even from preachers in the pulpits in his presence,
were the foundations on which his ministers raised themselves above all other ranks" (p. 240).
"He acquired a pride so colossal that, truly, had not God implanted in his heart the fear of
the devil, even in his worst excesses, he would literally have allowed himself to be worshipped.
What is more, he would have found worshippers; witness the extravagant monuments that
have been set up for him" (p. 252). There is also evidence that building and war were indeed
the major concerns of Louis XIV. This is visible in his letter to M. Bret Le Brun in Provence
in th 1690s (BN fr. 8962). These pieces with their concern about land and its improvements
are quite unlike Colbert's letters, which show his obsession with money, military provision,
and commodities. See Colbert 1868.
2 Vauban 1726, 1736.
3 Konvitz 1978; Sargent 1968, ch. 3; Cole 1964, vol. II, chs. 10–12; Neymarck 1970, livre II,
ch.1.
4 See diaries of visitors such as Lister (Lough 1985) and Locke (1953).
5 For a description of the relation of land to empire under the Romans, see Mann 1986, ch. 9;
and Armstrong 1982. This kind of territorial identity is deeply tied to the transition to capitalism, developing in one way in seventeenth-century France and manifesting itself in
Eastern Europe today in another related form. It is an aspect of the culture of capitalism that
students of materialism need to understand, even if they come to the subject mainly to
analyze economic life. This is because territorial identities affect the development and meanings of material culture and thus have great economic importance. Belonging to a region of
the world is often equated with a way of life, meaning a mode of consumption. In my earlier
research I paid particular attention to the play between local and international styles of dress

and their economic consequences. What I did not notice at the time was that these geographical patterns of fashionable change were predicated on a territoriality that I had taken for granted. Perhaps more important for the study of materialism, though, is the fundamental recognition that it has a political as well as an economic dimension. Western history itself has been written in terms of a politics of territoriality, and this part of our materialist culture has been masked by our tendency to naturalize rather than analyze it.

6 This political orientation was part of a larger materialist culture that was developing in early modern Europe. Europeans were turning toward material/technological solutions to their problems in many spheres, including the political one. This culture, without a discussion of political territoriality, is presented in Mukerji 1982. See also Konvitz 1987 for a good description of how France became territorial through cartography in this period.

7 If states seek territories just as animals do, as places to demonstrate domination, then there is nothing much to say about the territoriality of a state. Alternatively, if countries "own" their territories in much the way individuals can own property, then there is no special explanation needed for state territoriality. The history of cartography from the seventeenth century suggests that neither of these simple assumptions holds (Revel 1990; Burguière and Revel 1989).

8 See Mukerji 1984, Lister 1970, and Tooley 1978. Duranthon 1978 argues that the history of maps in France emanates from military and religious needs to administer lands.

9 Mallet 1684, Chastelet 1668.

10 See Le Clerc 1669. See also Konvitz 1987, Lister 1970, and Tooley 1978. For a description of the roots of territorial gardens in the nobility earlier than this, see Mariage 1990; for more discussions of techniques of land control in the gardens, see Mique 1992.

11 The château at Versailles was being only slightly modified when Le Nôtre started important work in the gardens. The famous first fête at Versailles took place before major renovations made the château large enough to function as the center of court life. See Adams 1979, pp. 79–80; Hazlehurst 1980, pp. 59–64; Walton 1986, and Marie 1968, pp. 26–27.

12 Thierry Mariage 1992 has discovered that the written designs for gardens were often made by surveyors after the practical work of building the gardens was over. This is an interesting way to understand the relationship between material practices and ideals of geometry in the gardens. They were much more inheritors of traditions of technical practice than of ideals of drawing. Mariage demonstrates that practical surveyors were hired for their skills in doing this kind of drawing, so their practices were also part of the cultural presentation of these gardens. They translated the land-use practices of the gardens into the written language of surveyors, tying the gardens to land management outside of the gardens.

13 For a discussion of geometries and boundaries as territorial markers, see Hazlehurst 1974.

14 See Clifford 1963, p. 73.

15 See Carroll 1996.

16 Félibien 1672.

17 Ranum 1979, particularly ch. 12; Anderson 1974, part I, ch. 4. For the thesis that financiers were recruited into a more feudal culture of statecraft than most histories suggest, see Dent 1973 (introduction).

18 Anderson 1974, p. 94.

19 For descriptions of this mobility in France, see Anderson 1974, pp. 94–95; see also Locke 1953, pp. 154, 164–67. The problems of legitimacy raised by these practices, albeit in an earlier period, are documented in Ladurie 1979.

20 Ladurie 1979.

21 Schalk 1986, Dens 1981.

22 Anderson 1974, pp. 94–101. For a brief but useful discussion of Colbert's relationship to Mazarin, see Murat 1984, ch. 3. For his role in constructing the French state, see Murat 1984, ch. 6.

23 This highly centralized and interventionist state took over activities that had been sources of power for the nobility and bourgeoisie. The state no longer derived its military power from the nobility, but developed a professional army, where members of the aristocracy could serve and maintain their identities as warriors, but they no longer held the power of the military as they had before, and they shared their world of warriors with non-aristocrats, again blurring the social ranks. At the same time, the world of commerce was linked to the state, reducing the autonomy of merchants and financiers to act in the economic realm. The state took control of many forms of manufacture and most international trade, allowing aristocrats who were prohibited from engaging in trade a means for gaining commercial wealth. Both nobles and bourgeois were pressed to seek their power through the state, found places there to explore new social possibilities, and provided economic and military support for that state. This state became a new kind of vehicle for political action, containing and exploiting bourgeois economic ambition and feudal authority.

24 Burke 1992.

25 Anderson 1974, p. 100; Elias 1983. The French developed a peculiar way of integrating the bourgeoisie and the nobility, the market and feudal relations. The two groups did not remain as separate as they did in Italy, where different sources of power were cultivated (see Burke 1974). Neither did they become merged as a fundamentally bourgeois elite, as in England. Bourgeois individualism had a long history in England, helping to make the success of bourgeois culture in this period understandable. See MacFarlane 1978. Instead, bourgeois culture in France was encapsulated within an aristocratic culture that diverted the bourgeoisie from investing in commerce (getting them to invest in state offices instead) and placed economic development within the hands of a state that gained its legitimacy from the nobility and its Catholicism. The role of Catholicism in this scenario is very interesting. It seems that the acceptance of Protestants coincided with the rise of the bourgeoisie in France, and the revocation of the Edict of Nantes coincided with the successful incorporation of the bourgeoisie into a noble-dominated elite. For a discussion of bourgeois investment in offices over businesses, see Anderson 1974, p. 97.

26 For a description of the materialism and private character of French bourgeois culture in the period, see Mangredien 1948, ch. 3. For a description of aristocratic ceremonial culture and its relationship to gardens in Italy and France in the sixteenth century, see Adams 1979, pp. 63–67.

27 Land was invested with complex layers of symbolism, giving it an aura of power without clear meaning. Comparable obscurity was evident in the painting of the period. See Montagu 1968. The layered symbolism from artwork gave the French formal garden a complexity and multivocality that belied its apparent simplicity as an expression of Cartesian rationality and made it also a marker of French wealth and ambition. There was indeed a visible mathematization of design in the gardens of the period (see Pérez-Gómez 1983). But the French garden was a political object, deployed to claim a cultural authority for France. This was achieved not only through the geometrical measurement of the landscape but also through its decoration and engineering to demonstrate French abilities to control the countryside.

28 Thomas 1983. He talks specifically about the system of domination that placed "man" over women and the creatures. For this reason, I use the term "man" rather than "humans" or "people."

29 See Strauss 1987.

30 For a discussion of French gardens and the celebration of power in the Baroque period, see Clifford 1963, p. 74. There is an interesting link between Clifford's ideas about the French landscape and the gardens, and the argument presented here. Clifford sees French garden designers responding to a physical environment that made land more two- than three-dimensional. That is why it could look more like a map or estate survey without having any cultural reason to. But I contend that designers were responding to a social environment that contained within it a particular cultural relationship to land, and that the meaning of land was undergoing change (Burke 1974). See the role of the clergy in Italy.

31 The English who cultivated these gardens on their property often had their portraits painted in their gardens, showing their families in the foreground with their landholdings behind. These paintings were simultaneously landscape paintings and property inventories. Nature was less a source of pleasure to them than a measure of their own worth, both economically and socially. In these portraits, land is fertile, but it is also as idle as they are. Yet each is part of an ordered and sensible universe. See Bermingham 1986.

32 Dumbarton Oaks 1974, Thacker 1972, and Clifford 1963.

33 Champigneulle 1961, pp. 40–41.

34 For a discussion of Italian Baroque versus French gardens, see Clifford 1963. Clifford (p. 71) argues that French gardens in the period were never really derived from the Baroque. He sees baroque gardens developing only in Italy, Spain, and central Europe. The use of canals and the flatness of the designs created a different tradition in France, one much more closely related to the Netherlands than to Italy. On the idea that French gardens owed much of their style to Dutch models of urban as well as garden design, see Hopper 1982. For the destruction of towns to build gardens, see Clifford 1963, p. 73. For a discussion of diversity and centralization in the Baroque, see Jansen 1962, ch. 6, and also Hauser 1951, vol. 2, ch. 8. Thierry Mariage also argues that Italian gardens were more affected by French models than earlier scholars have assumed (Mariage 1990, ch. 1). The "natural" evolution of garden forms that we see in most art histories may turn out to be more interesting as cultural artifacts than good history.

35 Hazlehurst 1966. This conception of the orderliness and diversity of nature remained a powerful element in French garden writing through the eighteenth century. See Liger 1776, pp. 353–55.

36 Hazlehurst 1980.

37 Mariage 1992 points out that garden books were post hoc readings of garden projects and hence could be given a veneer of scientism that did not necessarily drive their construction. The exercise of technique (engineering) preceded the activity of showing the orderliness in it (scientific theorizing).

38 Proctor 1991, Machiavelli 1965a.

39 Shapin 1994, Shapin and Schaffer 1985, Proctor 1991, Koyré 1958.

40 See Hedin 1983, p. 188.

41 Cronon 1991.

42 Rabinow 1989.

2 Military ambitions and territorial gardens

1 Serres 1611, Mollet 1981, Boyceau 1638 (particularly bk I, ch. 13 and bk III, ch. 2).

2 Hodge 1992, Vitruvius 1960, Roseneau 1959, Pepper and Adams 1986 (particularly ch. 8).

3 Boyceau 1638, bk I, ch. 13; bk III, avant-propos and ch. 2.

4 Androuet du Cerceau 1972, Boyceau 1638, Hazlehurst 1966, and Pepper and Adams 1986, p. 21.

5 Bourdin 1661, Le Clerc 1669, Vérin 1993, pp. 173–78.

6 Mariage 1990, p. 43; Bourdin 1661, Le Clerc 1669.

7 Vérin 1993, particularly ch. 4.

8 Salamagne 1986, pp. 47–49.

9 Cipolla 1965, ch. 1.

10 Salamagne 1986.

11 See Mariage 1990, pp. 51–53.

12 Ibid, pp. 42–45.

13 Ibid, p. 118.

14 Tilly 1975; see particularly Tilly's introduction, "Reflections on the history of European state making." The essay in this volume by Samuel Finer (Finer 1975) contains extended references to the importance of territoriality to modern Western states, but it does not associate the territoriality with a part of the landscape. It associates it with an abstract notion of space and the role of the military in defining that space. He also treats the nation as the culture of the state and not its territorial manifestation.

15 For Saint-Simon on Louvois' power over the king, see Saint-Simon 1958: "'Flattery fed the desire for military glory that sometimes tore him from his loves, which was how Louvois so easily involved him in major wars . . .'" (p. 248). For a discussion of the expenses of war and their role in the famines at the end of the regime, see Parker 1983 pp. 140–44; Rebelliau 1962, pp. 251–66; and Lachiver 1991.

16 Brewer 1989.

17 For the development of a full-time military under Louis XIV, see Parker 1983, p. 123 and Dugué MacCarthy 1984, pp. 34–68. For the development of the militia during the last decades of this regime, see Escoupérie 1986.

18 For noble military culture in the period, see Clare 1983 (particularly parts I and II). The diminishing of noble involvement in the army in the period was not so much Louis XIV's hope as his legacy. The cost in lives and noble fortunes from wars in the reign made it impossible later to restrict the officer corps to members of the nobility. While in 1629 nobles were expected to compose a quarter of the fighting forces, by 1661–78, this was no longer possible to sustain. Venality of offices, which had been abolished officially but continued in reality, had to be suppressed if not abolished so that those without private fortunes but with military skills could lead the army into battle. A set of new officer ranks evolved which did not require the officers to supply their own troops. See Corvisier 1979, pp.100–101, 162–65. Turenne was instrumental in bringing about this change (Weygand 1930, pp. 114–15).

19 See Ladurie 1979, p. 80, and Masson 1986.

20 See Vauban 1736; Dugué MacCarthy 1984, p. 63; Creveld 1989, pp. 99–101, 104–105; and Carrias 1960, pp. 148–49. See also Salamagne 1986 and Dollar 1983, pp. 11–23.

21 Creveld 1989, pp. 81–97. See Carrias 1960, p. 149 for Turenne's preference for field over siege warfare.

22 "*M. le Cardinal... informé* que cet héroique prisonnier *avait quelque intelligence dans les fortifications*, se le fit amener, estimant qu'un tel ennemi serait une acquisition précieuse" (Rebelliau 1962, p. 20). See also Vauban's role in Turenne's taking of Dunkirk (Weygand 1930, p. 82).

23 For the history of building citadels and tearing down old ones, see André 1974, chs. 8 and 9. For the continuity of this practice with policies by Richelieu, see Parker 1983; Carrias 1960, p. 113; and Rebelliau 1962, p. 104. For a map of the fortresses made or improved by Vauban, see Rebelliau 1962, pp. 312–13. Here as elsewhere there is evidence of a policy of centralization started by Richelieu but only realized later. The reasons for the effectiveness of the policy

under Louis XIV may lie in the greater significance of territoriality to the politics of this period.

24 For a discussion of arms manufacture in this period, see Bonnefoy 1986 and Cipolla 1965, pp. 66–70.

25 Parent and Verroust 1971, pp. 129–31, 147–61. It is important to note that places like La Rochelle, a center of Protestant power that had been devastated by Louis XIII, but then revived under Louis XIV, was given an arsenal. This location helped to keep the military hand of the state nearby. See Gutkind 1970, pp. 207–209. For earlier problems of military discipline, see Masson 1986. Vauban also tried to build housing near the arsenals in his fortified cities to keep the workers happy. He tried to place the church, housing and political buildings together in order to show physically the interconnectedness of the three. See Konvitz 1978, pp. 114–15. These efforts to populate border cities also helped to locate and stabilize the borders of France, not necessarily with soldiers, but with people with military jobs dependent on military success. Vauban also tried with less success to keep the perimeter of France stable in the Pyrenees. See Sahlins 1989, pp. 69–73.

26 The two lines of defenses proposed by Vauban were part of his vision of making France into a *pré carré* or great square. See Carrias 1960, p. 149; Rebelliau 1962, pp. 49–51; Sahlins 1989, pp. 69–73; Pujo 1991, ch. 6; Zeller 1928, ch. 5; and d'Albissin 1970 (particularly ch. 3). Nelly d'Albissin (ch. 2) demonstrates how unstable the boundaries were in this area even after the early wars by Louis XIV, and how much Vauban's plan was an attempt to stabilize them on the ground.

27 Salamagne 1986, Vauban 1736.

28 Pujo 1991, particularly chs. 2, 3 and 22.

29 For the idea of France as a *pré carré* and Vauban's early proposals for lines of defenses, see Pujo 1991, ch. 6; Carrias 1960, p. 149; Rebelliau 1962, pp. 49–51. For a map of the fortresses made or improved by Vauban that served to produce something close to his dream, see Rebelliau 1962, pp. 312–13 and Pujo 1991, p. 99. See also Sahlins 1989, particularly pp. 68–70, for the relationship between this notion of territorial development and the policies in the Pyrenees. Vauban also advocated a census as well as overseeing many surveys that helped to render the French state as a singular and measured entity. For Vauban's treatment of France as a managed territory, including his interest in both mapping and making a census of the state, see Parent and Verroust 1971, pp. 200–206.

30 Parent and Verroust 1971, pp. 137, 147–74, 191–206.

31 Vauban 1736, Mallet 1684.

32 When Vauban was rebuilding Quesnoy, there were even complaints sent to his superiors about the destructiveness of his engineering schemes. He was cutting down thousands of trees in the forest outside of the city to enlarge the battlement walls. The complaints were rejected; this was exactly what Vauban was expected to do. The physical resources of the state were meant to be put in the service of state power, and building fortresses was certainly one way of doing this (Salamagne 1986). Importantly, Vauban was used elsewhere to survey, protect, and develop royal forests and privately-held ones where the timber was conceivably useful to the military. Where timber was not needed immediately for his engineering, it was to be preserved as another kind of material resource for the state (Parent and Verroust 1971, pp. 191–94).

33 Rebelliau 1962, pp. 44–45, 92–93.

34 Morris 1979, pp. 122–37, 156–84; Machiavelli 1965b. Louis XIV's reign was supposed (by his publicists) to match the glory of Rome, including its military successes. When the king was married and the royal couple was presented to the Parisians, the decorations for the festivi-

ties celebrated Paris as a new Rome, where the king could rightfully rule his empire. See Néraudau 1986.

35 Burke 1974.

36 Néraudau 1986.

37 Yates 1947.

38 See Roux 1990. See also Parent and Verroust 1971 (esp. p. 122 and the appendix, pp. 288–97).

39 Durnerin 1983, La Quintinie 1693, vol. I, pp. 117–25. For other works in this tradition, see Laurent 1675 and Estienne 1687.

40 Bellaigue 1982.

41 The *plan en relief* of this château produced at Versailles in 1705 shows dramatically the military origins of this sort of design. See the plan-relief on display at Les Invalides in Paris. For contemporary comments on the Château Trompette and its new citadel, see Veryard 1701, p. 82.

42 This kind of great wall adds to the sense of power of the garden and château. On the garden side of Versailles, the wall behind Latona is imposing, and gives the château a more elevated standing. The same sense of power is associated with the walls rising up in the avant-cour at the front of the château. The stones seem to rise up from the streets to raise the château high above street level. At the Trianon side of the canal, a similar effect is produced by the high wall rising behind the fountain that abuts the end of the canal. A massive face of stone rises up from the water, giving the building above it a remoteness and grandeur. Similarly at Chantilly, a high wall between the courtyard and garden on the grotto side of the garden adds to the military posture of the house.

43 See Dugué MacCarthy 1984, pp. 9, 13, 24–26, 37. For discussion of Louis XIII's willingness to do battle against the Huguenots, see Parker 1983, pp. 53–57. For the growth of the French military under Louis XIII, see Parker 1983, pp. 60–64. For Louis XIII's devotion to military life, see Dugué MacCarthy 1984, pp. 9, 25–26. For the problem his absence created for yielding an heir, see Bluche 1986, pp. 27–30. For the importance to military technology of gunpowder and the role of cannon and guns in military tactics, see Creveld 1989, ch. 6, Child 1982, pp. 132–41, and Dugué MacCarthy 1984, pp. 9–33. For the French role in arms manufacture in the period, see Bonnefoy 1986. Compare with Machiavelli's use of classical military strategies (Machiavelli 1965b, bk III). See also Cipolla 1965, pp. 66–70.

44 See Adams 1990, pp. 28–52. On changes in military strategies during the Thirty Years War, see Dugué MacCarthy 1984, p. 13, and on the war itself (ibid. pp. 27–33).

45 For evidence of Louis XIV's desire for military glory, see Weygand 1930, pp. 154–59; Dugué MacCarthy 1984, p. 37; and André 1974, pp. 194–98. This regime followed Richelieu's lead in building up and centralizing the army. See, for example, Parker 1983, pp. 37, 123–25, 146–50. For an indication of the size of the French army at the end of this reign, see Corvisier 1979, p. 113. He claims that France had 300,000 troops under its command, three times more than Austria and four times more than Great Britain and Ireland.

46 Louis XIV 1806.

47 For a description of Versailles as a site for the French military, see Verlet 1985, pp. 244–45.

48 The king's guards were a fighting force and not just a unit based at Versailles for ritual purposes. See Dugué MacCarthy 1984, pp. 35, 39–44. For their place at Versailles, see Verlet 1985, pp. 244–45.

49 For the development of garrisons at fortresses, see Child 1982, pp. 186–87, 196–97; Parker 1983, p. 124; Corvisier 1979, pp. 79–92; and Salamagne 1986.

50 Creveld 1989, pp. 81–109; Carrias 1960, pp. 113–19; Parker 1983, pp. 61–64; Dugué MacCarthy 1984, p. 13; and Salamagne 1986, p. 45.

51 For a discussion of the Swiss guard and the use of pikes, see Creveld 1989, pp. 89–92; for a description of the Swiss guards and the garden, see Verlet 1985, pp. 203–204 and Lery 1926; and for a description of the military games played in the gardens, see Clare 1983.

52 For images of the topiary, see the "veues" and perspectives by Pierre Aveline. The clearest views of the topiary are not at Versailles; rather, see the *veue et perspective du château royale de Vincennes* and the one on the orangerie at Saint-Cloud. For images of French fortified towns that showed their landscaping, see Faucherre 1986 and also Roux 1990. For a description of a promenade in which there was military parading, see Thacker 1972.

53 Montclos 1991, p. 378.

54 The Fronde was significantly the moment when Louis XIV's most intensive political education began. In this period, Mazarin began to take him to political meetings, and began presenting him with political puzzles to solve to his satisfaction. This period of apprenticeship to Mazarin seems to have stuck with him in a way that all his earlier education in the classics had not. Many of the lessons seem to have guided him through the rest of his regime. See Mousnier 1984, p. 12. For the Fronde itself, see Mousnier 1984, pp. 611–30; Ranum 1979, pp. 203–28; and Parker 1983, ch. 3. See Dugué MacCarthy 1984, p. 37 and Weygand 1930, p. 55 on the royal family fleeing the city for Saint-Germain under the protection of the duc de Condé after they had been held in Paris. For discussion of the Fronde and this fountain, see Montclos 1991, p. 378.

55 Montclos 1991, p. 378.

56 Mariage 1980.

57 Scudéry 1979, esp. pp. 66–102.

58 Boyceau described garden design as nature seen through science. See Boyceau 1638, bk I, esp. ch.1; and bk III, chs. 4 and 5.

59 For English deforestation and its effect on France's forest policy, see Evelyn 1679. See Merchant 1980, pp. 66–68, 236–40, on Evelyn and English deforestation. See also Brewer 1989, p. 197 on the loss of ships in British conflicts with Louis XIV. This suggests the kind of demand placed on the forests by the navy and merchant shipping in the period. For the relationship between forests and rivers in making French forest reserves particularly useful to the navy, see Bamford 1956, p. 49. On Colbert, see Bamford 1956, ch. 1.

60 Devèze 1962, part 1, chs. 2–3 and Bamford 1956, pp. 14–19. Corvol (1984, ch. 1) argues that the problems of the forest were not remedied by the forest-management system put in place by Colbert because it was designed on the basis of insufficient knowledge of the forests and the conditions necessary for growth. It would be interesting to look at parallels between the problems of forests generally in this period and the particular problems encountered at Versailles in keeping the trees alive. To what extent were the foresters acting in ignorance when they had trouble keeping the forests alive at Versailles, and to what extent were the trees there suffering from particularly poor conditions?

61 For an exhaustive description of what the new foresters did in each forest, see Devèze 1962, part 2 and Bamford 1956, pp. 18–20. For an example of the fines levied on the local elite in one area, see Devèze 1962, pp. 114–15. Corvol (1984, pp. 17–28) argues that the surveys were not as well executed as many others writing on this subject have suggested. Devèze (1962, esp. pp. 76–77) is particularly insistent that these reforms were more important for the revenues they raised and the economic rationality behind them than their espoused military purposes.

62 See Devèze 1962, part 2, chs. 2–3; Merchant 1980, pp. 240–41, and Bamford 1956, pp. 18–29. The superiority of naval interests over economic ones in the forests later became more a matter of principle than practice. See Bamford 1956, pp. 30–37 for a discussion of how entrepreneurs affected the contracts for timber cutting that shaped French naval access to the

forests as the navy was growing, particularly in the eighteenth century. But in Colbert's period, the regulations were geared toward naval interests.

Colbert's first surveyors also noted the kinds of trees that grew in each region. They might not have penetrated all the forests and done this accurately, but they did attempt to find out enough about the contents of the forests to manage them more carefully. They tried to make their regulations reflect the fact that not all forests were the same. Some grew the large pole pines needed for masts or large oaks used for beams in shipbuilding. Both of these required long growth periods. Others had faster-growing trees for smaller-scale building needs. With the new forest-management program, the forests would still be marked out with geometrically similar plots of trees as they had before, and they would be harvested for lumber, but they had different kinds of regulations depending on what they grew. Some plots would be harvested in a few years, while others were left to grow for up to 120 years to provide ship timbers. Devèze shows the extent to which differences in the recommendations for the forests were a result of local resistence (as in Languedoc), differences in the trees, or differences in the environment in which the trees were supposed to grow. Corvol (1984, pp. 17–28) argues that the parcels were not so carefully differentiated, but the parcel sizes did vary, in part because of poor surveying. Sahlins (1994, pp. 52–56) argues that this kind of management system was in opposition to the local customs of forest use that emphasized "jardinage" or gardening within the forest. This was a primarily female activity that was based on the relations among plants in localities rather than on large systems of control. This kind of gardening, based on a kind of home gardening trope, was comparably at odds with formal gardening as it was with managed forests.

63 Devèze 1962, pp. 237–45; Sahlins 1989, chs. 1–3; Bamford 1956, pp. 18–29; Merchant 1980, p. 241; and Corvol 1984, ch. 2. Corvol and Devèze in particular suggest that the result of the forest reform was more juridical than either economic or military. Still, the point was not simply an institutional ordering of the responsibilities and rights vis-à-vis the forest, but rather a change in the material resources of the state. If one measures the military effects in terms of the size of the navy, or the economic effects in terms of improved revenues of the forest, this conclusion seems warranted. But the material restructuring of the forests themselves was more remarkable, and not really discussed well enough. The forests may not have been managed better but they were permanently marked as political resources and sites of state control in distant regions of France.

64 Devèze 1962, pp. 160–61 and Corvol 1984, pp. 28–29 on the roadbuilding projects. See Corvol (1984, ch. 2, section 1) on the general impulse in this period to mark perimeters in a material fashion, to make them manifest and to help police them.

65 Corvol 1984, ch. 2, section 1. Corvol makes the interesting point that the surveys in this period often only involved the forests being measured around their perimeters, and they were marked by their boundaries in ways consequential to their use. But actually little was known about their interiors. The aim was to mark and fortify old boundaries of royal forests and those with collective patterns of ownership, and to make users of these areas submit to royal regulations. The lack of autonomy felt by local officials was intentional (Corvol 1984, pp. 32–37). In this, the organization of the forest was a microcosm of the organization of the territorial state.

66 In 1699 Colbert ordered 1,000 young trees (4 to 5 feet high) and 200 fully-grown ones. In 1700 he authorized 1,500 livres to plant all the trees necessary to revegetate the gardens. He also authorized 8,000 livres for replacing plants in the orangery. See Archive Nationale ser. 0' #1809 for some of the orders for trees needed to replant the gardens in 1699 and 1700.

67 Bamford 1956, ch. 1; Corvol 1984, chs. 1–2; and Devèze 1962, part 1, ch. 1.

68 For a discussion of merchants' needs for skill at measuring volume by sight, see Baxandall 1974, pp. 86–94.

69 Le Clerc 1669. Although there was a long-standing tradition in European publishing of decorating books with illustrations that had no strong relation to the text, this practice had diminished by the seventeenth century and illustrations of the sort in this book, designed specifically to demonstrate exercises from the text, were clearly tailored to the books' content. Hence, their decorative content was intentional, and bore some relation to what the author or publisher thought of the intended readership. See Mukerji 1982, ch. 2.

70 Le Clerc 1669. Israel Silvestre was particularly fond of using these kinds of figures in his prints.

71 Thacker 1972.

72 Scudéry 1979; Félibien 1672, 1874.

73 Hazlehurst 1980.

74 The book, like other texts of the period on military strategy, contained geometry lessons. These were sometimes presented against the background of formal gardens and sometimes presented against images of warfare – battlefields and siege scenes. Again, as in Le Clerc's book, these pictures invite the viewer to measure these spaces using a common system of mathematics, suggesting that warfare and garden appreciation shared a common relation to space.

75 For a discussion of the plan-relief as a source of play or distraction, see Pujo 1991, p. 317, where he argues that Vauban's papers suggest that the first one may have been built for the dauphin as a source of amusement.

76 See the edition of *Monuments Historiques* dedicated to *Les Plans-Relief* (1986, no. 148, pp. 24–48). See also Roux 1990.

77 Francastel 1970, pp. 249–59. See Cipolla 1965, ch. 1, and Pepper and Adams 1986, ch. 1. The French were actually behind the Italians in their metalworking capabilities when they began to make the statues for Versailles. The French could only use gilded lead in the early fountains while the Italians were already proficient in casting bronze. So, even though the statuary at Versailles might have been quite flashy and impressive, golden and gaudy, the early lead statues were actually evidence of how far behind in metalcraft the French were. Félibien, interestingly, in his description of the fête of 1668, characterized the *Dragon* group of statues as bronze pieces, although they were made by the Marsy brothers from lead. They were gilded, so they glittered brightly enough, but they were from a soft pliable metal, not the more sturdy but demanding bronze. Félibien may have made a mistake in his writing, but this great propagandist was quite capable of describing a reality he wanted others to believe rather than what was true (Félibien 1994, p. 34). The Italians had been better at bronze sculpture from the period of Henri IV (Ranum 1979, p. 75), but although French skills in the area of casting had improved, French sculptors (having failed at gilding bronze) were making gilded lead work at the arsenal (Francastel 1970, pp. 58–60, 249–63). See also Francastel 1970, p. 163 for Girardon's work at the arsenal at Toulon. For the backwardness of French metalworking and artillery, see Cipolla 1965, ch. 1 (esp. pp. 66–70).

78 See Verlet 1985, p. 193 for information about another project commissioned from the Kellers for the gardens. They also seem to have cast some cannon for the miniature warships on the canal at Versailles.

79 Félibien 1994, pp. 142–53.

80 Thacker 1972.

81 Thacker 1972, p. 57:

1 En sortant du château par le vestibule de la Cour de marbre, on ira sur la terrasse il faut sar-
   rester sur le haut des degrez pour considerer la situation des parterres des pieces d'eau, and
   les fontaines des Cabinets.
2 Il faut ensuite aller droit sur le haut de Latonne, et faire une pause pour considerer Latonne,
   les Lesars, les rampes, les Statües, l'allée Royale, l'Apollon, le Canal, et puis se tourner pour
   voir les parterres et le Château.
3 Il faut apres tourner a gauche pour aller passer entre le Sfinx, en marchant il faut faire une
   pause devant le Cabinet pour considerer la gerbe and la nape en arrivant aux Sfinx on fera
   une pause pour voir le parterre de midy, et apres on ira droit sur le haut de l'Orangérie, d'ou
   l'on verra le parterre des Orangers et le lac des Suisses.
4 On tournera a droit, on montera entra l'Apollon de bronze, et le Lantin, et l'on fera une
   pause au corps advancé d'ou l'on voit Bacchus et Saturne . . ."

3 Material innovation and cultural identity

1 Elias 1983. For a sense of how important issues of taste and manufactures were in French
   life in the seventeenth century, see William Reddy's argument about cloth and the Revolution
   in France (Reddy 1986).
2 For an extended discussion of the Italian influences on early work at Versailles, see Francastel
   1970, ch. 2.
3 Reddy 1986; Cole 1964, vol. II, pp. 502–12; Lachiver 1991; and Ranum 1979. pp. 252–53.
4 Weber 1976. This pattern makes even more sense of Reddy's work on cloth and political
   meaning in France in the eighteenth century. If political identity in France was forming
   around a territory and the commodities made in it that were used to distinguish this area of
   Europe from others, then connoisseurship was a political stance in France at the beginning
   of the eighteenth century.
5 Murat 1984, ch. 10; Hahn 1971; Bonifas 1994; Frégnac 1976, pp. 120–24, 157–60; Auscher
   1905, pp. 1–27; and Laprade 1905. For the political character of this art, see especially Levey
   1971, pp. 160–63, and Arnold Hauser 1951, vol. II, pp. 187–207.
6 Saint-Simon 1958 and 1990; Burke 1992, p. 169. The odd fact that the king was spending
   huge sums of money when in financial trouble was not a personality flaw, but part of aristocratic culture. Jonathan Dewald describes in detail the odd way in which the money
   economy both was used and strangely ignored by French aristocrats in the seventeenth
   century (see Dewald 1993).
7 The omnipresent French writings comparing the Ancients and the Moderns help to illustrate
   how powerful a concern this was to seventeenth-century French intellectuals. See, for
   example, Perrault 1979, Pérez-Gómez 1983, and Lougee 1976.
8 See Burckhard 1958, vol I, part III; Scudéry 1979; Félibien 1689 and 1874.
9 See Félibien 1689 and 1874.
10 Mukerji 1982, ch. 5; Wallerstein 1974; Néraudau 1986.
11 Mukerji 1982, ch. 5; Apostolidès 1981, pp. 25–26; Appleby 1978, particularly ch. 9.
12 Cole 1964, vol. II, chs.10–11; and Apostolidès 1981, pp. 25–37. This view of the dual cultural
   and economic significance of trade was part of the argument made for establishing a trading
   company for trade with India. See BN CCC 207 (fols. 9vo-10). The cosmopolitan view of
   manufacture, and commodity substitution also developed in smaller industries like soapmaking. See BN CCC 207 (fols. 87–88) on the production of black soap in the north of
   France in a bid to stop the import of Dutch soap.

13 Murat 1984, ch. 10; Burke 1992, p. 51; Levey 1971, pp. 160–63; Apostolidès 1981, pp. 31–33. For condemnation of Le Brun's authoritarian control of the academy, see Stranahan 1888, pp. 47–52; Janson 1962, pp. 444–46. For a more sympathetic view of Le Brun, see Marly 1987, p. 34. A more nuanced view is also in Hedin 1983 and Francastel 1970, pp. 59–60 and ch. 5. Compare the discussion of Le Brun's control over the *Galerie d'Apollon* in the Louvre, and the discussion of the freedom of artists to veer from his sketches, in the discussion of the Marsy brothers' fountain of the Bacchus group (Francastel 1970, pp. 34–38, 63–64).

14 See Marly 1987, ch. 4 and p. 53 for the relationship of trade restrictions and the growth of the silk industry. For a discussion of internal trade in France, see Cole 1964, vol. I, pp. 357–83, and Beik 1985, ch. 12.

15 Cole 1964, vol. I, chs. 7 and 8; vol. II, chs. 9 and 12.

16 Mukerji 1982, p. 188; Laver 1979, pp. 109–30. See Burke 1978 for an examination of how this spread of fashion worked within the commercial culture of the period.

17 Simmel (1978) noted the importance of this kind of consumption but failed to see its political role. And although Veblen (1953) saw the significance of the social power of consumption for bourgeois families, he couched his analysis so much in a nineteenth-century individualism that the creation of collectivities through consumption did not come into his theory. Apostolidès 1981, pp. 37–40 demonstrates how the culture of the academies produced a rupture between elite and popular culture, hence reproducing and extending the social rift between nobles and ordinary people, but the culture produced by the academies nonetheless contributed to the fashioning of a French style that ordinary people helped to reproduce and used to make sense of themselves as members (albeit poorly treated ones) of France.

18 Cole 1964, vol II, chs. 12–13; Beik 1985, pp. 287–97; Ranum 1979, ch. 12; Metropolitan Museum of Art 1989.

19 Ranum 1979, ch. 12; Chatelain 1971, ch. 15 and pp. 468–85; for an explanation of Fouquet's fall without reference to his cultural position, see Murat 1984, ch. 5. Murat emphasizes Fouquet's role in diplomacy and his accumulation of naval power, suggesting that this was the real reason for Colbert's suspicion of Fouquet; but interestingly, Colbert took this as a model for his own interest in the navy, which did not increase his power significantly. Colbert imitated Fouquet in this regard, while the king imitated his approach to culture.

20 Ranum 1979, pp. 253–56; Bergin 1985.

21 Chatelain 1971, chs. 3, 4, 7–11, 13, 15; Ranum 1979, pp. 253–56.

22 For a description of Fouquet's collection of orange trees, see Murat 1984, pp. 113–14; Chatelain 1971, ch. 13.

23 Ranum 1979, pp. 252–59. Dent argues that the financiers were not the only group using land for making social claims. People from the higher ranks of the state bureaucracy were doing the same thing – albeit with less resistance. He also argues that the financiers were not a particularly capitalist group, in large part because of their importance to state finances, which involved them with the deep irrationality of the state financial system. Still, financiers had a peculiar social position. They were distrusted because of their economic importance. Thus, while their use of land to acquire titles and enter into the nobility was not in itself clear evidence of the entrance of the world of commerce into court life, it was still resented because finance was seen as deeply at odds with nobility. Moreover, Dent argues that the financiers were vulnerable to social distaste (and violence) because they were individualistic rather than corporatist. They had no group culture to protect them. In this way, they displayed an individualism that is usually associated with capitalism and commercial culture. They were carriers of a commercial culture that was seen to be at odds with court life, but was so essential

to it that they were able to experience mobility in spite of the cultural resistance to it. See Dent 1973, ch. 9, and particularly, pp. 235–42.

24 Chatelain 1971, chs, 3, 4, 7–10; Ranum 1979, pp. 253–56.

25 Chatelain 1971, pp. 135–41.

26 Ibid., ch. 6.

27 Ibid., chs. 7–8; for a description of the intellectual milieu in Paris in this period, see Ranum 1979, ch. 8. Note Le Brun's debt to his culture (pp. 161–66).

28 Chatelain 1971, ch. 14.

29 Ibid., chs. 13–14.

30 Ibid., ch. 13; Ranum 1979 (p. 256) claims Fouquet hated Paris and sought to leave it, but this did not diminish his immersion in Parisian culture.

31 Not surprisingly, given the lack of traditional respect for the intellectual and aesthetic contributions of women, most of the *précieuses* or women of the salon were Moderns. See Perrault 1979, Pérez-Gómez 1983, Lougee 1976, Picard 1943, and Backer 1974. For Molière and the *précieuses*, see Chatelain 1971, pp. 464–68.

32 Backer (1974) downplays the importance of Jansenism to this cohort, and particularly for Mlle de Scudéry, but other scholars oppose this view. See Chatelain 1971, pp. 84–89; for a discussion of Jansenism in this reign, see Grever 1990, ch, 10, particularly pp. 164–65, 172–75. For Perrault's tolerance of the new, including Jansenism, see Perrault 1979.

33 Chatelain 1971, p. 346.

34 Ibid., ch. 17, and p. 458.

35 Ibid, chs, 13, 15, and 18 (particularly pp. 303–313, 364–73). For Molière at Vaux, see Chatelain 1971, pp. 464–70.

36 Ranum 1979, p. 253. For Colbert's responsibility in amassing some of this fortune, see Murat 1984, pp. 21–28.

37 Compare the descriptions of Colbert and Fouquet in Chatelain 1971, Ranum 1979 (pp. 253–69), Cole 1964, Murat 1984, and Neymarck 1970.

38 Ranum 1979, pp. 253–59.

39 Manufacture des Gobelins 1962, pp. 8–15; Janson 1962, pp. 444–46; Stranahan, 1888, pp. 42–57.

40 Elias 1978; Ranum 1979, pp. 257–58.

41 Mukerji 1982, p. 69. See also Agnew 1986; McKendrick, Brewer, and Plumb 1982; Brewer and Porter 1993; Schama 1988; and Haskell and Teichgraeber 1993. For the complex ways in which commodities can have value, see the introduction to Appadurai 1986.

42 See Elias 1978 and Veblen 1953. No wonder Reddy (1986) found that both connoisseurship and government regulations of production became important political issues in the Revolution.

43 Mukerji 1982, ch. 5; Reddy 1986.

44 Mousnier 1974, pp. 682–712.

45 See Ranum 1979, pp. 259–72. For Colbert and the *petite académie*, see Murat 1984, pp. 115–16; and Perrault 1909. Colbert is depicted in many histories as rational and only concerned with economics (see, for example, Cole 1964 and Murat 1984). Elsewhere I have argued that conspicuous consumption was, in the early modern period, just as bourgeois as economic asceticism. Both were part of the new materialism developing in European culture. Colbert, as superintendent of the king's buildings and later the king's household, necessarily dedicated much of his career to celebrating the king's greatness. He had to participate in decisions about the expansion of the château at Versailles and the reconstruction of the Louvre. He chose artisans to work at the royal residences, and even though he had counsel

from Le Brun, Mansart, and others for these things, he was still burdened with the responsibility of making these decisions further the political goals of the king. Why would we think the king's *gloire* did not also play a role in Colbert's economic policies? Perhaps the tax reforms yielded money, not glory, but the point of the treasury was to give the king resources to pursue his glory and the glory of France. The factories were a different story. The production of elite consumer goods may have been good for the economy, but the pieces produced had to be of sufficiently fine quality to suit the king so that they could be sold to his courtiers. For a discussion of how the careful differentiation of linguistic/cultural categories has essentially been unsuccessful in Western culture, see Latour 1993.

46 Mukerji 1982, ch. 5; Cole 1964, vol. II, chs. 10–11.

47 For a clear statement of the competing economic theories in the period, see Appleby 1978. For discussion of fashion and economy in the period, see Mukerji 1982, chs. 5–6 (particularly pp. 198–202 and 258–59).

48 Cole 1964, vol. II, p. 133.

49 Cole 1964, vol. II, chs. 10–11; Apostolidès 1981, pp. 25–37. See BN CCC 207 (fols. 9vo–10) on textiles, BN CCC 207 (fols. 87–88) on soapmaking, BN CCC 207 (fols. 88vo–89, 137 vo) on pine tar for shipbuilding, and BN CCC 207 (fols. 112–119) on lacemaking.

50 Cole, vol. II pp. 134–35, 137.

51 Cole 1964, vol II, pp, 132–303. To understand how these rules were seen as essential to the cultural attractiveness of the goods produced, and hence to the economic success of the textile trade in France, see the 1665 letter in BN MC132 (fols. 304–304vo).

52 See Mettam 1988, ch. 5 on the general lack of rationality in the administration and pp. 269–88 for an examination of the ways in which political processes and negotiations over jurisdiction and rights entered into the process of taxation and the problems of its reform. See also Dent 1973, part 1; Beik 1985, pp. 87–91; Mousnier 1974, pp. 729–42; Neymarck 1970, bk III, ch. 1. Mettam (1988, p. 194) made it clear that the king's power depended on his reputation, so the promotion of his glory was not a minor issue, but one that drove all other parts of the regime.

53 Bourdieu 1984.

54 Cole 1964, vol. II, pp. 141–45, 149; and Chaplain 1984, pp. 15–21. Chaplain's book, although mostly addressing a later period of textile manufacture in France, is particularly sensitive to the spatial aspect of industrial development – the way in which location inside the geography of the state as well as regional location were important to industrial development in Louviers.

55 Cole 1964, vol. II, pp. 137–38; Schaeper 1990, ch. 2; and Neymarck 1970, bk II, ch.1.

56 Cole 1964, vol.II, pp. 156–71; Beik 1985, pp. 287–91.

57 Cole 1964, vol. II, ch. 12; Neymarck 1970, book II, ch.1. The clear design to make French laces distinctively French, even though based on Venetian styles, can be seen in BN CCC 207 (fols. 18vo–19). A proposal to manufacture textiles to replace English ones is documented in BN CCC 207 (fols. 174vo–186vo).

58 Cole 1964, vol. II, pp. 187–95; see Marly 1987, ch. 4 and p. 53 for the relationship between trade restrictions and the growth of the silk industry .

59 Mukerji 1982, p. 188. Marly 1987, ch. 2 (particularly pp. 54–55 and 58–59).

60 Cole 1964, vol II, pp. 239–86; Laprade 1905, chs. 1 and 2. For a description of Colbert and the entrepreneurs, see Cole 1964, vol. II, pp, 239–40. For the growth of the fashion for lace, see Marly 1987, pp. 80–81. On lacemaking as a means of substituting French for Venetian laces, see BN CCC 207 (fols. 112–19).

61 Metropolitan Museum of Art 1989, pp. 27–37.

62 Burke 1992, pp. 51, 156; Cole 1964, vol II, p. 288; Gerspach 1893, pp. 13–20

63 Burke 1992, pp. 51, 156; Cole 1964, vol. II, pp. 287–91; Gerspach 1893; Lacordaire 1852; Havard and Vachon 1889; Francastel 1970, pp. 137–41; Metropolitan Museum of Art, 1989, pp. 27–37.

64 Cole 1964, vol. II, pp. 291–95; Lacordaire 1852, p. 30; Havard and Vachon 1889.

65 Rule 1990, ch. 6, particularly p. 96.

66 d'Argenville 1972, part I, ch. 4, pp. 44–57.

67 d'Argenville 1972, p. 46; Mariage 1990, pp. 78–79.

68 Thacker 1979, pp. 140–43, argues that the parterres were derived from Italian sources. This view is shared by Francastel 1970, ch. 1 (particularly p. 80); but the newest research on Le Nôtre's gardens by Mariage (1990) suggests just the opposite. For the little discussion of fabrics and gardens available, see Beck 1978. For continuities between embroidery designs and lace designs, see the extensive embroideries on the clothes depicted in the *Almanac Royal*, 1682, "Bal à la Françoise" (reproduced in Marly 1987, p. 81).

69 Martinus Petrus, *Liure contenant passement de moresques tres utile a toutes gens exercant lecdict art en l'an 1563* in Marolles Collection, Bibliothèque Nationale; Mukerji 1982, pp. 185–96.

70 Berain 1660. See also Le Brun's fountain designs (Le Brun 1675).

71 Goody 1993; Gouldner 1965.

72 Museum of Modern Art 1989, pp. 27–37. Interestingly, in the *Venus and Adonis* tapestry from the Gobelins (made between 1686 and 1692), the pattern of using garlands in tapestries appears to have been for the moment reversed. Scenes from tapestry-making were used as a border of a central picture of Venus and Adonis. These figures were, however, set in a garden where Adonis was being crowned with a garland.

73 For a history of lacemaking in France in this period, see Laprade 1905 and Lefébure 1912. For the relationship between parterre designs and lace patterns of the period, compare the lace in the collar in the portrait of Colbert by Larmessin to the parterre design in Perelle's print, "Veue du Jardin des Thuileries comme it est à present." Paris: Chez Mariette (R16087 at the BN); or compare the lace in the Portrait of Boussuet by Rigaud with the "Veue de l'Orangérie ou Iardin de la Reine à Fontainebleau." Paris: chez N. Langlois (R16329 at the BN); or compare the portrait of the duchesse de Nemours by Rigaud with Perelle's "Veue Generale de Fontainebleau." Paris: Mariette (P7406 at the BN). This lace may be derived from Italian laces from the period, but the earlier Italian parterres tended to be much more geometrical in design. See, for example, Pianta de Giardino de Ser Luca di Parma sul Monte Palatino, Rome: Rossi.

74 Francastel 1970, ch. 4; Verlet 1985, ch. 2.

75 See illustration in Walton 1986, p. 207.

76 See Walton 1986, p. 199 for illustration. See Mollet 1981, pp. 19, 21, 22, 24–26, and compare with Montclos 1991, p. 108.

77 See Bonifas 1994, pp. 38–109. It is interesting that one book of parterre designs by Pierre Betin was published by Iean Boisseav, who described himself as a decorator and printer of marine charts. The line between cartography, describing land in political terms, and parterre design, decorating the land for power, was blurred at this interesting cultural intersection. See Betin n.d.

78 Ranum 1979, pp. 165–66; Burke 1992, pp. 66–67; Colbert, vol. V, pp. 245–65.

79 Colbert, vol. V, pp. 245–65.

80 Ibid.

81 Colbert, vol. V, particularly letter 21, pp. 258–65.

82 Picon 1989, chs. 8 and 9.

83 Burke 1992, pp. 66–67.

84 Hoog 1989, pp. 16–26.

85 Hoog 1989. Thacker (1979, p. 150) notes how unlike French sculpture Bernini's piece was.

86 Colbert's correspondence with Charles Errard is among the most plentiful in the collection of letters on the arts and buildings. Clearly, Colbert had need of the students to provide the artwork for royal residences and their gardens. He writes most frequently about the care which students should apply to the work. Sometimes he allows Roman artists to fill his requests, as long as it does not cost too much. To get a sense of the density of the exchanges, in 1679 Colbert wrote seven letters to Errard about training the students, getting funded, and providing adequate work for the French court. See Colbert 1868, vol. V, letters 147, 149, 150, 157, 162, 164, 169.

87 Murat 1984, pp. 124–25. See Francastel 1970, pp. 137–41; Cole 1964, vol. I, pp. 315–19; Burke 1992, p. 51; and Neymarck 1970, book IV, ch. 1

88 Murat 1984, pp. 124–25; Perrault 1909; and Burke 1992, p. 51. Interestingly, Le Brun seems to have cultivated Colbert's wife, giving her a present to show his satisfaction with his treatment by her husband (see Neymarck 1970, pp. 223–24). For the *petite académie* and its relationship to the other academies, see Apostolidès 1981, pp. 29–34; Burke 1992, pp. 58–59. See also Charles Perrault 1909.

89 Francastel 1970, pp. 86–88, 93–98, 106–25.

90 Apostolidès 1981 (particularly ch. 2); Burke 1992, p. 51. See also Perrault 1909.

91 Francastel 1970, p. 11.

92 Boyceau 1638, Mollet 1981, Mollet 1663, and Serres 1611.

93 Félibien 1672, pp. 1–3.

94 Francastel 1970, ch. 3. For the role of the *petite académie* see Burke 1992, p. 51; Apostolidès 1981, pp. 29–34; and Perrault 1909.

95 Much of this information was distributed in pictorial prints, in the illustrations and writings on almanacs, and in the newspapers of the period that focused on court life. See Marly 1987 and Préaud 1995. See also prints by Israel Silvestre, Le Pautre, and Perelle, all of whom documented court life. See in addition, Félibien 1668, 1672, 1689, 1874, and 1994.

96 For the conscious molding of political identity, see Anderson 1983. For state regulation of industry and the role of cities, see Cole 1964, vol. II, particularly ch. 12; for construction of tradition in this period, see Mukerji 1982, pp. 116–28.

4 Techniques of material mobilization

1 Colbert 1868, vol. V, letter 49, pp. 296–97, dated May 5, 1670. Colbert explains to the king that some of the statues are slow in arriving for the garden, and that one of the reflecting pools was damaged by ice, but is being repaired. In letter 56 to M. Arnouil at Marseilles Sept. 6, 1670, Colbert explains that the royal residences require large quantities of flowers, so he needs the Intendant to find in Provence all kinds of jonquils and tuberoses, and any other exotic flower that might ornament the gardens. In letter 89 (p. 334) he asks the same Arnouil for seashells to decorate the grotto, and says a ship will arrive soon to pick them up. Colbert wrote to the Chevalier de Terlon (letter 90, pp. 334–35) that he needed swans for the gardens, and wants him to seek them out in Denmark. Colbert requested 100 at a good price to be shipped immediately in good boxes so they will arrive healthy for the gardens. In 1674, Colbert wrote to Arnouil again for flowers, this time emphasizing that he must be more prompt in delivering them and more careful in his accounts (p. 362). Later in

the letters, M. Brodard at Marseilles was asked to send the new flowers and exotic birds (pp. 412–13, 437). For problems of keeping the sculptures from being ruined by visitors, see Archive Nationale ser.0' #1790. And for the orders for replanting the gardens or replacing trees in the orangerie, see Archive Nationale ser.0' #1809

2 Ranum 1979, ch. 12.

3 Mariage 1990 and Hazlehurst 1980. See also Pradel 1979.

4 Hazlehurst 1980; Mariage 1990, pp. 43–45.

5 Mariage 1990, particularly section 1.

6 Goody 1993.

7 Mariage 1990, pp. 39–41.

8 Bellaigue 1982, pp. 1–3.

9 Bellaigue 1982, ch. 2.

10 Mariage 1990, ch. 1; Ranum 1979, ch. 12.

11 Mariage 1990, pp. 23–36, particularly p. 25.

12 Mariage 1990, pp. 11–13, 17, 26–27, 33, 83–104. For drainage canals in France, see Pinon 1986, pp, 20–22.

13 Mariage 1990, pp. 9, 23–25; Mukerji 1982, ch. 6. The problem that French nobles faced in managing their finances and their privileges is discussed in Bitton 1969, particularly pp. 65–76, 124.

14 Boudon 1991. See also Mariage 1990, pp. 82–104.

15 Beaumont-Maillet 1991, pp. 71–79.

16 Mariage 1990, pp. 17–21; Pinon 1986, pp. 4–13.

17 Cole 1964, vol. I, ch. 2; Mariage 1990, pp. 17–21; Pinon 1986, pp. 20–22.

18 Mariage 1990, pp. 11–12. See also Fagniez 1975, ch. 1. The Protestant heritage of French ideas about gardening are just as present in Bernard Palissy's work in the mid–sixteenth century. Palissy was also a vigorous Protestant thinker, and a fountain-designer. His major work was in pottery, which he began to investigate because of his heritage as a member of the impoverished nobility. This allowed him only to profit from the land if he wanted to retain privileges. Pottery was developed from the soil, so it did fit the technical requirements of being a land-derived activity. As a Protestant noble, Palissy was in an interesting position to rethink the meanings and uses of land. He devoted himself in both his art and his writings to describing and using land in new ways (see Dupuy 1970, particularly parts I and II). His influence on Serres, if any, would be an interesting avenue to explore, and prove a useful addition to the ideas on Protestantism in Mariage (1990). See also Cole 1964, vol. I, ch. 2. Jacques Boyceau was also a Protestant who lived during the period of Henri IV. Although it would be easy to argue that his very theoretical approach to gardening as art was the opposite of this so-called Protestant land-management tradition, it may not be the best understanding of his efforts as a gardener. He was like Palissy in wanting to think about gardening in the context of nature. He was like Serres in thinking that gardening ought to be taken more seriously. His interest in gardens as a site of theorizing drew attention to land as a site of human intervention. It was not an historical necessity to extend ideas about architecture as an art to gardening. It made sense in the context of estate development, where the construction of a great house was incomplete without the decoration and celebration of the land around it. Boyceau provided a theoretical system for thinking about the second half of this project. See Hazlehurst 1966, particularly ch. 6.

19 Serres 1971. According to Cole (1964, vol. I, pp. 34–38) and Mariage (1990, p. 19), Laffemas was a major proponent of Serres' scheme for raising silkworms, and made it part of a more general entrepreneurial view of French well-being.

20 Serres 1611, particularly the preface, vol. I, pp. clxxxiij–cxcij.

21 Serres 1611, section 6, vol. II.

22 Serres 1611, preface, and section 6, particularly, vol. II, pp. 217–20.

23 Serres 1611, vol. I, p. 106.

24 Serres 1611, section 1, particularly vol. I, pp. 19–20.

25 For the parterre designs themselves, see Serres 1611, vol. II, p. 300, plates 1–3; vol.II, pp. 3–1, plates 1–11. For the role of parterres in organizing gardens, see Serres 1611, vol. II, pp. 295–97, 301. For sixteenth-century garden books containing evidence of the knot patterns before parterres, see for example, Hill 1568. For a mix of knot and vine-like parterre designs in a seventeenth-century garden, see de Caus 1981. For a description of the movement across the seventeenth century from knots to parterres, particularly in England, see Hadfield 1960, ch.3. For connections between knot designs and labyrinths or mazes in Renaissance gardens, see Carpeggiani 1991, pp. 84–87. For an example of the knot garden used for a botanical garden, see the plan of the botanical garden of Padua reproduced in Tomasi 1991, p. 81.

26 On medieval gardens, see Thacker 1979, pp. 85–86, 130, 134.

27 See Thacker 1979, p. 99.

28 Serres 1611, vol. II, pp. 302–306 and plates 13 and 14. Interestingly, this spiral plan was much like one used in the Jardin du Roi in Paris (now the Jardin des Plantes), which was the botanical garden sponsored and loved by Colbert.

29 See, for example, Serres 1611 and Laurent 1675.

30 Mariage 1990, ch.1; Hazlehurst 1966.

31 See Crumb 1928; Pérez-Gómez 1983, ch. 5; Estienne 1687; Gentil 1706; Laurent 1675; Estienne and Liébault 1702; Mollet 1981; Mollet 1663; de Caus 1973; d'Argenville 1972.

32 Serres 1611, Estienne 1687, Gentil 1706, Laurent.1675, and Bonnefons 1691. See Bonnefons 1654. The French edition of Bonnefons' book appeared in the mid-seventeenth century (1654) making it much closer to the estate-management tradition in France than this later date of 1691 suggests.

33 Palissy 1580; de Caus 1973, 1981; Gentil 1706; Morin 1651, 1655, 1658, 1680; Serres 1611; Bonnefons 1691.

34 For the tulip mania, see Mackey 1979, pp. 90–97. For information about raising tulips, see, for example, the catalogues of Pierre Morin (1651, 1655). See also Morin 1658, in which he distinguishes between plants for pleasure gardens and those for collectors' gardens, and Morin 1680.

35 La Quintiney 1717. See the section on melons beginning on p. 226. Compare this to the appendix to La Quintinie 1693, "Directions concerning melons by J. Evelyn."

   This proliferation of texts on gardening and horticulture in the seventeenth century was both profound and without precedent. Nonetheless, earlier information on plant culture was available in books; surprising amounts of information about plants had already been circulating in Europe even before the development of printing. See Baurmeister and Lafitte 1992, and Anon. 1980 (*Flowers in Books and Drawings c. 940–1840*). During the early secularization of books from the twelfth to fourteenth century, more texts were given realistic illustrations, many of which included plants and flowers. These images sometimes made different species identifiable, and showed visual relations among them. While intellectuals argued whether Creation brought evidence of God to the Earth, more plants, flowers, animals, and sea creatures appeared in and around texts. Some medieval books were even devoted to the culture and uses of plants. The Tacuinum Sanitatis (late fourteenth century, Italy), which presented common garden plants and their care, became a familiar literary genre in Italy and Germany in the late medieval period. Apparently this genre was derived from Arab intellectual precedents, and found an interested audience in Europe. Information about plants from the manuscript world may not have been widely spread, but it constituted another thread in the traditions of European gardening. To the extent that these works contained practical counsel for vegetable and herb gardening found in later herbals and horticultural works, they even may have been surprisingly early precursors to the seventeenth-century texts (see Arano 1976).

36 Virville, 1954, pp. 21–34.

37 It is interesting to note that the development of the Jardin des Plantes in Paris under de la Brosse was accomplished through the use of tracts on the design of botanical gardens in French. This successful piece of intellectual entrepreneurship was perhaps aided by the author's shift from the language of botany into the language of gardens in the first half of the seventeenth century when garden writing was so popular. Significantly, the books on regional flowering plants from the seventeenth century in France were alternately in French and in Latin, suggesting the dual interest in, and acceptance of, these works by those in gardening and in botany.

38 Palissy 1580, de Caus 1973, Mollet 1651, Boyceau 1638, Estienne 1687.

39 Locke 1953, Boyceau 1638, Pérez-Gómez 1983, ch 5.

40 See Gentil 1706. For the Italian priest's view of French gardens in 1664–65, see Blunt 1956, chs. 8–9.

41 Ranum 1979, pp. 203–28; Elias 1983.

42 Félibien 1679, 1874 (p. 24).

43 Serres was one of the earliest proponents of putting plants (especially melons and cucumbers) under glass. He also saw his work as serving the economic development of estates in particular and France in general. See Serres 1611, vol. II, section 6, on the *jardin potager*.

44 Durnerin 1983, p. 2.

45 For a description of the earth-moving machine invented to bring earth from the mountains to the potager, see Lery 1926, pp. 18–19. For a description of the earth-moving itself, see description from June 17, 1681 in Archive Nationale ser. 0' #1790. For descriptions of the king's rulings about the potager and its improvements in 1679, see Archive Nationale ser. 0' #1809 (reprinted in Morellet 1681).

46 Durnerin 1983, p. 2.

47 The French clearly knew about stoves since at least one book describing them and their uses was available in French. See Van der Groen 1669. There is evidence that the French were already building greenhouses in the early part of the eighteenth century, but not during the reign of Louis XIV. See Liger 1776, pp. 220–26.

48 Serres 1611, Van der Groen 1669, and Muijzenberg n.d.

49 La Quintinie 1693, vol. I, pp. 117–25

50 The price of glass in 1688 was 230 livres per square meter. In 1692, the price was 225 livres; in 1702, 4 square metres of glass cost 2,750 livres (see Varagnac 1971, p. 289). In 1682, La Quintinie received 2,000 livres in wages, but this was supplemented with 2,000 livres "de gratification." He was given 18,000 livres for "running the garden", i.e. paying laborers, buying manure, and getting seeds and seedlings. This amount did not include expenses for building and so the costs of glass could bring the total well above this amount (see Bellaigue 1982, p. 20). To get a sense of the amount of glass used over the beds of the potager, see the print by Aveline, *Veue et perspectiue du jardin potager de Versailles* (Paris: chez Crepy, rue St. Jacques à St. Pierre). The whole rear section of the gardens is covered with glass. For this use of glass in the context of the period, see Muijzenberg n.d.

51 La Quintinie 1693; Lenotre 1934, p. 62.

52 Estienne 1687.

53 Laurent 1675. The publisher Charles de Sercy specialized in garden books and advertised a list of ten of them in 1675, including books by Mollet, a royal gardener, and Laurent, the commercial florist. These books clearly had a market and a group of authors that linked commercial and royal gardeners, and provided publishers with profits. See the advertisement in Laurent's book. For evidence in La Quinitinie's own book about his trade in rare plants, see La Quintinie 1692, pp. 88, 104, 126, 141, 300, and 420. He mentions on these pages the combination of commercial growers, botanist-plant hunters, and estate gardeners with whom he exchanged plants.

54 Schnapper 1991; Harvey 1974, chs. 2–3; Virville 1954, pp. 21–34; Ranum 1979, ch. 6; Mackey 1979, pp. 90–97; Allan 1964, particularly chs. 6, 16, 17, 19. Webber (1968) describes the development of English market gardening and its rise as a profession. See also Hadfield 1960, ch. 4; and Grieve 1980.There was also clearly an active collection of botanical specimens in this period. The point to be stressed is that botanical collecting was not the only or even the driving force behind the trade in plants for collections.

55 Daston 1995. See Schnapper 1991, pp. 175–77; and Ranum 1979, ch. 6.

56 In the obsession with collecting, gardens became extensions of the house. Each housed exotic novelties from distant lands – chinoiserie inside and rare bulbs outside. Images of the same flora and fauna even appeared inside houses embroidered on fabrics for dress, upholstery, and draperies (see Beck 1978). Petted tender plants were even given their own houses. (Compare this to Veblen's ideas about horses being beloved by elites because they are so expensive to keep – Veblen 1953, p. 143.) Orangeries were built for wintering tender trees. Stoves (or heated glass houses) were developed for growing palms and other large tropical plants as well as medicinal plants (see Hix 1981). Rare animals were simultaneously sought and placed in specially prepared menageries. For a description of the collection of rare plants at Versailles, see Ferrier 1895, p. 147. Locke mentions a menagerie at Versailles and another at Chantilly (1953, pp. 153, 168–69.)

To understand this from a different point of view, one can draw on Bruno Latour's idea from *Science in Action* (1986) that nature can be recruited as a political ally. He argues that scientists routinely use nature this way when they promote their theories and the power of their institutions by claiming that the *data* from nature tell them what they know. Nature is made to speak on their behalf. In a similar vein, one can argue that nature in early modern gardens was use as an ally to attest to the power and high status of those developing the gardens. An exotic tree was a marker as well as a prize (or prized as a marker), locating its owner in social space just as the owner located the tree in the garden.

57 Mukerji 1982, ch. 5.

58 This is an interesting case of economic capital being changed into cultural capital, and may explain some historical sources of this circulatory dynamic. See Bourdieu 1984.

59 Schnapper 1991, Tomasi 1991, Webber 1968 and 1972. Veryard (1701, p. 8) has a description of the botanical garden in Leyden.

60 Allan 1964.

61 Webber 1968, 1972; Hix 1981; Hopper 1982.

62 Harvey 1974, ch. 2; Tournefort 1698, 1717.

63 Lister 1970, pp. 148–70 describes how many imported vegetables and flowers were arriving in Paris in this period. Veryard 1701, pp. 86–96 describes the south of France (Languedoc and the Midi in particular) as a natural garden because it was so full of wild flowers and flowering bushes and trees. This suggests that many flowers could have been dug up and shipped without commercial middlemen.

64 Mukerji 1982, ch. 1; Daston 1995.

65 Mackey 1979, pp. 90–97.

66 Ibid.

67 Morin 1651.

68 Morin, 1651, 1655, 1658 (in which he distinguishes between plants for pleasure gardens and those for collectors' gardens), and 1680. In his books on plant culture, he distinguished between plants appropriate for pleasure gardens and those for scientific or collectors' gardens. In the 1655 catalogue, he also made clear that, in spite of his commercial relation to plants and his relatively low social status, he was still in contact with aristocratic and scientific gardeners through the plant trade, bringing to Paris new species of plant that interested these other gardeners. He was no court figure, but he helped bring to France exactly the kinds of decorative bulbs and scented trees that were popular with Louis XIV, and graced parterres at Versailles close to the château.

69 Veryard (1701, pp. 86–87) argued that the whole area around Montpellier was like a "physick garden" because it grew so abundantly. Other areas of the south of France were also full of gardens, such as Toulon and Marseilles. He even spoke of fields filled with both cultivated and wild exotics (pp. 92–96).

70 Locke describes how orange trees were brought to Paris in the period.

> They are set in square cases and are a great many of them bigger then a man's thigh, but most of them with litle heads, having been lately transported, i.e. 2, 3, 4, 5, or 6 years since. They bring them, as he told me, from Italy to Rouen by sea, big as they are, & the better to transport them, cut of the stock where it is entire & not spread into branches, & cut (as the Gardener told me) all the roots. I believe they are most of them cut of, for the boxes seeme not capeable to hold the roots which are necessary for a tree of that bulke as many of them are, & soe, root & branches being cut off, they bring them exposd to the aire like soe many stakes at all times of the yeare without dyeing, but I am afraid in this later part of the story the gardiner made bold with truth. Wed. 7 Jul, 1677. (Locke 1953, p. 155)

See also Colbert 1868, vol. V, pp. 307, 334–35, 353–54, 362.

71 See Farmer 1905, p.100.

72 Farmer 1905, p. 84.

73 Registre où sont ecrits par dattes les ordres que Le Roy a donez à Monsieur Mansart Surintendant des Bâtiments de sa Majesté par tout ce qui est à faire, à changer, ou à réparer aux châteaux, jardins, petit et grand, Parc de Versailles, Trianon, la mesnagerie et dépendences dudit Versaille, Archives Nationale, Paris. 01# 1809. Du 5 Juillet, 1699.

74 Colbert 1868, vol. V, letter 174, p. 412: a letter to Sieur Bodard Intendant des Galères à Marseilles, March 22, 1680, in which Colbert shows that he expected to get at least some of his tuberoses through the use of naval vessels. See also Masson 1967, pp. 506–507; Hadfield 1960, p.141; and Laborde 1880.

75 Laissus and Torlais 1986, Webber 1968 and 1972, and Tomasi 1991. See Colbert (1868, vol. V, letter 174) for evidence of naval shipment of bulbs from Marseilles to Versailles. See particularly, Brockway 1979, ch. 3, on the development of European techniques for plant transfers, particularly seed exchanges.

76 Cole 1964, vol. I, pp. 280–86, 319–20. For manuscripts on the development of the Bibliothèque du Roi, see the "Memoire historique sur la Bibliothèque du Roy," BN fr. 8962, fol. 107.

77 Murat 1984, pp. 113–20; Burke 1992, pp. 97–99, 110–19; Perrault 1909; and Gerspach 1893. Colbert set up the Imprimerie Royale as a publishing house for the state, not just to control texts printed on politically sensitive issues, but also to provide copies of French works for the king's library. The royal library became the central repository for French literary works, identifying and elaborating an intellectual and artistic identity for France. (This library

eventually became the heart of the collection for the Bibliothèque Nationale.) See Cole 1964, vol. I, pp. 319–20. For Colbert's interest in collecting books from far distant reaches, see Masson 1967, pp. 506–507. For Colbert's interest in books while working for Mazarin, and in collecting for the king, see Murat 1984, pp. 22–23 and pp. 113–20, respectively.

78 Laissus and Torlais, 1986 pp.261–63, 289; Cole 1964, vol. I, pp. 319–20. For a discussion of plant collection as part of a broader pattern of collection of goods from the Levant organized by Colbert, see Masson 1967, pp. 506–507. See also Murat 1984, pp. 126–28. Veryard (1701, p. 67) described the Jardin du Roi in appropriately laudatory fashion.

79 For a description of the collection, see Farmer 1905, p. 104; and Dunlop 1970, p. 27. For Colbert's interest in the Ménagerie, see Murat 1984, pp. 126–27. For the connection with the collection of the Jardin des Plantes, note that when the Ménagerie was destroyed, the animals were either transferred to the Jardin des Plantes or destroyed (Farmer 1905, p. 105n).

80 Levron 1968, p. 112.

81 Clément 1980, vol. V, pp. 307, 334–35, 353–54, 362.

82 These tender plants seemed to trade places with the statuary of the garden, which brought forms of art that paralleled what was found in the house into the elements, while the palms and citruses were kept in containers and seasonally wheeled into the Orangerie for protection (Saint-Simon 1990, p. 163).

83 Chandernagor 1981, p. 316. See Liger 1776, pp. 211–15, on the use of nurseries for growing seedlings and young plants to fill in parterres and replace damaged trees.

84 For a description of how at the same time the reformation of the forests was also joining the flora from the north and south of France into a single system of order, see Devèze 1962, pp. 108–167.

85 Latour 1986.

86 Schama 1995, pp. 244–306.

87 Néraudau 1986, ch. 6, particularly pp. 202–10. For hydraulic works written in French in the seventeenth and early eighteenth century, see, for example, de Caus 1657, Perrault 1674, La Fonchere 1718, Pinon 1986, Mariotte 1708, and Pujol 1725. Verin spends surprisingly little time discussing this area of engineering in France, instead highlighting fortification techniques. This bias of attention is appropriate on one level, but it does not do justice to the seriousness of the enterprise of hydraulics in the period.

88 The easy joining of military technique and water engineering in this period is evident in a book published at the end of Louis XIV's reign by La Fonchere (1718), which mixes discussions of fortification techniques with an essay on the machine at Marly.

89 Beaumont-Maillet 1991, ch. 2.

90 Barbet 1907, part 1. Since Barbet was so concerned about water quality, it is hard to know how far he was projecting back into the past. The distinction may not have had the same resonance as it did around the turn of the twentieth century when public hygiene was such an issue. For a discussion of relations between water systems, see Mariage 1990, pp. 122–25.

91 Pujol 1725, preface. In linking interest in the practical movement of water to the garden, Pujol says (pp. aij–aiij):

Je prends la liberté de vous presenter ce Traité sur le Mouvement & la Mesure des Eaux. J'ai crû MONSIEUR, qu'une matiere si agréable & si utile ne seroit pas indigne de votre attention. Les differens movemens des Eaux son aujourd'hui le plus bel agrément des principaux Jardins de la France & de l'Italie. La merveilleuse Machine de Marly & les Jets d'eaux sans nombre du magnifique Parc de Versailles, montrent assez que les plus grand Héros & les plus grands Rois en ont fait l'objet de leurs amusemens & de leurs plaisirs. Et pour l'utilité, MONSEIGNEUR, personne n'ignore ce que des Eaux bien conduites & bien ménagées peuvent porter dans un Pays, de richesses & d'abondance...

See Lister 1970, pp. 213–14, for the use of the same kinds of pumps in the gardens at Versailles that were found in the mines of both England and Germany.

92 See Mousset 1930, ch. 2. Even the layout of the garden at Versailles may have had some commercial roots in the form of Dutch garden designs that were derived from Dutch models of ideal cities, commercially served by canal systems (Hopper 1982).

93 Barbet 1907, pp. 23–27

94 Ibid., pp. 28–30

95 Ibid., pp. 31–48.

96 Ibid.

97 Ibid.

98 Ibid., pp. 48–73. Mariage 1990, p. 121. For details about the arguments over engineering these systems, see BN Mélanges Colbert 1671 bis (fols. 476–81) where Thomas Lambert is arguing against the criticism of his plan for a canal linking the Estang de Bouviers to the reservoirs by the grotto. He claims M. Petit criticized his plans for political reasons, not technical ones.

99 Beaumont-Maillet 1991, ch. 2. It is interesting that Veryard makes a point of noting that soldiers were being used for canal building. He equates this practice with the Roman use of soldiers in engineering schemes to keep the soldiers in good shape for battle (Veryard 1701, p. 85).

100 Barbet 1907, pp. 68–73; Beaumont-Maillet 1991, ch. 2; Mariage 1990, pp. 121–22.What they did manage to build of the Canal de Midi was so elaborate and expensive that it did not have as much economic success as Colbert had wanted. Veryard (1701, pp. 84–85) ascribes the limited use of the Canal de Midi to its expense. While one might have expected major merchants to use the canal the most, they did not. The number of locks, installed to take the canal over the many hills, made a trip along the whole length of the canal too expensive. Merchants found that going by sea was often more efficient. But farmers and small-scale producers who wanted simply to reach markets beyond their usual ones made a great deal of use of the canal. Veryard also noted that merchants with fully laden cargo vessels might now go by sea, but in times of war would happily pay the expense of using the canal. Here the connection between military and commercial interests came alive.

101 Barbet 1907, pp. 52–54; Mariage 1990, p. 121.

102 Barbet 1907, pp. 74–81.

103 Gondouin 1803; La Fonchere 1718, pp. 137–56.

104 Scudéry 1979; Locke 1953. Books of this time on hydraulic engineering more often described existing practices than proposed new ones; for the hydraulic engineering of the day, see Mariotte 1708 and Pujol 1725.

5 Social choreography and the politics of place

1 See Félibien 1668 and 1874, and Scudéry 1979. Marin (1981) quotes Colbert's instructions for writing a history of a battle won by Louis XIV. Marin uses this case to consider how the writers who represented this reign intended to make its power absolute by writing of it as timeless. A history that was written for posterity, making no assumptions that the readers would recognize all the players in the events, would make the actors into timeless figures and the power of the king limitless. For the full discussion, see Marin 1981, pp. 49–108.

2 Burke 1992; Saint-Simon 1990, pp. 39–40, 71–75, 100–103, 112–15; Ziegler 1966, pp. 193–200.

3 Saint-Simon 1990, pp. 69–134. It seems that speaking against the king gave rise to a new form of punishment: cutting off the tongue. A woman who spoke against the king was

celebrated in the period for uttering not a word while being severely whipped (see Ziegler 1966, pp. 28–29, quoting Lefèvre d'Ormesson). These lessons were learned by the nobility as well as the victims and their peers, otherwise the nobles would not have felt compelled to write about these incidents.

4 Saint-Simon may have become a hero to later revolutionaries because of his criticism of the king, but he was fully a monarchist and simply felt Louis XIV was not worthy of his position.

5 Elias 1983, Burke 1992, Robert Darnton 1982. See also Saint-Simon 1980, pp. 50–51.

6 Habermas 1989. For a discussion of some differences between the bourgeois public sphere and French political life in the Ancien Régime, see particularly, pp. 27–42.

7 For the merging of church and court ritual, see particularly the description of the coronation in Bluche 1986, ch. 1. For a discussion of the continuities between court and Church ritual, see also Isherwood 1973, pp. 63–67.

8 Bluche 1986, ch. 1; Marin 1981, pp. 7–22; Kirsten 1970, pp. 50–51; Apostolidès 1981, ch. 1 (particularly pp. 16–19); Blum 1928, pp. 21–22. For a discussion of rituals and ceremonies before and after the reign of Louis XIV, see Isherwood 1973, pp. 57–59, 61–67, 281. For an example of the religious allusions used in the fêtes under Louis XIV, see Marin's analysis of the reason why the fêtes of 1674 were spread over six days, as in the Creation (Marin 1981, pp. 242–43).

Interestingly enough, the end of the king's progress, when the seat of court was permanently established at Versailles, coincided with the growth of pleasure travel to hot springs and other areas of France by aristocrats. See Mongredien 1948, pp.114–17. The tour, using surveys of transportation systems, defined the land as a political locale as well as a site of aristocratic privilege (Mukerji 1982, pp. 121–24).

9 Isherwood 1973, pp. 55–57.

10 For the interesting life and ideas of Palissy, see Dupuy 1970 and Pérez-Gómez 1983. For descriptions of the massacre and its relationship to the court entertainments of Catherine de Medici, see Yates 1947, chs. 10–11; Kirsten 1970, p. 50. For a description of how Huguenots incorporated this event into their faith, see Diefendorf 1993, pp. 41–63. For the importance of ritual in political conversion, and the voiceless politics of religion in France in the seventeenth century, see Luria 1993, pp. 65–81.

11 Isherwood 1973, pp. 88–93, 97–113; Kirsten 1970, pp. 54–55.

12 Isherwood 1973, pp. 63–67. Religious processions and musical pageantry were criticized by Agrippa as too much like *mascarades*, even though there was an outpouring of religious feeling in them. The processions were steeped in biblical allegories and chanting that did indeed make them visually and musically similar to the court ritual of the Valois era, but this form, too, declined.

13 Isherwood 1973, pp. 88–93; Kirsten 1970, pp. 62–63. It is hard to know exactly how much to attribute this growth in importance of the *ballet de cour* to the king or to Richelieu, who also apparently had a fondness for the *ballet de cour*. See Pierson 1990, ch. 14, particularly, pp. 222–23.

14 Isherwood 1973, pp. 94–103; Magne 1944, pp. 21–61. For the early Italian roots of *carrousels* and their links to feudal games, see Néraudau 1986, pp. 47–49. Marin makes the case that, according to medieval thought, the king was the possessor of two bodies: one physical and the other the embodiment of power. The former could die, but the latter, the power of the king, was eternal (Marin 1981, introduction). It is interesting to consider the appearance of these nobles' bodies in the *ballet de cour* as not simply healthy noble bodies but also embodied representations of an eternal power, the natural superiority of the nobility supposedly also derived from the Divine.

15 Kirsten 1970, pp. 78–79.

16 Ibid.; Marin 1981, pp. 17–22.

17 Haraway 1989, White 1987. As Marin (1981) points out, these signs of absolutism were sites beyond the world of the mundane in which power was not merely represented but created through representation. In the images of the powerful, the meaning of power itself could be explored and made manifest. The cultural meanings of absolutism, according to Marin, were played with and played out in/through representations. Goody (1977) argues that new meanings and possibilities for action are facilitated by writing because the written forms can then be viewed, thought about self-consciously, and then rearranged to promote further thought and action. Marin suggests that much the same can be said of all forms of representation. That is why they are generative of power, and not just markers of it. They create a secondary space in which cultural possibilities can be worked upon in new ways. See Marin 1981 (particularly pp. 7–17) and 1993 (particularly pp. 25–39, 194–95).

18 Schutz 1967, part III.

19 Crest 1990, pp. 1–6; Blum 1928, pp. 122–25; Christout 1987, pp. 22–23.

20 See Nolhac 1925, pp. 64–65. For the relation of pleasure to its renunciation in this fête, see Apostolidès 1981, pp. 98–101. The story was based on the romance, *Roland furieux* or *Orlando furioso* by Ariosto, which combined seduction, heroism, and feudal chivalry in an attractive mix for the French aristocracy. See Crest 1990, pp. 4–6.

21 Néraudau 1986, pp. 51–55. Apostolidès 1981, ch. 5.

22 Magne 1944, pp. 103–17.

23 Molière 1853, pp. 1–21; Crest 1990, pp. 4–6; Magne 1944, pp. 104–107; Nolhac 1925, pp. 67–68; Ziegler 1966, pp. 38–39.

24 Molière 1853, pp. 21–28; Crest 1990, p. 7; Magne 1944, pp. 107–108; Nolhac 1925, p. 68; Isherwood 1973, pp. 266–68.

25 Molière 1853 pp. 28–117; Crest 1970, pp. 7–11; Magne 1944, pp. 108–12; Nolhac 1925, pp. 69–70.

26 Magne 1944, p. 111.

27 Crest 1990, pp. 11–12; Magne 1944, pp. 112–13; Nolhac 1925, pp. 70–71; Isherwood 1973, pp. 268–69.

28 Crest 1990, p. 12; Magne 1944, p. 114; Nolhac 1925, p. 71.

29 Crest 1990, p. 12; Magne 1944, p. 114; Nolhac 1925, p. 71; Dewald 1993.

30 Crest 1990, p. 13; Magne 1944, p. 114; Nolhac 1925, p. 71; Foucault 1979, part III, ch. 3.

31 Mazouer 1993, pp. 86–88, 181–82; Magne 1944, pp. 78–88, 114; Nolhac 1925, p. 72; Crest 1990, p. 13; Kirsten 1970, pp. 81–82. Christout (1987, p. 18) argues that, unlike the later *comédie-ballets*, *Les Fâcheux* was scored by Pierre Beauchamps, not Lully, but it was still a *comédie-ballet* of the sort that Molière made famous with Lully. Lenotre and Kirsten, on the other hand, say that the dance master, Beauchamps, choreographed the dances while Lully composed the music (or revised Beauchamps' musical efforts). Lully and Beauchamps were both working for Fouquet, and were certainly able to help each other. See Lenotre 1934, p. 19, and Kirsten 1970, p. 82. Isherwood (1973, p. 143) argues that Molière and Lully began collaborating to produce *comédie-ballets* in 1664 with the production of *Le Mariage forcé*. The different accounts suggest that *Les Fâcheux* was a kind of transitional piece that already set out many characteristics of the *comédie-ballets* of Molière and Lully, but was too much the work of Beauchamps to fit comfortably in the category of their *comédie-ballets*. In any case, this novelty was developed to please the king and court, was used by Fouquet to show his taste and power as well as his respect for these social "betters," and displayed the simultaneous lightness of touch and pretentiousness that typified the work he preferred. Apostolidès (1981, pp. 61–62) describes how the visual medium of dance was

newly tied to the written word in this piece. The triviality of the words was in stark contrast to the solemn importance imputed to the written myths and legends used to shape earlier dances, and yet the dances in this case were used to comment on the narrative being carried centrally by the lines of the comedy. This strange opening up and yet closing down of voice was a crucial aspect of the novelty of this form. The fact that it was indeed incorporated into *Les Plaisirs* remains a provocative fact, no matter who did the score.

32 Magne 1944, p. 114; Nolhac 1925, p. 72; Mongredien 1948, pp. 104–105.

33 Wollen 1992.

34 Magne 1944, pp. 114–15; Nolhac 1925, p. 72; Ziegler 1966, pp. 39–40.

35 Magne 1944, pp. 115–16; Nolhac 1925, p. 71.

36 See Isherwood 1973, p. 269.

37 Magne 1944, p. 116.

38 For the press coverage of the fête, see Isherwood 1973, p. 269. Notice Marigny's wariness of the king's political intent as the exception to prove the rule (Bonney 1988).

39 Magne 1944, pp. 104–107; Nolhac 1925, pp. 63–64. It is certainly true that La Vallière had suffered from the gossip against her, and that the king had maintained his relations with her in spite of the anger of the queen, and many of the nobles. There was good reason to give her a week of pleasures and respite from the gnawing talk, and to claim at the same time his right to her love. It is just that he was unlikely to have kept the political possibilities of these events out of his mind, given his passion for political details. See Ziegler 1966, pp. 41–49.

40 Molière 1853, pp. 20–21.

41 Molière 1853, p. 4; Elias 1983.

42 Molière 1853, p. 4; Isherwood 1973, p. 269; Magne 1944, pp. 104–32.

43 Apostolidès 1981, ch. 6; Marin 1981, pp. 49–108.

44 Félibien 1994, pp. 34–39.

45 Apostolidès 1981, pp. 109–13; Crest 1990, pp. 22–37; Magne 1944, pp. 132–51; Nolhac 1925, pp. 75–76; Isherwood 1973, pp. 270–80; Ziegler 1966, pp. 60–63. For the importance of fruits in the development of a French identity, see chapter 6. For now, it is important to see why it was that getting La Quintinie to grow his famous pears was an issue that would (so to speak) bear fruit in the next decades. See Lenotre 1934, pp. 55–62. It is interesting that this fête began with a promenade which allowed the king to view the newly developed bosquets in the garden. In this kind of parade-review of the gardens, he enacted in miniature a survey of his territories in the wake of successful warfare. See Crest 1990, p. 24. It is also important to note that while the *divertissement* was filled with images of the antique, still associating the participants with the new Rome, the events were not choreographed to reproduce a guiding story of triumph of warrior-elites in some past time (Crest 1990, pp. 24–35, particularly pp. 27–28), but to mark a new historical moment of power (see Apostolidès 1981, pp. 122–31; Marin 1981, pp. 242–50).

46 Farmer 1905, pp. 126–27.

47 Crest 1990, pp. 38–62; Magne 1944, pp. 132–51; Nolhac 1925, pp. 75–76, 91–102; Isherwood 1973, pp. 270–80; Ziegler 1966, pp. 60–63. For the change in the representation of royal power in this *divertissement*, see Apostolidès 1981, ch. 6. Dewar (1993) suggests how little impoverishment seems to have been recognized as an issue to the aristocracy of this period. It may have been a consequential fact that reduced the autonomy of the aristocracy, but it did not seem to stop their pursuit of material satisfactions.

48 Félibien 1668 (BN Lb37. 360), particularly p. 60. For a discussion of how the antique, medieval, and contemporary themes were woven together at *Les Plaisirs,* see Crest 1990, pp. 13–21; Apostolidès 1981, ch. 5. For this regime's theme of the new Rome, see, Néraudau 1986.

49 For a description of these garden decorations, see Nolhac 1924, pp. 67–69; and Félibien 1994, p. 104. It should also be noted that the king stopped performing in ballets in 1670. His last role was as Apollo. He continued to patronize the dance, but he was no longer a participant in this form. The *ballet de cour* in France had finished its trajectory toward the celebration of the political present, and away from the narratives of past glory. Now the desire for the restoration of narrative in musical forms began a journey in French music toward the opera, where dance and music could again transport audiences out of contemporary time and place. But this was not a medium for engaging court nobles in ritualized enactments of social superiority as the *ballet de cour* had been. See Isherwood 1973, pp. 147–49. For the connection between the development of professional dancers and this break from court performers, see Migel 1972, pp. 5–7.

50 Félibien 1994; Apostolidès 1981, p. 126; Marin 1981, pp. 49–108.

51 Dens 1981; Saint-Simon 1990, pp. 23–24, 28–31, 50–51. See also Ranum 1980 for a description of how decorum and politics were coordinated in this period.

52 For witnesses of *Les Plaisirs*, see Isherwood 1973, p. 267. For the opening of the gardens and fêtes, see Apostolidès 1981, pp. 110–11.

53 Following his lead we can take the bourgeois public sphere less as a model of political participation than a means for the social production of the bourgeois individual. See Habermas 1989.

54 The relation between interaction controls and politics is alluded to by Goffman 1969, pp. 98–103. Others in the symbolic interactionist tradition paying attention to political processes include Gusfield 1963 and 1981; Skolnick 1966; and Cicourel and Kitsuse 1963 – although the latter broke away from this tradition.

55 Goffman 1959, 1963, 1967.

56 The breakdown of microsociology in the 1970s into competing schools of thought has obscured the distinctiveness and value of this tradition. With the turn toward language-based notion of microsocial processes to the exclusion of performance, even Goffman's work moved away from dramaturgy. See Goffman 1974. Even some of those who remained concerned with the dramaturgical model and elaborated it in interesting ways, such as Joe Gusfield (in his introduction to Burke 1989, pp. 1–49) have been more concerned with issues of scripting and language in performance. The historical example in this chapter, perhaps more than many other cases, makes clear to me that performance analysis in sociology is needed to make sense of particular times and places, where performance of power is more important than its ideological manifestations. Clifford Geertz has, of course, analyzed political culture, but with an emphasis on non-Western cultures that has made his ideas easy to contain as non-Western (Geertz 1980).

57 O'Connor 1990, pp. 154–55.

58 Davis 1986.

59 Goffman 1959.

60 Molière 1755.

61 Ibid., p. 198.

62 Ibid., pp. 199–200 (marked 204 in text).

63 Ibid., p. 203

64 Ibid., p. 203

65 Saint-Simon 1990, pp. 23–24, 28–30, 48–49.

66 Molière 1755, p. 213.

67 For the ways by which courtiers could get at one another, see Saint-Simon 1990, pp. 28–31.

68 Molière 1755, p. 219.

69 For Marie Adelaide's effect on the court and the continuation of the demands of fashion

even late in the reign, see Marly 1987, pp. 99–101, 119–23; Saint-Simon 1990, pp. 82–86; and Elliott 1992, particularly, chs. 5–10. For the intrigues and gaming at Versailles, see Ziegler 1966, chs. 1 and 2 (particularly p. 55). For the move to Versailles, see Ziegler 1966, p. 192. For descriptions of the duchesse de Bourgogne's character and effect on the court, see Ziegler 1966, ch. 21. For the importance of the king's permanent entourage to his absolutism, see Marin on Pascal in Marin 1981, pp. 21–23.

70 Steen 1990, pp. 66–67.

71 The boredom is well described by Elisabeth Charlotte in a letter to Amalie Elisabeth on May 16, 1705 (Forster 1958, pp. 158–59). She begins by saying, " No Carthusian monk leads a quieter and more solitary life than I do. I think I shall end up by forgetting how to speak" (p. 158).

72 Le Roi 1862; see also Marin 1981 (particularly pp. 251–90).

73 Meyer 1982, pp. 45–46; Ziegler 1966, p. 147; Devismes 1974, pp. 20–25. The times at which these events transpired are not entirely clear; Saint-Simon (1990, p. 160) says the king rose at 8.00 a.m.

74 Forster 1958, pp. 38–39; Ziegler 1966, pp. 146–55; Saint-Simon 1990, pp. 221–26; Meyer 1982, p. 45.

75 Ziegler 1966, pp. 147–49; Devismes 1974, pp. 24–25.

76 Lenotre 1934, pp. 66–68; Devismes 1974, pp. 25–26, 31–38. Saint-Simon (1990, pp. 166–67) describes the stomach troubles that resulted from this eating. For the boredom at court, see Mongredien 1948, ch 1.

77 Ziegler 1966, pp. 149–151; Meyer 1982, pp. 46–48; Lenotre 1934, pp. 63–72.

78 Ziegler 1966, p. 151; Meyer 1982, p. 48. Devismes (1974, pp. 26–27) says that he worked in the afternoon in his *Cabinet*.

79 Ziegler 1966, pp. 152–55, 192–93; Meyer 1982, pp. 49–50; Mongredien 1948, pp. 102–4; Apostolidès 1981, pp. 55–58; Devismes 1974, pp. 27–30; Dewald 1993.

80 Marly 1987, pp. 74–79. Marin (1981, pp. 19–21) discusses the importance of costuming and other aspects of appearance to the assertion of personal rule/state-based absolutism by Louis XIV.

81 Elias 1983. For evidence of the costs of being at court, see Mongredien 1948, pp. 17–18, 21–23, 70–71.

82 These fashions also were inscribed on the bodies of elite Parisians as well as those at court. See Mongredien 1948, pp. 67–70.

83 Mukerji 1982, ch. 5.

84 Marly 1987, pp. 38–39.

85 Ibid., chs. 1 and 2.

86 Ibid., pp. 61–63. The relationship of these guards to others installed at Versailles is described by Devismes 1974, pp. 16–20. The other honorary guards were also dressed in blue with gold or red trim. The Gardes Françaises and Gardes Suisses were more working guards and true soldiers than the others.

87 Marly 1987, p. 63.

88 Ibid., pp. 61–64, 68.

89 Mukerji 1982, ch. 5.

90 Saint-Simon (1990, p. 101) argues that the king actually had a strong personal distaste for homosexuality, but did not express it publicly. Whether this was out of respect for his brother, or the result of political calculation, is not clear. It is only clear that the king was very expressive of his feelings in most domains, but not in this area. For a description of the king's brother, see Saint-Simon 1990, pp. 71–75. For a description of the homosexuality at

court (not always written by sympathetic witnesses/gossips) and the way in which the king both expressed his dislike for it and yet constrained his actions to suppress it at court, see Ziegler 1966, ch. 12.

91 For explanation and description of the king's brother's cross-dressing, see Marly 1987, p. 26; Elliott 1992, p. 292; and Saint-Simon 1990, pp. 71–75.

92 Lister 1967, pp. 32–35; Berger 1972.

93 Saint-Simon 1990, pp. 171–72; Marly 1987, pp. 64–65.

94 Marly, p. 69; Christout, p. 23.

95 For a description of the role of dance at court in the seventeenth century, including the role of dancing masters in the court of Louis XIV, see Christout 1987, particularly p. 11; and Migel 1972, pp.4–6. For examples of the postures, see contemporary prints and images (particularly the prints by Silvestre) in the books by Mallet (1684) and Le Clerc (1669).

96 Wollen 1992.

97 Foucault 1979, pp. 135–39.

98 Saint-Simon 1990, p. 141–42, 202–205.

99 Wollen 1992. Foucault 1979, pp. 141–49.

100 The prints of the royal gardens, including Versailles, provide ample evidence of this connection in a most unassuming way. The bulk of these prints were said to be made to document great buildings of France or the residences of the king, but they are not just visual inventories of properties; they are almost always populated with human figures, illustrating some element of social life at court. The gardens are marked with stylish figures standing, bowing, sitting, strolling, fishing, hunting, or pointing to elements of the gardens. The good breeding of these characters is indicated in the prints both by the quality of their clothing and by their posture and stature. The purpose of the figures is not to provide ethnographic information about court life, but to locate the royal gardens as social sites. With their very French inhabitants, these are marked as French gardens, not to be confused with Italian gardens, which in prints are more often populated with mythological figures than courtiers. The aristocrats on French garden prints visually mark these places as the sites for political performance that they were meant to be. The size of the figures, for example, provide a scale for measuring the scope of the garden features; by being overwhelmed by the greenery around them, they exaggerate the size of the king's domain.

101 Lully developed highly gestural and solemn processional music. See Isherwood 1973, pp.142–43, 204–14; Pierson 1990, p. 235; and McClary 1992. For a sense of the relationship between music and space in this period, pay attention to the extent to which music was combined with other forms in the court of Louis XIV. The fêtes, *ballets de cour*, promenades, carrousels, *comédie-ballets*, operas, and military marches were all events that combined music with bodies in motion, tied to some kind of gestural language or narratives told with bodies as much as voices. The degree of improvisation in the performances required by the limited notation of the period helped to make even the act of making music a gestural activity which was flexible enough to respond to the moment in which it was being played. The fact that Lully collaborated so frequently with the stage designer Vigarini also helps to point out the way in which the space of performance was integral to the music. See Pierson 1990, particularly pp. 230–33. For the rejection of Italian influences by Lully, see Masson 1972, pp. 18–19. For the ways in which French music was influenced by but remained distinct from Italian music, see Masson 1972, pp. 26–31, and Christout 1987, pp. 17–18.

102 See Isherwood 1973, p. 259, for the importance of the promenade and the use of music on these walks. The musicians of the Grande Ecurie played for hunts and promenades. They were a military band of sorts, playing wind and percussion instruments (Pierson 1990, p. 224).

103 Wollen (1992) has argued, following Foucault, that the discipline exercised in this situation
    provided a means of social surveillance. The king and his ministers could keep an eye on
    the nobles who were at Versailles, and also script their daily activities through ritual. For a
    description of the way music in this period was used to unite all the body disciplines and
    arts of the period, see Masson 1972, particularly pp. 15–18.

6 Naturalizing power in the new state

 1 In case it seems that this idea was only held by the king's French publicists and proponents, it
    is important to note that Ellis Veryard picked up exactly this theme in describing Versailles,
    while traveling through France: "The Gardens want nothing that Art and Nature can con-
    tribute to charm the Senses, and abundantly satisfy the curiosity of the Traveller" (1701, p. 68).
 2 Fontenelle 1990, p. 36.
 3 Félibien 1672.
 4 Fontenelle 1990, p. 36.
 5 Fontenelle 1990, p. viii.
 6 For the idea of France as a *pré carré* and Vauban's early proposals for lines of defenses, see
    Pujo 1991, ch. 6; Carrias 1960, p. 149; Rebelliau 1962, pp. 49–51. For Vauban's treatment of
    France as a managed territory, including his interest in both mapping and making a census
    of the state, see Parent and Verroust 1971, pp. 200–206.
 7 Félibien 1994, p. 151. These elements were also depicted in statues in the park (see Néraudau
    1986, pp. 225–26).
 8 For an extensive description of the water system when Locke visited it, see Locke 1953, pp.
    164–67, 175, 178, 180. For specific remarks about the circulation of water in the system at
    Versailles, see Locke 1953, p. 154 and Scudéry 1979, pp. 80–81. For a description of the vor-
    tices and Cartesian science, as it was presented in popular form, see Fontenelle 1990, pp.
    19–20, 52–54.
 9 Fontenelle 1990, pp. viii–x, 9–22; Tocanne 1978, ch. 2.
10 For the establishment of the scientific institutions in France, and Colbert's championing of
    this development, see Hahn 1971, ch. 1; and Picon 1989, pp. 42–44. For Colbert and his close
    advisors, see Murat 1984, pp. 115–16; Perrault, 1909; Neymarck 1970; and Apostolidès 1981,
    ch. 2.
11 Church 1969, part 2; Bergin 1985; and Bonney 1988.
12 See Tocanne (1978, ch. 3, particularly pp. 182–86) on Pascal, secularization of natural phi-
    losophy, and problems of political legitimacy in France.
13 For a discussion of seventeenth-century scientists' views of God, including those of
    Gassendi, see Osler 1994, particularly ch. 6, and Koyré 1944, section 3.
14 Locke (1953, p. 153) provides an interesting analysis of the geometry around the canal. He
    talks of the Ménagerie, Trianon, and château setting out a great triangle with the cross of the
    canal in the middle, and a secondary cross adding to the pattern.
15 Burke 1992, particularly ch. 7.
16 Burke 1992, particularly, chs. 4–6.
17 Habermas 1975.
18 Ibid.
19 Weber 1978, vol. I, pp. 234–41.
20 Jay 1993.
21 In the nineteenth century, the proliferation of images (due the the development of new tech-
    nologies for their mass production) started to raise questions about the meaning of images;

the political mobilization of material culture for purposes of legitimation has become much less important than what is said politically. But this was not the case in the seventeenth century. What we can *see* in French formal gardens from this early period is the descent of the king to Earth and the unleashing of natural powers. This imagery provides not just a change in the representations used to legitimate the king's reign, but a movement in the constitution of the category, power, that is shown rather than told to garden visitors.

22 Burke 1992. Scudéry, in memorializing artworks, shows how the power of the word in this period was linked through the classical tradition to monuments. She argued that great monuments would not last as long as words; therefore, they needed words to make their glories endure. The flip-side of this was that words devoted to keeping monuments visible were underscoring the importance of material markers of power and glory. See Scudéry 1979, p. 9.

23 See Apostolidès 1981 for the spectacle of power and the way in which it linked different sources of power. See Bluche 1986 on the significance of French life to the king and his period.

24 Pujo 1991, ch. 6; Carrias 1960, p. 149; Rebelliau 1962, pp. 49–51; Sahlins 1989, pp. 69–73.

25 Wilford 1981, pp. 111–12.

26 Roger 1971, p. 170; Yates 1947; Institute de France 1967, ch. 1; Stroup 1990.

27 Stroup 1990, ch.1. For the symbolic imposition of a territorial bias in the work on natural history, see Stroup 1990, pp. 73–74, and Roger 1971, pp. 176–77.

28 Science was most clearly useful to the delineation and analysis of French territory. No wonder so much of the science eminating from French scientific societies at this time was concerned with problems of accurate land measurement. Not only were mathematicians concerned with the problems of survey mathematics, but astronomers were looking for means of using measurements of the heavens as a basis for locating sites on the Earth. Even the great natural history project of the Académie was oddly connected to this project through mechanistic philosophy. Reduction of animal and plant physiology to mechanistic models made creatures measurable entitites just like the Earth itself. Moreover, scientific dissections for the natural history project yielded a kind of topographical approach to comparative animal physiology. The outside shapes of whole animals set up natural boundaries for the "machine" under study. The "innards" of the animals were presented as separate parts of the mechanism, rendered in contour drawings that reduced organs to their surface features. They were depicted as highly ordered natural landscapes in themselves. Mechanistic philosophy in this period of French science might have placed greatest emphasis on the problems of knowing and representing nature, but the kind of knowing and representing served by a mechanical view of the world emphasized extension, proportion, and motion. All three turned out to be particularly important for measuring territory. Extension and proportion were clear parts of surveying, and the motions of the heavens were vital pieces of information required for careful measurement of the Earth. See Wolf 1902 (particularly chs. 1 and 7); Cassini 1720; and Konvitz 1987, ch.1.

29 Cassini 1720; Wilford 1981, ch. 8.

30 Wilford 1981, ch. 8; Duranthon 1978.

31 Cassini 1720; Duranthon 1978, p. 4; Chapin 1990.

32 Wilford 1981, ch. 8; Chapin 1990.

33 Wilford 1981, ch. 8.

34 Proctor 1991; Koyré 1957.

35 Osler 1994, ch. 6; Tocanne 1978, part 1, ch. 2; Vickers 1984.

36 Fontenelle 1990, pp. 19–54; Vickers 1984; Tocanne 1978, part I; Osler 1994, ch. 2; Mukerji 1984.

37 Le Clerc 1669, introduction.

38 Scudéry 1979, pp. 8, 85–86.

39 See Bluche 1986, p. 583; Burke 1992, pp. 129–130.

40 Koyré 1944, pp. 80–87; Tocanne 1978, ch. 2.

41 Koyré 1944, pp. 21–22, 33–35, 52–68; Osler 1994, ch. 9.

42 Koyré 1944, pp. 80–84. Osler 1994, p. 5.

43 Néraudau 1986, ch. 6; Girard 1985, pp. 27–54, 173–88.

44 Mariage 1992.

45 Lough 1985, pp. 114–15, 323–24; Lister, pp. 185–86.

46 Fontenelle 1990, p. 11.

47 Osler 1994, ch. 6.

48 Fontenelle 1990, p. 11.

49 Interestingly, as much as the marquise (Fontenelle's fictional student in this book) wanted to learn about the order of the heavens, she was reluctant to analyze the Earth around her. When Fontenelle, the narrator, tried to draw geometrical figures in the dirt near them to explain a concept to her, the marquise even stopped him, not wanting to impose such a structure on the ground. This was an odd sensitivity for a character who was supposedly sitting in a formal garden. In seventeenth-century French parks, it was just such forms that were being used to render visible on the land itself the mathematical qualities of nature assumed by science.

50 Tocanne 1978, pp. 182–86; Merchant 1980.

51 Tocanne 1978, pp. 182–86.

52 Marin 1981, pp. 14–21.

53 Marin 1981, particularly the introduction and pp. 251–60; Apostolidès 1981, pp. 137–40.

54 Marin 1981, pp. 14–21.

55 Osler 1994, pp. 3–9, 156–57.

56 Marin 1981.

57 Saint-Simon 1990, pp. 140, 148–49; Marin 1981; Apostolidès 1981, ch. 1.

58 For a description and discussion of the Trianon as a location for the king's intimacies, and its remodeling for Maintenon, see Lenotre 1934 and Verlet 1985, pp. 195–202.

59 For the significance of the Trianon in the period, and particularly its place in the representation of the king, see Marin 1981, pp. 236–50. See also Néraudau 1986, pp. 249–53, and Verlet 1985, p. 104.

60 For the politics of representation around the king and the importance of halting the aging process, see Apostolidès 1981, part 2. See also Verlet 1985, p. 104. For the story of the flowers and their replacement in the parterres at the Trianon, see Chandernagor 1981, p. 316.

61 Schalk 1986.

62 See for example, Molière's *Tartuffe*. See also Steen 1990, pp. 66–67.

63 Schalk 1986.

64 Bitton 1969, Wollen 1992.

65 For the dauphin's education, see Elliott 1992.

66 Thomas 1983, ch. 1.

67 Picon 1989, particularly pp. 44–88; Tocanne 1978, pp. 82–83; Roger 1971 pp. 51–94, 338–44. For the debate about animals' souls, see Roger 1971, part I, ch. 3; and Thomas 1983, ch. 1.

68 Foucault 1979, ch. 3; Daston 1995. For Colbert's interest in the Ménagerie, see Murat 1984, pp. 126–27; for his interest in the Jardin des Plantes, see Laissus and Torlais 1986, pp. 261–63, 289, and Cole 1964, vol. I, pp. 319–20.

69 Picon 1989, ch. 4; Stroup 1990, pp. 39, 54, 59, 194.

70 Roger 1971, particularly part 2, ch. 3.

71 See Elliott 1992, p. 162 on the use of fables in education in the period. See Conan 1982, pp. 91–92.

72 Perrault 1982, pp. 20–21, 40–41.

73 In his book, Perrault lists 39 fables illustrated as fountains but he states that there are 40.

74 For examples of labyrinths designed for gardens before this period, see Hill 1652.

75 Perrault 1982.

76 Tocanne 1978, pp. 182–86.

77 Bluche 1986, ch. 21.

78 Verlet 1985, pp. 193–94, shows how the canal spoke to politics. The canal had a miniature fleet of warships and other vessels. It provided a play space for acting out war games. This bringing together of the powers of the heavens and the Earth in the canal addressed directly not just the meaning of the state as a territory, but also the state as a military power.

79 Francastel 1970, ch. 2.

80 Francastel 1970, pp. 35–42.

81 Ibid.

82 See Burke 1992, pp. 25–26, 50–59.

83 Racine 1981, pp. 23–33.

84 Tocanne mentions that the Renaissance interest in magic and spiritual powers in nature drew attention to the Earth as a site of signs and symbols, in which natural forces were manifest. This thinking, which was so evident in the cartography of the sixteenth and seventeenth centuries, was probably the source of the power symbols in the territorial gardens at Versailles. See Tocanne 1978, pp. 18–19, and Néraudau 1986, ch. 6 (particularly pp. 202–10). Félibien specifically speaks of the use of the obelisk and sun and other mysterious symbols of power used in the fêtes at Versailles (Félibien 1994, p. 149). For one example of how Renaissance naturalism entered into French thinking, see Hine 1984, pp. 165–76. For the role of occult thinking in French science through the sixteenth and seventeenth centuries, see Roger 1971, pp. 39–40; also Courtilz de Sandras 1695, p. 45. Simon Schama also picks up this theme in *Landscape and Memory* (1995).

85 Félibien 1689, Scudéry 1979, and Mariage 1992, pp. 15–18.

86 Even the symbols of nature and power in the park at Versailles were not so much preconceived and imposed on the gardens. Certainly, the theme of the Sun King was self-consciously developed and elaborated, and particular pieces like statues of France or French rivers were commissioned just for the park. But much of the classical statuary that was copied from ancient works or antique pieces themselves arrived in France as "found objects" for the gardens. Their uses and meanings had to be constructed over time. Even pieces that were specifically commissioned for the park were often moved about until they found a permanent home. The Apollo grouping from the grotto was repositioned on more than one occasion, once the grotto was destroyed for the expansion of the château. Importantly, the canal itself began as a linear structure like most of Le Nôtre's canals. The possibility of crossing it only developed slowly, when the garden came to be used as a central royal residence.

87 The importance of representation and demonstration to science in this period is spelled out in Shapin and Schaffer 1985. A wide variety of demonstrations used both inside and outside science have been analyzed by Rosental 1996.

88 d'Argenville 1760.

7 A history of material power

1 Strong 1979 and 1986.

2 Sahlins 1976.

3 Dan Schiller has recently argued that neo-Marxist theory has once again kept theorists away from seeing the material character of cultural relations. The turn toward culture has obscured the labor behind all forms of cultural production (Schiller 1996). For the sociology of cultural tradition that does focus on labor, see Berger 1995. I would add that this turn has also been one toward consciousness and language, and away from a materialism that might root cultural analysis in the world of things.

4 For the enduring hope that purification can indeed make the study of the social scientific, see Schneider 1993 and Berger 1995.

5 Schama 1988 and 1995 .

6 Gianfranco Poggi mentions state territory but does not have a systematic way to include it in his theory of the state (Poggi 1990, particularly p. 22). Finer (1975) is even clearer about the centrality of territoriality to state-formation, although not much more helpful about why it was important.

7 For some of the many recent books that talk of the French state in this period that pay little or no attention to territorial development, even when they talk about regionalism and/or culture, see Hatton 1976, Holt 1991, Kimmel 1988, and Major 1994. Corrigan and Sayer (1985) argue that state politics required a legitimacy, a cultural revolution, to become socially accepted as a system of power. They even point (in ch. 5) to some of the same kinds of material manipulation of land and manufacture in England that complemented what I have described as part of French state-formation in this period. But they do not describe the cultural revolution of state-formation as a material cultural process.

8 McNeil 1963 (particularly ch. 12), 1976, 1982 (particularly ch. 4); Foucault 1979; Braudel 1973 and 1990. For some of the voluminous literature on industrial development, see Mukerji 1982, ch. 6.

9 Tilly 1975; Mann 1986; Evans, Rueschemeyer, and Skocpol 1985; Skocpol 1979.

10 Corrigan and Sayer 1985.

11 Knapp 1992.

12 Baxandall 1974 and 1985; Strong 1979 and 1986; Schama 1988 and 1995; Alpers 1983; Latour 1993; Haraway 1989; Burke 1978 and 1992; Appadurai 1986; and Kemp 1990.

13 Jay 1993; Yates 1947; Baxandall 1974; Alpers 1983; Agnew 1986; Strong 1979 and 1986.

14 Foucault 1973.

15 Latour 1986.

References

Adams, Simon 1990. "Tactics or Politics? 'The Military Revolution' and the Hapsburg Hegemony, 1525–1648." In John A. Lynn (ed.) *Tools of War*. Urbana and Chicago: University of Illinois Press.

Adams, William Howard 1979. *The French Garden*. New York: George Braziller.

Agnew, Jean-Christophe 1986. *Worlds Apart*. Cambridge: Cambridge University Press.

Allan, Mea 1964. *The Tradescants*. London: Michael Joseph.

Alpers, Svetlana 1983. *The Art of Describing: Dutch Art in the Seventeenth Century*. Chicago: University of Chicago Press.

Anderson, Benedict 1983. *Imagined Communities: Reflections on the Origin and Spread of Nationalism*. London: Verso.

Anderson, Perry 1974. *Lineages of the Absolutist State*. London: Verso.

André, Louis 1974. *Michel le Tellier et Louvois*. Genève: Slatkine-Megariotes Reprints.

Androuet du Cerceau, Jacques 1972. *Le Premier volume des plus excellents bastiments de France; Le Second volume des plus excellents bastiments de France*, Farnborough: Gregg.

Anon. 1980. *Flowers in Books and Drawings c. 940–1840*. New York: Pierpont Morgan Library.

Apostolidès, Jean-Marie 1981. *Le Roi-Machine: Spectacle et politique au temps de Louis XIV*. Paris: Editions de Minuit.

Appadurai, Arjun (ed.) 1986. *The Social Life of Things: Commodities in Cultural Perspective*. Cambridge: Cambridge University Press.

Appleby, Joyce 1978. *Economic Thought and Ideology in Seventeenth-Century England*. Princeton: Princeton University Press.

Arano, Luisa Cogliati 1976. *The Medieval Health Handbook: Tacuinum Sanitatis*. New York: George Braziller.

Armstrong, John 1982. *Nations Before Nationalism*. Chapel Hill, NC: University of North Carolina Press.

Auscher, E. S. 1905. *A History and Description of French Porcelain*. London: Cassell and Company.

Backer, Dorothy A. L. 1974. *Precious Women*. New York: Basic Books.

Bakhurst, David 1991. *Consciousness and Revolution in Soviet Philosophy: From the Bolsheviks to Evald Ilyenkov*. Cambridge: Cambridge University Press.

Bamford, Paul W. 1956. *Forests and French Sea Power 1660–1789*. Toronto: University of Toronto Press.

Barbet, L. A. 1907. *Les Grandes Eaux de Versailles: installations mécaniques et étangs artificiels, descriptions des fontaines et de leurs origins*. Paris: H. Dunod et E. Pinat.

Baurmeister, Ursula and Marie-Pierre Lafitte, *Des Livres et des rois: la bibliothèque royale de Blois*. Paris: Bibliothèque Nationale 1992.

Baxandall, Michael 1974 [1972]. *Painting and Experience in Fifteenth-Century Italy*. New York: Oxford University Press.

    1985. *Patterns of Intention: On the Historical Explanation of Pictures*. New Haven: Yale University Press.

Beaumont-Maillet, Laure 1991. *L'Eau à Paris*. Paris: Hazan.

Beck, Thomasina 1978. *Embroidered Gardens*. New York: Viking.

Beik, William 1985. *Absolutism and Society in Seventeenth-Century France: State Power and Provincial Aristocracy in Languedoc*. Cambridge: Cambridge University Press.

Bellaigue, R. de 1982. *Le Potager du roy 1678–1793*. Versailles: Ecole Nationale d'Horticulture.

Berain, J. 1660. *Parterres de broderies. Ornements inventez par J. Berain*. Paris: Bonchard-Huzard.

Berger, Bennett 1995. *Essay in the Sociology of Culture*. Berkeley: University of California Press.

Berger, John 1972. *Ways of Seeing*. London: Penguin.

Bergin, Joseph 1985. *Cardinal Richelieu: Power and the Pursuit of Wealth*. New Haven: Yale University Press.

Bermingham, Ann 1986. *Landscape and Ideology*. Berkeley: University of California Press.

Betin, Pierre n.d. *Le Fidelle Jardinier ou differantes sortes de parterres tant de broderie que mesle de pieces a metre fleurs pour servir dinstruction a ceaux qui ce delectent en ces art novellement designez*. Paris, Iean Boisseuv.

Bitton, Davis 1969. *The French Nobility in Crisis, 1560–1640*. Stanford: Stanford University Press.

Bluche, François 1986. *Louis XIV*. Paris: Fayard.

Blum, André 1928. *Histoire du Costume. Les modes au XVIIe et au XVIIIe siècle*. Paris: Hachette.

Blunt, Wilfrid 1956. *Sebastiano*. London: James Barrie.

Bonifas, Janine 1994. *Faïences du Nord de la France*. Sevres, Musée National de Céramique: Réunion des Musées Nationaux.

Bonnefons, Nicolas de 1654. *Le iardinier francois : qui enseigne a cultiver les arbres, & herbes potageres: avec la maniere de conserver les fruicts, & faire toutes sortes de confitures, conserves, & massepans ...* Cinquiesme edition / reveue par l'autheur. A Amsterdam: Chez Iean Blaeu.

    1691. *The French Gardiner*. John Evelyn (trans.). London: B. Took.

Bonnefoy, François 1986. "Maximilien Titon et le développement des armes portative en France sous Louis XIV," *Revue Historique des Armées* 162: 34–44.

Bonney, Richard 1988. *Society and Government in France under Richelieu and Mazarin 1624–61*. New York: St Martin's Press.

Boudon, Françoise 1991. "Garden history and cartography." In Monique Mosser and Georges Teyssot (eds.) *The Architecture of Western Gardens*. Cambridge, MA: MIT Press, pp. 125–34.

Bourdieu, Pierre 1984. *Distinction*. R. Nice (trans.). Cambridge, MA: Harvard University Press.

Bourdin, R. P. 1661. *Cours de Mathématiques dédié à la noblesse*. Paris.

Boyceau, Jacques 1638. *Traité du jardinage selon les raisons de la nature et de l'art*. Paris: Michel Vanlochom.

Braudel, Fernand 1973. *The Mediterranean and the Mediterranean World in the Age of Philip II*. S. Reynolds (trans.). New York: Harper & Row.

1990. *The Identity of France*. S Reynolds (trans.). London: Collins.

Brewer, John 1989. *Sinews of Power*. New York: Knopf.

Brewer, John and Roy Porter (eds.) 1993. *Consumption and the World of Goods*. London: Routledge.

Brockway, Lucile 1979. *Science and Colonial Expansion: The Role of the British Royal Botanic Gardens*. New York: Academic Press.

Burckhardt, Jacob 1958. *The Civilization of the Renaissance*. New York: Harper.

Burguière, André and Jacques Revel (eds.) 1989. *Histoire de la France. L'Espace français*. Paris: Editions du Seuil.

Burke, Kenneth 1989. *On Symbols and Society*. J. Gusfield (ed.). Chicago: University of Chicago Press.

Burke, Peter 1974. *Venice and Amsterdam*. London: Temple Smith.

1978. *Popular Culture in Early Modern Europe*. London: Temple Smith.

1992. *The Fabrication of Louis XIV*. New Haven: Yale University Press.

Carpeggiani, Paolo 1991. "Labyrinths in the gardens of the Renaissance." In Monique Mosser and Georges Teyssot (eds.) *The Architecture of Western Gardens*. Cambridge, MA: MIT Press.

Carrias, Eugene 1960. *La Pensée militaire française*. Paris: Presses Universitaires de France.

Carroll, Patrick 1996. "Nature vexed and disturbed." Paper delivered at Mephistos, The XVth Annual Graduate Student Conference for the History, Philosophy, and Sociology of Science, Technology, Medicine and Related Fields, Toronto.

Cassini, Jacques 1720. *De la Grandeur et de la figure de la Terre. Suite des memoires de l'Academie Royale des Sciences, année MDCCXVIII*. Paris: Imprimerie Royale.

Chandernagor, Françoise 1981. *L'Allée du Roi: Souvenirs de Françoise d'Aubigne, Marquise de Maintenon, epouse du roi de France*. Paris: Julliard.

Chapin, Seymour L. 1990. "Science in the reign of Louis XIV." In P. Sonnino (ed.) *The Reign of Louis XIV*. London: Humanities Press.

Chaplain, Jean-Michel 1984. *La chambre des tisseurs. Louviers: cité drapière*. Champ Vallon.

Chastelet, Paul Hay de 1668. *Traité de la guerre ou politique militaire*. Paris: Theodore Girard.

Chatelain, Urbain-Victor 1971. *Le Surintendant Nicolas Fouquet, Protecteur des Lettres, des Arts et des Sciences*. Genève: Slatkin Reprints.

Child, John 1982. *Armies and Warfare in Europe 1648–1789*. Manchester: Manchester University Press.

Christout, Marie-Françoise 1987. *Le Ballet de Cour au XVIIe Siècle*. Genève: Editions Minkoff.

Church, William F. (ed.) 1969. *The Impact of Absolutism in France Under Richelieu, Mazarin, and Louis XIV*. New York: John Wiley.

Cicourel, Aaron and John Kitsuse 1963. *The Educational Decision-Makers*. Indianapolis: Bobbs-Merrill.

Cipolla, Carlo 1965. *Guns, Sails and Empires. Technological Innovation and the Early Phases of European Expansion 1400–1700*. New York: Minerva Books.

Clare, Lucien 1983. *La Quintainé, la course de bague et le jeu des tête: Etude historique et ethno-linguistique d'une famille de jeux equestres*. Paris: Editions du CNRS.

Clément, Pierre 1980 [1874]. *Histoire de Colbert et son administration*. Genève: Slatkin Reprints.

Clifford, Derek 1963. *A History of Garden Design*. New York: Praeger.

Colbert, Jean-Baptiste 1868. *Lettres, instructions et mémoires de Colbert.* Pierre Clément (ed.). Paris: Imprimerie Impériale.

Cole, Charles W. 1964. *Colbert and a Century of French Mercantilism.* Hamden, CT: Archon Books.

Conan, Michel 1982. "Postface." In Charles Perrault (ed.) *Le Labyrinthe de Versailles 1677.* Paris: Editions de Moniteur.

Corrigan, Philip and Derek Sayer 1985. *The Great Arch: English State Formation as Cultural Revolution.* London: Blackwell.

Corvisier, André 1979. *Armies and Societies in Europe 1494–1789.* A. Siddall (trans.). Bloomington: Indiana University Press.

Corvol, Andrée 1984. *L'Homme et l'arbre sous l'Ancien Régime.* Paris: Economica.

Courtilz de Sandras, Gatien 1695. *The life of the famous John Baptist Colbert, late minister and secretary of state to Lewis XIV. the present French king. Done into English from a French copy printed at Cologne this present year 1695.* London (printed for R. Bentley, J. Tonson, H. Bonwick, W. Freeman, S. Manship).

Crest, Sabine du 1990. *Des Fêtes à Versailles.* Paris: Aux Amateurs de Livres.

Creveld, Martin van 1989. *Technology and War.* New York: The Free Press.

Cronon, William 1991. *Nature's Metropolis.* New York: Norton.

Crumb, Phyllis 1928. *Nature in the Age of Louis XIV.* London: Routledge.

d'Albissin, Nelly G. 1970. *Genèse de la frontière Franco-Belge: Les variations des limites septentionales de la France de 1659 à 1789.* Paris: Editions A. & J. Picard.

d'Argenville, Antoine Joseph Dezallier 1972 [1760]. *La Théorie et la practique du jardinage.* New York: Hildesheim.

Darnton, Robert 1982. *The Literary Underground of the Old Regime.* Cambridge: Harvard University Press.

Daston, Lorraine 1995. "Curiosity in early modern science," *Word and Image* 11, 4: 391–404.

Davis, Susan 1986. *Parades and Power.* Philadelphia: Temple University Press.

de Caus, Isaac 1657. *Nouvelle invention de lever l'eau. Nouvelle invention de lever l'eau: plus haut que sa source avec quelques machines mouvantes par le moyen de l'eau, et un discours de la conduit d'icelle.* Londres: Imprimé pour Thomas Davies.

de Caus, Salomon 1973 [1615]. *Les Raisons des forces mouvantes, avec diverse machines tant utiles que plaisantes.* Livre II. [Fontaines. Frankfort 1615.] Reprinted with an introduction by W. L. Sumner. Amsterdam: Uitgeverij Frits Knuf B.V.

    1981. *Le Jardin Palatin.* Editions de Moniteur.

Dens, Jean-Pierre 1981. *L'Honnête Homme et la critique du goût.* Lexington Kentucky: French Forum Publishers.

Dent, Julian 1973. *Crisis in Finance: Crown, Financiers and Society in 17th-Century France.* New York: St. Martins.

Desargues, Gerald 1648. *Manière universelle de M. Desargues pour pratiquer la perspective par petit pied.* Par A. Bosse. Paris: De l'imprimerie de Pierre Des-Hays.

Devèze, M. 1962. "Une admirable réforme administrative: la grande réformation des forêts royales sous Colbert (1662–1680)," *Annales de L'Ecole Nationale des Eaux et Forêts et de la Station de Recherches et Expériences.* Vol. 10, pp. 10–295. Nancy: Ecole Nationale des Eaux et Forêts.

Devismes, Roland 1974. *La Cour à Versailles, première partie: Versailles sous Louis XIV.* Paris: La Pensée Universelle.

Dewald, Jonathan 1993. "The ruling class in the marketplace: nobles and money in early modern France." In T. Haskell and R. Teichgraeber III (eds.) *The Culture of the Market*. Cambridge: Cambridge University Press, pp. 43–65.

Diefendorf, Barbara 1993. "The Huguenot psalter and the faith of French Protestants in the sixteenth century." In B. Diefendorf and C. Hesse (eds.) *Culture and Identity in Early Modern Europe (1500-1800)*. Ann Arbor: University of Michigan Press.

Dollar, Jacques 1983. *Vauban à Luxembourg, place forte de l'Europe (1684–97)*. Luxembourg: RLT Edition.

Dugué MacCarthy, Marcel 1984. *Soldats du Roi: Les armées de l'Ancien Regime XVIIe et XVIIIe siècles (1610–1789)*. Paris: Les collections du musée de l'armée.

Dumbarton Oaks 1974. *The French Formal Garden*. Washington, DC: Dumbarton Oaks.

Dunlop, Ian 1970. *Versailles*. New York: Taplinger Publishing Co.

Dupuy, Ernest 1970 [1902]. *Bernard Palissy*. Genève: Slatkin Reprints.

Duranthon, Marc 1978. *La Carte de France*. Paris: Solar.

Durnerin, A. 1983. "Le Potager du Roi 1683–1983." Versailles: ENSP.

Elias, Nobert 1978 [1939]. *The Civilizing Process*. New York: Urizen Books.
    1983 [1969]. *The Court Society*. New York: Pantheon.

Elliott, Charles 1992. *Princess of Versailles: The Life of Marie Adelaide of Savoy*. New York: Tricknor and Fields.

Escoupérie, Rose-Blanche 1986. "Une modeste communauté d'habitants du Bas-Quercy fournit des hommes pour la milice au siècle de Louis XIV et Louis XV," *Revue Historique des Armées* 162: 24–33.

Estienne, Charles and Jean Liébault 1702 [1570]. *L'Agriculture et la maison rustique*. Lyons: A. Laurens.

Estienne, Dom Claude S. 1687. *Nouvelle instruction pour connoistre les bons fruits selon les mois de l'année*. Paris: Charles Sercy.

Evans, Peter B., Dietrich Rueschemeyer, and Theda Skocpol (eds.) 1985. *Bringing the State Back In*. Cambridge: Cambridge University Press.

Evelyn, John 1679. *Sylva or Discourse on Forest Trees*. London: John Martyn.

Fagniez, Gustave 1975. *L'Economie sociale de la France sous Henri IV (1598–1610)*. Genève: Slatkin Reprints.

Farmer, James Eugene 1905. *Versailles and the Court under Louis XIV*. New York: The Century Co.

Faucherre, Nicolas 1986. "Outil stratégique ou jouet princier?" *Monuments Historiques* 148: 38–44.

Félibien, André 1668. *Relation de la Feste de Versailles du 18e Juillet 1668*. Paris: Pierre le Petit (Bibliothèque Nationale Lb37. 360).
    1672. *Description de la Grotte de Versailles*. Paris: Chez Sébastien Mabre-Cramoisy.
    1679. *Description de Versailles*. Paris.
    1689. *Recueil de descriptions de peintures et d'autres ouvrages fait pour le roy*. Paris: Veuve de S. Mabre-Cramoisy.
    1874. *Memoires pour servir à l'histoire des maisons royalles et bastiments de France*. Paris: J. Baur.
    1994 [1674]. *Les Fêtes de Versailles, chroniques de 1668 & 1674*. Paris: Editions Dédale, Maisonneuve et Laros.

Ferrier, Richard 1895. *The Journal of Major Richard Ferrier while Travelling in France in the Year 1687*. London: Camden Miscellany, New Series 53, vol. IX.

Finer, Samuel E. 1975. "State- and nation-building in Europe: the role of the military." In

Charles Tilly (ed.) *The Formation of National States in Western Europe.* Princeton: Princeton University Press.

Fontenelle, Bernard le Bovier de 1990. *Conversations on the Plurality of Worlds.* N. R. Gelbart (ed.) and H. A. Hargreaves (trans.). Berkeley: University of California Press.

Forster, Elborg 1958. *A Woman's Life in the Court of the Sun King: Letters of Liselotte von der Pfalz, Elisabeth Charlotte, Duchesse d'Orleans.* Baltimore and London: Johns Hopkins University Press.

Foucault, Michel 1973. *The Order of Things: An Archaeology of the Human Sciences.* New York: Vintage Books.

1979. *Discipline and Punish.* New York: Vintage.

Francastel, Pierre 1970 [1930]. *La Sculpture de Versailles.* Paris: Mouton.

Frégnac, Claude 1976. *La Faïence Européenne.* Paris: Editions Vilo.

Geertz, Clifford 1980. *Negara: The Theater State in 19th-Century Bali.* Princeton: Princeton University Press.

Gentil, François 1706, *The Retir'd Gard'ner.* London and Wise (trans.). London.

Gerspach, E. 1893 *Répertoire détaillé des tapisseries des Gobelins de 1662 à 1892.* Paris: A. Le Vasseur et cie.

Girard, Jacques 1985. *Versailles Gardens: Sculpture and Mythology.* London: Sotheby's Publications.

Goffman, Erving 1959. *Presentation of Self in Everyday Life.* New York: Anchor Books.

1963. *Behavior in Public Places.* New York: Free Press.

1967. *Interaction Ritual.* New York: Anchor Books.

1969. *Strategic Interaction.* New York: Ballantine Books.

1974. *Frame Analysis.* New York: Harper.

Gondouin, A. M. 1803. *Sur la machine de Marly.* Paris: l'Auteur.

Goody, Jack 1977. "What is a list?" In Jack Goody (ed.) *Domestication of the Savage Mind.* Cambridge: Cambridge University Press.

1993. *The Culture of Flowers.* Cambridge: Cambridge University Press.

Gouldner, Alvin 1965. *Enter Plato: Classical Greece and the Origins of Social Theory.* New York: Basic Books.

Grever, John H. 1990. "The religious history of the reign." In Paul Sonnino (ed.) *The Reign of Louis XIV.* London: Humanities Press.

Grieve, Hilda 1980. *A Transatlantic Gardening Friendship 1694–1777.* Essex Historical Society.

Gusfield, Joseph 1963. *Symbolic Crusade.* Urbana, IL: University of Illinois Press.

1981. *The Culture of Public Problems.* Chicago: University of Chicago Press.

Gutkind, E. A. 1970. *Urban Development in Western Europe.* Vol. 5: *France and Belgium.* New York: Free Press.

Habermas, Jürgen 1975. *Legitimation Crisis.* Thomas McCarthy (trans.). Boston: Beacon Press.

1989. *The Structural Transformation of the Public Sphere.* Cambridge, MA: MIT Press.

Hadfield, Miles 1960. *A History of British Gardening.* London: John Murray.

Hahn, Roger 1971. *The Anatomy of a Scientific Institution: The Paris Academy of Sciences, 1666–1803.* Berkeley: University of California Press.

Haraway, Donna 1989. *Primate Visions: Gender, Race, and Nature in the World of Modern Science.* New York: Routledge.

Harvey, John 1974. *Early Nurserymen.* London: Philimore.

Haskell, Thomas and R. Teichgraeber (eds.) 1993. *The Culture of the Market*. Cambridge: Cambridge University Press.

Hatton, Ragnhild 1976. *Louis XIV and Absolutism*. London: Macmillan.

Hauser, Arnold 1951. *Social History of Art*. New York: Vintage.

Havard, Henry and Marius Vachon 1889. *Les Manufactures nationales: Les Gobelins, la Savonnerie, Sèvres, Beauvais*. Paris: Georges Decaux, Librairie Illustré.

Hazlehurst, F. Hamilton 1974. "Le Nostre at Conflans." In Dumbarton Oaks, *The French Formal Garden*. Washington, DC: Dumbarton Oaks.

Hazlehurst, H. Franklin 1966. *Jacques Boyceau and the French Formal Garden*. Athens, GA: University of Georgia Press.

　1980. *Gardens of Illusion*. Nashville: Vanderbilt University Press.

Hedin, Thomas 1983. *The Sculpture of Gaspard and Balthazar Marsy*. Columbia, MO: University of Missouri Press.

Hill, Thomas 1568. *The Profitable Art of Gardening*. London: Walde-Grave.

　1652. *The gardeners labyrinth; or, A new art of gardning: wherein is laid down new and rare inventions and secrets of gardning not heretofore known. For sowing, planting, and setting all manner of roots, herbs, and flowers ...* London: (printed by) Jane Bell.

Hine, William L. 1984. "Marin Mersenne: Renaissance naturalism and Renaissance magic." In Brian Vickers (ed.) *Occult and Scientific Mentalities in the Renaissance*. Cambridge: Cambridge University Press.

Hix, John 1981. *The Glass House*. Cambridge, MA: MIT Press.

Hodge, A. Trevor 1992. *Roman Aqueducts and Water Supply*. London: Duckworth.

Holt, Mack P. (ed.) 1991. *Society and Insitutions in Early Modern France*. Athens, GA: University of Georgia Press.

Hoog, Simone 1989. *Le Bernin Louis XIV, un statue "déplacée."* Paris: Adam Brio.

Hopper, Florence 1982. "The Dutch classical garden and André Mollet," *Journal of Garden History* 2: 25–40.

Institut de France 1967. *Académie des Sciences: Troisième Centenaire 1666–1966*. Paris: Gauthier-Villars.

Isherwood, Robert M. 1973. *Music in the Service of the King*. Ithaca and London: Cornell University Press.

Janson, H.W. 1962. *History of Art*. New York: Abrams.

Jay, Martin 1993. *Downcast Eyes*. Berkeley: University of California Press.

Kemp, Martin 1990. *The Science of Art: Optical Themes in Western Art from Brunelleschi to Seurat*. New Haven: Yale University Press.

Kimmel, Michael S. 1988. *Absolutism and its Discontents*. New Brunswick, NJ: Transactions Press.

Kirsten, Lincoln 1970. *Movement and Metaphor*. New York: Praeger.

Knapp, A. Bernard (ed.) 1992. *Archaeology, Annales, and Ethnohistory*. Cambridge: Cambridge University Press.

Konvitz, Joseph 1978. *Cities and the Sea*. Baltimore: Johns Hopkins University Press.

　1987. *Cartography in France, 1660–1848*. Chicago: University of Chicago Press.

Koyré, Alexandre 1944. *Entretiens sur Descartes*. Paris and New York: Brentano's.

　1957. *From the Closed World to the Infinite Universe*. Baltimore: Johns Hopkins University Press.

La Fonchere, M. de 1718. *Nouvelle Methode de fortifier les plus grandes villes suivi de dissertations sur la machine de Marly, sur les pompoes du Pont Nôtre Dame et de la*

Samaritaine, avec des remarques très curieuses sur l'hydraulique, la mechanique, et la fortification. Paris: Florentin Lelaulne.

La Quintinie, Jean de 1692. *Instruction pour les jardins fruitiers et potagers.* Amsterdam: Henri Desbordes.

    1693. *The Compleat Gard'ner or Directions for Cultivating and Right Ordering of Fruit-Gardens and Kitchen-Gardens with Divers Reflections on Several parts of Husbandry.* John Evelyn (trans.). London: Matthew Gillyflower.

La Quintiney, Jean de 1717. *The Complete Gard'ner: or Directions for Cultivating and Right Ordering of Fruit-Gardens and Kitchen Gardens.* John London and Henry Wise (trans.). London: A & W. Bell.

Laborde, L. de 1880. *Comptes des Batîments de Roi.* Paris: J. Baur.

Lachiver, Marcel 1991. *Les années de misère: la famine au temps du Grand Roi.* Paris: Fayard.

Lacordaire, A. L. 1852. *Notice sur l'origine et les travaux des manufactures de tapisserie et de tapis réunis aux Gobelins et catalogue des tapisseries qui y sont exposées.* Paris: Manufacture des Gobelins.

Ladurie, E. Le Roy 1979. *Carnival in Romans.* New York: George Braziller.

Laissus, Yves and Jean Torlais 1986. *Le Jardin du Roi et le Collège Royal dans l'Enseignment des Sciences au XVIIe Siècle.* Paris: Hermann.

Laprade, Laurence de 1905. *Le Poinct de France et les centres dentelliers au XVIIe et au XVIIIe siècles.* Paris: Lucien Laveur.

Latour, Bruno 1986. *Science in Action.* Milton Keynes: Open University Press.

    1993. *We Have Never Been Modern.* Cambridge, MA: Harvard University Press.

Laurent, Jean 1675. *Abrégé pour les arbres nain et autres.* Paris: Charles Sercy.

Laver, James 1979. *The Concise History of Costume and Fashion.* New York: Charles Scribner's Sons.

Le Brun, Charles 1675. *Recueil de divers dessins de fontaines ... inventez et dessignez par Le Brun.* Paris: Chez Andran.

    1727. *Expressions des passions de l'âme representées en plusieurs testes gravées d'apres les desseins de feu Monsieur le Brun.* Paris: Jean Audran.

Le Clerc, Sébastien 1669. *Practique de la geometrie sur le papier and sur le terrain.* Paris: Chez Thomas Jolly.

Lefébure, Ernest 1912. *Les Poincts de France.* M. Johnston (trans.). New York.

Lenotre, G. 1934. *Versailles au temps des Rois.* Verviers (Belgium): Marabout.

Le Roi, J.-A. 1862. *Journal de la Sante du Roi Louis XIV de l'année 1647 à l'année 1711, ecrit par Vallot, D'Aquin et Fagon.* Paris: Auguste Durard.

Lery, E. 1926. "Les Travaux du potager de Versailles: la machine à transporter les terres," *Conférences des Sociétés Savantes de Seine et Oise* 8, pp. 18–20.

Levey, Michael 1971. *Painting at Court.* New York: New York University Press.

Levron, Jacques 1968. *Daily Life at Versailles in the Seventeenth and Eighteenth Centuries.* New York: Macmillan.

Liger, Louis 1776. *La Jardinier Fleuriste ou La Culture Universelle des fleurs, arbres, arbustes, arbrisseaux, servant à l'embelissement des jardins.* (13th edn). Paris: Chez Saugrain.

Lister, Martin 1967. *A Journey to Paris in the year 1698.* R. Stearns (ed.). Urbana: University of Illinois Press.

Lister, Raymond 1970. *Antique Maps and their Cartographers.* London: G. Bell.

Locke, John 1953. *Locke's Travels in France 1675–1679.* John Lough (ed.). Cambridge: Cambridge University Press.

Lougee, Carolyn 1976. *Le Paradis des Femmes: Women, Salons, and Social Stratification in 17th-century France*. Princeton: Princeton University Press.

Lough, John (ed.) 1985. *France Observed in the Seventeenth Century by British Travellers*. Stockfield: Oriel Press.

Louis XIV 1806. *Mémoires de Louis XIV, écrits par lui-même, composés pour le grand dauphin, son fils, et adressés à ce prince*. J. L. M. de Gain-Montagnac (ed.). Paris: Garnery.

Luria, Keith 1993."Rituals of conversion: Catholics and Protestants in seventeenth-century Poitou." In B. Diefendorf and C. Hesse (eds.), *Culture and Identity in Early Modern Europe (1500-1800)*. Ann Arbor: University of Michigan Press.

MacFarlane, Alan 1978. *The Origins of English Individualism*. Cambridge: Cambridge University Press.

Machiavelli, Niccolò 1965a. *The Prince*. W. K. Marriott (trans.). Introd. by H. Butterfield. London : Dent.

1965b [1521]. *The Art of War*. E. Farneworth (trans.). New York: Da Capo Press.

Mackey, Charles 1979 [1852]. *Extraordinary Popular Delusions and the Madness of Crowds*. New York: Harmony Books.

Magne, Emile 1944. *Les Plaisirs et les fêtes en France au XVIIe siècle*. Genève: Editions de Frégate.

Major, J. Russell 1994. *From Renaissance Monarchy to Absolute Monarchy*. Baltimore: Johns Hopkins Press.

Mallet, Allain Manesson 1684. *Les Travaux de Mars ou l'art de la guerre*. Amsterdam: Jan et Gillis Janson à Waesbergue.

Mangredien, Georges 1948. *La Vie Quotidienne sous Louis XIV*. Paris: Librairie Hachette.

Mann, Michael 1986. *The Sources of Social Power*, vol. I. Cambridge: Cambridge Unviersity Press.

Manufacture des Gobelins 1962. *Charles Le Brun, Premier Directeur de la Manufacture Royale des Gobelins*. Paris: Musée des Gobelins.

Mariage, Thierry 1990. *L'Univers de Le Nôtre*. Bruxelles: Pierre Mardaga.

1992. "De la validité des documents graphiques pour juger de l'evolution des jardins de Versailles." In Richard Mique (ed.) *Les Jardins de Versailles et de Trianon d'André Le Nôtre*. Paris: Réunion des Musées Nationaux, pp. 15–18.

Marie, Alfred 1968. *Naissance de Versailles*. Paris: Editions Vincent, Fréal, et Cie.

Marin, Louis 1981. *Portrait du Roi*. Paris: Editions de Minuit.

1993. *Des pouvoirs de l'image*. Paris: Editions de Seuil.

Mariotte, M. 1708. *Traité de Mouvement des eaux et des autres corps fluides, divise en V. parties*. Paris: Chez Jean Jombert.

Marly, Diana de 1987. *Louis XIV and Versailles*. London: Batsford.

Masson, Bernard 1986. "Un aspect de la discipline dans les armées de Louis XIII: La lutte contre la désertion du soldat 1635–1643," *Revue Historique des Armées* 162: 11–23.

Masson, Paul 1967 [1911]. *Histoire du Commerce dans le Levant au XVIIe siècle*. New York: Burt Franklin.

Masson, Paul-Marie 1972. *L'Opéra de Rameau*. New York: Da Capo Press.

Mazouer, Charles 1993. *Molière et ses comédies-ballets*. Paris: Klincksieck.

McClary, Susan 1992. "Politics of the body and the body politic." Paper presented at the Clark Library Conference: *Body Politics and the Body Politic*. Los Angeles.

McKendrick, Neil, John Brewer, and J. H. Plumb 1982. *Birth of a Consumer Society*. London: Europa.

McNeil, William 1963. *The Rise of the West*. Chicago: Chicago University Press.

1976. *Plagues and Peoples.* Garden City NY: Anchor Press.

1982. *The Pursuit of Power: Technology, Armed Force and Society since AD 100.* Chicago: Chicago University Press.

Merchant, Carolyn 1980. *The Death of Nature: Women, Ecology, and the Scientific Revolution.* San Francisco: Harper and Row.

Metropolitan Museum of Art 1989. *French Decorative Arts during the Reign of Louis XIV, 1645–1715.* New York; Metropolitan Museum of Art.

Mettam, Roger 1988. *Power and Faction in Louis XIV's France.* London: Basil Blackwell.

Meyer, Daniel 1982. *Quand les Rois régnaient à Versailles.* Paris: Fayard.

Migel, Parmenia 1972. *The Ballerinas.* New York: Macmillan.

Mique, Richard 1992. *Les Jardins de Versailles et de Trianon d'André Le Nôtre.* Paris: Reunion des Musées Nationaux.

Molière 1755. "L'Impromptu de Versailles." In *Works,* vol. 5. London: D. Browne and A. Millar.

    1853 [1665]. *Les Plaisirs de l'Isle enchantée. Course de bague, collation ornée de Machines, Comedite de Molière de las Princesse d'Elide, meslée de Danse et de Musique, Ballet du Palais d'Alcine, Feu d'Artifice: Et autres Festes galantes et magnifiques; faites par le Roy à Versailles, le 7. May 1664. Et continuées plusieurs autres Jours.* Paris: Chez Robert Ballard. Réimpression de Louis Lacour. Paris: Librairie des Bibliophiles.

Mollet, André 1981 [1651]. *Le Jardin de Plaisir.* Paris: Editions de Moniteur.

Mollet, Claude 1663. *Théâtre des jardinages.* Paris: C. de Sercy.

Mongredien, Georges 1948. *La Vie Quotidienne sous Louis XIV.* Paris: Librairie Hachette.

Montagu, Jennifer 1968. "The painted enigma and French seventeenth-century art," *Journal of the Warburg and Courtauld Institutes,* 31: 307–35.

Montclos, Jean-Marie Pérouse de 1991. *Versailles.* New York: Abbeville.

Morellet, Laurent 1681. *Explication historique de ce qu'il y a de plus remarquable dans la maison royale de Versailles et en celle de Monsieur à Saint-Cloud.* par le sieur Combes (Laurent Morellet). Paris: C. Nego.

Morin, Pierre 1651. *Catalogue de quelques plantes à fleurs qui son de présent au jardin de Pierre Morin le jeune, dit troisième, fleurist scitué au fauborg Saint Germain proche la Charité.* Paris: François Le Cointe.

    1655. *Catalogue de quelques plantes à fleurs* (2nd edn), Paris: François Le Cointe.

    1658. *Remarques necessaires pour la culture des Fleurs. Diligement observé par P. Morin.* Paris: Charles de Sercy.

    1680. *Instruction Facile pour connoitre toutes sortes d'orangers et citronniers.* Paris: Charles de Sercy.

Morris, A. E. J. 1979. *History of Urban Form.* London: George Godwin Ltd.

Mosser, Monique and Georges Teyssot 1991. *The Architecture of Western Gardens.* Cambridge, MA: MIT Press.

Mousnier, Roland 1974. *The Institutions of France under the Absolute Monarchy, 1598–1789.* Chicago: University of Chicago Press.

    1984. *Absolute Monarchy 1598–1789.* A. Goldhammer (trans.). Vol. II. Chicago: University of Chicago Press.

Mousset, Albert 1930. *Les Francine: Créateurs des eaux de Versailles, intendants des eaux et fontaines de France de 1623 à 1784.* Paris: August Picard.

Muijzenberg, Erwin W. B. dan deer n.d. "A history of greenhouses." Wageningen (typescript).

Mukerji, Chandra 1982. *From Graven Images: Patterns of Modern Materialism.* New York: Columbia University Press.

1984. "Visual language in science and the exercise of power," *Studies in Visual Communication* 10: 30–45.

1994."Visualization and science." Paper presented at the Conference on Visualization and Science, Galveston, Texas.

Murat, Inès 1984. *Colbert*. Cook and Asselt (trans.). Charlottesville: University Press of Virginia.

Néraudau, J. P. 1986. *L'Olympe du Roi-Soleil*. Paris: Société d'Edition Les Belles Lettres.

Neymarck, Alfred 1970 [1877]. *Colbert et son temps*. Genève: Slatkin Reprints.

Nolhac, Pierre de 1924. *Les Jardins de Versailles*. Paris: Henri Floury.

1925. *Création de Versailles*. Paris: Louis Conard.

O'Connor, John T. 1990."Diplomatic history of the reign." In P. Sonnino (ed.) *The Reign of Louis XIV*. London: Humanities Press.

Osler, Margaret 1994. *Divine Will and the Mechanical Philosophy*. Cambridge: Cambridge University Press.

Palissy, Bernard 1580. *Recepte Véritable*. Paris: M. Le Jeune.

Parent, Michel and Jacques Verroust 1971. *Vauban*. Paris: Editions Jacques Fréal.

Parker, David 1983. *The Making of French Absolutism*. London: Edward Arnold.

Pepper, Simon and Nicholas Adams 1986. *Firearms and Fortifications: Military Architecture and Siege Warefare in Sixteenth-Century Siena*. Chicago: University of Chicago Press.

Pérez-Gómez, Alberto 1983. *Architecture and the Crisis of Modern Science*. Cambridge, MA: MIT Press.

Perrault, Charles 1909. *Mémoires de ma vie*. Paris: P. Bonnefon.

1979 [1692]. *Parallèle des Anciens and des Modernes*. Genève: Slatkin Reprints.

1982 [1677]. *Le Labyrinthe de Versailles 1677*. Paris: Editions de Moniteur.

Perrault, Pierre 1674. *De l'Origine des fontaines*. Paris: Pierre le Petit.

Picard, M. 1684. *Traité du Nivellement*. Paris: Estienne Michallet.

Picard, Roger 1943. *Les Salons Littéraires et La Société Française 1610–1789*. New York: Brentanos.

Picon, Antione 1989. *Claude Perrault ou la curiosité d'un classique*. Paris: Picard Editeur.

Pierson, Peter 1990. "Music in the reign of Louis XIV." In Paul Sonnino (ed.), *The Reign of Louis XIV*. London: Humanities Press.

Pinon, Pierre (ed.) 1986. *Un Canal ... Les Canaux ...* Paris: Caisse Nationale des Monuments Historiques et des Sites.

Poggi, Gianfranco 1990. *The State: Its Nature, Development and Prospects*. Cambridge: Polity Press.

Pradel, Abraham du 1979 [1878]. *Le Livre Commode des Adresses de Paris pour 1692*. Edouard Fournier (ed.). Liechtenstein: Kraus Reprint.

Préaud, Maxime 1995. *Les Effets du soleil: Almancs du règne de Louis XIV*. Paris: Réunion des Musées Nationaux.

Proctor, Robert 1991, *Value-Free Science? Purity and Power in Modern Knowledge*. Cambridge, MA: Harvard University Press.

Pujo, Bernard 1991. *Vauban*. Paris: Albin Michel.

Pujol, Abbé 1725. *Traité du mouvement et de la mesure des eaux coulantes and jaillisantes avec un traité preliminaire du mouvement en general, tiré des ouvrages manuscrits du feu M Varignon*. Paris.

Rabinow, Paul 1989. *French Modern: Norms and Forms of the Social Environment*. Cambridge, MA: MIT Press.

Racine, Michel 1981. *Architecture rustique de rocailleurs*. Paris: Moniteur.

Ranum, Orest 1979. *Paris in the Age of Absolutism*. Bloomington: Indiana University Press.
  1980. "Courtesy, absolutism, and the rise of the French state, 1630–1660," *Journal of Modern History* 52: 426–51.
Rebelliau, Alfred 1962. *Vauban*. Paris: Fayard.
Reddy, William M. 1986. "The structure of a cultural crisis: thinking about cloth in France before and after the Revolution." In A. Appadurai (ed.), *The Social Life of Things: Commodities in Cultural Perspective*. Cambridge: Cambridge University Press.
Revel, Jacques. "La connaissance du territoire." Conference paper, Maison des Sciences de l'Homme, 1990.
Roger, Jacques 1971. *Les Sciences de la vie dans la pensée française du XVIIIe siècle: la génération des animaux de Descartes à l'encyclopédie*. Paris: Armand Colin.
Roseneau, Helen 1959. *The Ideal City: Its Architectural Evolution*. Boston, MA: Boston Book and Art Shop.
Rosental, Claude 1996. "Fuzzyfying the world. Social practices of 'showing' the properties of fuzzy logic." Princeton history of Science Workshop.
Roux, Antoine de 1990. *Perignan à la fin du XVIIe siècle*. Caisse Nationale des Monuments Historiques et des Sites.
Rule, John C. 1990. "The administrative history of the reign." In Paul Sonnino (ed.) *The Reign of Louis XIV*. London: Humanities Press.
Sahlins, Marshall 1976. *Culture and Practical Reason*. Chicago: University of Chicago Press.
Sahlins, Peter 1989. *Boundaries: The Making of France and Spain in the Pyrenees*. Berkeley: University of California Press.
  1994. *Forest Rites*. Cambridge, MA: Harvard University Press.
Saint-Simon 1958. *Saint-Simon at Versailles. Selected and Translated from the Memoirs of M. Le Duc de Saint-Simon*. Lucy Norton (ed.). London: Hamish Hamilton.
  1990, *The Age of Magnificence*. Ted Morgan (ed.). New York: Paragon.
Salamagne, Alain 1986. "Vauban et les fortifications du Quesnoy," *Revue Historique des Armées* 162: 45–51.
Sargent, A. J. 1968. *The Economic Policy of Colbert*. New York: Burt Franklin.
Schaeper, Thomas 1990. "Economic history of the reign." In Paul Sonnino (ed.) *The Reign of Louis XIV*. London: Humanities Press.
Schalk, Ellery 1986. *From Valor to Pedigree: Ideas of Nobility in France in the Sixteenth and Seventeenth Century*. Princeton: Princeton Univesity Press.
Schama, Simon 1988. *The Embarrassment of Riches: An Interpretation of Dutch Culture in the Golden Age*. London: Fontana.
  1995. *Landscape and Memory*. New York: Knopf.
Schiller, Dan 1996. *Theorizing Communication*. Cambridge: Cambridge University Press.
Schnapper, Antoine 1991. "Gardens and plant collections in France and Italy in the seventeenth century." In Monique Mosser and George Teyssot (eds.), *The Architecture of Western Gardens*. Cambridge, MA: MIT Press.
Schneider, Mark 1993. *Culture and Enchantment*. Chicago: University of Chicago Press.
Schutz, Alfred 1967. *Collected Papers I: The Problem of Social Reality*. Maurice Natanson (ed.). The Hague: Matinus Nijhoff.
Scudéry, Madeleine de 1979. *La Promenade de Versailles*. Genève: Slatkin Reprints.
Serres, Olivier de 1611. *Le théâtre d'agriculture et mesnages des champs*. Genève: Mat Hiev Berjon.
  1971 [1607]. *The Perfect Use of Silk-Wormes*. Amsterdam and New York: Da Capo Press.

Shapin, Steven 1994. *A Social History of Truth: Civility and Science in Seventeenth-Century England*. Chicago: University of Chicago Press.

Shapin, Steven and Simon Schaffer 1985. *Leviathan and the Airpump*. Princeton: Princeton University Press.

Simmel, Georg 1978 [1900]. *The Philosophy of Money*. London: Routledge and Kegan Paul.

Skocpol, Theda 1979. *States and Social Revolutions: A Comparative Analysis of France, Russia, and China*. Cambridge and New York: Cambridge University Press.

Skolnick, Jerome 1966. *Justice Without Trial*. New York: Wiley.

Sonnino, Paul (ed.) 1990. *The Reign of Louis XIV*. London: Humanities Press.

Steen, Charles R. 1990. "Social history of the reign." In P. Sonnino (ed.) *The Reign of Louis XIV*. London: Humanities Press.

Stranahan, C. H. 1888. *A History of French Painting*. New York: Charles Scribner's sons.

Strauss, Linda 1987. "Automata: a study in the interface of science, technology, and popular culture." Dissertation, History Department, University of California, San Diego.

Strong, Roy C. 1979. *The Renaissance Garden in England*. London: Thames and Hudson.
   1986. *Henry, Prince of Wales, and England's Lost Renaissance*. New York: Thames and Hudson.

Stroup, Alice 1990. *A Company of Scientists: Botany, Patronage, and Community in the Seventeenth-Century Parisian Royal Academy of Sciences*. Berkeley: University of California Press.

Thacker, Christopher 1972. "La manière de montrer les jardins de Versailles," *Journal of Garden History* 1: 49–69.
   1979. *The History of Gardens*. Berkeley: University of California Press.

Thomas, Keith 1983. *Man and the Natural World*. New York: Pantheon.

Tilly, Charles 1975. *The Formation of National States in Western Europe*. Princeton: Princeton University Press.

Tocanne, Bernard 1978. *L'Idée de nature en France dans la seconde moitié du XVIIe siècle*. Strasbourg: Klincksieck.

Tomasi, Luisa Tongiogi 1991. "Botanical gardens of the sixteenth and seventeenth centuries." In Monique Mosser and George Teyssot (eds.) *The Architecture of Western Gardens*. Cambridge, MA: MIT Press.

Tooley, R. V. 1978. *Maps and Mapmakers*. New York: Crown.

Tournefort, Joseph Pitton de 1698. *Histoire des plantes qui naissent aux environs de Paris*. Paris: De l'Imprimerie Royale.
   1717. *Relation d'un voyage du Levant: fait par ordre du Roy*. Lyon: Annison and Pseul.

Van der Groen 1669. *Jardinier hollandais*. Amsterdam: Marc Doornick.

Varagnac, André 1971. "En marge de l'histoire du verre." *Mélanges de Préhistoire d'Archéocivilisation et d'Ethnographie*. Paris: Sevpen.

Vauban, Sébastien le Prestre de 1726. *Maximes et instructions sur l'art militaire*. Paris: Chez Denis Mariette, Jean-Baptiste Delespine et Jean-Baptiste Coignard.
   1736. *De l'attaque et de la défense des places*. The Hague: Chez Pierre de Hondt.

Veblen, Thorstein 1953 [1899]. *The Theory of the Leisure Class*. New York: Mentor Books.

Vérin, Hélen 1993. *La Gloire des Ingénieurs: l'intelligence technique du XVIe au XVIIIe siècle*. Paris: Albin Michel.

Verlet, Pierre 1985. *Le Château de Versailles*. Paris: Fayard.

Veryard, Ellis 1701. *An Account of Divers Choice Remarks as well as Geographical, Historical, Political, Mathematical and Moral; Taken in a Journey through the Low Countries, France,*

Italy, and Part of Spain with the Isles of Sicilty and Malta. London: S. Smith and B. Walford.

Vickers, Brian (ed.) 1984. *Occult and Scientific Mentalities in the Renaissance.* Cambridge: Cambridge University Press.

Virville, Davy de 1954. *Histoire de la botanique en France.* Paris: Société d'Edition d'Enseignement Supérieur.

Vitruvius 1960. *The Ten Books of Architecture.* M. H. Morgan (trans.). New York: Dover.

Wallerstein, Immanuel 1974. *The Modern World-System.* New York: Academic Press.

Walton, Guy 1986. *Louis XIV's Versailles.* Chicago: University of Chicago Press.

Webber, Ronald 1968. *The Early Horticulturalists.* Plymouth: David & Charles.

1972. *Market Gardening: The History of Commercial Flower, Fruit, and Vegetable Growing.* London: David & Charles.

Weber, Eugen 1976. *Peasants into Frenchmen: The Modernization of Rural France 1870–1914.* Stanford: Stanford University Press.

Weber, Max 1978. *Economy and Society.* G. Roth and C. Wittich (eds.). Berkeley: University of California Press.

Weygand, Max 1930. *Turenne, Marshal of France.* London: George Harrap & Co. Ltd.

White, Hayden 1987. *The Content of the Form: Narrative Discourse and Historical Representation.* Baltimore: Johns Hopkins University Press.

Wilford, John Noble 1981. *The Mapmakers.* New York: Vintage.

Wolf, C. 1902. *Histoire de l'Observatoire de Paris de sa fondation à 1793.* Paris: Gauthier-Villars.

Wollen, Peter 1992. "Government by appearances." Paper presented at the Clark Library Conference: *Body Politics and the Body Politic.* Los Angeles.

Yates, Frances 1947. *The French Academies of the Sixteenth Century.* London: Warburg Institute.

Zeller, Gaston 1928. *L'Organisation défensive des frontières du nord et de l'est au XVIIe siècle.* Nancy: Berger-Levrault.

Ziegler, Gilette 1966. *At the Court of Versailles: Eye-Witness Reports from the Reign of Louis XIV.* New York: Dutton.

Index